D0205419

POPULAR FILMGOING
IN 1930s BRITAIN

Exeter Studies in Film History
General Editors: Richard Maltby and Duncan Petrie

Exeter Studies in Film History is devoted to publishing the best new scholarship on the cultural, technical and aesthetic history of cinema. The aims of the series are to reconsider established orthodoxies and to revise our understanding of cinema's past by shedding light on neglected areas in film history.

Published in association with the Bill Douglas Centre for the History of Cinema and Popular Culture, the series includes monographs and essay collections, translations of major works written in other languages, and reprinted editions of important texts in cinema history. The series editors are Richard Maltby, Associate Professor of Screen Studies, Flinders University, Australia, and Duncan Petrie, Director of the Bill Douglas Centre for the History of Cinema and Popular Culture, University of Exeter.

Exeter Studies in Film History

Parallel Tracks: The Railroad and Silent Cinema
Lynne Kirby (1997)

The World According to Hollywood, 1918–1939
Ruth Vasey (1997)

'Film Europe' and 'Film America': Cinema, Commerce and Cultural Exchange 1920–1939
edited by Andrew Higson and Richard Maltby (1999)

A Paul Rotha Reader
edited by Duncan Petrie and Robert Kruger (1999)

A Chorus of Raspberries: British Film Comedy 1929–1939
David Sutton (2000)

The Great Art of Light and Shadow: Archaeology of the Cinema
Laurent Mannoni, translated by Richard Crangle (2000)

Alternative Empires: European Modernist Cinemas and Cultures of Imperialism
Martin Stollery (2000)

University of Exeter Press also publishes the celebrated five-volume series looking at the early years of English cinema, *The Beginnings of the Cinema in England*, by John Barnes.

Popular Filmgoing in 1930s Britain

A Choice of Pleasures

John Sedgwick

UNIVERSITY
of
EXETER
PRESS

To Bernard Hrusa-Marlow

First published in 2000 by
University of Exeter Press
Reed Hall, Streatham Drive
Exeter EX4 4QR
UK
www.ex.ac.uk/uep/

British Library Cataloguing in Publication Data
A catalogue record for this book is available
from the British Library.

ISBN 0 85989 660 9

Typeset in 11/13pt Monotype Imprint
by XL Publishing Services, Tiverton

Printed in Great Britain by Short Run Press Ltd, Exeter

Contents

Tables and Figures

TABLES AND FIGURES

Figures

The information in those tables and figures that do not have source
attributions has been established by the author as a result of his research
methodology.

Acknowledgements

This book builds upon a thesis for which I was awarded a PhD by London Guildhall University in 1995. But in a way its origins go back to 1981–83 when as a postgraduate student I studied Economic and Social History at Birkbeck College, London University, and wrote a dissertation on the very early economic history of the British film industry, 1896–1908. Two figures at Birkbeck College in the early 1980s have had a marked influence on the way I have approached my research—Roderick Floud and Ben Fine. Roderick, I'm pleased to say, took me on as a doctoral student and with Mike Cowan saw me through to the end. I'm grateful to all three.

Few economic historians have shown much interest in film, or for that matter issues of consumption in the modern world. Most of the academic support that I have received in writing the book has come from a group of film historians who collectively emphasize context and evidence rather than theory. To Tony Aldgate, James Chapman, Mark Glancy, Kevin Gough Yates, Sue Harper, Ian Jarvie, Vincent Porter, and Jeffrey Richards, I am indebted for their learning, interest, scepticism, tolerance and friendship. Jeffrey's book *The Age of the Dream Palace* continues to serve as an inspiration in capturing time and place, and to my mind is as fine a film history as any that have been written. In the case of Sue and Vincent I owe a special vote of thanks for their painstaking critiques of my methodological statement found in the Introduction.

I am also indebted to my colleagues in the Economics Group at the University of North London. Stuart Archbold, John Curran, John Grahl, Photis Lysandrou, Bob Morgan, Mike Pokorny, Norman

Stang, Martin Topple and Guglielmo Volpe all have taken time with me over aspects of the work. With Mike Pokorny I have developed a collaboration in the area of film economics which has led to a number of journal articles. Mike has given me a lot of guidance in the conceptual aspects of this work, making it much better than it otherwise would have been.

The same is true of Richard Maltby, my editor for this book, who has helped to shape its final structure through his perceptive reading of the text. In addition I would like to record my appreciation to the staff at the University of Exeter Press, who have been unfailingly helpful and courteous. David Culbert, the editor of *Historical Journal of Film, Radio and Television* also deserves my thanks on two accounts. Between 1994 and 1998 David published all of my early papers. Without this support it is quite possible that this book would never have been born. Further, David has given me permission to use the research reported in these papers, as the basis of a number of chapters in the book.

Finally, I have to thank Carole, Martha and Rachel in keeping faith with a sometimes emotionally erratic husband and father. Martha spent a good part of her eleventh and twelfth years contributing (voluntarily) to the database which sources the book. What a lucky father I am. She was joined in this apprenticeship by my friend and former school teacher Bernard Hrusa-Marlow. A man of great learning and humanity and kindness, Bernard has experienced this project, from beginning to end, almost as acutely as myself. It is to Bernard that I dedicate this book.

Introduction

Rose and Edward, however, being children of this age, may have found more in the film than would superficially appear from this description of it; there may have been an almost profound appeal in the rapidity of the tempo alone; its cheerful irresponsibility, dimmed only by the easiest of sentiment, may have meant more to them than we can guess; and even its world may have been an amusing parody of the world that they preferred to see, a world of quick change, of easy light relations with people and things, without rigid standards and heavy responsibilities, cleansed of despair and madness and death.

J.B. Priestley, *They Walk in the City*[1]

This is a book about popular cinema in Britain during the 1930s. As such, it examines the activity of cinemagoing and, in particular, the choices made by audiences in preferring one film to another. It demonstrates that British audiences were enamoured of films made in Hollywood, but that as the decade wore on they came increasingly to appreciate and value films emanating from British studios. The corollary to this is that British cinema cannot be understood separately from the dominating presence of Hollywood. Hollywood posed a continuous challenge to indigenous film-makers by providing a standard that had either to be matched or circumvented though genre and product innovation. Audiences adjudicated on the efforts of British producers to compete effectively. They did so in a dispassionate manner, not seeing British films because they were British but because they were good, entertaining and yielded pleasure. This study should

1

be viewed as an appreciation of the importance of cinema to the lives of British people, as well as an examination of those systems which enabled filmgoers in urban Britain to make choices between rival film products placed on the market by rent-seeking capitalist producers, distributors and exhibitors.

Film popularity matters because it reflects how people choose to spend their time and, in going to the cinema, their preferences among films. In this respect, film provides valuable evidence about the appetites and emotions of social groups who otherwise leave little trace. Films themselves are the outcome of a combination of business and aesthetic strategies designed to attract the largest possible audience. Most importantly, these strategies are made within, and are generally sensitive to, prevailing social, institutional and international contexts.[2] Popular filmgoing, then, engages a series of agencies—consumers, production, distribution, and exhibition businesses, financial institutions and markets, censorship bodies, interest groups and the state— in the visual presentation and consumption of ideas about a world of relations—past, present and future—that in turn bear some relation to our collective imagination.

The principle of informed choice is critical to any idea of popular cinema. The rationale behind differential box-office performance— first expounded by Simon Rowson in 1936[3]—is that within any single urban locality, potential audiences have a range of film programmes, at similarly priced cinemas, from which to make choices. In attending cinema A to watch film Y the filmgoer, for that interval of time at least, forgoes the opportunity to view film Z in cinema B. Indeed, in an essay published in 1937, Alexander Korda argued that cinema, perhaps for the first time, gave the people the right of veto over what they consumed.[4] This is not to deny that some cinemagoers in the past attended habitually, irrespective of programme, but to recognize that this aspect of attendance did not determine the relative popularity of films.[5] Nor is it to propose that cinemagoers were a homogeneous mass, as has been implied by some socio-philosophical commentators. They were not, and in this fact lies the fascination of the appeal of particular films to particular social groupings. And, as Annette Kuhn has discovered, cinema was only one aspect of the leisure activities enjoyed by cinemagoers.[6]

The approach taken throughout the book is that audiences consisted of individuals exercising their intelligence (as well as their emotions) in the fulfilment of their own pleasure: that they reacted pro-actively and critically with films in first acquiring and then assessing meaning.

As Marcia Landy among others has argued, popular cinema works from the assumption that 'the spectator is not mindless. The films do not place the spectator in a position of total subordination to the text…The narratives replay situations that have their roots in the world familiar to the spectator, the world within film and the world in which the spectator lives.'[7] Janet Thumim, in expressing a growing concern about the role of audiences in popular cinema, has written, 'For the cultural historian it is the very success of this ('hit') film which provokes questions about its content: what pleasures did it offer, what wide-spread desires did it satisfy, in short how was it *used* by its audiences.'[8]

Jeffrey Richards has drawn attention to the socializing aspect of popular British films, claiming that during the 1930s:

> The actual films were used either to distract or to direct the audiences into approved channels, by validating key institutions of hegemony, such as monarchy and Empire, the police and the law, and the armed forces, and promoting those qualities useful to society as presently constituted: hard work, monogamy, cheerfulness, deference, patriotism.[9]

More recently, he has extended this thesis, elaborating on the role of cinema in 'nationalizing taste'[10] and 'propagating national image, both in reflecting widely held views and constructing, extending, interrogating and perpetuating dominant cultural myths'.[11]

For a film to be popular it must be seen widely and enjoyed. The extent of its diffusion will depend significantly upon the reputation it develops. Whilst distributors will expect to influence this reputation through pre- and post-release publicity activities involving a variety of media, ultimately their efforts will be successful only where the 'pitch' for any single film is congruent with the strength and intent of the flow of information which spreads by word of mouth from its initial audiences. It is possible to conceive of a framework of reaction which ranges from *deep*—where considerable commotion is associated with the release of a film—to *shallow*, and from strongly *positive*—where audience response is very favourable—to strongly *negative*. A deep positive reaction is a necessary condition if the film is to be popular. A deep negative reaction will lead to the film's 'bombing'. Shallow reactions are less likely to be strongly felt. Levels of popularity may be measured absolutely. One film may be seen by more people than another; may be shown on more screens; may generate greater box-office revenue.

3

Accordingly, it is possible to rank films using such criteria. However, popularity can be scaled or targeted relative to a studio's conception of a film.[12] Thus, a big-budget film made by a major Hollywood studio with an extensive distribution network, and backed by intensive publicity, will need to be popular (absolutely) if it is to generate a positive rate of return for the producer/distributor. This is as true for the 1930s as it is today. In contrast, for moderate- and low-budget productions, the requirements of target popularity, relative to their concepts, are not so rigorous. For these films, middling scores of absolute popularity will suffice to produce rates of return that satisfactorily fulfil their producer's 'concept' expectations. Occasionally the achieved absolute popularity score far exceeds these expectations, giving rise, in trade terminology to a 'sleeper'. In the heyday of the Hollywood studio system, a notable 'sleeper' was *It Happened One Night* (1934). More recent examples are the British productions *Four Weddings and a Funeral* (1994) and *The Full Monty* (1997). The phenomenon of the 'sleeper', with its 'dual aspect' of popularity, shows that the term 'popular' needs to be tempered by knowledge of the structural circumstances of a film's production, distribution and exhibition—a configuration that will be later defined as a 'system of provision'.[13]

Film popularity is fundamental to capitalist cinema. As is well understood, the popularity of each film is transmuted into box-office revenue from which, after taxation, the respective production, distribution and exhibition agents take their contractually negotiated cut (rent). The profitability of each film is then measured as the difference between the producer's rent, received from the distributor, and the costs incurred in production: likewise, the profitability of each cinema is obtained by the deducting those fixed and variable costs associated with exhibition from the exhibitor's rent.

Without cognizance of the size of the market, and the rivalry between firms competing for shares of it, no true understanding of the development of commercial cinema can be arrived at. In effect this is to argue that the scale of the resources (quantitative and qualitative) which flowed into the industry, the types of organization which emerged, the pace and nature of the technological developments which affected the characteristics of the product, the look of the product, the conventions for effective communication, and, finally, the way in which these facets changed over time, are predicated upon the assumption that opportunities for profit existed, and were pursued with vigour.

4

Ian Jarvie contextualizes film as a commodity very effectively in distinguishing between 'high' and 'popular' culture:

> Mass culture, unlike traditional or high culture, was not the unique product of artisans or of a cottage industry; its items were produced on a large scale, part of a consumption-orientated economic system driven to expand its markets and its controls over markets, regardless of national boundaries. Mass culture did not claim to offer disembodied and timeless aesthetic experience but rather delivered concrete pleasure to suit the quotidian life and fantasies of ordinary people. Such materials responded to, and reflected, the expectations of their audiences. Thus mass cultural commodities contained popular self-representation of the originating society.[14]

This reinforces the point that audiences need to be understood as consumers with limited budgets and time for leisure, who bring to the act of consumption a set of expectations and desires, but are mindful of alternative opportunities for fulfilment within the sphere of films and outside it. As Sue Harper and Vincent Porter, in a study of audience behaviour in Britain in 1950, have argued '...gender, social class and, to a lesser extent, age were paramount in determining the nature and intensity of film response'.[15] They maintain that although films and their stars are important in shaping the experience of audiences, the latter, in turn, bring their own world-views and experiences to the cinema and these act as filters through which meaning and pleasure are derived. From their re-evaluation of the 1950 Mass-Observation study into the incidence and reasons behind crying at the cinema, Harper and Porter found that filmgoers, classified into gender and social class categories for the purposes of analysis, gave differentiated responses to both the act of crying and the films which stimulated this behaviour.

Film consumption as an *ex-ante* gamble

In keeping with this approach to audiences it is argued that a critical attribute of first-time viewing is that of *ex-ante* risk. In attending a screening of a new film, audiences cannot have a full conception of the forthcoming experience. That they are there in the first place reveals probably a preference for some distinguishing film characteristic(s) such as genre, star, or director. However, the fact that they have not yet experienced how the package of film characteristics has been put

5

together implies that, on viewing a new film, each consumer enters into a discovery process. De Vany and Walls have argued that 'Film audiences make hits or flops and they do it, not by revealing preferences they already have, but by discovering what they like'.[16] It is important, however, to qualify this by noting that the *extent* of discovery will vary from film to film. Indeed, films can also become 'hits' by confirming preferences, for example, in sequels and runs of films where stars play similar roles, such as the Astaire/Rogers films of the 1930s, or become 'flops' by disconfirming preferences, as in ill-conceived sequels and star films where role-familiarity is perceived as staleness, or where the attempt to avoid staleness results in an unacceptable disjunction from the familiar persona (e.g. Joan Crawford in *The Gorgeous Hussy* (1936) and Clark Gable in *Parnell* (1937)).[17]

Historically, during the embryonic period of the film industry, film programmes included actualities, travelogues, event reconstructions, as well as dramatic and comic films. That hedonic film aesthetics prevailed over those which were more educational or interest specific, suggests that pleasure was at the core of what audiences most enjoyed about the experience of filmgoing. It became intrinsic to the purpose for which films were made. A theoretical approach to film consumption, along these lines, is developed in Chapter 1.

Before developing this approach to film consumption, it is important to substantiate the claim that people in their billions went to the cinema primarily to watch films, normally under conditions of quiet and comfort. Although such an assertion may appear obvious, certain outcomes of the rise in interest in cinema audiences and their motives for going to the cinema may have detracted from this essential point. David Fowler, for instance, cites evidence that cinemas functioned as places where young people could meet, court and parade. He is concerned to moderate the view that cinema served solely as an instrument of social control, maintaining that 'cinemas were by no means simply institutions where a passive working-class audience would sit in silence and receive, unquestionably, all of the images and messages peddled in the films shown to them'.[18]

On another tack, Robert Allen has written 'it is easy to overlook the fact that in the 1920s in America, for example, many viewers were not particularly interested in what film was playing',[19] and he lists the physical qualities of cinemas, such as the aura of luxury, fantastic architecture and air conditioning, as sources of attraction. Whilst these were undoubtedly important,[20] and certainly should be factored into any account of cinemagoing, they were not sufficiently important to override the influence of any particular film upon any particular box-office take. To put it another way, if considerations other than the qualities of films themselves had been dominant, then the differential performance of films screened at any single cinema would have been slight. A scrutiny of the monthly box-office data printed in *Variety* from cinemas across the US, leaves no doubt that this was not the case. Different films attracted different sizes of audience at the same cinema. The results that emerge from the empirical investigations into film popularity outlined in later chapters, demonstrate that what was true for the US was also true for Britain. Indeed, the concept of a 'hit' film or a film 'star' is meaningless otherwise.

Film as a commodity

The risk-situation entered into by filmgoers in choosing between films is mirrored by that faced by producers in attracting audiences to their films. If audiences are engaged in a discovery process in learning what they like, the same is, of course, true for film entrepreneurs.[21] The search for novelty on the part of both parties creates an arresting and uncertain environment. The rewards to 'hit' production are very great indeed and are made possible by the fact that the potential productivity of a film, and its stars, is considerable: where distribution arrangements are in place, it can be exhibited wherever demand for it exists at very little extra cost. The technological properties of the film commodity make this possible, and the pursuit of these potential returns drives the evolving configuration and aesthetics of commercial film-making. The industrial district known as Hollywood has been largely successful in capturing these returns on a global basis for much of the twentieth century.

Producers, then, are confronted with the task of setting and then meeting, and perhaps pleasantly surprising, audience expectations and desires. In doing this they will be, at the same time, aware of their own past successes and mindful of the 'hit' films produced by rival producers. As a result, the product is moved on in a more-or-less dynamic and unpredictable fashion as producers search, within this rivalrous environment, for a novel (but not too novel) package which will serve this purpose. In this context, Marcia Landy writes:

> The texts (of genre films) are not static instances of the super-imposition of standardised attitudes foisted on innocent audiences but exemplary of a dynamic interplay between producer, director,

text and audience[22] ... The spectator not only plays a role in the production of meaning but also plays an economic role in the perpetuation and decline of various genres, and if the texts do not speak to the spectators' needs and aspirations, they are consigned to oblivion. Positive audience response results in further reproduction, or modification, of genres to suit contemporary realities.[23]

In that audiences, historically, have revealed preferences for a particular sub-genre (sometimes leading to sequels), stars or directors, film producers will expect to attenuate risk by deploying these devices. The nearer stars come to being cast-iron box-office draws, however, the greater their market value, and where this is reflected in salary, the greater the costs associated with the project.[24] Indeed, theoretically, in an efficient market, stars' salaries would rise to that point just sufficient to reflect their unique contribution to the box-office take.

It is clear that the analysis up to this point is predicated upon the idea of film as a commodity.[25] Commodities can be thought of as having two distinct but interrelated forms. Not only do they exist as physical entities—with each example consisting of a separate bundle of characteristics—but also as carriers of prices. The first of these forms may be thought of as encompassing a fantastic array of utility-generating things including ideas and services, of which film is but one type. A thing's physical properties are those which are proper to it independently of human intentions or beliefs. In contrast 'being a commodity' is a mode of classification in economics in which human intention is part of the definition. Hayek's conception of 'praxeological' to describe this type of classification is pertinent here. He observed:

> Careful logical analysis of these concepts will show that they all express relationships between several (at least three) terms, one of which is the acting or thinking person, the other some desired or imagined effect, and the third a thing in the ordinary sense...The point is that they are abstractions from *all* [Hayek's emphasis] the physical attributes of the things in question and that their definitions must run entirely in terms of the mental attitudes of men towards the things.[26]

At a minimum, a commodity must have a producer/supplier who seeks a desired effect (profit) from the exchange of the item-as-commodity with a purchaser seeking an effected desire (such as to be entertained) at an acceptable price. (Normally, of course, exchange relations are very much more complicated than this.) As carriers of prices, commodities are homogeneous and stand in direct relation to each other. They can be thus be compared and evaluated according to the return—the ratio of utility (use value) to price (exchange value)—that they offer the potential consumer. They are confirmed as commodities through exchange, requiring that a sufficient number of transactions takes place at a given price to satisfy the supplier. Rejection may lead the suppliers to lower prices, or to remove the thing in question from the commodity market altogether. In certain circumstances, where an entity's potential as a commodity does not meet the motives and intentions of agents in the market, or where the importance of a failing commodity transcends the particular interests of its producer(s), its existence as a commodity may be made possible or sustained by extra-market agencies such as the State through devices such as subsidies or quotas.

To summarize: all commodities are in some sense 'produced' or 'supplied'. This may be a minimal activity such as that of a beachcomber collecting bric-à-brac and bringing it to market, or one of great complexity, e.g. the process of organizing all of the inputs needed to make and distribute a film. All commodities are in some sense 'exchanged' for a price and 'consumed', again in various degrees of complexity.

In the case of film, what is exchanged for the price paid by a member of the audience is the projected sequence of on-screen images which are 'consumed' in the mind of that member of the audience. Figure 0.1 expresses these relations in a simple flow chart. On the supply side, it is traded by means of price though a series of rental agreements between rent-seeking agents—producers, distributors and exhibitors. It takes the material form of strips of celluloid carrying visual images, perfectly reproduced from an original template—the film negative.[27] On the consumption side, film may be thought of as a sequence of those images projected onto a screen of some description. Thus the exhibitor may be thought of as a second-order 'producer' in relation to audiences, in that the cinema's projection system 'transforms' the material strips of celluloid into the immaterial audio-visual images 'consumed' by individual members of the audience through their senses and cognitive processes. As argued earlier, the collective reception of these projected images by audiences confirms, or otherwise, the existence of any particular film as a commodity, and this reception is based on those expectations of pleasure which audiences bring to the experience of film viewing. Of course, there are many examples of non-commoditized films, often involving govern-

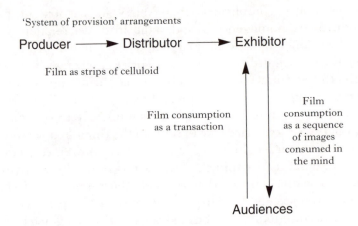

Figure 0.1: *Production and consumption relations*

ment agencies and serving information/propaganda objectives.[28] Such films do not owe their existence to the market.

Further, the production and distribution of feature films made in Communist economies can be described as quasi-commodities in that, typically, the film market was not fully developed. However, the films to which the people were attracted in the capitalist economies—annually in their billions during the classical period 1920 to 1950—constitute what is commonly understood as popular cinema, and were most certainly part of what Marx termed that 'immense collection of commodities' which make up the 'wealth of societies in which the capitalist mode of production prevails'.[29]

Film as a commodity-type

Noël Carroll has developed an ontological conception of mass art, which he defines as follows:

> x is a mass artwork if and only if 1. x is a multiple instance or type artwork, 2. produced and distributed by a mass technology, 3. which is intentionally designed to gravitate toward those choices which promise accessibility for the largest number of untutored (or relatively untutored) audiences.[30]

Film corresponds precisely to these criteria.[31] To understand why this is so requires an exploration of those characteristics which distinguish film commodity from other commodity types, including other mass art commodities such as audio records and books. I identify five. These are:

- the non-diminishable, indefinitely enlargeable, infinitely reproducible, but excludable nature of the film image;
- uniqueness;
- the rapidity with which pleasure derived from consumption declines relative to the anticipation of new pleasures—rapidly diminishing marginal utility;[32]
- the slow physical deterioration of the means of producing the film image;
- the dedicated expenditure of time and attention on the part of consumers which could be put to alternative uses.

Taking each in turn, it is possible to distinguish between technologically-based characteristics—the first and fourth characteristics in the list—and those which emerge from how the commodity is consumed—the third and fifth. The second characteristic—uniqueness—derives from the third and is made possible by the first. A more detailed description of the characteristics will convey the distinctiveness of film-as-commodity.

The non-diminishable, indefinitely enlargeable and infinitely reproducible nature of the film image

The strips of celluloid—the film negative—are the outcome of manifold acts of co-ordination within an organizational framework. However, the negative itself is not what is consumed by audiences, but rather the screen images which it makes possible in its role as template for the projection prints sent to the cinemas. These images have the property of being perfectly non-diminishable: their physical properties are not reduced as a consequence of consumption. It makes no difference to the physical condition of the image-commodity whether it is viewed by one consumer or one million.

Although in principle the film image is capable of indefinite enlargement, implying that the size of screen and therefore potential audience at any single viewing is also indefinite, in practice the size of the immediate local market for film products determined that the seating capacity of local exhibition venues rarely exceeded 3,000 seats during the heyday of cinema, and on average it was much smaller than that.[33] The principal reason for the apparent small scale of cinemas,

11

when compared with professional sporting stadia, for instance, lay in film's capability of precise mechanical reproduction which allowed the same visual information to be produced *ad infinitum*, anywhere, at any time, on demand.

As a new technology the invention and innovation of cinemato-graphic techniques made possible the universalization of a particular set of images that made up a film, including its stars. Further, the capability of exclusion meant that particular film images could only be obtained at a price. Clearly, the effect of this technology on the productivity of that bundle of factor inputs engaged in the production of a film commodity was potentially enormous and explains the importance of distribution as well as the enormous salaries com-manded by the most successful stars/directors/producers of their day.[34]

There were, therefore, no limits on the potential size of an audience, since physical constraints imposed by cinema architecture and environmental considerations could be overcome through additional cinema building and the manufacture of more prints and their sub-sequent distribution. The greater the diffusion of any particular film, the greater the productivity of its protagonists. Further, the extension of the media that now carry film, notably television and video, serves to give even more emphasis to the importance of these features.

The cinema, as it emerged from the music hall in Britain and vaudeville in the US, continued the practice of limiting audiences through seating capacity and pricing, whilst the relatively slow diminishability—technical deterioration—of the negative meant that the exercise could be repeated, on the next day, or the next month, without any significant loss of image quality. In this context, it is easy to understand that cinema runs evolved, separated by temporal and spatial clearance zones, as a means of economizing on the number of prints necessary to meet the planned distribution of any single film. The distributor also realized that the strict supervision of the temporal diffusion of film products would enable first-run cinemas to charge higher prices than second-run cinemas, which in turn would be able to charge higher prices than third-run cinemas and so on, on the grounds that a significant proportion of audiences was prepared to pay a premium to watch films at an earlier rather than a later date. Given that distributors took a flat rate sum plus a proportion of the box-office gross, this price discriminatory practice ensured that net revenues to the distributor were greater than would have been the case had cinemas charged the same price everywhere. The practice of 'continuous performances' and also 'double-feature' programming was introduced during the 1930s in response to a sharpening of competitiveness resulting from the downturn in economic activity.

Commodity uniqueness

Each film is unique in that it comprises a set of characteristics which differentiate it from other films. Such a set typically includes genre, plot, screenplay, star billing, direction, cinematography, art direction, supporting actors, sets, locations, wardrobe and make-up, music and length. However, this complexity creates a major problem for film production companies because of the uncertainty it poses for audiences. Since box-office revenues are based upon the reception of each film by consumers who make choices between rival unique products, studio heads and producers will be concerned to reduce the degree of uncertainty that uniqueness entails.[35] They will seek to influence consumer choice and hence film earnings by incorporating certain deliberate design features into the product, the most important of which, historically, have been narrative storytelling conventions, stars, genre, production studio and director. The bundle of characteristics which defines the uniqueness of the film commodity came to be used to arouse a set of expectations in filmgoers. Thus, publicity signalling that James Stewart was appearing in a Frank Capra romantic comedy, or Jessie Matthews in a Gaumont-British musical, directed the consumer towards certain terrains of pleasure.

We can view this business behaviour as a form of 'branding', where producers of differentiated products invest in quality signals with the objective of generating favourable (quality) image perceptions on the part of filmgoers. The publicity departments of film production studios hence set out not simply to promote each new film, but also the stars who were appearing in it and other tangible qualities associated with it. Indeed, loyalty to the studio itself was promoted through its own company logo and fanfare at the start of each film. Catherine Kerr quotes from Halsey, Stuart and Co.'s 'Bond Financing' prospectus of 1927 to the effect that:

> The 'stars' are today an economic necessity to the motion picture industry. In the 'star' your producer gets not only a 'production' value…but a 'trademark' value, and an 'insurance' value which are very real and very potent in guaranteeing the sale of this product to the cash customers at a profit.[36]

However, unlike typical commodity producers whose output consists of standardized items within differentiated product ranges, film production companies can only approximate a set of standards based loosely on genre categories. This is because of the risk inherent in predicting filmgoers' reactions to the artistic and personality aspect of a film's imagery. Sneak previews with poll-tested audience responses provide some information for revising a finished film, but there always was (and is) an irreducible element of uncertainty.[37]

For the consumer, this creates a non-typical set of information conditions. At the same time that a film production company attempts to convey assurances to customers that its product will fulfil the desired set of expectations, filmgoers, as has been argued above, know from experience that the uniqueness of each film means that differences between *ex-ante* expectations and *ex-post* evaluations are common. This is quite unlike the normal pattern of consumer experience in relation to rigorously standardized products which meet precisely a set of *ex-ante* expectations built upon repetitive consumption experience.

Historically, the major production companies created portfolios of unique commodities, each of which was subject to an amortization schedule: films were commonly written off as having no resaleable value in the American market after 12 months during the period 1930–50.[38] In Britain and the US during the 1930s, the major players typically produced a range of different quality commodities which were marketed in categories ranging from 'super' to 'regular' productions. The different grades reflected cost differences based upon star, production and publicity values. Following the Cinematograph Film Act of 1927, which made blind block booking illegal in Britain, these commodities had to be marketed separately.

As indicated above, however, hard though the studios tried to attenuate the uncertainties associated with a 'hit' production, they were never entirely able to do so. The *ex-ante* recipe for box-office success was necessarily elusive—the ingredients of 'star' and 'production values' may have been necessary but they were not sufficient conditions for 'hit' production. Sedgwick and Pokorny have shown that the portfolio approach to production allowed the major Hollywood studios during the classical period to pool their risks over a product range, thus reducing the significance of the success, or failure, of individual film commodities.[39]

Rapidly diminishing marginal utility of the film commodity
With the existence of a plentiful supply of rival film commodities in accessible localities at comparable prices, consumers will tend to

consume a particular commodity once only, since the opportunity cost of a repeat viewing might entail the lost opportunity to watch an alternative film. This is not to say that consumers never repeat view a particular film, but that the event is still comparatively rare in the cinema and might be explained by the much lower sensual arousal generated by a second, or third viewing, in relation to the anticipated stimulation associated with the prospect of viewing a film of choice for the first time.[40] It is interesting to note that it was only towards the end of the 1930s that re-releases of earlier successful films became commonplace, and even then the additional box-office generated was in most cases only a small fraction of the original take.[41] Of course, this is less likely to be the case with the advent of the home consumption of films brought about, post-1950, by the wide diffusion of television and more recently the general diffusion of video technology and satellite and cable television.[42]

The principle of diminishing marginal utility is a key factor in understanding the rapid amortization schedules adopted by the Hollywood majors during the classical period. With re-releases becoming common only during the later 1930s, the general absence of repeat viewing meant that a film's commercial potential had been exhausted by the end of its geographical distribution. This would take some 12–15 months, during which time it was distributed through the various 'run' categories of cinemas. After this time, if the costs incurred in production had not been recovered, they were unlikely ever to be. Part of the explanation for this rapid consumption of what is a complex product can be explained through the organization of film characteristics into forms of which the consumer had prior experience, and could hence codify rapidly.

Relatively slow physical diminishability of the film commodity
Unlike the rapid commercial diminishability of the film commodity, the rate of physical depreciation is relatively slow; indeed, with the application of modern techniques of preservation and restoration it is effectively zero. This characteristic, coupled with the relatively low cost of making copies, implies a potential mismatch between supply and demand sides of the market for film commodities, with supply exceeding demand. Given the limited market for any single film, distribution based upon the exchange of full property rights will result in a ranked series of seconds and rental markets awash with films of an extensive vintage range. Such a market would discourage the production of new films, particularly where the respective first and

seconds markets were not sealed off from one another and substitution between the two occurred.

The organizational solution to this problem was the emergence of distribution companies that regulated the supply of film products onto the market by means of rental agreements with exhibitors. Initially, only special event actualities or major new films were distributed by procedures restricting exhibitors to limited temporal access. However, the general adoption of the system in the United States, following the demise of the MPPC (Motion Picture Patents Company) cartel and the emergence of the longer feature film *circa* 1908–14 and its parallel development in Britain, brought the existence of a seconds markets to an end.

The dedicated expenditure of time and attention necessary in the
consumption of the film commodity which could be put to alternative uses
The act of film consumption in the cinema is time-intensive in that it entails, for the greater part, the focused attention of an audience who have travelled to a cinema and paid the price of admission to a programme in preference to alternative uses of their time, including those pleasures available at rival cinemas.

Film as a system of provision

In moving analytically from the abstract conception of commodity production to actual production of film as a commodity, it has been possible to identify a combination of characteristics which not only distinguish it from other commodity types, but also provide a framework for understanding the unique form of industrial configuration which film has taken and the ownership patterns which have been superimposed upon this. All the key elements in the history of film as a commodity can be traced back analytically to the commodity characteristics I have enumerated: the separation of the industry into the spheres of production, distribution and exhibition; the emergence of the differentiated commodity; the change in the system from assigning price on the basis of footage to one based upon anticipated popularity; the evolution of price discriminatory practices not only within cinemas but, and more importantly, as an inherent element in the system of distribution; the development of storytelling conventions; the emergence of features, and genres; the importance of stars to sales; the development of vertically integrated business forms; the extension of the commodity to new media forms; and the international predominance of Hollywood in world markets.

This depiction of film fits comfortably into a new theoretical approach to the study of consumption in capitalist economies developed by Ben Fine and Ellen Leopold.[43] They eschew what they term 'horizontal' approaches to consumption, in which analysts 'search for common elements across all aspects of consumption', in favour of a vertical approach which 'unites a particular pattern of production with a particular pattern of consumption...(in) ways in which each is moderated by the connections between them'.[44] They term any such vertical pattern a 'system of provision'. For Fine and Leopold, the study of 'systems of provision'

> requires an examination, both historical and social, of the connected causal links by which commodities are distinctly and materially made available, in a way that encourages more fruitful speculation about the future of consumption as well as a deeper understanding of both the present and past.[45]

In a similar vein they argue that

> each commodity or commodity group is best understood in terms of a unity of economic and social processes which vary significantly from one to another, each creating and reflecting upon ... its own 'system of provision'.[46]

Outline of the project of this book

This book explores aspects of film as a 'system of provision' in Britain during the 1930s. In particular it is concerned with the issue of film popularity and establishes a distinctive empirical methodology for measuring it in the absence, in Britain, of detailed box-office information. Janet Thumim's observation, quoted earlier, that film 'hits' are valuable sources of evidence concerning the kinds of pleasure which cinema audiences derived from film may be taken as a starting point. The empirical issue of how to establish popularity is not, however, unproblematic. Both Thumim[47] and Sue Harper,[48] for instance, draw upon those selective secondary sources found in specialized magazines and trade journals—*Picturegoer*, *Motion Picture Herald* and *Kinematograph Weekly* (hereafter abbreviated to *Kine Weekly*)—for evidence. Indeed, Harper writes:

> All the evidence of audience response in the 1930s has gone through some type of filter; letters to magazines have been selected and

possibly amended and Mass-Observation material may be coloured by the bias of the interviewer. But a representative selection of material can be made, so long as different kinds of journals and geographical regions are covered.[49]

Thumim uses annual poll evidence from the same or similar sources to list ten or so films which were the most popular during the 1950s and into the 1960s. Another example of this procedure is Jeffrey Richards' use of the *Motion Picture Herald*'s annual ranking of stars amongst British audiences to champion the positions of George Formby and Gracie Fields as the foremost male and female stars of their day.[50] The popularity data found in these sources present a number of difficulties, however. Not only do the records of the selection practices and the ensuing data no longer exist, making inspection and evaluation impossible, but the form in which they are presented prevents any further analytical manipulation. Also, a list of the most popular films is one which excludes evidence of popularity within the body of remaining films released in the course of any one season. During the 1930s when some 600–700 films were released per annum, such a practice leaves out an awful lot of evidence. Moreover, it is difficult to see how the evidence found in nationally distributed trade journals can adequately reflect differences, if any, in regional patterns of consumption.

In proposing a new methodology for establishing contemporaneous film popularity, rooted in observation and collection of data, and organized in the framework of falsifiable theory,[51] it would appear that I run foul of the charge of 'crude empiricism', to use Jackie Stacey's disapproving phrase.[52] Empiricism as a methodology should never be crude. Deciding what data to collect, and how to organize them as a means of producing a set of results which represents fully the phenomenon of film popularity, requires a close practical and theoretical understanding of the institutional practices and arrangements of film as a 'system of provision'. Conversely, any measure of popularity which pays scant attention to institutional detail, such as one derived solely from the writings of critics or contemporary social surveys, can be criticized in terms of incompleteness: it will not reflect the film choices available to audiences and their subsequent decisions.

Chapter 1 develops a theory of filmgoing choice. It is a theory of choice and not consumption and takes as a starting point a 'system of provision' which has emerged historically and takes a particular form. From this position an account is offered of the nature of risk involved in consumer choice. Further, it is argued that the uncertainty faced by consumers translates directly to the risk inherent in film production, and in turn to the business practices designed by film studio entrepreneurs to attenuate it. Another strand of the argument works from the empirical observation that different films, produced by similarly endowed studios with similar budgets, regularly achieve quite different levels of popularity and leads to the conjecture that the reason for this is that filmgoers wittingly engage in a bounded discovery process: one based upon a well-defined set of aesthetic preferences that have been formed and shaped through repeated experience over time. In analytically separating individual choice from the general environment of consumption it is possible to garner fresh insights into how the 'system of provision' operates. For instance, it is clear from a political economy perspective that the reasons behind the adoption of blanket release practices from the mid-1970s are intimately connected to a more intensive sales and merchandizing strategy pursued by the major Hollywood studios. This fits comfortably into a monopoly capital framework that has global economy consequences. But what of these changes from the perspective of the individual filmgoer? In understanding how these selling activities influence the filmgoer we need to have a framework for understanding the consumer as a receiver of information. In what ways are filmgoers' expectations formed and changed over time? How do they respond to new aesthetic information? How is it that some films seem to strike a chord with filmgoers and others do not? These questions lead back to the high risks associated with individual film production, even when undertaken by major Hollywood studios, which do all that they can—through market segmentation, stars, and portfolio practices—to attenuate risk.

My argument is that you need a theory of film choice to complement that of film supply, and that by abstracting from historical practice, if just for a moment, it is possible to come to a deeper understanding of that historical practice. There have been lots of social reasons why people have gone to the cinema in their hundreds of billions this century. As argued earlier, part of the explanation for cinema's popularity, is that films have brought a range of aesthetic pleasures to mankind, bringing about an improved sense of well-being. As each film offers a distinct bundle of pleasure characteristics it seems not unreasonable to conjecture that filmgoing decisions are, at least in part, based on expectations of pleasure, where different films in a choice set offer the prospect, but not necessarily the realization, of different levels of pleasure.

Chapter 2 does three things. It sets the historical context of cinema-going in Britain during the 1930s, and is followed by an account of the reasons why British film production failed in the decade following the end of the First World War, based upon the writings of Kristin Thompson and Rachael Low. The chapter closes with an analysis of the reasons for, and impact of, the 1927 Cinematograph Films Act. It argues strongly that the Act is of critical importance in understanding the re-birth and revived fortunes of British film production during the 1930s.

Chapter 3 is devoted to underpinning and explaining a methodology for measuring film popularity in the absence of box-office records: what I term the POPSTAT index of film popularity. The chapter starts with an analysis of the commercial life of film commodities, based upon the exhibition programmes of a nation-wide sample of approximately ninety London West End and provincial city cinemas, and proceeds to an explanation of the mechanics of, and principles behind, the cascade system of film distribution in Britain during the period. It further provides systematic evidence of how films moved out in time and space from high- to low-order cinemas across Britain, and deals with some crucial problems concerning the representativeness of the cinemas found in the sample. A detailed account of London's premier 'flagship' cinemas and their principal film attractions during the period is set out in the appendix to the chapter. Finally the chapter develops the concept of POPSTAT, a measure (index) of individual film popularity derived from the exhibition exposure that any single film received in those cinemas which make up the sample.

The POPSTAT methodology is made operational in Chapters 4, 5 and 6 and applied to three sample sets of cinemas: respectively, a national sample previously explained and described in Chapter 3; and two local samples, those of Bolton and Brighton.[53] The chapters provide evidence of differences in the pattern of popularity across the three samples of cinemas, with Chapter 4 explicitly focusing on the comparative popularity of British films in relation to their more illustrious Hollywood counterparts.

The claims for this methodology are as follows:

i.   The researcher has no influence on the selection of those films which appear to be the most popular of the day.

ii. All films marketed have an equal chance statistically of being amongst the 'hits' of the day. The sampling methodology excludes only those films which have not received at least one screening in the sample set of cinemas.

iii. The index of popularity (POPSTAT) allows the researcher to rank films in order of popularity.

iv. Its premises and procedures are explicit. Accordingly, it is answerable to analytic criticism which might show it to be misconceived or, less seriously, faulty.

v. It is transferable between communities, regions and nations in which the 'systems of provision' have similar characteristics.

In Chapters 7, 8 and 9, the POPSTAT rankings are used to explore the relationship between popularity and film budgets, popularity and genre, and popularity and stardom, respectively. This investigation draws heavily upon the business ledgers of MGM, Warners and RKO. Chapter 8 introduces the idea of film lineages as a means of tracing the life-cycles of certain styles of film, while in Chapter 9 the adaptation of the POPSTAT methodology is demonstrated by a measure of star popularity (STARSTAT) derived from the POPSTAT scores of the annual Top 100 films screened in Britain during the period.

The last three chapters are drawn from two recent publications in the *Historical Journal of Film, Radio and Television*.[54] Chapters 10 and 11 are devoted to an exploration of the issues which arise from the size of the British domestic market and the ubiquitous presence of the Hollywood film. The problem for British film-makers was that their domestic market was not large enough to sustain big-budget film production. The conundrum facing them was that high production values were expensive, but if they were to compete effectively with the top films emanating from the principal Hollywood studios this expense was a necessary one. Access to the British and American markets was, however, uneven. The vertically integrated American majors, along with United Artists, held a near monopoly of the US distribution network, making it extremely difficult for British producers to get their films screened as a matter of routine in that market. In Britain, with the revival of domestic production, the Americans lost market share. Nevertheless, they were still extremely potent players and collectively remained the dominant force in the British market. The asymmetry of these arrangements made it difficult for indigenous film-makers to sustain profitability.

One strategic response to this conundrum was Gaumont-British's decision to establish its own New York based distribution company. Chapter 10 draws heavily upon the internal memorandums, private letters, telegrams and reports found in the Michael Balcon Special Collection housed at the British Film Institute. For the strategy to be successful, the films made at its two London studios needed to do well in first-run American cinemas. The chapter describes the box-office performance of the twenty-eight films sent to the US by the company for in-house distribution. The information was obtained from the box-office data published monthly in *Variety* on cinemas across the US, and to my knowledge constitutes the first systematic use of this rich source of data.

Chapter 11 presents a contextual view of the industry late in the period, by which time Britain had in place a well-developed film production infrastructure, with major studios at Shepperton, Denham, Elstree and Pinewood. As well as providing detailed evidence concerning the asymmetry between the market opportunities for British and Hollywood producers, the chapter provides an account of the debates which led up to, and the immediate effects of, the 1938 Cinematograph Films Act.

The concluding chapter draws attention to the achievements of British production during the period. In this chapter I emphasize the importance for the film historian of thinking *ex ante* about decisions taken by film-makers. The problem with structural models of social phenomena is that they relegate as secondary the role of agency in human affairs in favour of structures and mechanisms by which pertinent phenomena are explained. Conversely, I would argue that whilst structures are likely to help our understanding of the constraints faced by agents they impede our understanding of the future perceived by them at the moment of decision-making. This future is likely to be uncertain, and one reason for this is that in taking a particular decision the agent will cause the structure to be changed, no matter how minutely, from what it would have been had the decision not been made, or indeed had a different decision been made. If this is true of one agent, then the effect will be magnified for all agents, particularly as each will be making qualitatively different decisions in the light of their own assessment of the uncertainty which they face. In such ways, boundaries are redrawn in uneven and unforeseen ways. In my opinion, this agency-orientated framework of analysis is key to understanding the impact which the 1927 Cinematograph Films Act had upon film production, in particular, and film as a 'system of provision', in general, in Britain during the 1930s. In changing the institutional environment, the legislation encouraged British film-makers to push against the structural constraints of the prevailing 'system of provision', changing it in unpredictable ways with unknown consequences.

1

A Theory of Film Choice

A Matter of Taste[1]

Film is an unusual commodity in that prior to watching a film for the first time audiences can have only a limited idea of what it is that they are about to experience. This is because each film has the characteristic of being, in some respect, unique. Audiences have come to expect that their senses will be aroused in a not altogether predictable fashion by new narrative and aesthetic information consciously organized by producers to attract them away from other pursuits, including viewing other films. It is apparent from the early history of cinemagoing that audiences revealed preferences for films in which the story element was foremost, in contrast to actualities, travelogues and trick films in which information and spectacle predominated: audiences took greater pleasure from the narrative form. It is also the case that, as a general rule, contemporaneity and newness have been preferred to repeat viewing or films of an older vintage, a consumption characteristic which has generated a powerful incentive for producers working at the top end of the market to innovate.

The particular technology embodied in the film commodity means that, once made and marketed, its productivity potential is considerable. Clearly, the distribution function exists to ensure that the unique set of images which constitutes a film can be screened anywhere in response to the demand for it. The rational rent-seeking distributor wishes to handle films that are popular, as does the rational rent-seeking cinema owner. The rational rent-seeking producer aims to make such films. The dilemma is that pleasure-seeking audiences do not know definitively how they feel about a film until they have seen it.

In evaluating the pleasure derived from a film in relation to the price

23

of a cinema admission, the filmgoer is engaged in *ex-post* activity. Whilst this is true of all consumption, film is one of a number of commodity types where divergences between expectation and experience are commonplace, part of which might be explained by the advertisers' incentives to promote, in an artfully persuasive fashion, goods which cannot be fully evaluated prior to consumption and are generally only consumed once. Consumers can only work on what Nelson terms 'soft' information and are thus subject to misleading advertising.[2] This implies that the act of consumption entails a spread of risk which can be measured (discounted) in terms of the potential pleasures foregone. Hence, filmgoing represents a risky investment in pleasure for the consumer. Knowing this we shall assume that the rational filmgoer chooses between films with circumspection, balancing their respective characteristics (as far as she or he understands them) one against the other. Consumer uncertainty is mirrored on the supply side of the industry since each new film on release is presented to a potential audience which may or may not take to it: in not knowing fully how to please audiences, the producer runs the risk of not pleasing them very much at all. At the top end of the market, film-making is a particularly risky business, since audiences have demanded more not less innovation and producers have historically invested more in trying to please them. Film producers, knowing that film audiences will in general prefer high levels of riskless pleasure, cannot guarantee this because they are compelled to meet audiences' prior requirement for novelty and uniqueness.

Writing about audience preferences in Britain during the 1950s, Harper and Porter distinguish between three categories of filmgoer.

> It seems that the audience for each film consisted of indiscriminate, regular and occasional cinema-goers and that these were in varying proportions. The attitudes of these three groups were quite distinct. Indiscriminate audiences were attracted to the cinema and went to it, no matter what. For regular cinema-goers, films were an integral part of their weekly round of pleasure. Occasional cinema-goers were more discriminating, and would see only specific films.[3]

Harper and Porter are writing about a period of rapid decline in cinema attendances during which the indiscriminate segment of the audience was all but extinguished, giving greater weight to the decisions of the other two groups in establishing levels of popularity. They argue that the success or otherwise of a film was largely determined by the occasional attenders: those who needed to be attracted by a particular film away from other activities. Historically, the existence of a numerically significant marginal audience explains why it is that the box-office performance of similarly budgeted films and their stars varies so markedly. The corollary of this is that different films showing at the same cinema during the same part of a season generate quite different levels of box-office activity. From this it may be supposed that film audiences comprise sufficient numbers of filmgoers who, having discovered what it is that they like from past experience, make choices between films, or between films and other activities, along rational lines. Film popularity is a reflection of their preferences.

This chapter offers a theory of choice. This is different from a theory of consumption in that the latter is taken to be historically specific and entails a set of norms based upon prevailing social and cultural conventions.[4] The work presented here abstracts from time and place and seeks an explanation of film choice based on rational deliberation. It does so in order to draw out and examine the risk environment faced by filmgoers. It assumes the existence of a 'system of provision' in which agency arrangements have emerged about the production, distribution and exhibition of film as a commodity, such that a common characteristic of urban environments is the multiple and simultaneous opportunities for cinemagoing. The chapter is divided into four sections. The first establishes a dynamic framework for analysing consumer behaviour, in which taste is considered to be an essential element in the decision-making process. The second establishes a heuristic mechanism which enables the consumer to reject those films which are not consonant with the consumer's preconceived set of preferences. Shackle's approach to decision-making under uncertainty forms the basis of the third section. The fourth and final section brings the chapter to a conclusion with a discussion of the relationship between filmgoer choice and film popularity.

Behavioural assumptions

In choosing between films, consumers will use their personal resources of time, experience, information and knowledge as a set of input variables to some personal output function which each one of them is keen to maximize: each consumer would prefer to watch films which generate intense emotional rewards (termed pleasure from this point onwards), the precise nature of which varies from one consumer to another, rather than those which do not.

Time is scarce in that there are competing uses to which it can be put. It is relevant to the decision-making process on three counts: firstly, consumers will engage in search activity when identifying an initial choice set; secondly, they will operate some heuristic mechanism which allows them to select ultimately one film above all others; and finally, they will suspend all other activities for the duration of consumption.

Experience is accumulated through learning. Hence the stock of an individual's experience (human capital) at any point in time is derived from the accumulation of past encounters. In choosing between films an individual will use elements of this knowledge in the pursuit of a desired end. One way of thinking about how to make sense of the past is in terms of the quest for consonance and the rejection of dissonance, as elaborated by Gilad, Kaish and Loab.[5] In their model, individuals allow into the decision-making process only that information broadly compatible with a set of pre-existing (prior) commitments. Each individual has a threshold tolerance for dissonant information 'where a higher degree contributes to a more adaptive, or profitable behaviour'.[6] The action of filtering out dissonant information—what may be considered as an 'I know what I like' syndrome—has a rational basis up to the point at which it becomes apparent that the original commitment is wrong, and that point will be reached when the individual judges that the loss through denial, in terms of not accepting dissonant information, exceeds the benefits associated with not admitting that the commitment was mistaken.

With regard to films, it is possible to understand commitment in terms of previously established preferences (tastes) for particular genre, style or star types. These types will have rewarded the consumer in the past and serve as markers in the present decision-making process. The filmgoer may experience loyalty and association towards one or more of these markers which will prejudice future consumption decisions. Dissonance, on the other hand, will manifest itself in terms of dislike towards certain markers: e.g. actors who have failed to convince, directors whose style of film-making seems heavy handed, storylines which are offensive. However, commitments can be shown to be wrong-headed, or not stand the test of time when repeated exposure to such markers introduces fatigue and with it diminishing utility. The formation of tastes is likely to be more dynamic with respect to film than most other commodity types because of the peculiar set of characteristics which constitute film as a commodity.

In particular, its characteristic of uniqueness obliges the filmgoer to admit new information in the act of consumption, even where the set of markers flagged up by the film suggests strong commitment. The distinct possibility that this information may not confirm a filmgoer's previous set of commitments suggests that markers are likely to be less than foolproof, leading the filmgoer, where disappointed by a film, to a reappraisal and occasionally a change of commitment.[7] Furthermore, every now and then a new film comes along which has a seminal effect upon experiential paradigms leading to the widespread introduction of a new set of markers and the subsequent reappraisal of all existing ones. I would argue that the Astaire/Rogers film *The Gay Divorcee* (1934) was such a film, not only in presenting two new stars but also in terms of changing the style and aesthetics of the Hollywood musical from the time of its release.

This analysis can be adduced in support of the following principles: first, that tastes exist and second, that they change over time. Further, whilst it might be possible to map tastes retrospectively, it is not possible to project them forward, as we move beyond the immediate future, with any degree of probability. The model proposed here takes the form of a regressive geometric series in which the weights of the ith marker decline with the passage of time back from the moment in which the decision-maker is situated, but where the parameter values reflect the strength of a consumer's response to the jth performance at the time of that performance. The index value given to the ith marker for the jth performance can range from strongly negative to strongly positive. In effect, markers accumulate index values which can be checked against an already established, experientially derived threshold value, k. Where ongoing accumulated values are greater than the threshold k, the consumer stays with a particular marker. Where they fall below that value, markers are rejected by the consumer as commitment is lost. This can give us interesting inter-generational effects since the accumulation of weights would clearly be lower for younger people, whilst their sensory responses (parameter values) might be expected to be more intense than those of the next generation, indicating that young persons' marker commitments are likely to be much less stable, hence less reliable and more subject to change.

The approach to taste adopted here is at odds with the theory of choice developed by Stigler and Becker in which 'differences in tastes never becomes the explanation for differences in behaviour ... [and that] The establishment of the proposition that one may usefully treat tastes as stable overtime and similar among people is central'.[8] For them, advertising does not influence taste but reduces search costs; changes in fashion represent a constant preference for style; music appreciation increases with the productivity of the time spent listening to music. Tastes do not change. What does change is the efficiency with which the consumer uses his time to obtain utility. These are human capital arguments allowing differences in preferences to be explained by a combination of relative prices and incomes—the province of the economist—rather than taste, about which sociologists and psychologists may have more to say.

Although the Stigler and Becker analytical framework recognizes that individuals develop—they experience diminishing returns with respect to heroin addiction but increasing returns to musical appreciation, advertising and fashion—they do not allow this to affect the human capital variable in their household production function, which remains exogenously determined. The loop from experience to human capital formation is not made. This is of critical importance since it is the loop which connects experience to learning, to knowledge, and which enables consumers to make judgements and choose between things. Further, it is difficult to conceive that what Stigler and Becker term human capital does not contain an aesthetic/taste aspect since the household outputs of today become part of tomorrow's stock of experience. If, for example, an individual were to become more efficient in appreciating paintings as 'works of art', through say a series of visits to important galleries, we might expect that the person's appreciation and perception of aesthetics would change, not only in the realm of painting, but across everyday life. Clearly, if this were to be the case, all future decisions in which aesthetic considerations were important would be affected, such as choosing furniture. There is also likely to be a social dimension to this process in that by associating with a new group of people who have similar artistic interests, the individual will experience a new sense of self-esteem in regard to other household members and the broader community. The individual, in a profound way, moves on and is intangibly different as a result of the experience. Being more efficient in the use of time is likely to be a facet of this. Likewise, having a more developed sense of taste. Human capital formation is intimately linked to those outputs to which it is directed by the consumer, but is in turn affected and altered as a consequence of that consumption. Rather than as a uni-directional line of causation, it is better to think of consumption as a dialectical activity in which the self not only acts upon its environment in making choices between things but is, in turn, profoundly affected by what is chosen.

Initial choice set

Cinemagoing is often a joint activity. Where this is the case, the decision about what to see reflects an ensemble of preferences, implying a satisficing rather than a personal optimizing form of behaviour. For the sake of simplicity, however, let us suppose that the act of choosing between cinema programmes is a singular rather than group decision, and that in choosing between films a filmgoer goes through two procedures. Firstly, she or he organizes an *initial choice set*, defined as those x films available on release at conveniently situated and affordable cinemas, an assumption which removes time and transport costs as well as admission price differentials from the analysis. This can be justified in that not only has cinemagoing been historically a low-cost form of entertainment, but cinemas have been in plentiful supply in urban areas and potential audiences have had a variety of programmes to choose from at a set of similarly priced and accoutred cinemas. Next, suppose that the *initial choice set* is organized as illustrated in Figure 1.1 by ordering expectations along a continuum of pleasure, which ranges from antipathy to indifference and so on through low and middling pleasure bands to a final band where only those films which promise high levels of pleasure are assigned. The filmgoer can be expected to do this by using readily available information of both a formal (reviews, publicity etc.) and informal nature (word of mouth).[9] In making a selection, the filmgoer will not necessarily know a great deal about all films in the set but will be concerned to move to the second procedure which entails sifting those which are potentially attractive from those which are not. Hence, the supposition is that some kind of threshold device is used to sort films into two bins—a *reject bin* and a *final choice set* consisting of those films

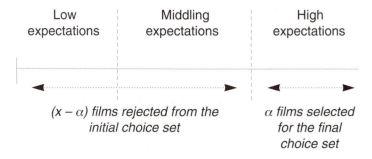

Figure 1.1: *The initial choice set*

towards which the filmgoer is most attracted.

This decision-making heuristic conforms to the general behavioural routine proposed by Peter Earl:

> As decision-makers get further into the process of choice, they will normally narrow down the range of possibilities that are being considered, at the same time as increasing the detail in terms of which they consider them. The use of hierarchies is something that we naturally fall into in order to simplify our decision-making.[10]

As argued earlier, a useful way of thinking about this is to imagine that filmgoers have developed particular tastes and that they search for those films containing markers to which they are committed. For instance, suppose that a filmgoer values two aesthetic characteristics in a film above all others. Let these be glamour and romance and let us suppose that the filmgoer sets high threshold levels of each. In Figure 1.2, only three films (films A, B and C) potentially satisfy these threshold levels. These films then constitute the filmgoer's *final choice set*. The remaining films fail in that they do not promise sufficient levels of either characteristic. Thus while film D is imbued with sufficient romance, it clearly fails the filmgoer in terms of glamour. Alternately, film G certainly satisfies the filmgoer in terms of sought-after levels of glamour but scores very badly on the romance measure.

The analytical procedure outlined emphasises a positive approach to selection. However, it may be the case that filmgoers adopt a negative

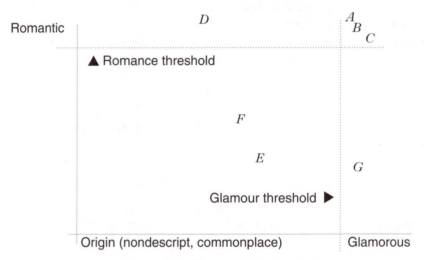

Figure 1.2: *Characteristics thresholds*

stance: rather than looking for characteristics that are attractive, the consumer may alternatively have strong aversions toward certain characteristics/markers. For instance, the filmgoer may be averse to a particular star (John Wayne) and genre (the western). Accordingly, a filmgoer of the late 1940s might well have committed *She Wore a Yellow Ribbon* (1949) to the reject bin.

The number and the interrelationships of characteristics which distinguish any particular film will be large and complex. One can think of narrative style, visual style, atmosphere, pacing, spatial setting, historical and social context, genre, before moving on to idiosyncratic star, star combination, and director and producer influences, to name but the most obvious. Complexity comes with the demand for novelty which ensures that the combination characteristics of any particular film will always carry some element of uniqueness. The juxtaposition of these characteristics implies that the number of points of comparison between films can be very great indeed.

Choosing between films

Having decided upon a final choice set, the filmgoer must choose between the films therein, assuming, of course, that there is more than one film to choose from. The distinction between expectations and experience can be usefully illustrated by reference to George Shackle's *principle of surprise*.[11] The argument here is that filmgoers know from previous experience that, in watching a new film, they may experience a reaction to it which surprises them to the extent that their expectations have not been perfectly matched. Thus, in choosing between films as well as between filmgoing and some other activity, consumers use their imaginations. These expectations are likely to be strongly formed within cultures in which filmgoing has been a genuinely popular leisure activity, implying that filmgoers will hold firm preferences for what they like. However, a filmgoer's expectations should not be regarded as forever bounded, but rather as a modifiable set of ideas subject to change as distinctive aesthetic regimes emerge and affect the way in which things are looked at and pleasures are derived. As Shackle suggests:

> Expectation is not a passive finished and settled state of thought but an activity of mind which can at no time say that it has completed the imaginative exploitation of its data; for these data are merely fragmentary suggestions in a paradoxical fertile void.[12]

The risk implicit in film consumption means that the expectations which consumers bring to the cinema may be exceeded or disappointed. The pattern of loss and gain can be depicted by means of an *ex-post* frequency distribution about a reference point marking an expected level of pleasure, denoted in Figure 1.3 as *e*. The knowledge upon which this is based is derived from an individual's personal history of filmgoing. A 'horizontal' distribution (i.e. parallel to the Pleasure axis) would imply that the difference between expectation and realization is randomly distributed. However, it is more likely that the distribution will be 'bell-shaped' about *e*, suggesting that filmgoers make informed choices and that whilst they can be wildly wrong in their prior assessment of a film, this is a relatively uncommon occurrence.

The frequency distributions drawn in Figure 1.3 are based on hypothetical historic patterns of loss and gain for a representative filmgoer. Each film seen has a place in the distribution and all of them together constitute the distribution. The *ex-post* experience of each film, then, when measured against the *ex-ante* expectation which it aroused, is recorded either as matching exactly that expectation or as a loss or gain. This is quite different from the situation facing the filmgoer when choosing between films, since each film in the *final choice set* offers only the imaginable prospect of a loss or gain relative to the

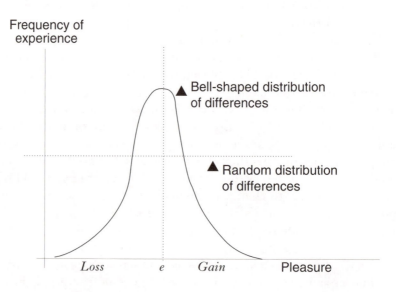

Figure 1.3: *Frequency distributions of the difference between expectations and realizations of multiple filmgoing over a long period*

measure of expectation it arouses. The past, although helping the filmgoer to form expectations, can only give that person an understanding of the chances of loss or gain. However, the uniqueness of each film ensures that the experience of watching will be to some extent novel and thus peculiar to that film. A strong version of this argument—one which perhaps does not give sufficient attention to the function of markers in film choice—is given by Hoskins, McFadyen and Finn:

> A feature film is a product that consumers must pay for before they know how much enjoyment they will receive. Attending large numbers of films provides little guidance in choosing a new movie... In other words, search activity and experience, which are valuable to consumers for many other products, are of little guidance to consumers in choosing which movie to attend.[13]

A Subjective Expected Utility Theory (SEU) approach to risk requires that probability values be ascribed to a range of consumer expectations (i.e. extreme disappointment to intense pleasure) formed for each of the films in the *final choice set*—films A, B, and C in Figure 1.2. The expected pleasure (value) from each film can be then be compared and a choice made. The filmgoer's attitude to risk will affect which films pass the threshold of the final choice set. It is easy to envisage that some films offer safer bets for consumers than others in that expectations are more clearly formed through promotional activities, the assignment of stars and other markers. However, as should be clear, insuperable difficulties arise from the separateness and uniqueness of each new film consumption experience. Though I might be fairly sure that the pleasure I am likely to derive from seeing film A will fall within a particular hedonistic range, it is quite different from saying that the chances of film A exactly meeting my expectations are 0.4 whilst small variations from this (gains or losses) have a 0.2 chance and so on. Film does not lend itself to additive models of consumer behaviour. As Shackle has argued:

> Hopes which are mutually exclusive are not additive; fears which are mutually exclusive are not additive. In each case the greatest prevails, and alone determines the power of the attractive or of the deterrent component of the venture's 'dual personality'. In this last sentence, the word 'greatest' is insufficiently precise... What we mean is the *most powerful element* among them.[14]

An approach to this type of audience experience, which eschews illusory mathematical precision in favour of a more intuitive approach, can be found in Peter Earl's adaptation of George Shackle's work on choice. Shackle's hostility to the SEU theory led him to propose an *ex-ante* reflection of risk in the form of *degrees of surprise*. In the case of film, although an individual cannot be surprised by a film that she or he has never seen, her/his previous filmgoing experience suggests, nevertheless, that she or he *might* be. Accordingly, it is proposed that in choosing between films, a filmgoer forms an imaginative map of a range of expectations set against a scale of surprise, which ranges from unsurprising to astonishing. The argument is as follows:

Ex ante I can use my imagination to consider the possible pleasures I would be likely to experience if attending a screening of film X. This is not to say that I can visualize, with any degree of completeness, how film X would look or the manner in which its narrative would unfold. Rather, I have a conception of the pleasure domain into which I can place the film and of the type of pleasure I would expect to derive.

It follows from the logic of the notion of surprise that if my expectations are met I will not be surprised, and my aesthetic and cognitive senses will have been stirred in the manner to which they are accustomed by what I have seen. However, I know from past cinemagoing experiences that I have regularly been disappointed or overcompensated by films that I have watched, and that a consequence of this is that for most films I go to see, I am able to imagine beforehand a set of surprised states, ranging from unsurprising to astonishing, which might befall me. These increase in intensity with the degree of loss or gain. Further, I perceive that different films generate distinctive surprise profiles, some being more difficult to call than others. In choosing between films, I am mindful of the risks associated with each film as captured by the separate surprise profiles I form of them. My choice will be affected by how, in general, I approach those risks associated with filmgoing, coupled with the capricious influences at work at the moment of choice.

These ideas are illustrated in Figures 1.4 and 1.5. In Figure 1.4 the horizontal axis measures the loss or gain that the filmgoer anticipates relative to some *best bet* (most likely) value of pleasure l associated with films found in the *final choice set*—the greatest value of the level of pleasure promised without surprise. It is critically important to remember that l lies at some position towards the right extreme of the absolute scale of pleasure set out in Figure 1.1—as captured analytically, in terms of the threshold criteria of the two pleasure-

inducing film characteristics (romance and glamour), indicated graph-
ically in Figure 1.2. Hence, the potential losses and gains imagined by
the filmgoer are measured relative to that position. Another filmgoer
may anticipate a different value, say *m* (based perhaps on different
characteristics such as humour and charm), as a *best bet* expected level
of pleasure for the same film, in which case that filmgoer's possible
loss and gain are measured with respect to *m* as the reference point.

Figure 1.4 shows how a filmgoer's expectations might be configured
for a hypothetical film, X. The surprise curve indicates that the
filmgoer will experience some surprise if the *best bet* level of expectation
l is not realized; small at first, the rapidly steepening slopes indicate
that further increments or decrements will be met with rapidly
escalating levels of surprise. This depiction of the filmgoer's risk
assessment of film X accords with the analysis that each new film
experience is in some respect unique and therefore difficult *ex ante* to
predict with any sense of precision. The actual shape of the curve would
be derived from previous personal experience of filmgoing coupled to
the information on the film garnered by the individual filmgoer. Points
a, b, c, d in Figure 1.4 represent four distinct *ex-ante* evaluations of
the likelihood that the filmgoing experience will depart from the *best
bet* level of expected pleasure, *l*. In the case of point *a*, if this were to
happen, the pleasure over and above that expected would leave the
viewer both elated and near to astonishment. Further, it can be
imagined that if this exhilaration of the senses were to happen it would
affect the filmgoer's assessment of future films containing the same
markers; star(s), director, genre, etc. The opposite would be true for

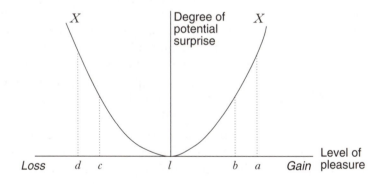

Source: Adapted from Earl (1995: 114).

Figure 1.4: *A filmgoer's potential surprise function for film* X

an experience marked by point *d*. The sense of disappointment would be pronounced, perhaps leading the viewer to a profound downward revision of expectations of future films associated with a similar combination of inputs. The respective gain and loss associated with points *b* and *c* represent the more common story of a filmgoer having been pleasantly surprised or mildly disappointed by a film, leading to a more moderate subsequent adjustment of marker expectations.

Although this analysis started from consideration of a filmgoer making a *final choice set*, the analytical model could just as easily apply to a film that filmgoers had not initially been strongly attracted to, but whose attention was subsequently drawn to it by a cascade of positive information emerging from filmgoers attending previous screenings. Such information flows confound the expectations of large numbers of filmgoers, causing them to re-evaluate the film and reposition it rightwards along the continuum of pleasure suggested in Figure 1.1. At some early stage in the distribution process, audiences will have been surprised greatly, if not astonished, by the qualities of the film known in the trade as *a sleeper*.

Finally, Figure 1.5 represents two films, *Y* and *Z*, which lie within a filmgoer's *final choice set*, where *n* and *p* respectively represent her or his *best bet* expectations of pleasure. It is clear that the two films present quite distinct risk profiles for the potential consumer, with the profile of film *Y* similar to that of film *X* in Figure 1.4—that is, symmetric about its *best bet* value—whilst the surprise function curve of film *Z* presents a profile asymmetric about its *best bet* value, suggesting that the filmgoer would not be greatly surprised if she or he were to gain significant levels of pleasure over and above her/his *best bet* expectation, *p*. Clearly, *p* and *n* are held with equivalent strength, in that if either level of pleasure were to occur, the filmgoer would not be surprised at all. The intriguing feature of these profiles is that while the *best bet* pleasure level value associated with film *Y* is greater than that of film *Z*, since *n>p*, film *Z* nevertheless holds the promise of higher levels of pleasure and the threat of greater disappointment. Which will the filmgoer choose? A determinate solution to the problem is possible if we know the filmgoer's attitude to risk. Intuitively, a risk-averse filmgoer is more likely to choose film *Y* whilst a risk-loving filmgoer would select film *Z*.

This result can be arrived at analytically as follows. In supposing that an individual can imagine a potential surprise profile for each of the films that constitute the *final choice set*, we can assume that the promise of high levels of pleasure at low levels of risk is preferred.[15]

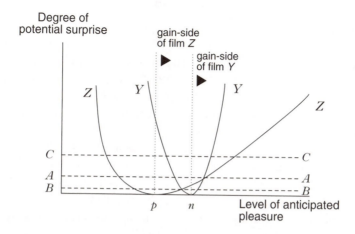

Source: Adapted from Earl (1995: 118).

Figure 1.5: *A filmgoer's potential surprise function for films* Y *and* Z

Let us suppose that the filmgoer is risk-loving, in that the prospect of a measure of gain outweighs the same measure of loss, and focuses, accordingly, on the gain-side of the *best bet* estimates of the films in the *final choice set*.[16] Let us further suppose that there is some threshold level of surprise which the risk-loving filmgoer is prepared to entertain. Consider a threshold represented by the line AA parallel to the X axis such that it cuts the surprise function curves at the point where they intersect on the gain-side. In this case, at this level of risk (potential surprise), the filmgoer is indifferent between the two films. Clearly, a filmgoer with a lower tolerance of risk, such as at level BB, will prefer film Y to film Z, since a lower threshold line will cut the curve for film Y at a greater value on the pleasure axis than that at which it cuts the curve for film Z. Conversely, a filmgoer who is more risk adventurous, e.g. at threshold level CC, will have a higher threshold for potential surprise and bet on film Z.

In the case of a risk-averse filmgoer, the loss-side will carry greater imaginative weight. Here the prospect of being disappointed is discounted fully since the filmgoer will have a zero tolerance for anticipated surprise. In effect, the filmgoer will choose that film which offers the greatest level of pleasure at the least level of surprise. In the case of the example shown in Figure 1.5 the *best bet* point n will dominate p and film Y will be preferred to Z.

Conclusion

Not surprisingly, there is a close correspondence between this theory of filmgoer choice and film popularity. At the level of the individual filmgoer, the discussion focuses on the process by which films are sifted and sorted into ranked groupings *ex ante* through an evaluation of their anticipated pleasures, whilst film popularity at the level of the market is conducted in an *ex-post* environment, in which initial audience reaction is known. Clearly, the link between the two is the quality and quantity of information which becomes available to the individual filmgoer, in his capacity as arbitrator between those films that make up his *final choice set*. De Vany and Walls have modelled those information flows, arguing: 'The evidence shows there is positive information feedback among film audiences ... and that the industry's flexible supply adaptation to this feedback produces increasing returns.'[17] Distribution and exhibition move rapidly and flexibly in response to positive feedback flows.

On occasions, relatively small budget films become popular—*The Blair Witch Project* (1999) being an extreme example—and do so primarily, at least during the early stages of release, through word of mouth: they become discovered. In terms of the theory being proposed, initial audiences will be sufficiently (pleasantly) surprised *ex post* with the film, that signals will be transmitted causing potential audiences to re-evaluate their expectations upwards. In so doing, the film will be levered into higher pleasure bands by filmgoers, leading greater numbers than initially predicted to feature it in their *final choice set*. Such films become extra popular relative to their concept. Conversely, big-budget productions have much less scope to build popularity in this way, but do have considerable scope for becoming a flop by unfavourable word-of-mouth.[18] The concept behind them is that they will be placed, with great frequency, in the higher reaches of filmgoers' expected pleasure ranges in the first place. Producers and distributors do this through the deployment of a set of story, style, genre and star conventions, together with massive publicity and multiple screen release. The intention is to generate confidently held expectations with high values of anticipated pleasure—n in Figure 1.4—with steep potential surprise profiles similar to that of film Y in Figure 1.5. With such films, not much surprise is anticipated: the films will become 'hits' if consumers in general experience little in the way of surprise. The theory, accordingly, helps to explain the marketing and distribution strategies adopted by the major Hollywood studios with respect to their big budget productions.

2

The Context

The truth was, of course, that Mr Smeeth's children *were* foreigners, not simply because they belonged to a younger generation that existed in a different world…They were children of the Woolworth Stores and the moving pictures…Edna's appearance, her grimaces and gestures, were temporarily based on those of an American Polish Jewess, who from her mint in Hollywood, had stamped them on these young girls all over the world.

J.B. Priestley, *Angel Pavement*[1]

This chapter draws together three distinct discourses, each of which impinges on the subject of film popularity in Britain during the 1930s, and which together provide a context to the remainder of the book. The first section serves as a social history, the second as a tribute to Rachael Low and Kristin Thompson for path-breaking histories of the period of cinema which precedes this study, and the third to report on and add to the revisionist perspective of the 1927 Cinematograph Act.

Britain during the 1930s

The uneven experience of living in Britain during the inter-war period, particularly in the 1930s, is now generally accepted. It is clear that the unrelenting grimness and insecurity of life where adult unemployment was common, which is so movingly depicted in Walter Greenwood's *Love on the Dole* (1933), is only part of the story. It is a part which led George Orwell to travel north in search of this environment—

described in *The Road to Wigan Pier*—and as late as 1981 caused Stuart Hall to admit that:

> It isn't by chance that very few of us are working in popular culture in the 1930s. I suspect there is something peculiarly awkward, especially for socialists, in the non-appearance of a militant radical mature culture of the working class in the 1930s when—to tell you the truth—most of us would have expected it to appear. From the viewpoint of a purely 'heroic' or 'autonomous' popular culture, the 1930s is a pretty barren period.[2]

It is interesting to note that cinemagoing does not appear to be a regular experience with Greenwood's fictitious community in North Street, in the industrial district of Hanky Park, in contrast to J.B. Priestley's young working-class characters in *Angel Pavement* (1930) and *They Walk in the City* (1936), who 'being children of their age' went to the cinema as a matter of course.

In his *English Journey*, published in 1933, Priestley distinguished between two types of urban experience. He described one as '19th century England': the England (Britain) of the Industrial Revolution built around the staple industries of coal, cotton, shipbuilding, iron and steel and mechanical engineering, where social (including work) conditions and customs were rooted in the past. The other was characterized by 'arterial and by-pass roads, of filling stations and factories that look like exhibition buildings, of giant cinemas and dance halls and cafes, bungalows with tiny garages, cocktail bars, Woolworths, motor coaches, wireless, hiking, factory girls looking like actresses, greyhound racing and dirt tracks, swimming pools and everything given away with coupons'.[3] More recently, John Stevenson and Chris Cook have argued that:

> For those in work, the 1930s were a period of rising living standards and new levels of consumption, upon which a considerable degree of industrial growth was based. This was a paradox which lay at the heart of Britain in the thirties, where new levels of prosperity contrasted with the intractable problems of mass unemployment and the depressed areas.[4]

Stevenson and Cook's thesis on the 1930s is given broad support by the statistics set out in Table 2.1. The dramatic increase in unemployment, to almost 3.5 million by 1932, is not surprisingly accompanied by a fall back in employment. The recovery from 1933 onwards took place in an environment in which the downward trend in prices—falling from 1925, if the immediate post-war boom and its aftermath are discounted, and accelerating over the years 1929–33— was gently reversed. Money wages remained remarkably constant from 1923 onwards, dipping only during the worst years of the Depression. Solomou and Weale's estimates of employment income indicate that those wage/salary-earners who remained in employment enjoyed, on average, a 40 per cent increase in real earnings between 1923 and 1938, the bulk (approximately three-quarters) of this increase occurring during the 1930s.[5]

For Stevenson and Cook:

> The fall in the cost of living, by almost a third during the interwar period meant that for many salaried people affluence began not in the 1950s but in the thirties... By the middle years of the decade, Britain was on average better paid, better fed, better clothed and housed, and hence healthier than it had ever been'.[6]

Of course, as a measure an average is opaque unless it is supported by associated measures of variance: it allows Walter Greenwood's agonized picture of working-class Britain to become subsumed into J.B. Priestley's rather broader canvas of working-class life built upon the presence of work rather than its absence. Some sense of the importance of work can be gleaned from *Love on the Dole*, in the incredulous bewilderment with which Harry and his dad respond to the jobs which Harry's sister Sally procures for them at the Bus Offices, and Harry's joint emotions of pride and shame which accompany his first wage packet—shame because of his inability to face his unemployed friend, Jack Lindsay, standing alone on the corner of North Street.[7]

Another manifestation of unevenness is provided by David Fowler, who argues that young working-class people in employment enjoyed a distinctive lifestyle based upon their collective purchasing power. Fowler reproduces census evidence to show that, between 1921 and 1931, the participation rate of young people in the workforce increased from 83.7 to 85.1 per cent for boys aged 14–19 and from 63.8 to 70.8 per cent for girls.[8] He uses Ministry of Labour data to produce tables of youth unemployment to demonstrate that young people could expect dramatically different levels of opportunity depending on where they lived.

Whilst youth unemployment rates in Liverpool varied between 13.1

Table 2.1: *British economy and cinema statistics, 1930–1938*

	1930	1931	1932	1933	1934	1935	1936	1937	1938
1. Population (000s)	45,866	46,074	46,335	46,521	46,666	46,868	47,081	47,289	47,494
2. Employment (000s)	19,115	18,665	18,753	19,136	19,685	20,037	20,670	21,364	21,418
3. Unemployment (000s)	2,379	3,252	3,400	3,087	2,609	2,437	2,100	1,776	2,164
4. Retail prices (1930 = 100)	100.0	93.5	91.0	88.4	89.0	90.3	92.9	98.1	98.7
5. Average weekly wage earnings (1930 = 100)	100.0	98.9	97.1	96.0	96.0	97.1	98.9	102.9	105.7
6. Employment income (£ms)	2,486	2,409	2,356	2,410	2,491	2,592	2,736	2,923	2,976
7. Consumer expenditure (£ms)	3,844	3,734	3,615	3,673	3,765	3,898	4,074	4,262	4,310
8. Expenditure on entertainment (£ms)	60.9	58.5	57.2	55.4	58.5	58.6	60.8	62.7	64.9
9. Entertainment admissions (ms)	1,378	1,333	1,253	1,234	1,315	1,332	1,400	1,447	1,497
10. Expenditure on cinema (£ms)					38.8	38.7	38.6	39.9	41.5
11. Cinema admissions (ms)					903	907	917	946	987
12. Average ticket price (d.)					10.3	10.2	10.1	10.1	10.1
13. Expenditure on cinema per caput (£)					0.83	0.83	0.82	0.84	0.87
14. Cinema admissions per caput					19.3	19.4	19.5	20.0	20.1

Sources: Row 1, Feinstein, tab. 55; rows 2–3, ibid., tab. 57; rows 4–5, ibid., tab. 65; rows 6–7, Solomou and Weale, tab. A1; rows 8–9, Stone and Rowe, tab. 36; rows 10–12, Browning and Sorrell.

Note: Unless otherwise stated all values are expressed in terms of current year prices.

and 22.3 per cent for the period 1930–36, those in London never rose above 4.2 per cent. Manchester's rates were a little higher than those in London, varying between 2.1 and 9.3 per cent, whilst those in Glasgow and Newcastle were similar to Liverpool's.[9] Fowler (1995: 15) explains that the 'insatiable' demand for juvenile labour in London and Manchester existed because young people were 'cheaper to employ than adults even during periods of high unemployment'. This situation was reflected in Harry's experience as an apprenticed engineer in *Love on the Dole* where, to avoid paying him 'men's wages', the owners of the engineering works made him redundant at the end of his apprenticeship. Furthermore, Fowler maintains, young working-class people in employment could expect to keep enough of their wages, to be able to afford a distinctive lifestyle. He writes:

> All the social investigators who studied the income and expenditure of working-class families were agreed, then, that the young wage-earners in such families retained about 50% of their earnings, and in some an even higher percentage...Age it seems was the most important determinant of disposable income...While 14- and 15-year olds might hand over their wage packets to their mothers and receive only a few coppers back, those of 16 and older insisted on keeping much more of their earnings.[10]

In 1935, young men under the age of 21 in Manchester could expect to earn over £1 a week during the 1930s, whilst young women earned as much as a third less. The most highly paid trade was working on the trams, in which young men averaged almost 32 shillings, as against 24s.5d. for young women.[11] If those in their later teens could expect to keep as much as half, or even more, of their wages, it meant that with some 3.5 million wage-earners in Britain between the ages of 14–20,[12] young people collectively were able to generate a distinct demand for the products of their choosing. It is this that leads Fowler to claim that:

> a distinctive teenage culture, based largely upon access to commercialised leisure and conspicuous consumption of leisure products aimed at the young, was in evidence in British towns and cities by the 1930s.[13]

Of the activities that made up this distinctive lifestyle, Fowler maintains that 'Cinemagoing was indisputably the most popular form of commercial recreation among the young people during the inter-war period'.[14] For Priestley's Edna Smeeth (mentioned in the epigraph to this chapter), cinemagoing was evidently an extremely important influence on her sense of self. The importance of films to young women such as Edna is confirmed by Joan Harley's investigation into the leisure activities of young female wage-earners in Manchester, written as an MEd. dissertation in 1937, and uncovered by David Fowler. According to Fowler:

She [Harley] was convinced, for instance, that the Hollywood musicals were having an affect upon the girls. Some girls she spoke to, she claimed, had adopted a 'Hollywood accent' and a number of others copied the dress styles, hairstyles, and mannerisms of their favourite film actresses to a ludicrous degree.[15]

It was not, however, just young people who went to the cinema. Cinema admissions accounted for approximately two-thirds of all expenditure on entertainment in Britain between 1934 and 1938 (see Table 2.1). Clearly, only a fraction of the expenditure on cinema tickets, rising annually from £38 to £41.5 million, came from Fowler's '1930s teenagers'.

Drawing upon a series of social surveys on social habits and welfare from around Britain,[16] Ross McKibbin confirms that the four main determinants of cinemagoing were age, social class, gender and geography:

> Among adults, all levels of working class went more often than the middle or upper classes. But skilled workers and clerical and distributive workers went 'significantly' more often than unskilled workers, who as adolescents were likely to go most but who in adulthood could least afford it. Though the non-working class went less frequently they bought more expensive seats and so spent per capita almost as much as anyone else.
>
> Cinema attendance was biased by gender as well as class: except during adolescence when boys were likely to go at least as often as girls, women always went to the cinema more than men...The cinema was ideally suited to women at a moment when their own cultural lives were necessarily passive, their routines largely determined by the demands of their husband and children.[17]

The principal source of our quantitative understanding of cinemagoing in Britain during the 1930s is Simon Rowson's 1936 evaluation of Entertainment Duty Returns made available to him by the Board of Trade. From these returns, Rowson estimated that there were 963 million admissions into British cinemas in 1934—a figure later scaled down by Browning and Sorrell (1954) to 903 million—paying an average admission price of 10.25d.[18] The mode price was even lower, with Rowson estimating that 28.3 per cent of cinemagoers paid either 6d. or 7d.[19] As 23.7 per cent of the population of population in 1931 were under the age of 15, this meant that on average each person aged 15 or over visited the cinema approximately twenty-six times a year.

They did so in all parts of the country. Rowson estimated that on average there was a cinema for every 10,500 people (8,000 if the population of 15 years and older is taken) and a seat for every twelve people. This ranged from 8,000 people per cinema (10 people per seat) in South Wales to 15,900 (14 people per seat) in the London postal area. Rowson further found that the size of cinemas was directly correlated to the density of population, indicating that the less highly densely populated a region the smaller its cinemas.[20] Whereas 51 per cent of London cinemas had upwards of 1501 seats, this fell to 27 per cent in Scotland (almost exclusively Edinburgh and Glasgow) and the Home Counties and 22 per cent in Lancashire, with the remaining regions ranging between 10 and 20 per cent, with the exception of North Wales where only 8 per cent of cinemas fell into this band.[21]

During the 1930s the British market for film entertainment was in size second only to that of the United States. Rowson estimated that there were 4,305 cinemas wired for sound in Britain in 1934, with the figure rising to 5,000 by the end of the decade.[22] With the emergence of sound technology in the late 1920s, making English language films less accessible in non-English speaking markets, coupled with the gradual loss of market share in Germany following the accession of Hitler and the Nazi Party in 1933, the British market became ever more important to Hollywood producers as the decade wore on.[23] Indeed, McKibbon argues that 'Going to the pictures was not simply the most important leisure activity of the English, at least outside of the home, it was more important to them than to any other nationality'.[24] Not surprisingly, British protection legislation was taken very seriously by the American producers, through their trade organization—the MPPDA (The Hays Office)—and the US State Department.[25] Hollywood film finances show that the principal studios covered their production and distribution costs in the North American market and relied on the rest of the world, primarily Britain, for their profits.

Although A.J.P. Taylor's observation that the cinema was 'the essential social habit of the age... [which] slaughtered all competitors',[26] signals the importance of cinemagoing for a generation, historians working outside of the area have paid scant attention to it either as a means of social representation or as an economic phenomenon. In the latter case, economic historians are primarily concerned with supply-side matters. It is clear from Table 2.1 that although close to a billion customers paid to go to the cinema annually during the mid to late 1930s this accounted for a little over 1 per cent of aggregate consumer expenditure. In conventional terms, cinemagoing was not a major contributor to the national economy. And yet each member of the population aged 15 years or over spent close on the equivalent of one and a half to two working weeks watching films each year. Moreover, these films fulfilled the function of providing filmgoers with a set of more or less coherent ideas with which to explain the world and themselves within it. Although people went to the cinema as a social activity, they came away from it not just entertained, but with a conceptual framework for understanding social forms such as the individual, gender, family, club, occupation, politics, crime, the armed forces, sport, religion, art, nation, state, social class and etiquette, and history. They did not necessarily always accept the framework of ideas or the visual representation of social form being put to them but, nevertheless, they were wittingly subject to them.

In his outstanding contribution to British cinema history, Jeffrey Richards (1984) maintains that cinema played a critical role during the 1930s in reflecting the aspirations of the people for a better life and reassuring them that the establishment could be trusted to oversee an environment—essentially democratic—necessary to this end:

> Beyond the personal level, film stars function also on a broader societal level, performing the same ideological role as films themselves. Given the framework of capitalist production and middle-class censorship, the stars can be used to promote conformity to patterns of behaviour favoured by the Establishment. They can be used to gloss over ambiguities and instabilities in society by individualising social and economic problems and resolving them on a personal level by the use of their star charisma.[27]

Gracie Fields and George Formby were, for Richards, the two British stars *par excellence* who fulfilled this role during the 1930s. Of them he wrote: 'The classic cases in the British cinema are the use of the native working-class stars Gracie Fields and George Formby to promote consensus, the values of decency and hard work, and the overcoming of problems by individual effort.'[28] In the context of the Depression, the undoubted popularity of Fields and Formby amongst the working class, Priestley's constituencies of 'new' and 'industrial' England, sits comfortably alongside the two substantial General

Election victories of 1931 and 1935 achieved by the Conservative Party (thinly veiled as the Nationalist Party), and the genuine emotion which surfaced following the death in 1935 of George V.[29] A reading of the provincial daily newspapers of the period, with their combination of national, international and local news and local advertisements, leaves little doubt that at a local level Britain was a socially and politically cohesive and coherent nation. Even in the face of mass unemployment and poverty, local institutions such as the town council, the courts and police acted with legitimate authority and maintained order. It is quite clear that a complaisant working-class culture pervaded Britain, albeit with distinctive regional characteristics: one that was not radical in Stuart Hall's sense since it was not concerned to transform society by challenging the apparatus of the British State, but took the pragmatic line of working within it for what it judged was possible. Within this environment, cinema performed the important role of diffusing widely an aesthetic experience which served the dual function of increasing the general level of well-being while reinforcing the status quo.

The legacy of Kristin Thompson and Rachael Low in explaining the early failure of the British film industry

The poor performance of the British film industry during the silent era is widely recognized, and can be dated from the end of the embryonic and pioneering period, *circa* 1907/8. Kristin Thompson's seminal account of Hollywood's international reach during the early period provides evidence to indicate that British producers took as little as 10 per cent of their domestic market during the period immediately before the 1927 legislation.[30] This record of failure is difficult to reconcile with the fact that: (a) Britain was the single largest market outside North America for moving pictures and (b) its international trading networks were unsurpassed.[31]

In the period before the First World War most American companies (with the exception of Vitagraph) based their European and world selling operations in London. Britain was attractive to American companies for three reasons: firstly, until 1915 there was no tariff on film imports; secondly, Britain was America's biggest foreign market; and thirdly, the British shipping system was extremely extensive and 'British business people had knowledge of international commerce and could cope with the different currencies, languages and other special problems involved'.[32] For Thompson, the existence of this pre-war trading infrastructure enabled British distributors to act 'as the re-exporter for America and other foreign films, dispatching them to all parts of the globe...until the war intervened'. The consequences appear clear:

> By down playing production in favour of distribution and exhibition, the British firms left the field open for foreign films; with so little screen time being devoted to native production, it became increasingly difficult to interest investors in making British films.[33]

The speed at which the American producers were able to dominate world markets outside Europe was undoubtedly influenced by the effects of the First World War, which brought about 'the breakdown of European production'.[34] Through impediments to shipping, the war made it increasingly difficult for London to function as the world centre for re-exportation and stimulated the new set of US production companies to develop a direct sales strategy. International direct selling required global distribution networks, which is exactly what the major American producers undertook during the latter half of the 1910s.[35]

Towards the end of the war, the American company Essanay started a process which ended with the complete destruction of the open distribution system in Britain. Using the market power of its Chaplin films, the company issued nothing but exclusive contracts to individual exhibitors. Thompson observes that over the five years from 1916:

> Britain went from being one of the most flexible open markets in the world to one of the most rigid closed ones. The system perpetuated the American firms' advantage, since it kept the theatres tied to their larger outputs, eliminating open play dates into which other countries' films might slip.[36]

American firms' share of the British market rose from around 75 per cent of new film output during the war years to close to 90 per cent during the 1920s. The British market was worth approximately 35 per cent of all overseas revenue to American producers.[37]

In setting out to explain the hegemony of the Hollywood product in international markets, Thompson has concentrated upon the behaviour of a new breed of American film production companies.[38] The historian of the British industry conversely needs to explain why British studios at first failed to match and subsequently challenge foreign film-makers in the domestic market. Rachael Low, in her monumental seven-volume history of the British industry between 1896 and 1939, tackles this very problem.[39] Her argument is presented below in detail, as it remains the only developed account of the industry in the period before 1930.

For Low, the problems faced by the industry were caused by the failure of production, for which she castigates the amateurish ethos of many of those involved. Indeed, the continual crisis in production was part of a wider malaise affecting British industry, namely that of entrepreneurial failure:

> The bustling enterprise which had once led the world was also the first to become set in its ways. There was a strong class structure, in which those who succeeded in industry and trade tended to become traditionalists themselves, and adopt the ways of the upper classes.[40]

Social prejudice worked against talented individuals entering the industry. Indeed, even as late as the late 1920s:

> (t)he social traditions which had by now relaxed sufficiently to accept certain leading members of the theatrical profession as respectable members of society stood fast when it came to the cinema, and many actors regarded their film work simply as an embarrassing necessity.[41]

Until the advent of the 1927 Act the British film industry was seriously underfunded. On the period immediately before 1914 Low observes:

> If in conclusion some explanation of the disappointing state of the British film at this time should be attempted, it can be said that the central commercial defect seems to have been the insufficiency of capital. From this, it can be argued, stemmed the attendant defect in the artistic sphere of the paucity of first-class talent, or original and creative vitality. One is left with the impression that in Britain the film had to overcome a resistance of a particularly inelastic social and intellectual pattern. In France and Italy the film might be a younger sister of the arts, in America art itself. In England it was a poor relation, and, moreover, not a very respectable one.[42]

As for the effect of the First World War on the industry:

In general the key people in British production were not affected by mobilisation. The greatest difficulty likely to be suffered by a luxury producing industry of this nature in time of war is a shortage of capital. But the shortage of capital for British film production, its fundamental weakness, dated from before the war. There is no reason whatever to suppose that, had there been no war, British production would have been able to withstand the irresistible growth of the American output.[43]

Undercapitalization resulted in small production companies '(r)un by men of little imagination, who were reluctant to back anything unusual or unproved', making films of little merit on parsimonious budgets.[44] Of these industry leaders she writes scathingly:

> All that we can say is that because of the poor quality of commercial leadership in the film industry at this time the surrender to mediocre professionalism was widespread, and many of those who were allowed play the largest part in making the British films of the day were hacks.[45]

Charles Pathé, the head of the principal French production company Pathé Frères, had made a similar observation about the quality of British film industry entrepreneurs in an interview in *Bioscope* in 1914: 'I am afraid that the trouble is due to lack of enterprise. There is no continuity of effort among your producers. They work too hastily and in too small a way.'[46] British film production companies made poor investment prospects:

> The reluctance of banks to finance production, frequently deplored and contrasted with the happy situation in America, was hardly unreasonable in view of the poor prospects of the investment.[47]

Further, the prejudice against the industry meant that films were often made by 'hacks' and production companies run by second-rate businessmen who were unable to overcome either economic or non-economic constraints. Indeed, many of the ingredients of the wider historiographical debate on the decline of Britain as an economic power are exemplified in Low's depiction of the British film industry before the 1930s, leading her to the sour conclusion:

> The vicious circle of bad quality and lack of money resulting from

the basic conditions of the country's climate, size and history made the British film industry less and less able to stand up to American competition.[48]

In explaining that business cultures have deep historical roots, Coleman and Macleod advance the argument: 'Just as today's new technique embodies the experience of the past, so today's response cannot be divorced from yesterday's understanding.'[49] For these authors, it is those very qualities of individualism and enterprise—described by Low in the context of film-making in Britain—which characterized British business culture around the turn of the century and proved to be so unsuited to the emerging methods and organization of mass-production:

> Precisely because it arose from spontaneous and uncoordinated efforts of small businessmen creating a structure of many small businesses, the British industrial revolution gave rise to powerful currents of individualism in business behaviour. They continued to be manifest in some of the attitudes of the business community after the 1860s. An unwillingness to make standard components; a pride in being able to produce a multiplicity of different wares to suit a variety of markets from the local town to overseas Empire; a pervasive, secretive and obstinate individualism: such continuing qualities proved ill-suited to the competitive environment emerging in the twentieth century and peculiarly antipathetic to mass production.[50]

The transformation of the film industry during the 1930s from the moribund state portrayed by Low was triggered by the 1927 Cinematograph Act, which at a stroke changed the risk environment facing those ambitious British producers who wished to challenge Hollywood's domination of the British market.

The 1927 Cinematograph Films Act

The 1927 Act stipulated that distributors and exhibitors operating in the domestic market should handle a growing proportion of British films, measured in footage and foot-screenings respectively, rising to a ceiling of 20 per cent by 1936.[51] It is important to recognize that this protection did not guarantee producer bookings. The legislation was passed at a time when Britain was still a free-trade nation and indicates the concern on the part of leading figures in the British establishment that the absence of an indigenous film industry endangered the distinctiveness of the British way of life. According to Dickinson and Street,

> Although the Films Act was formulated in a context of heightened official awareness and concern about the propaganda of film and its general importance in national life, the mechanism adopted to combat the 'Hollywood invasion' was not really appropriate as a means of establishing a British film industry which would be independent of American economic and cultural influence.[52]

In devising legislation to encourage the production of British films, the Board of Trade officials were acting in line with the largely non-interventionalist stance of the British State in matters of industry and commerce. Although this policy may not have produced the distinctive films that Dickinson and Street may have wished for, it certainly did produce films; domestic production expanded from 96 in the 1929–30 season to 228 in 1937–38.[53] By emphasizing quantity control, rather than price control in the form of a tariff, the film Quota in effect sealed an incrementally expanding section of the slowly expanding domestic market for indigenous producers.

The 1927 legislation had a truly profound effect on the British production sector. It progressively tilted access to the British film entertainment market in favour of domestic producers by requiring distributors and exhibitors to take a rising quota of British productions (quantity control) rather than by raising the price of overseas (Hollywood) product relative to domestic output in the form of tariffs (price control). However, the 'Quota' did not specify which films should be taken. This is critically important. Given that exhibitors preferred to show films that audiences wanted to see, together with the fact the great majority of British people lived in urban areas well supplied with cinemas, and were therefore able to choose between programmes, it follows that the legislation was bound to provide a strong incentive to quality producers by allowing them to compete narrowly with other British producers in a protected segment of the market from which all distributors and exhibitors were required to draw supply.[54] The demand for successful British films (i.e. films capable of attracting audiences from alternative uses of their time) was enhanced as a consequence. Furthermore, although exhibitors were compelled to show a rising proportion of British films, not all exhibitors in any single locality would be screening British films simultaneously; thus British film-makers, by force of circumstance, were also competing openly against the Hollywood product. Where British films were poor, the guarantee of distribution and exhibition was not sufficient to generate adequate box-office revenue. But, where they were not, the legislation certainly helped diffuse the product amongst a wider audience than otherwise would have been the case. Immediately following the 1927 Act the incentive to engage in 'quality' film production encouraged the Gaumont-British and ABC organizations to vertically integrate backwards, upstream from exhibition into distribution and production, while encouraging newly formed production studios such as ATP and Twickenham to forward integrate downstream into distribution during the early years of the 1930s. As Robert Murphy has argued:

> The major advantage enjoyed by vertically integrated companies was that their studios were able to launch more ambitious production programmes, secure in the knowledge that the films would be shown in their cinemas and that box-office profits would finance subsequent productions. State protection was therefore responsible for a fundamental change in the structure of the industry and a revival in production.[55]

In addition, the temporal provisions in the legislation (i.e the rising quota over time) also created the opportunity for film-makers and business managers to learn through doing and so improve their future competitiveness.

Although the 1927 Cinematograph Films Act led to the production in volume of cheaply made films—most of which were of poor quality, and collectively known as 'Quota Quickies'[56]—made by a plethora of short-lived companies, often for American renters who had no interest in developing 'quality' in the British production sector, the principal effect of the legislation was to encourage indigenous investment in British production, resulting in the emergence of a handful of domestic 'quality' producers.[57] Indeed, as Tom Ryall claims, 'The 1927 Act was responsible for the emergence of a "studio system" not dissimilar to that of Hollywood with its interrelated cluster of major, minor and "B" picture companies.'[58] As will be shown in Chapter 4, by the mid-1930s the major and top end of the minor producers were between them making approximately sixty films per annum, which generated above average box-office returns. Jarvie has referred to this process as one of 'pushing back' the Hollywood product.[59]

The lack of recognition for this achievement can be put down to two factors. The first is that information was scattered and fragmentary, and on the key topic of detailed British box-office takings, almost non-existent. In Chapter 3 the methodological construct, POPSTAT, is introduced as a proxy for the absent records of revenues. The second factor is more speculative because it involves normative issues. These are evident in the earlier quotation from Dickenson and Street about combatting the 'Hollywood invasion'. Those who thought (and still think) that the 1927 Act was misconceived had an idea of what a British popular film ought to be and (usually more covertly) what audiences ought to want. For these critics, the discovery that there was a commercial 'quality' British film production sector was part of the problem as they saw it, in that Hollywood served as a general model of film-making, to the detriment of a unique British aesthetic.

Discontent with the Act became focused on the Quota Quickies which were well-known through all manner of anecdotal notoriety. When coupled with the crises in domestic production in 1936–38, caused by the retraction of the production plans of the leading British studios and the growth in the speculative financing of film production, and the unceasingly consistent quality and quantity of Hollywood major studio output, this has led to the general view that the 1927 legislation was poorly conceived and encouraged volume rather than quality. Indeed, Rachael Low maintains that:

> The 1927 quota legislation intended to solve all the industry's problems was a failure. Film production doubled during the thirties, but the increase consisted almost entirely of cheap and inferior films, the famous quota quickies and others not much better, which took advantage of the protected market and went far to ruin the reputation of British production as a whole.[60]

In revising this interpretation it needs to be shown that both British films and the stars who appeared in them were genuinely popular with British audiences. Further, it will be argued that had there been no legislation it is doubtful that much of the body of work that goes to make up British Cinema in the 1930s would have been made.

3

Measuring Popularity

For this was his usual Saturday night programme, if he had the money: first, tea at one of the big teashops, which were always crowded with girls and always offered a chance of a pick-up; then a visit to one of the great West End cinemas, in which, once inside, he could spin out the whole evening, perhaps on the edge of adventure all the time.

> J.B. Priestley, *Angel Pavement* [1]

'Let's go and see a good picture or down to the second house at Finsbury Park or something like that, and sit in the best seats, and you buy yourself a cigar and buy me some chocolates for once, and let's do it properly. Come on, boy. What do you say?'

> Mrs Smeeth to Mr Smeeth in *Angel Pavement* [2]

Film historians have typically measured the market penetration achieved by a film studio or a national cinema by computing its share of the films annually put onto the market. Implicit in such an approach is the treatment of film as a homogeneous commodity: each film counts equally. Such a method, however, is contrary to the spirit of film as a distinctive 'system of provision' based upon a peculiar set of commodity characteristics. Films compete on the basis of their uniqueness, and performance is measured in part in terms of the size of audience attracted to them. Assessing popularity hence requires a means of measuring differential audience reaction. In response to this problem, given the general absence of British box-office information, I collected and analysed the advertised film programmes of between 81 and 92 of the leading London West End and provincial city cinemas, located throughout Britain, for the period 1 January 1932 to 31 March 1938. The changing sample numbers reflect the entry and exit of cinemas from the market. The initial source of information was the 'Showing Next Week' listing in the *Kine Weekly*. Where the *Kine Weekly* records are incomplete, or questionable, London and provincial city-based newspapers were used. The cinemas are listed in Appendix 1 along with their owners, seating capacity, and mid-range price.[3] The choice of period represents a stage in which the configuration of the industry had largely settled following the burst of new firms' activity which emerged immediately after the 1927 Act; the transformation of the industry from silent to sound technology had been accomplished; and the operations of the industry were bounded by a common set of administrative rules laid down by the 1927 Act.[4]

As has been argued at length in the Introduction, this approach to measuring film popularity entails an empirically based analysis of audience preferences, founded not on the stated preferences of audiences—partially and intermittently recorded through social investigations of the time, and questionnaire surveys conducted by both the Bernstein and Korda organizations—but on what they actually saw.

The general system of distribution

The commercial life of a feature film during the 1930s was typically brief. Even the 126 films identified later in the chapter as West End 'hits', and listed in Appendix 2, had for the most part completed their passage through the system of British cinemas within twelve months. Less popular films, of course, experienced much shorter exhibition spans. Although re-releases became more common towards the end of the period under investigation, they were never an important element in pre-Second World War filmgoing.

This brief life-cycle was reflected in the amortization schedules used by the major Hollywood studios in assessing the profitability of their outputs. Greenwald described the principle of film amortization as follows:

> Even though the physical condition of a film may remain the same, the entire value of a film can be eliminated leaving no residual value. The obsolescence of films is frankly noted in a film's inability to bring any additional income and is recognised by a fast depreciation.[5]

Table 3.1: *The film amortization (percentage) schedules of the major Hollywood studios in 1935*[a]

| | Weeks | | | | | | | |
	4	8	12	16	24	26	52	65
Loew's (MGM)	15	36	51	60	67	-	89	100
Paramount	35	-	80	89	-	96	100	-
Warners	-	-	52	-	-	73	93	-
20th Cent. Fox	14	35	50	60	73	75	94	-
RKO	17	38	52	63	74	-	95	-
Columbia	9	28	50	68	84	86	98	-
Universal	11	26	40	50	64	67	97	-

Source: Greenwald (1950, Table VI-2).

Notes:
a. It is not clear from Greenwald's account whether these schedules include foreign sales. In his Table VI-3 he lists the types of amortization schedules practised by the studios with respect to foreign sales. He identifies four main conventions:
    1) all films written-off in the domestic North American market—USA and Canada;
    2) all films written-off in the world market (including US domestic) at the same rate;
    3) all films written-off with different rates for the US domestic and foreign market;
    4) all films written-off with different rates for the US domestic and British market and foreign markets other than British.

The amortization schedules adopted by the principal Hollywood studios for 1935 are reproduced in Table 3.1. Although similar information has not to date been uncovered for the British studios of that time, the general implication of the American schedules is clear: if costs were not covered world-wide within 12–15 months, the films in question made losses.[6] A key feature of the schedules is their approximation to the form of a geometric progression, with most studios expecting to meet at least half the production costs of any one film within twelve weeks of release. This is important for the claim that the POPSTAT index of film popularity—developed and explained later in the chapter—is representative of the British market as a whole. From the fact that the cinemas in the sample consist almost entirely of higher-order cinemas in the selected cities—excluding suburban London first-run houses—and given the similarity of British and American distribution practices, Greenwald's data show that pre-release and first-run cinemas made a disproportionate contribution towards a film's box-office performance. It was inconceivable that a film could be a 'hit' without being popular in the sample set of cinemas.

The system of film distribution in Britain was similar to that of the United States[7] and can be explained in terms of price discriminatory practices, whereby distributors entered films at the highest feasible point in the exhibition hierarchy and then allowed them, subsequently, to 'cascade' down over time through clearly demarcated cinema 'runs', from higher- to lower-order cinemas. The critical factor in this system was the economic rent generated by individual films at each point of exhibition. Distributors were concerned to maximize their returns, and the system which emerged during the 1920s in the US, whereby the vertically integrated majors were able to ration the spatial and temporal distribution of their product and demand higher prices from audiences wishing to see a film sooner rather than later, was perfectly designed to achieve this. This contrasts with the current practice of saturation release where the initial distribution of a film is based upon *a priori* expectations of demand and subsequently adjusts rapidly to actual demand patterns. If these expectations are high the distribution will be dense at the moment of release. Rather than exploiting the scarcity value of a film, the current mode is designed to overcome that scarcity as rapidly as possible.[8]

The logic behind the 'cascade system' of distribution/exhibition can be illustrated by means of the following schematic example. Let us suppose we have a monopoly distributor who rents films to a set of 100 cinemas, each of which is independently owned, has a single admission price of £1 and a weekly exhibition capacity of 20,000 seat-screenings (number of seats multiplied by number of separate shows). Further, let us assume that all the exhibition programmes consist of a single-billed film which runs simultaneously throughout this environment for a week and that all the cinemas experience identical attendance figures of 50 per cent capacity. Finally, suppose that the monopolist is dedicated to the objective of maximizing box-office take and accordingly imposes a rental contract which has both fixed and variable rate components. The former is intended to guarantee the distributor a minimum revenue whilst the latter is designed to gain an economic rent derived from the revealed preferences of audiences. The distributor will use his monopoly position to secure the highest marginal rates feasible in a zero-sum game with the exhibitor—a game in which the gains of one party are identical to the losses of the other. The rental contract in effect specifies the price that the exhibitor will pay to screen the film. The uniform release system of distribution will generate a gross revenue of £1 million prior to the deduction of the respective shares of the renter and exhibitor.

However, the monopolist is also aware that by selecting from the set a small number of cinemas, with a more luxurious ambience, and allowing these to exhibit the same film at an earlier date, the cinema owner will be able to charge higher admission prices. The monopolist knows this to be the case because market research has indicated that a body of customers would be prepared to pay a higher price to watch films sooner rather than later, to appreciate the appurtenances of a more comfortable cinema, or perhaps simply to enjoy the status associated with going to higher-order cinemas. Conversely, the research also shows that a body of filmgoers is not prepared to pay a higher price for such pleasures and accordingly will wait for the film of its choice to be screened at a later date. Acting on this information, the distributor designates five cinemas as pre-general release first-run houses and secures the agreement of the exhibitor to set a price of £3, whilst designating a further five cinemas as pre-general release second-run cinemas with £2 admission price. Assuming an identical set of attendance figures, box-office revenue now would rise to £1,150,000. Given that both fixed and variable rates remain unchanged, both the distributor and owners of the ten designated cinemas are better off whilst none of the remaining ninety cinema owners is worse off. As far as the distributor is concerned the 'cascade system' of distribution/ exhibition is preferable to an undifferentiated general release system.

The foregoing story demonstrates the logic behind the 'cascade system' of distribution/exhibition as far as the renter is concerned. Simultaneously, the exhibitor also seeks to maximize box-office revenue, given a set of film rental costs. Under a system of film rental contracts with both fixed and variable elements, the exhibitor could not be expected to take a film where the fixed charge element exceeded the box-office takings net of cinema operation costs. This may provide a limiting factor to the distribution of films, as cinemas at the bottom of the cascade, which tended to be smaller than the mean cinema size and charged very low admission prices during the 1930s (e.g. regularly as little as twopence for matinee screenings), might not be expected to cover the fixed rental fees associated with films of the principal distributors. Under such conditions the cinema programmes of lower-tier cinemas will differ from those of higher-order ones.

At the top of the cascade, higher-order cinemas with greater capacity and operating costs needed to attract audiences and fill capacity by exhibiting films which competed effectively with those showing on rival screens. Films which were thought to be unlikely to generate sufficient box-office returns to cover rental costs would be less likely to receive such desirable exhibition placements as those that had been favourably assessed. This is not to say that films which did not start from such high-status, high-profile positions in the cascade were not financially successful. Indeed, it is clear from my earlier work on the profit and loss ledgers of RKO and Warners during this period that lower-budget films tended to generate higher and more consistent rates of return than those of the studios' major releases.[9]

As a general rule, a pre-release cinema would exhibit films at an earlier date than a general release first-run cinema, which in turn would have the exhibition opportunity before second-run houses. The scale of prices dropped very rapidly as a film was distributed downwards and outwards through the various 'runs'.

It has been established in Table 2.1 that nominal cinema prices were largely stable during the 1930s. They were also invariant between the respective programmes of individual cinemas, although intra-cinema price discriminatory practices were evident in the common practice of cinemas at all levels to charge lower admission prices for matinee screenings, and sometimes higher prices for Saturday evening shows. Whereas the renter was able to set premium rates for those films expected to be highly popular with audiences—charging between 25–60 per cent of box-office grosses for major features—the exhibitors, mindful of the extent of local competition, maintained their price structure irrespective of the film being shown.[10] The distributor and exhibitor were engaged in a zero-sum game where, for any given film, the relative gains of one party were at the expense of the other. Yet, clearly, both exhibitor and distributor had an interest in handling popular films, with the exhibitor receiving a windfall gain where the distributor underestimated audience interest.[11] By the rules of an unfettered commercial practice, it was in neither the distributor's nor the exhibitor's interest to handle films of an inferior quality, given the existence of discriminating audiences, and the supply of alternative film programmes available within localities at similar prices. As Simon Rowson argued:

> It is probable indeed that one of the most valuable contributions to the exceptional popularity of the cinema is the existence of a power of selection among alternative programmes in various accessible houses.[12]

Certainly, the existence of the Cinematograph Films Act quotas may at times have resulted in distributors and exhibitors dealing in films that they would not freely have chosen, and having to select the least inferior in their estimation. Indeed, it was the unsubstantiated exaggeration of such situations which contributed to the 'Quota-Quickie disaster' interpretation of the effects of the Act.

The national sample cinema set

As recorded in Chapter 2, Rowson calculated that there were 4,305 wired cinemas in operation in Britain in 1934, whilst returns from Western Electric suggest 4,205 in 1933, 4,383 in 1934, 4,471 in 1935 and 4,582 in 1936.[13] Clearly, the sample size of between 81 and 92 cinemas represents a tiny proportion of the overall cinema population. Further, as mentioned earlier, it is skewed to (biased in favour of) the top end of the market. Cinemas in the sample set were almost twice as large as the average size cinema calculated by Rowson—approximately 1,700 seats compared with 900.[14] They were also much more expensive, with the sample mid-range price of approximately 2 shillings being over twice the average cinema admission price for all cinemas.[15]

It is possible to assert with some confidence that the sample cinema set adequately captures the exhibition characteristics of cinemas at the top end of the market. Using price as a yardstick, it has been possible to find only six cinemas—one in London, one in Newcastle, and four in Liverpool—which might have been added to the list of cinemas whose exhibition programmes were published in the *Kine Weekly*.[16] This is important information since if it can be shown that those films that are popular at the top end of the market continue to be popular as they are distributed out through the 'cascade system' of distribution/exhibition, then it follows that the cinema sample adopted here is sufficient to reflect national taste as a whole.

Approximately half of the cinemas in the sample were owned or controlled by the two leading British combines, with ABPC's share of seating varying between 16 to 18 per cent and that of Gaumont-British being between 33 and 36 per cent.[17] A similar set of proportions emerges from the calculation of gross revenue potential, with APBC's share ranging from 12 to 15 per cent and that of Gaumont-British between 36 and 38 per cent. These sample cinema-seating shares are disproportionately large in relation to the market presence of the two vertically integrated organizations with respect to the total population of cinemas, of which ABPC had 200 (0.4 per cent) and Gaumont-

British 324 (0.7 per cent) in 1934.[18] Undoubtedly, the films of the production wings (producing under the trade names of British International Pictures, and Gaumont-British and Gainsborough respectively) of the two organizations were privileged through in-house programming. To think otherwise would be foolish. The critical question is, did these films play to empty houses? If they did not—and there is no evidence to suggest that this might have been the case— then it must be supposed that these films competed more-or-less effectively with films produced by rival producers in rival cinemas.

From Table 3.2 it can be seen that the geographical dispersion of the sample cinema set is strongly biased towards London's West End

Table 3.2: *The geographical characteristics of the national sample set of cinemas, 1932–1937*[a]

	Number of cinemas in sample	Average no. of seats	Weighted average mid-range price (shillings)	Average cinema seating	Percentage of sample seats	Percentage of sample revenue
London West End	16 to 19	31,024	3.98	1,825	21	41
Birmingham	5 to 6	6,903	1.84	1,383	5	4
Bristol	8 to 9	14,494	1.26	1,610	10	6
Croydon[b]	1	3,712	1.80	3,712	3	2
Edinburgh	8	13,873	1.28	1,734	9	6
Glasgow	9 to 11	18,977	1.46	1,898	13	9
Leeds	7 to 8	13,317	1.56	1,736	9	7
Liverpool	7 to 9	11,970	1.36	1,495	8	5
Manchester	8 to 9	14,001	1.80	1,645	10	9
Newcastle	5	8,787	1.64	1,757	6	5
Sheffield	7	10,159	1.24	1,451	7	4
All cinemas	81 to 92	147,212	2.02	1,721	100	100

Sources: *Kine Weekly*; *Kine Year Books* 1932–1939; Eyles (1993); Eyles and Skone (1991).

Notes:
a. All averages are weighted arithmetic means.
b. The programmes of the massive Davis, Croydon (with a seating capacity second only to that of the 4,200 seater Green's Playhouse, Glasgow—also in the sample) were listed under London West End Cinemas in both the *Kine Weekly* and London's *Evening Standard*.

cinemas. They make up approximately 20 per cent of the sample cinemas but account for 40 per cent of the potential revenue capacity, because the average mid-range price of West End cinemas is more than twice that of the mean of the sample, whilst their seating capacity was only slightly larger than the mean. Otherwise the number of cinemas varies between five in Newcastle and Birmingham to eleven in Glasgow, with the latter boasting 13 per cent of the number of seats in the sample but, along with Manchester, generating only 9 per cent of the sample's revenue capacity.

The flagship cinemas

The pre-release London West End cinemas were either owned or leased by major producer-distributors or distributors. They were perceived as 'flagship' cinemas in which their films could be presented in the full glare of publicity. Further, the practice of maintaining a large temporal clearance interval between the pre-release and general release dates—generally between two and five months—gave them time to organize the distribution pattern of the film, including the necessary number of prints, as well as fixing its rental price. These cinemas also acted as trade show venues. Not all major players were formally tied to these exhibition venues, however. Until the late 1930s, of the American players only MGM (with the Empire, Leicester Square), Paramount (with the Capitol and Plaza) and United Artists (with the Leicester Square Theatre and London Pavilion from 1934) maintained a direct link between distribution and exhibition. To put this differently, Columbia (after it terminated its distribution agreement with United Artists in 1932), Fox (20th Century-Fox from 1936), RKO, Universal, and Warners-First National all required pre-release exhibition access to cinemas under the control of rival companies.[19]

Perhaps surprisingly, there is a varied pattern of exhibition amongst these premier cinemas: single feature, double feature, weekly change, occasional extra week holdovers, and multi-week runs can all be observed in the programme details described below. Eyles and Skone suggest that some of the cinemas attracted a regular and loyal audience—for instance the Plaza.[20] It certainly would appear that the management of individual cinemas (or their owners) had distinct exhibition policies, based upon operational and strategic factors such as location, size, price structure, number of friendly cinemas in the group, and the behaviour of rival managements.

For example the Empire, Leicester Square, increasingly resorted to double-bill programmes over the period, a practice chiefly explained by the need to conform to the Quota levels set down by the 1927 legislation. To this end, many MGM lesser 'A' features were shown with minor British studio films acquired by the parent company's British distribution arm. In 1932 the Empire showed just three British films—*Two White Arms* (Cinema House), *Diamond Cut Diamond* (Cinema House), *Last Coupon* (British International Pictures). Thereafter, with the exception of 1935, the management exhibited more than ten British films a year—fifteen in 1933, eleven in 1934, four in 1935, eleven in 1936 and twenty-two between 1 January 1937 and 31 March 1938. Of these, only the first two of the aforementioned films in 1932, in addition to *Perfect Understanding* (Gloria Swanson Productions) in 1933 and *This'll Make You Whistle* (Herbert Wilcox) in 1937, played as single features. Of the remaining sixty-three films, all except *Mimi* (BIP) were listed second on the billing, with *Southern Roses* (Capitol-Grafton) the only British film of the entire set to run for a second week—second billed with *Love on the Run* (MGM) in February 1937.[21]

Another example of this commercial focus can be seen in the criterion which determined the length of run any single film received. For the Empire, in what appears to be the sole surviving example of such data for a British cinema, Eyles (1989) lists the cinema's complete programmes 1928–61 together with an almost complete set of attendance figures. During the 1930s, it appears that a weekly audience in excess of 40,000 would generally be sufficient to warrant a further week's exhibition. For example, the exhibition record of *Mutiny on the Bounty* reads:

Period	Attendance	Notes
First day	11,094	Opened on 26 December 1935. Next seven days 73,894
Second week	65,584	
Third week	59,488	
Fourth week	40,472	Closed 21 January 1936, following the death of George V.
Fifth week	43,492	No matinee on 28 January 1936. George V's funeral.
Sixth week	38,532	

A detailed account of London's West End 'flagship' cinemas including their principal attractions between 1932 and 1937 is given in the Appendix to this chapter.

General release patterns

Earlier it was argued that the unrepresentative nature of the sample set of cinemas does not invalidate the statistical exercise aimed at establishing an index of film popularity, since popularity reveals itself initially in the upper levels of the 'cascade system' of distribution/ exhibition and is later confirmed, or not, as a film 'cascades' outwards in time and space from pre-release to general release showings and from higher- to lower-status cinemas. As has been established earlier in the chapter, implicit to this argument is the assumption that distributors chose to enter films at the highest possible level of exhibition, thereby enhancing a film's chances of big gross box-office success. It is further assumed that a film which received extended circulation at the higher exhibition levels enjoyed widespread distribution at the second-, third- and other-run levels of exhibition. Conversely, a film which failed to secure a pre-general release distrib- ution in London's West End cinemas would be expected to generate poorer box-office results than those that did. The objective of this section is to provide further evidence for these assertions and in doing so demonstrate the validity of POPSTAT as a general measure of film popularity.

In the analysis of London's West End 'flagship' cinemas, 126 films are listed as having, for the most part, extended single billing. If the above propositions concerning the cascading pattern of distribution are substantially correct, the expectation is that each of these 126 films would continue to show extensively as they filtered down through lower-status cinemas during the course of their exhibition history. An idea of the pattern of distribution may be obtained in microcosm from within the sample cinema set itself. In monitoring the exhibition profile of these 126 films as they pass through the sample set, a clear 'cascade' pattern of diffusion emerges with cinemas positioned according to how quickly (in what order) they could have expected to screen any particular film following its release.

The sample cinema set, organized into different 'run' groupings, is presented in Table 3.3. Cinemas which consistently show films at an earlier date than others will find themselves in a higher grouping, calculated by establishing the pecking order in which each of the sample cinemas exhibited films from the 126–film selection, with the highest rank set at one, i.e. marking out cinemas showing films hitherto not exhibited in Britain: that is films receiving their premieres. For instance, all 17 films of the 126–film selection screened at the New Gallery, Regent Street, were premieres, so generating a mean Exhibitor Status Rating (ESR) of 1.0 for that cinema. The results demonstrate a marked distinction between the cinemas in the sample with regard to their ability to secure these 126 'hit' productions as well as their position in the pecking order of exhibition dates. In selecting those films which had considerable pre-release West End exposure and which may consequently be thought to have been desirable acquisitions for the exhibitor, it is possible to show that the 'cascade' effect claimed for the population of cinemas in Britain as a whole is captured in the sample cinema set.

The relatively small number of films handled by the London pre-release cinemas is, of course, explained by their extended runs. Clearly, a weekly change cinema will run many more programmes than one in which extended runs are the norm. From Table 3.3, twelve (13 per cent of) cinemas played more than 50 (39 per cent) of the 126 films, whilst over half the cinemas (55) showed fewer than a fifth (25) of the films in the selection. The cinemas exhibiting the greatest number of this selection of films were the London cinemas—Marble Arch Pavilion, New Victoria, Dominion and Stoll—the huge London suburban Davis, Croydon, with 3,712 seats; and the following provincial city cinemas: the Regent, Bristol; the Regent, Sheffield; the Picture House, Glasgow; the New Victoria and New Picture House, Edinburgh; the Queens Theatre, Newcastle; the Trocadero, Liverpool; and Gaumont, Birmingham. Apart from the Stoll and the Davis these cinemas belonged to the Gaumont-British organization.

Earlier in the chapter it was argued that a clear distinction existed between London first- and second-run pre-release cinemas. Typically, the flagship cinemas premiered films three to five months prior to their general release. These films were shown a second time in London, two to four weeks before this, generally as part of a weekly change double-bill programme, at one of a set of pre-general release second-run cinemas. The proportion of the 126 films shown by the Dominion, the New Victoria and, to a lesser extent, the Marble Arch Pavilion is notable.

Amongst the principal provincial first-run cinemas, the Paramount cinemas in Birmingham, Glasgow, Leeds, Liverpool, Manchester and Newcastle, were dedicated to the exhibition of Paramount's major films prior to wider distribution.[22] This bias explains why these cinemas do not feature prominently in terms of the number of the 126 films exhibited and yet are highly ranked with respect to the early stage at which they screened films in the 'cascade' process.

The ABC cinemas appear to have performed less well than those in

Table 3.3: *The exhibition status of cinemas in the national sample*

	City	Number of 126 West End 'hits' shown[a]	Mean exhibition status ranking (ESR)[b]
Principal pre-release London cinemas			
Empire	London	24	1.3
Carlton	London	22	1.1
Tivoli	London	18	1.1
New Gallery	London	17	1.0
Leicester Square Theatre	London	13	1.0
Plaza	London	10	1.2
Regal	London	9	1.0
London Pavilion	London	7	1.0
Odeon	London	3	1.0
Principal second pre-release London cinemas			
New Victoria	London WE	80	3.7
Dominion	London WE	73	3.6
Marble Arch	London WE	51	3.8
Astoria	London WE	30	3.7
Metropole	London WE	20	3.2
Capitol	London WE	7	5.7
Other London cinemas			
Stoll	London	105	12.8
Davis	Croydon	61	13.0
Paramount	London WE	4	6.0
Provincial first-run cinemas			
Gaumont	Birmingham	47	8.9
Futurist	Birmingham	40	7.7
Forum	Birmingham	24	8.0
Paramount	Birmingham	5	6.6
Regent	Bristol	61	8.1
Kings	Bristol	29	8.8
New Palace	Bristol	29	10.9
Whiteladies	Bristol	26	9.2
New Victoria	Edinburgh	63	9.9
New Picture House	Edinburgh	56	10.6

Table 3.3 continued	City	Number of 126 West End 'hits' shown[a]	Mean exhibition status ranking (ESR)[b]
Playhouse	Edinburgh	32	11.3
Caley	Edinburgh	8	6.9
Picture House	Glasgow	58	7.3
New Savoy	Glasgow	39	10.1
Paramount	Glasgow	24	6.6
Regal	Glasgow	22	5.9
Coliseum	Glasgow	21	5.9
Majestic	Leeds	41	11.9
Paramount	Leeds	36	6.0
Scala	Leeds	15	13.2
Ritz	Leeds	19	11.9
Rialto	Leeds	13	12.0
Trocadero	Liverpool	51	9.0
Rialto	Liverpool	35	12.1
Forum	Liverpool	28	11.4
Royal Hippodrome	Liverpool	26	12.2
Paramount	Liverpool	19	6.6
Paramount	Manchester	37	6.4
Gaumont	Manchester	22	7.0
Market Street	Manchester	18	11.8
New Oxford	Manchester	18	11.8
Queens	Newcastle	55	10.2
Pavilion	Newcastle	36	12.2
Paramount	Newcastle	27	5.1
Regent	Sheffield	60	14.7
Central	Sheffield	32	13.6
Hippodrome	Sheffield	26	16.3
Cinema House	Sheffield	17	13.3

Provincial second-run cinemas

Stoll	Bristol	34	18.7
Embassy	Bristol	29	14.8
Triangle	Bristol	23	18.3
Hippodrome	Bristol	21	12.2
Empire	Bristol	21	18.1
Scala	Birmingham	43	16.4

Table 3.3 continued	City	Number of 126 West End 'hits' shown[a]	Mean exhibition status ranking (ESR)[b]
West End	Birmingham	31	12.1
Palace	Edinburgh	42	16.8
Rutland	Edinburgh	26	10.0
St Andrews	Edinburgh	25	12.5
Cranstons	Glasgow	47	17.6
La Scala	Glasgow	20	11.5
Green's Playhouse	Glasgow	11	15.5
Bedford	Glasgow	10	9.6
Grand	Glasgow	10	19.4
Regent	Glasgow	34	14.7
Assembly	Leeds	45	16.1
Tower	Leeds	38	19.1
Coliseum	Leeds	15	18.9
Futurist	Liverpool	34	16.2
Palais de Luxe	Liverpool	26	20.3
Scala	Liverpool	14	18.9
Piccadilly	Manchester	30	15.5
Deansgate	Manchester	22	16.9
Gaiety	Manchester	10	16.7
Regal	Manchester	9	19.9
New Westgate	Newcastle	24	15.2
Stoll	Newcastle	14	15.0
Electra	Sheffield	23	20.3
Albert Hall	Sheffield	14	21.6
Union Street	Sheffield	4	18.3

Sources: *Kine Weekly* supplemented by provincial city daily and evening newspapers.

Notes:
a. This is derived from the number of occasions in which films from the 126 'hits' which had extended runs in the principal London West End cinemas formed part of a programme in the listed cinemas.
b. This is a measure of a cinema's exhibitive status (or 'clout') where a mean of 1.0 implies that a cinema has only screened premiers whereas a mean of 2.0 implies that on average the films screened had one previous exhibition run. In general a mean ESR value x implies that on average the films screened have had $(x-1)$ previous exhibition-runs. Accordingly, the lower the mean ESR value the higher the exhibition status of the cinema and *vice versa*. The weighted average Exhibitive Status Ranking (ESR) of the sample cinemas is 10.9

the chains owned by the rival Gaumont-British organization. The Coliseum and Regal, Glasgow and Kings and Whiteladies, Bristol, were the only provincial city ABC cinemas with a mean Exhibition Status Rating (ESR) above the sample mean rating of 10.9. In all four cases they exhibited between a sixth and fifth of the 126–film selection.

Many of the Gaumont-British-owned cinemas achieved a mean ESR above that of the sample mean as well as exhibiting a higher proportion of films from the 126 selection than those of their ABC rivals. The Gaumonts of Birmingham and Manchester; the Picture House and the New Savoy, Glasgow; the Regent and the New Palace, Bristol; the Trocadero, Liverpool; the New Victoria, the New Picture and the Rutland, Edinburgh; and the Queens, Newcastle all achieved this.

A reworking of the information, by city, indicates a temporal pattern of release in which audiences in some cities saw films consistently before those in other cities. The city-by-city weighted mean ESRs rise from 11 for Birmingham, Glasgow and Newcastle, to 12 for Manchester and Edinburgh, 13 for Bristol and Liverpool, 14 for Leeds, and 16 for Sheffield. Such differences imply that distributors used a regional policy of staggered releases, which enabled them to economize on print costs amongst other things.

The index of film popularity—POPSTAT

POPSTAT is relative measure of film popularity. It is calculated for each film that was programmed at least once at a cinema in the sample set during the period under investigation on the basis that box-office revenue is generated through exhibition. From Appendix 1 it is clear that cinemas in the sample were of unequal size. Further, their commercial status, manifest in their ability to obtain films from the major distributors before, at, or after the date of general release, significantly affected the prices they could charge. It follows, then, that their gross and net box-office revenue capacities differed considerably from one to another. In order to represent these differences, each cinema in the sample is given a weight based upon its potential gross revenue capacity, obtained by multiplying its mid-range ticket price by the number of seats and expressing the result as a proportion of the mean potential gross revenue of all cinemas in the sample.[23] This relative measure of potential revenue clearly does not reflect the variations in the capacity utilization of each cinema which occurred according to which particular film was being screened. This means that all films at a given cinema are treated as if they generated the same capacity utilization, an assumption which discriminates against the most popular films. The data used in assessing potential box-office revenue of each cinema are listed in Appendix 1 for those cinemas whose film programmes form the basis of the POPSTAT calculations. For example, in 1932 the Revenue Potential (2,518 seat-shillings) of the Forum Birmingham is given by its seating capacity (1,259) multiplied by its mid-range price (2 shillings). The cinema's weighting (0.68) is established by dividing its Revenue Potential by the average Revenue Potential (3,686.33 seat-shillings) of all cinemas listed in the table. The value being less than 1.0 implies that the Forum Birmingham generated lower box-office receipts than the average for the sample set of cinemas. The weights hence reflect the relative commercial status of sample cinemas, indicating that the revenue capacity of the Empire, Leicester Square was, for example, approximately twice that of the Davis cinema, Croydon, four times that of the Piccadilly, Manchester, and eight times that of the Regent, Glasgow. As the sample varied slightly over the period—monitored in Appendix 1—with a number of cinemas closing or new ones emerging, so the average cinema Revenue Potential changed marginally and with this the weight of each cinema. New weights were calculated accordingly for each year of the investigation.

The box-office potential of cinemas was not the only factor that determined the box-office revenue potential of a film when screened at a cinema in the sample set. The length of run—particularly significant in the West End cinemas—and the billing status of the film—whether it played on a single- or double-billed programme—were also important. The index reflects these factors by multiplying the cinema weight by the length of run, where multiples of whole and half weeks are used, and by a weight of 0.5 where the film shares a double-billing programme and 1.0 in the case of a single billing. Again the measure discriminates against the most popular films in that where a highly popular film shares the programme with a much less popular film each film is treated equally.

The popularity of each film is thus given:

$$POPSTAT_{it} = \sum_{j=1}^{n} a_j * b_{ij} * l_{ij}$$

Where POPSTAT = popularity statistic

t = time duration in weeks of the commercial life of a film from its entry into the sample set of cinemas to its exit

71

i = ith film

j = jth cinema

n = number of cinemas in the sample set at which the ith film was screened

a_j = the weighting of the jth cinema

b_{ij} = the weighting of the billing status of the ith film at the jth cinema where 0.5 represents a shared and 1.0 equals a single billing

l_{ij} = the length of exhibition of the ith film at the jth cinema in weeks and half-weeks

* represents 'multiplied by'

The notation should be read as follows: the POPSTAT score of the ith film at the end of its commercial life of t weeks—say *Mutiny on the Bounty* (1935, MGM)—is given by multiplying the cinema weighting of the jth cinema at which it was exhibited—say the Empire, Leicester Square—by the billing status and length of run at that cinema, and then summing for all n cinemas found in the sample (from j = 1 to n) at which the film was screened. This is done for all films which were registered as 'long films' with the Board of Trade between 1 January 1932 and 31 March 1938 in accordance with the regulations laid down in the 1927 Cinematograph Films Act, thus providing a POPSTAT score for each film that had at least one exhibition booking.

The POPSTAT index treats all billings at each cinema in the sample equally. That is to say that it does not factor in either the part of the week in which a film was shown or the time of year.[24] It is widely known that cinema attendances were higher at the weekend. This would not affect the POPSTAT scores of films booked for weekly runs, the dominant practice for cinemas in the national sample set outlined in this chapter. However, there are repercussions at the level of lower-order cinemas found in the subsequent analysis of cinemagoing in Bolton and Brighton in which half-weekly double-bill programmes were the norm. A film which was billed from Thursday to Saturday would expect to earn more revenue than one screened during the earlier part of the week. Accordingly, one could fix weights to the POPSTAT scores derived from such cinemas reflecting this factor. I have not done this because my impression from the data is that for the most part there was no obvious pattern as to when particular films were screened during the week at lower-order cinemas, and therefore the weighted effect would even out for those films which received multiple bookings at such cinemas. Further, in relation to higher-order cinemas, the potential seat-revenues of lower-order cinemas were small, and consequently the difference which part-of-the-week weights might make to the overall POPSTAT performance of a film would also be small and not affect in general the ranked order of the most popular films.

A more serious problem emerges from the time of the year in which a film receives the bulk of its higher-order cinema bookings. Again it is commonly understood that cinema attendance was higher in the winter months, particularly in the period leading up to and over Christmas, than in the summer. Should this not be reflected in the POPSTAT scores of films in the same way that it would have been reflected in box-office returns? The simple answer to this would be yes, but there is to date insufficient evidence about this effect in the public domain to provide a statistically reliable scaling tool. A corollary to this thesis is that those films which were released during the summer months would have performed better at the box-office had they been released later in the year. Accordingly, it could be argued that actual box-office performance is in fact insensitive to this counterfactual proposition, whereas POPSTAT, in not reflecting seasonal patterns of cinema attendance, perhaps provides a truer sense of popularity.

Conclusion

The purpose of this chapter has been to describe the 'cascade system' of distribution/exhibition. The 'flagship' cinemas of London's West End cinemas were of vital importance to renters as showcases for their product, prior to general release. Not only did films which enjoyed extended runs at these cinemas generate substantial box-office revenues, but the degree of their popularity also provided important information in the fixing of rental charges. In the course of this description, 126 films were identified as having had exceptional West End exposure. These films then formed the basis of an investigation into the pattern of temporal and spatial film diffusion out from the West End to lower-level provincial cinemas in the sample.

From the base of cinema exhibition it has been possible to develop a methodology for estimating film popularity. The proposed POPSTAT index draws upon the programmes of a sample of cinemas featured in the *Kine Weekly* over the period January 1932 to March 1938. The information collected is biased in that it is drawn from the top stratum of pre-release London West End and first-run provincial city cinemas. However, whilst not representative of the population of cinemas in Britain as a whole over this period, the 'cascade system' identified within the sample cinema set suggests a replication of exhibition patterns at subsequent-run cinemas. The hypothesis which is later tested in local studies of cinemagoing in Bolton and Brighton, is that films that do well in the national sample cinema set continue broadly to do so in lower-order cinemas, with a small number becoming the 'hits' of their day, whilst those that had a spasmodic second billing record in the sample cinemas would do less well, except for the occasional 'sleeper'.

Appendix to Chapter 3: London's West End flagship cinemas

Capitol, Haymarket
This 1,700 seat cinema was part of the GTC circuit, which had been under the ownership of Gaumont-British since May 1928. From April 1933 until its closure for refurbishment on 18 January 1936 it specialized in the pre-release exhibition of one-week double-bill programmes. Overall, approximately 80 per cent of its programmes consisted of shared billings. The major studios represented in exhibition were Fox (23 per cent), Universal (13 per cent), Columbia (12 per cent), Gaumont-British/Gainsborough (10 per cent), Warners-First National (9 per cent) and RKO (8 per cent). After refurbishment it opened again on 4 February 1937 as the Gaumont, Haymarket (1,328 seats).

Its principal attractions during the period under investigation were the following: *Goodnight Vienna* (B&D)—seven weeks from 28 March 1932; *Love on Wheels* (Gainsborough)—six weeks from 9 May 1932; *The Good Companions* (Gaumont-British)—five weeks from 27 February 1933; *Foreign Affaires* (Gainsborough)—four weeks from 23 December 1935; *Lloyds of London* (20th Century-Fox)—four weeks from 12 April 1937, after it had become the Gaumont, Haymarket.[25]

Carlton, Haymarket
Owned by Paramount, this 1,159 seat cinema was used to premiere its principal films. Across the 325 weeks of the sample period only 72 programmes were seen of which 13 were shared billings. Not surprisingly, the programme profile was dominated by films of the parent company, with 51 Paramount films occupying two-thirds of all possible screenings. This was a cinema which specialized in lengthy runs with the average Paramount film running for more than four weeks. However, as can be seen below, prominent films from other studios were also shown at the Carlton.

The most extensive runs were the following: *Shanghai Express* (Paramount)—twelve weeks from 21 March 1932; *One Hour With You* (Paramount)—eight weeks from 4 July 1932; *Devil and the Deep* (Paramount)—six weeks from 29 August 1932; *Movie Crazy* (Harold Lloyd)—six weeks from 10 October 1932; *Trouble in Paradise* (Paramount)—six weeks from 19 December 1932; *Sign of the Cross* (Paramount)—eight weeks from 30 January 1933; *Bedtime Story* (Paramount)—six weeks from 22 May 1933; *Bitter Sweet* (B&D)—six weeks from 21 August 1933; *I'm No Angel* (Paramount)—eleven weeks from 27 November 1933; *One Night of Love* (Columbia)—thirteen weeks from 24 September 1934; *The Lives of a Bengal Lancer* (Paramount)—eighteen weeks from 28 January 1935; *The Crusades* (Paramount)—six weeks from 26 August 1935; *Top Hat* (RKO)—fourteen weeks from 7 October 1935; *The Milky Way* (Paramount) — six weeks from 2 March 1936; *The General Died at Dawn* (Paramount)—six and a half weeks from 12 October 1936; *The Charge of the Light Brigade* (Warners)—eight weeks from 29 December 1936; *I Met Him in Paris* (Paramount)—nine and a half weeks from 14 June 1937; *The Life of Emile Zola* (Warners)—nine and a half weeks from 18 October 1937; *The Buccaneer* (Paramount)—seven weeks run from 31 January 1938.

One interesting aspect of the exhibition profile of the Carlton is the absence of MGM films, and the small number of British productions screened during these years. My investigation of screenings indicates that the cinema failed to meet its Quota obligation, as defined by the 1927 Act, for all years except for the Quota year 1932–3 in which *Bitter Sweet* played for six weeks. The Exhibition Quota year ran from 1 October to 30 September. My calculations for the Carlton are found in Table 3.4 (overleaf).[26]

Empire, Leicester Square

Opened on November 1928, the Empire (3,226 seats) was MGM's 'flagship' cinema. Given its size, it is not surprising that the length of run achieved by prominent films was considerably less than that at the Carlton, which had about a third of the Empire's seating capacity. However, like the Carlton's, the Empire's exhibition profile was dominated by films from the parent company.[27] Of the 311 films shown at the Empire during the investigation period, 209 (67 per cent) carried the MGM trade mark. Unlike the Carlton, the Empire ran a significant number of double bills, the great majority of which teamed US parent company productions with British films made from minor domestic

Table 3.4: *A profile of the Carlton's film programmes, 1932–1937*

	1932–33	1933–34	1934–35	1935–36	1936–37
British films	2	0	0	2	2
Total films	13	18	10	12	15
British film weeks	7	0	0	6.5	3
British film weeks (per cent)[a]	13	0	0	13	6
Quota Minimum	12.5	15	15	20	20

For sample period 1 January 1932 to 31 March 1938

British films	8
Total films	72
British films (per cent)	11
British film weeks	19.5
Total film weeks[b]	337
British film weeks (per cent)	6

Sources: *Kine Weekly*; *Evening Standard*.

Notes:
a. This row represents a first approximation of the screen time as defined by the 1927 legislation. A fuller estimation would require information about the length of the films as well as the number of their screenings.
b. This figure exceeds the 325 weeks covered by the sample because of a small number (12) of double billings.

production companies. Altogether 78 of the 233 programmes (33 per cent) were double features. Another dissimilarity from the Carlton appears to be the management's attitude to the Quota legislation: 67 of the 311 films (22 per cent) were British, occupying 18 per cent of screen time.

Of the 209 MGM films exhibited at the Empire, 120 (57 per cent) were single-billed MGM films. Overall, parent company films occupied 296.5 of the 411 (72 per cent) aggregate exhibition weeks: the mean run being less than 1.5 weeks.

The major attractions during the period were the following: *Hell Divers* (MGM)—three weeks from 21 March 1932; *Queen Christina* (MGM)—four weeks from 19 February 1934; *Riptide* (MGM)—three weeks from 16 April 1934; *The Barretts of Wimpole Street* (MGM)— three weeks from 15 October 1934; *The Merry Widow* (MGM)—three weeks from 26 November 1934; *The Painted Veil* (MGM)—three weeks from 31 December 1934; *China Seas* (MGM)—three weeks from 16 September 1935; *Anna Karenina* (MGM)—three weeks from 7 October 1935; *Broadway Melody of 1936* (MGM)—three weeks from 9 December 1935; *Mutiny on the Bounty* (MGM)—six weeks from 30 December 1935; *A Tale of Two Cities* (MGM)—four weeks from 13 April 1936; *Libelled Lady* (MGM)—three weeks from 16 November 1936; *Camille* (MGM)—four weeks from 8 March 1937; *Captains Courageous* (MGM)—three weeks from 10 May 1937; and *Marie Walewska*—four weeks from 20 December 1937.[28]

MGM pursued a policy of pre-releasing its most prestigious films at a number of London West End theatres. Four films opened at the Palace Theatre before transferring to the Empire. These were *Grand Hotel* (MGM)—fourteen weeks, from 3 September 1932, at the Palace before a further two weeks at the Empire in December 1932; *Dinner at Eight* (MGM)—twelve weeks, from 4 September 1933, at the Palace before a further two weeks at the Empire in November 1933; *David Copperfield* (MGM)—eight weeks, from 4 March 1935, at the Palace before a further two weeks at the Empire in June 1935; and *The Good Earth* (MGM)—twelve weeks, from 24 March 1937, at the Palace before a further two weeks at the Empire in June 1937.

Two other major MGM films opened at His Majesty's Theatre: *The Great Ziegfeld* (MGM)—seven weeks, from 31 August 1936, at His Majesty's Theatre followed by seven weeks at the London Hippodrome from 12 October 1936; and *Romeo and Juliet* (MGM)—nine weeks at His Majesty's Theatre, from 12 October 1936, both appearing later at the Empire for one and two weeks respectively.

The management of the Empire rarely promoted the major films of rival producers, although a few films from Universal, RKO, Columbia, and latterly 20th Century-Fox were exhibited, primarily as supporting features to the main MGM feature. Only *She Married Her Boss* (Columbia)—shown from 18 November 1935 for two weeks; *Mary of Scotland* (RKO)—from 30 August 1936 for two weeks; and *The Road to Glory* (20th Century-Fox)—from 2 November 1936 for two weeks—played as single features with runs exceeding one week.

Leicester Square Theatre, Leicester Square
Opened on 19 December 1930, the cinema, for a period between March and July 1932, was known as the Olympic. Its original name restored, it presented non-stop variety from August 1932, closing and re-opening as a cinema once more in September 1933 under the control

of Jack Buchanan and leased to United Artists.[29] From then until 18 July 1937 the Leicester Square Theatre acted, along with the London Pavilion, as United Artists' premier-run cinema. As such, it featured the films of London Film Productions—whose managing director, Alexander Korda, became a full owner-director of United Artists in 1935—British and Dominions, 20th Century and Goldwyn. The films of the first of these companies were particularly prominent in the programme. Altogether, the twelve London Films productions played for 72 weeks. The 1,760 seat cinema specialized in extensive runs. Indeed, between November 1933 and the end of the period of the survey, the cinema played a mere 55 programmes, of which only six were double bills.

The principal attractions were: *The Private Life of Henry VIII* (London Films)—nine weeks from 27 November 1933; *Catherine the Great* (London Films)—seven weeks from 12 February 1934; *Roman Scandals* (Goldwyn)—ten weeks from 16 April 1934; *Nell Gwyn* (B&D)—seven weeks from 17 September 1934; *The Scarlet Pimpernel* (London Films)—nine weeks from 24 December 1934; *Sanders of the River* (London Films)—nine weeks from 1 April 1935; *Cardinal Richelieu* (20th Century)—seven weeks from 24 June 1935; *The Ghost Goes West* (London Films)—ten weeks from 16 December 1935; *Things to Come* (London Films)—nine weeks from 24 February 1935; *Show Boat* (Universal)—nine weeks from 15 June 1936; and *Garden of Allah* (Selznick)—six weeks from 14 December 1936.

From September 1937 the cinema became the leading West End house of General Film Distributors. During this period *Victoria the Great* (Imperator) had a nine and a half weeks run from 13 September 1937 and *100 Men and a Girl* (Universal) sustained eleven weeks run from 6 December 1937.

London Pavilion, Coventry Street

From 5 September 1934 the newly refurbished London Pavilion (1,209 seats) served as a second United Artists' showcase pre-release cinema and, like the Leicester Square Theatre, it was principally an extended-run single-billing house. Between February 1935 and March 1938 only five of the 54 programmes were double billed. However, the runs were considerably shorter and film production company representation more evenly spread than was the case at its companion cinema, the Leicester Square Theatre. The most frequently represented studio was Goldwyn, seven films of which were exhibited over the period, taking up almost 20 per cent of screen time. Amongst the other production companies distributed by United Artists were British and Dominions, 20th Century (USA), Reliance (USA), Criterion, Selznick (USA), Pickford (USA), London Films, Trafalgar Films, Saville Films, Wanger (USA), and Grafton.

The most notable film runs were the following: *Kid Millions* (Goldwyn)—six weeks from 28 January 1935; *Escape Me Never* (B&D)—ten weeks from 8 April 1935; *Strike Me Pink* (Goldwyn)— six and a half weeks from 16 March 1936; *Little Lord Fauntleroy* (Selznick)—five and a half weeks from 27 April 1936; *Dreaming Lips* (Trafalgar)—five weeks from 1 February 1937; *Knight Without Armour* (London Films)—six weeks from 27 September 1937; and *Nothing Sacred* (Selznick)—five weeks from 7 February 1938.

Marble Arch Pavilion, Marble Arch

Seating 1,189 customers, the Marble Arch Pavilion, according to Eyles and Skone, '...came to be on the small side and a little remote, taking films on transfer from bigger, more central cinemas'.[30] This is borne out by its exhibition record. Owned by the Gaumont-British organization, only two first runs of any significance were recorded during these years: *FP1* (UFA of Germany)—six weeks from 3 April 1933; and *Jack of All Trades* (Gainsborough)—four weeks from 17 February 1936.

Otherwise the cinema specialized in exhibiting films which had transferred from more centrally sited West End cinemas. Six notable examples were the following: *Cavalcade* (Fox)—twelve weeks from 12 June 1933, following a sixteen-week run at the Tivoli; *Catherine the Great* (London Films)—five weeks from 2 April 1934, following seven weeks at the Leicester Square Theatre; *It Happened One Night* (Columbia)—four weeks from 28 May 1934, following a four-week run at the Tivoli; *The 39 Steps*—eight weeks from 15 July 1935, following five weeks at the New Gallery; *Modern Times* (Chaplin)— twelve weeks following a thirteen-week run at the Tivoli; *Mutiny on the Bounty* (MGM)— four weeks from 3 August 1936, following six weeks at the Empire; and *Lost Horizon* (Columbia)—six weeks from 23 August 1937, following an eighteen-week run at the Tivoli.

However, more characteristic were shorter runs of films from the production wings of the parent company (Gaumont-British or Gainsborough) after a premier run at either the New Gallery or Tivoli cinemas. Films in this category were *Rome Express*, *I Was a Spy*, *The Constant Nymph*, *The Man of Aran*, *Evergreen*, *The Tunnel* and *OHMS*.

Altogether, 35 of the 91 films shown at the Marble Arch Pavilion were made at either the Gaumont-British or Gainsborough studios, whilst 58 were distributed by the parent company's distribution organization. Finally, both Fox and 20th Century-Fox released or transferred minor 'A' pictures (including *Cavalcade*, which was, exceptionally, a super 'A' picture) to the cinema, having thirteen films screened over the period.

New Gallery, Regent Street
Owned by the Gaumont-British organization, the New Gallery, with a seating capacity of 1,450, premiered many films from its parent company's production wing. Notable runs were recorded by: *Soldiers of the King* (Gainsborough)—four weeks from 20 March 1933; *A Cuckoo in the Nest* (Gaumont-British)—four weeks from 30 October 1933; *The Man of Aran* (Gainsborough)—six weeks from 23 April 1934; *Evergreen* (Gaumont-British)—four weeks from 4 June 1934; *The Camels are Coming* (Gainsborough)—six weeks from 29 October 1934; *The Man Who Knew Too Much* (Gaumont-British)—four weeks from 10 December 1934; *The 39 Steps* (Gaumont-British)—five weeks from 10 June 1935; *The Clairvoyant* (Gainsborough)—four weeks from 5 August 1935; *The Guv'nor* (Gaumont-British)—four weeks from 23 December 1935 with *Baxter's Millions* (Universal); *Pot Luck* (Gainsborough)—four weeks from 6 April 1936 with *It Happened in Hollywood* (RKO).

Altogether, films from the parent company's stable occupied more than 40 per cent of the screen time during this period. Also, as at the Marble Arch Pavilion, Fox and 20th Century-Fox had a significant exhibition representation, occupying approximately 10 per cent of the screen time, again with predominantly minor 'A' pictures on a shared billing. Warners had an even more significant exhibition presence at the cinema, securing approximately 20 per cent of the screen space. As with those of Fox, most of the Warner films were in the minor 'A' category and shown on a shared billing, although *The Green Pastures* (Warners) was premiered at the cinema and achieved a five-week run, from 30 November 1936.

Other notable attractions at the cinema were two New World Productions: *Wings of the Morning* and *Under the Red Robe*, both of which secured four-week runs in 1937; and at the beginning of the period *A Night Like This* (British and Dominions)—five and a half weeks from 14 March 1932; and *The Bowery* (20th Century)—four weeks from 25 December 1933.

Odeon, Leicester Square

Seating 2,116, and contractually tied to United Artists, the Odeon, Leicester Square opened on 2 November 1937 with a five-week run of Selznick's *The Prisoner of Zenda*. During its brief spell of operation during the survey period, the cinema screened an exclusive roster of United Artists releases including: *Hurricane* (Goldwyn)—six weeks from 31 January 1938; and *The Goldwyn Follies* which premiered on 14 March 1938.

Plaza, Regent Street

Eyles and Skone have described the 1,896 seater Paramount-owned Plaza as the company's second pre-release house, after the Carlton, Haymarket, dedicated to the screening of the parent company's less prestigious output, 'usually with weekly changes, [and] cultivating a regular audience.'[31] Michael Powell lends this statement some contemporary support, writing: 'For four years we were inseparable… Working, playing, hunting girls, gossiping, biting, scratching, creating, going to the Plaza cinema every Saturday to see the new Paramount movie.'[32]

Certainly the programming of the cinema was dominated by the films of the production wing of its American parent which occupied more than 60 per cent of screen time. Most of these ran for a single week as part of a double-bill programme. The only other notable studio representations were the films of RKO which attained approximately a 12 per cent share of screenings. Those films which had single-billing runs of three or more weeks were: *Blonde Venus* (Paramount)—three weeks from 31 October 1932; *Spitfire* (RKO)—three weeks from 11 June 1934; *Ruggles of Red Gap* (Paramount)—four weeks from 18 March 1935; *Follow the Fleet* (RKO)—five weeks from 13 April 1936; *The Plainsman* (Paramount)—four weeks from 8 February 1937; *Farewell Again* (Pendennis)—three and a half weeks from 3 May 1937; *Souls at Sea* (Paramount)—four weeks from 6 September 1937; and *True Confession* (Paramount)—three weeks from 20 December 1937.

The cinema's management appear to have shown no more than the minimum number of domestic films required by the 1927 legislation. Through the period of investigation only some 14 per cent of screen space was occupied with British-made films, rising towards the end of the period with the increasing Quota requirement.[33]

Regal, Marble Arch

This large cinema with a seating capacity of 2,400 was the showcase theatre of the ABC chain during the 1930s. Perhaps because of its size and its westward location from the Leicester Square heartland of London's West End, only a few films achieved a run greater than three weeks, with the remainder mixed between weekly change double-billed and single-billed features. Those that did were: *42nd Street* (Warners)—four weeks from 1 May 1933; *The Affairs of Voltaire* (Warners)—four weeks from 1 January 1934; *Little Women* (RKO)—four weeks from 29 January 1934; *G Men* (Warners)—four weeks from 17 June 1935; *Mr Deeds Goes to Town* (Columbia)—six weeks from 24 August 1936; *Swing Time* (RKO)—four weeks from 26 October 1936; *Theodora Goes Wild* (Columbia)—four weeks from 15 February 1937; *Shall We Dance* (RKO)—four weeks from 17 May 1937; and *Stage Door* (RKO)—four weeks from 3 January 1938.

Not one of these films was produced by the production wing of the parent company. In general, the films of British International were not as prominent at the Regal as those from the Gaumont-British and Gainsborough studios were at the New Gallery, Tivoli, and Marble Arch Pavilion, occupying a mere 15 per cent of screen time. The studio most represented in the programmes at the Regal was Warners with just less than 40 per cent of screen time. Fox and 20th Century-Fox, RKO and Columbia with approximately 16, 12 and 10 per cent respectively of screen time were also important exhibitors.

Rialto, Coventry Street

Before becoming an ABC cinema in January 1934, the 700 seat Rialto specialized in premiering major French and German productions. *A Nous La Liberté*, *Blue Angel*, *The Blue Light*, *Il Est Charmant*, *Le Million*, *L'Ordonnance*, and *Poil de Carotte*, were all introduced to domestic audiences at the Rialto. Thereafter, the cinema specialized in weekly change double billings featuring either films from its parent company or films acquired by the in-house distribution wing, Wardour, predominately from minor United States studios such as Liberty, Majestic and Peerless. The only BIP runs of any significance were *Lucky Girl* which played for eleven weeks from 15 August 1932 with the UFA film *Back to Nature*—this was before it became an ABC cinema—and *Forgotten Men* (Jewel Productions) which received a ten-week run as a single feature from 12 December 1934. Towards the end of 1936 and throughout 1937 the cinema began operating as a second-run pre-release cinema offering more obviously commercial films from the major Hollywood studios. For example, *Mr Deeds Goes to Town* (Columbia) had an eleven-week run from 12 October 1936 and *Swing*

Time (RKO) played for seven weeks from 28 December 1936 as part of a double feature with *Grand Jury* (RKO), both having premiered at the Regal, Marble Arch.

Tivoli, Strand

Listed in the *Kine Year Books* as seating more than 2,000[34], the Tivoli was the second of the Gaumont-British showcase cinemas in the London West End, prior to the opening of the Gaumont Haymarket in February 1937. Even more than its counterpart, the New Gallery, the Tivoli was a single-bill multi-week run cinema. Only 26 of the 325 weeks of the investigation saw double-bill programmes. Some of the runs were very long indeed, as can be gauged from the list below, with an average run of single-billed programmes of more than four weeks. The most notable runs were: *Arrowsmith* (Goldwyn)—seven weeks from 28 March 1932; *Jack's the Boy* (Gainsborough)—ten and a half weeks from 20 June 1932; *Cavalcade* (Fox)—sixteen weeks from 20 February 1933; *I Was A Spy* (Gaumont-British)—six weeks from 4 September 1933; *The House of Rothschild* (20th Century)—twelve weeks from 28 May 1934; *Jew Süss* (Gaumont-British)—six weeks from 8 October 1934; *The Iron Duke* (Gaumont-British)—seven and a half weeks from 26 November 1934; *Roberta* (RKO)—five weeks from 27 May 1935; *On Wings of Song* (Columbia)—seven weeks from 2 September 1935; *Modern Times* (Chaplin)—thirteen weeks from 10 February 1936; *Lost Horizon* (Columbia)—eighteen weeks from 19 April 1937; *A Star is Born* (Selznick)—eight weeks from 13 September 1937; and *Tovarich* (Warners)—six and a half weeks from 24 January 1938, one of which was shared with *The Radio Murder Mystery* (Warners).

Again, the films of Gaumont-British/Gainsborough feature prominently, taking up approximately 30 per cent of the cinema's screen time. Of the other studios, the films of RKO occupied approximately 20 per cent, Fox 17 per cent, and Columbia 11 per cent of screen time, with the remaining studios achieving less than 10 per cent.

4

Shares in the British Market

My examination of British genres suggests that whether the British critics wished to acknowledge it or not, Britain did in fact have a viable national cinema.

Marcia Landy[1]

In Chapter 3 the method of measuring film popularity (POPSTAT) was explained. Based upon the exhibition records of between 81 and 92 leading cinemas spread throughout the urban centres of Britain, the methodology captures the diffusion of each film as it passes through the sample set of cinemas. Whilst these cinemas represented the top end of the market, exhibiting films at an earlier date than cinemas outside of the sample, I have argued that the cascade system of distribution/exhibition ensured that these same films would then filter down through runs of lower-order cinemas. As a consequence, those films which were popular in the sample set of cinemas would continue to be popular in those cinemas outside of the sample. Although this assumption is later modified in the light of the investigation of cinemagoing preferences in Bolton and Brighton and Hove, the national sample set of cinemas provides for the first time a body of objective and reclassifiable knowledge concerning film popularity in Britain during the 1930s.

Characteristics of the national sample results

One of the stipulations of the 1927 Cinematograph Films Act was that all commercial films, both features (long films) and shorts, should be registered with the Board of Trade for Quota purposes. From the POPSTAT formula established in Chapter 3, it follows that each feature film that was billed at least once at a cinema in the sample set of cinemas during the period will generate a POPSTAT score greater than zero. In this way it is possible to rank all of the films marketed in Britain during these years, where a higher POPSTAT value implies a more popular film.

Basic statistical information drawn from the sample is presented in Table 4.1. The sheer scale of film consumption, rising from 649 features in 1932 to 803 by 1937, is immediately observable. Undoubtedly, the emergence of double-bill programmes fuelled the demand for this growth. However, the mean POPSTAT score remains fairly steady for the first five of the six years of the study, the small variation being explained by the small increase in the number of cinemas in the sample set, causing the relative weights of all cinemas to change, and by the annual increase in the numbers of films competing for exhibition. The lower mean POPSTAT for 1937 can principally be attributed to the termination of the study at 31 March 1938 which does not allow sufficient time for the releases of late 1937 to diffuse fully through the sample set of cinemas.[2] This particularly affects the POPSTAT scores of films which enjoyed extensive pre-release West End runs at that time such as *A Star is Born* (Selznick, 1937).

Table 4.1: *General POPSTAT characteristics of the national sample data*

	Films registered	Mean POPSTAT	Standard deviation	Coefficient of variation
1932	649	6.11	6.53	1.07
1933	668	6.05	7.44	1.23
1934	664	6.21	7.10	1.14
1935	701	6.34	7.83	1.24
1936	743	6.29	8.15	1.30
1937	803	4.93	7.43	1.51

Sources: Board of Trade Film Register; *Kine Year Book* and *Kine Weekly*.

Note: The 'Films registered' column totals 4,205. This differs from the 4,748 'Total Films' recorded in Table 4.4 since it does not include those films registered in 1931 but still playing in 1932 and those films registered between 1 January and 31 March 1938.

Along with the annual mean POPSTAT score, the associate statistics of standard deviation and coefficient of variation are also stable, indicating a repetitive annual frequency distribution of POPSTAT scores among the whole population of films. The standard deviation is important because it measures the spread of POPSTAT scores around the arithmetic mean and hence contributes to a fuller picture of the data. Table 4.1 shows that the magnitude of the annual standard deviation statistics is greater than that of the arithmetic mean over the time period, indicating that the data were widely dispersed. Because standard deviation statistics are derived from particular data sets, difficulties arise when comparing them from two or more distinct data populations. This problem is rectified by means of the coefficient of variation, which serves to standardize the measure of dispersion of the data by expressing the standard deviation as a proportion of the arithmetic mean, thus making it possible to compare dispersion, in this case, from one year to another.

I have pointed out some of the peculiar properties of film as a commodity in my analysis of its consumption characteristics in the Introduction. It is clear from the mean POPSTAT (a proxy for revenue) and standard deviation data in Table 4.1 that the production side has, as a consequence, its own peculiarities, compared to more conventional commodities. For the producers of most commodities, having a standard deviation of the same magnitude as its referential mean would be bizarre, but in the commercial film industry of the 1930s, that was a norm to which its budget controllers were accustomed.

The consistency of the statistics in Table 4.1 over the time period of the investigation together with the wide dispersion of the data around the arithmetic mean is evident from the frequency distributions presented in Table 4.2. If, for any one year, the number of films in each POPSTAT interval is plotted against POPSTAT intervals, as in Figure 4.1, the resultant curve is typically concave upwards falling - less formally, 'C' shaped—indicating a distribution in which the modal (i.e. most frequent) value is either 0 or less than 1 for all years, with only a small proportion of films achieving high POPSTAT scores. As the POPSTAT statistic is in effect a relative measure of box-office performance, it means that the most popular films of each year earned upwards of 60 times that of those films falling into the modal classification and 10 times that of those at the arithmetic mean.[3] It is clear that only a small number of films could expect to become 'hits', with approximately 65 per cent of films earning less than average box-

Table 4.2: *The frequency distribution of POPSTAT scores for films marketed in Britain, 1932–1937*

POPSTAT interval	Number of films in each POPSTAT interval					
	1932	1933	1934	1935	1936	1937
= 0	62	72	80	99	131	200
>0 to 1	68	93	69	61	74	104
>1 to 2	48	51	41	58	67	67
>2 to 3	56	57	50	55	34	65
>3 to 4	56	49	56	72	49	65
>4 to 5	67	53	59	49	64	34
>5 to 6	40	38	53	46	50	37
>6 to 7	52	38	46	35	42	39
>7 to 8	26	37	26	21	27	21
>8 to 9	26	30	26	21	27	21
>9 to 10	26	28	24	26	13	22
>10 to 11	26	23	22	25	23	16
>11 to 12	20	15	10	24	18	7
>12 to 13	7	16	11	14	14	10
>13 to 14	4	4	13	3	7	13
>14 to 15	11	12	4	12	14	6
>15 to 20	24	20	27	27	42	30
>20 to 30	19	24	22	18	20	20
>30 to 40	5	4	5	9	7	8
>40 to 50	2	2	4	5	6	5
>50 to 60	1	1	0	2	2	0
>60 to 70	0	0	1	1	0	0
>70 to 80	0	0	0	0	0	0
>80 to 90	0	0	0	0	1	1
>90 to 100	0	1	0	0	0	0
Total	649	668	664	701	743	803

Note: The 1933 data are amended slightly from that which appeared in Sedgwick (1998a).

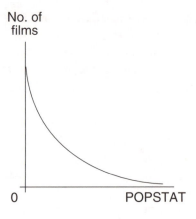

No. of
films

0   POPSTAT

Source: Table 4.2

Figure 4.1: *A typically 'C'-shaped annual distribution of POPSTAT scores*

office receipts. At the other end of the distribution only some 10 per cent of films scored more than twice the arithmetic mean and only 2 per cent of films had scores more than two standard deviations above the mean. The information produced in Table 4.2 is vital to an understanding of the competitive framework faced by film producers. Although it may be supposed that the major film studios aspired to 'hit' production, very few of their products collectively achieved this goal.[4]

The situation I am describing is one in which, year after year, at the end of each financial year the film producers know *ex post* that there has been a small number of 'hits', and they know precisely which films were the 'hits' and by whom they were produced. But *ex ante*, for the financial year to come, all that they can feel certain of is that there will be a small number of unspecifiable 'hits'. Such situations typify, in a non-technical way, what is meant by saying that hit production seems to be a stochastic process. For statisticians, such situations provide an exciting technical challenge which is to find out (in the case of film production) if there is a statistical relationship between the inputs into film production and the output of 'hits', a topic explored further in Chapter 7.

Barry King captures this phenomenon incisively:

> Looking at the global level of activity, we find that every season produces its hits, but that no particular producer can be absolutely certain of monopolising the 'hit' product. What this means is that any season of releases resembled, at first sight, a zero sum game

with some producers having a time-dated monopoly of the total available market, theoretically speaking, since their film or films are the most popular.[5]

Moreover, audience demand for 'hit' films was sufficient to transcend vertical integration boundaries. This meant, for instance, that in the North American market, prime site cinemas owned by the parent organization of one of the major studios would often screen the 'hit' films of rival studios, particularly where available in-house releases were perceived as being relatively uncompetitive.[6] For King 'What the lucky producer has, therefore, is a monopoly (copy) right to a film which will give his company access to his competitor's screen time for a price.'[7]

POPSTAT zero-rated films

Those films which failed to achieve a single booking at any of the national sample cinemas realize a zero POPSTAT score. Table 4.2 indicates that the number of such films increased over the period.[8] Details of the national origins and principal production companies of zero-rated films are given overleaf in Table 4.3. What becomes clear from a detailed inspection of the data is that other than those films that British and Dominion (B&D) made for Paramount's Quota requirement, the British producers of zero-rated films were small occasional concerns. Their American counterparts specialized in portfolios of low-budget films: westerns for the greater part. If these films were not showing in the sample cinema set, then where were they playing? The *Kine Weekly* reviews of such films suggest that they were likely to play to 'industrial audiences' in 'industrial halls' and were particularly attractive to juveniles.[9] Many of the French, German and Soviet films which failed to secure circulation within the sample cinema set, on the other hand, were films of 'artistic' importance, imported primarily for exhibition by Film Societies.[10]

Shares in the British market

By aggregating the POPSTAT scores of films from each of the production companies for each of the years in the study it is possible to arrive at a measure of market shares for the period as a whole. This is derived by dividing the Aggregate POPSTAT generated by the films

Table 4.3. *The national origin and principal producers of POPSTAT zero-rated films*

	1932[a]	1933[b]	1934[c]	1935[d]	1936[e]	1937[f]
Australia	0	4	3	2	0	2
Britain	17	34	27	25	29	46
France	1	1	6	6	9	4
Germany/Austria	4	4	4	7	8	8
USA	33	29	38	52	70	133
USSR	3	0	0	1	4	3
Others	4	0	2	7	11	5
Total	62	72	80	100	131	200

Sources: *Kine Year Books*, 1932–7; Eyles (1993, 1996); Eyles and Skone (1991).

Notes: Most prolific POPSTAT zero-rated producers were:
a. in 1932, Equity (Br) 3 films; Kent (USA) 4 films; Monogram (USA) 4 films.
b. In 1933, Freuler (USA) 3 films; Monogram (USA) 5 films; Sound City (Br) 5 films; Warners British (Br) 8 films.
c. In 1934, Big Four (USA) 4 films; British and Dominions (Br) 4 films; British International Pictures (Br) 3 films; Hoffberg (USA) 4 films; Monogram (USA) 10 films; Reliable (USA) 3 films.
d. In 1935, British and Dominions (Br) 3 films; Columbia (USA) 3 films; Monogram (USA) 10 films; Reliable (USA) 8 films; Superior (USA) 8 films; Universal (USA) 3 films.
e. In 1936, British and Dominions (Br) 3 films; Diversion (USA) 3 films; Guarantee (USA) 3 films; Majestic (USA) 6 films; Puritan (USA) 5 films; Reliable (USA) 12 films; Republic (USA) 5 films; Superior (USA) 3 films and Universal (USA) 5 films.
f. In 1937, Ace (Br) 3 films; Beacon (USA) 3 films; Beaumont (USA) 7 films; Berke (USA) 4 films; British and Dominions (Br) 3 films; Columbia (USA) 8 films; Fox British (Br) 5 films; Grand National (USA) 6 films; Hackel (USA) 8 films; Hoffberg (USA) 4 films; Principal (USA) 3 films; RKO (USA) 8 films; Republic (USA) 14 films; Universal (USA) 14 films; and Warners (USA) 5 films.

of each production studio by the Total Films Aggregate POPSTAT, and hence differs from the supply share which is derived by dividing the films produced by each studio by the Total Films put on to the market by all production companies. Table 4.4 ranks American and British production companies accordingly. It is apparent that market shares were fairly widely dispersed, with the eight leading players—counting Fox and 20th Century-Fox as a single firm—taking a 70 per cent share of demand over the period. This is reflected in a Herfindahl

Table 4.4: *Summary production company POPSTAT for films released in Britain, 1932–1937*

Production company	Films released	Aggregate POPSTAT	Share of supply (%)	Share of market (%)	Mean POPSTAT per film	No. of Top 50 films	No. of Top 100 films
Principal Hollywood studios							
Paramount	415	3,745.54	8.71	14.11	9.03	33	103
MGM	293	3,206.42	6.15	12.08	10.94	55	95
Warners	381	2,697.29	7.99	10.18	7.08	18	53
RKO	304	1,907.5	6.38	7.19	6.27	16	33
Columbia	305	1,591.02	6.4	5.99	5.22	13	20
Fox	219	1,573.81	4.6	5.93	7.19	13	28
Universal	243	1,101.82	5.1	4.15	4.53	8	12
20th Century-Fox	103	783.78	2.16	2.95	7.61	8	21
Goldwyn	27	588.03	0.57	2.22	21.78	13	20
20th Century	17	387.47	0.36	1.46	22.79	9	15
Total	2,307	17,582.66	48.41	66.25	7.62	186	400
Occasional Hollywood producers							
Selznick	5	148.55	0.1	0.56	29.71	4	4
Reliance	7	112.6	0.15	0.42	16.09	3	7
Wanger	6	73.27	0.13	0.28	12.21	2	3
Total	18	334.42	0.38	1.26	18.58	9	14
Poverty Row studios							
Monogram	120	199.09	2.52	0.75	1.66	0	0
Republic	91	171.76	1.91	0.65	1.89	0	0
Chesterfield	24	68.81	0.52	0.27	2.87	0	0
Mascot	15	56.72	0.31	0.21	3.78	0	0
Invincible	23	55.44	0.5	0.21	2.34	0	0
Majestic	23	53.33	0.48	0.20	2.32	0	0
World Wide	17	34.71	0.36	0.13	2.04	0	0
Total	315	643.64	6.61	2.43	2.04	0	0
Principal British studios							
G-B/ Gainsborough	125	1,898.16	2.63	6.98	15.19	50	79
BIP/ABPC	131	750.1	2.76	2.84	5.73	4	13
B&D	106	695.05	2.23	2.63	6.56	16	22
London Films[a]	32	608.31	0.67	2.31	19.01	14	20
Total	394	3,951.61	8.3	14.77	10.03	84	133
Occasional British producers							
Wilcox[b]	15	157.31	0.32	0.60	10.49	1	5
Capitol[c]	12	138.88	0.25	0.53	11.57	3	4
Criterion	4	58.35	0.08	0.22	14.59	1	3
New World	3	38.23	0.06	0.14	12.74	1	2
Total	34	392.77	0.71	1.49	11.55	6	14

Table 4.4 continued

Production company	Films released	Aggregate POPSTAT	Share of supply (%)	Share of market (%)	Mean POPSTAT per film	No. of Top 50 films	No. of Top 100 films
Secondary British studios							
Twickenham[d]	48	250.36	1.01	0.95	5.22	1	3
Warners	103	225.78	2.15	0.86	2.21	0	0
ATP	28	207.45	0.59	0.79	7.41	2	5
British Lion	40	206.30	0.84	0.78	5.16	0	1
Real Art	45	131.30	0.95	0.50	2.92	1	1
Paramount British	10	69.42	0.21	0.26	6.94	1	1
Fox British	52	52.23	1.09	0.20	1.00	0	0
Total	326	1,143.27	6.87	4.33	3.51	5	11
Complete Hollywood[e]	3,243	19,652.64	68.03	74.14	6.06	201	426
Principal + occasional Hollywood	2,325	17,917.08	48.97	67.9	7.71	195	414
Complete British[f]	1,301	6,552.61	27.4	24.60	5.04	98	170
Principal + occasional British	428	4,344.38	9.01	16.26	10.15	90	147
Other Films	222	334.30	4.67	1.27	1.50	1	4
Total Films	4,748	26,386.30	100	100	5.51	300	600[g]

Notes:

This table is an amended version of Table 1.2 in Sedgwick (1998a)

a. Also includes Denham Films, Pendennis Films and Saville Productions.

b. Also includes: Imperator Films.

c. Also includes: Cecil Films, Grafton Films, and Trafalgar Films.

d. Also includes: JH Productions and St Margaret Films

e. Represents all films registered as originating in the US including those produced by the studios not listed above.

f. Represents all films registered as British including those produced by studios not listed above.

g. The 28 Top 100 films produced by studios not listed above are as follows: *Congress Dances* (UFA-Germany), *Age of Love* (Caddo-USA), *Movie Crazy* (Lloyd-USA), *Tell Me Tonight* (Cine Alliance-Br/Ger), *Sky Devils* (Caddo-USA), *Blue Light* (Sokal-Germany), *Scarface* (Caddo-USA), *Mr Robinson Crusoe* (Elton-USA), *A Nous La Liberté* (Tobis-France), *Congorilla* (Johnson-USA), *Rain* (Feature-USA), *Corsair* (Art Cinema-USA), *Baroud* (Ingram-Br), *FP1* (UFA-Br/Ger) *Dick Turpin* (John Stafford Productions-Br), *The Prince of Arcadia* (Nettlefold-Fogwell-Br), *The Battle* (Liono-French), *The Cat's Paw* (Lloyd-USA), *18 Minutes* (Allied-Br), *The Love Affair of the Dictator* (Toeplitz-Br) *Becky Sharp* (Pioneer-USA), *Song of Freedom* (Hammer-Br), *As You Like It* (Interallied-Br), *Modern Times*, Chaplin-USA), *Gay Desperado* (Pickford-USA), *The Sky's The Limit* (Buchanan-Br), and *Thunder in the City* (Atlantic-Br).

Index of industrial concentration of just 0.068, where in a possible range of 0 to 1.0 the latter value represents a pure monopoly.[11] As will become evident, a number of prominent producers co-existed during the period. Beyond them and the dozen or so firms which achieved at least a 1 per cent share of demand was a myriad of firms whose individual performance was negligible by industry standards, but who between them contributed some 25 per cent of market supply.

The penultimate row of Table 4.4 shows that films originating from countries other than Britain or the United States account for only just over 1 per cent share of the British market, with indigenously made films taking just under a quarter share. From this it is clear that any assessment of British film performance must be made within a market context dominated by the Hollywood product.

For both sets of Hollywood and British producers, a distinction has been made between principal, occasional, and secondary studios. The principal studios all took at least a 1 per cent share of the market, with Paramount, MGM, and Warners each attaining over a 10 per cent share. The most significant British producer in this respect was Gaumont-British/Gainsborough, which took just under 7 per cent of the market, placing it on a par with RKO and ahead of Columbia and Universal, whilst making far fewer films. Indeed, the scale of Hollywood's principal volume producers' output in comparison to that of Britain's three leading volume studios is overwhelming, each producing between two to four times that of Britain's largest studios. Between them, MGM and Paramount contributed 88 of the 300 annual Top 50 films and 180 of the 600 annual Top 100 films. Even more notable than its market share performance, however, was the market presence of Gaumont-British, which was second only to that of MGM when measured by the number of Top 50 productions. The popularity of its product in the national sample cinema set can be gauged by the studio's mean POPSTAT per film, which at 15.23 is a third higher than that of the films emanating from the Paramount and MGM studios. This remarkable performance gives an insight into the reasons behind its attempt, described in Chapter 10, to replace *ad hoc* distribution deals in the US by establishing an in-house distribution organization in the American market between late 1934 and early 1936.

Both Goldwyn and London Films can be described as big-budget, low-volume, 'hit' producers. Unlike the other principal producers, with the exception of the B&D, neither Goldwyn nor London Films was integrated into distribution and exhibition: each made films only and had their film output distributed through United Artists. Their small output levels reveal a high risk production strategy in which almost the whole of their respective film outputs were designed to appear in cinemas as major attractions, requiring extensive pre-release runs on both sides of the Atlantic. Such a strategy may be contrasted with the management of risk approach to film production associated with the larger portfolios of the principal vertically integrated organizations. The mean POPSTAT per film results for the two studios—each near to four times the population (Total Films) mean—reveal the considerable success achieved by their films in the British market.

Although relatively low-volume producers, both Goldwyn and London Films owned their studios.[12] In comparison, the set of what are termed 'occasional' producers operating out of Hollywood and London, did not. Although similarly concerned with the production of major attractions, these independent quality producers worked *ad hoc,* bringing small numbers of individual projects to fruition. For the most part they employed human resources on a film by film basis and hired their studio facilities from existing principal producers.[13] Of these, Selznick was the most well known, and even in this pre-*Gone with the Wind* period, heads the listings of film popularity when measured by mean POPSTAT per film.

Undoubtedly the emergence in 1936 of new first-rate production facilities at Denham and Pinewood stimulated the growth in what Rachael Low has termed 'tenant producers'. The production companies linked to Max Schach (Capitol, Cecil, Grafton and Trafalgar) and Herbert Wilcox (Wilcox and Imperator), as well as those listed in note 'a' to Table 4.4 under London Films, fitted this category, as did the attempt by the Fairbanks to establish themselves in production in Britain in the form of Criterion Films. New World Pictures represented the first example of one of the major Hollywood studios taking a position at the quality end of the British production sector: in this case 20th Century-Fox, soon to be followed by MGM and Columbia. All these producers made films which on average scored significantly more than the population (Total Films) mean.

The 'secondary' producers were mainly concerned with supplying support features, to supplement those produced by the 'principal' studios, for double-billing programmes. In Britain, production of this type of film was very much stimulated by the existence of the Quota. Of the British companies, the films of British Lion and Associated Talking Pictures (ATP), Twickenham—including later variants in the form of J.H. Productions and St Margaret's Productions—form a particular category, in that although they can hardly be described as 'hit' producers, they aspired in this direction, and some of their films achieved a quite respectable distribution within the national sample cinema set. As with B&D, there is a clear distinction between those films made for the Quota purposes of the principal Hollywood renters and those distributed by their respective in-house rental arms. In the case of ATP, several Top 50 hits were recorded and the releases of 1934, 1936 and 1937 generated a mean annual POPSTAT above 10, whilst those of Twickenham and British Lion fared less well, recording mean POPSTAT scores per film a little below those of the population (Total Films) mean of 5.51, results which partly reflected the lack of contract performers as popular as ATP stars Gracie Fields and George Formby. In this respect, relegating ATP to a 'secondary' status may be a little unkind.

The remaining studios listed in Table 4.4 made films which received only a marginal distribution, if any at all, in the national sample cinema set. Monogram and later Republic in the United States and Warners British in Britain put out large numbers of films—over 300 between them—but failed to attain a single Top 100 ranking for any of the years during the period. Again, the films of the British companies in this category were generally handled by the major Hollywood distributors and made for Quota purposes. Those of their American counterparts, for the most part, were made by companies specializing in the genre form of the western. The outputs of Universal and Columbia also consisted in large numbers of westerns. Earlier, the argument was put that zero-rated POPSTAT films had a limited distribution amongst 'industrial audiences' in 'industrial halls'. This was also the case for those American films in the just above zero-rating classification. For the British films in this category the story is complicated by the effect of the Quota on domestic production, which caused films to be made which would otherwise not have been.

The relative performance of British film makers

From Table 4.4 it is possible to deduce that those British companies listed made less than 60 per cent of domestic film output, accounting for some 84 per cent of the market taken by domestic productions. As all the volume producers are listed, this implies that approximately 40 per cent of indigenous film production was produced by short-lived small-scale companies. The proportion of American films not accounted for by firms in the list is much smaller, at less than 20 per cent, taking up only 6 per cent share of the market for films of American origin.

This has a bearing on the question of the comparative popularity of Hollywood and British films. On this topic, beset with controversy over the years, Table 4.4 yields some revealing answers. The 'Complete Hollywood' and 'Complete British' rows of the Table display data based on all Hollywood and British films registered with the Board of Trade. The respective mean POPSTATs per film are 6.06 and 5.04. The rows labelled 'Principal + Occasional Hollywood' and 'Principal + Occasional British' display data based on the studios producing the films which audiences (nation-wide) most wanted to see. In effect the American 'Poverty Row' product and, for the greater part, the British 'Quota Quickies' have been stripped out. The respective mean POPSTATs per film are 7.71 and 10.15. The advantage which US films seemed to have enjoyed now disappears because the 428 British films in *this* category score double the mean POPSTAT per film derived from British films as a whole.

Undoubtedly, the magnitude of this statistic is influenced by the Quota requirements which renters and exhibitors were obliged to conform to. Although any particular British film could still, in principle, be rejected, the Act's constraints meant that some British films had to be accepted for screening. However, instead of the pessimistic view, according to which the 1927 legislation was the engine of a Gresham's Law disaster in which the reputation of British films sank under the tide of Quota Quickies, driving audiences even more firmly into loyalty to Hollywood than had been the case before the Act, Table 4.4 reveals that although large numbers of Quota Quickies were produced, the POPSTAT scoring system makes it possible to demonstrate empirically that they were only masking the achievement of a thriving British 'quality' film production sector, whose films were not merely popular with British audiences but as popular as comparable Hollywood films. These results, then, are in line with Simon Rowson's claim, in his 1936 address to the Royal Statistical Society, that for the year 1934 he had demonstrated 'quite conclusively the superior general average attractiveness of British films to British exhibitors, and presumably British audiences'.[14]

Evidence presented to the Moyne Committee

Further support for the contention that on average those films emanating from the studios of 'principal' and 'occasional' producers on either side of the Atlantic were of comparable popularity may be obtained from evidence presented to the *Board of Trade Committee on Cinematograph Films*, chaired by Lord Moyne, which met in 1936 to hear evidence and make recommendations concerning the replacement of the 1927 Cinematograph Films Act.

The distribution records for 1933–34 and 1934–35, aggregated in Table 4.5, show that, with the exception of United Artists,[15] the major American distributors distributed very little more than the legally defined minimum amount of British film footage. This suggests that, had the Quota legislation not existed, these films would not have been made. In 1934, of the 186 British films registered during the year, 102 were distributed by the major American distributors (excluding United Artists). From this it would appear that well over half of domestic production of that year owed its existence to protection legislation.[16] Furthermore, of the remaining 84 films, over half (49) were produced and distributed by the two domestic vertically integrated combines, Gaumont-British and ABPC.

In his evidence to the Committee, a Board of Trade official, Mr R.D. Fennelly, drew attention to the qualitative differences between domestic films distributed by British- and US-controlled renters. Using the Cinematograph Exhibitors' Association markings, Mr Fennelly produced statistics to show that 62 per cent of British film output distributed by domestic renters scored sufficient points to be considered 'good' or better, whereas this same mark applied to only 13 per cent of domestic films distributed by American controlled renters.[17]

A consequence of this arithmetic, and one to which Mr Fennelly alluded, is that given the Exhibitors' Quota of 15 per cent—rising to 20 per cent in 1935–6—there was a shortage of 'good' domestic films relative to demand. For the discriminating independent exhibitor at the top end of the market, who found it difficult to obtain the films of the two principal domestic combines—at least at the first-run stage— supply was restricted to approximately 35 (84 – 49) 'good' British films. A first-run cinema screening a once-weekly double-bill programme would require approximately 15 domestically produced films in 1934 increasing to 20 by 1936 in keeping with the Quota requirements. In view of distributor insistence upon zoning and barring—so as to establish both geographical and temporal exclusive rights over the product—the degree of freedom with respect to choosing programmes which met the Quota specifications, was severely constrained. This may well have led some exhibitors to show 'inferior' British films, not

Table 4.5: *The distribution of British films by the major American and British renters, 1933/4 and 1934/5*

	Quota requirement (000s feet) (1)	Actual distribution (000s feet) (2)	Column 2/ column 1
American distributors			
United Artists	86	142	1.65
Columbia	105	105	1.00
Warners/First National	190	192	1.01
Fox	134	135	1.01
MGM	187	187	1.00
Paramount	205	206	1.00
RKO-Radio	176	178	1.01
Universal	113	113	1.00
British distributors			
ABFD	61	110	1.8
APD	10.5	39	3.71
British Lion	23	81	3.52
Butchers	24	71	2.96
Gaumont-British	91	416	4.57
Pathé	70	72	1.02
Wardour	49	229	4.67

Source: *Minutes of Evidence* (1936).

Note: The distribution year as defined by the 1927 legislation ran from 1 April to 31 March.

out of choice, but out of necessity. However, the evidence uncovered by Rowson, and repeated by Mr Fennelly, suggests that domestic distributors considerably exceeded their Quota obligations with respect to British films. It would appear that the relative shortage of 'quality' domestic productions, partially caused and certainly fuelled by the Quota legislation requirements, contributed to the expansion in 'quality' domestic film output at least until 1936. If this is the case, then far from being the disaster that Low and others have claimed, the legislation was instrumental in leading to the production of British films which competed successfully with American films in the domestic market, in terms of quality and box-office returns.

Both Rowson and Mr Fennelly made much of the system of marking classifications adopted by the Cinematograph Exhibitors' Association (CEA), in its weekly review of releases. To predict the scale of box-office returns, films were given a mark out of ten, with a base below seven for 'very poor' films moving upwards in quarter mark steps to 'outstanding' productions scoring nine or more. A benchmark of 8.0 was used for those films that constituted 'good' entertainment.[18] Rowson suggested that the relationship between the rating and quality was non-linear, arguing:

> How much a picture marked 8 is better than one marked 7 is probably unknowable and certainly unknown, but it is intended to imply, and it is probably true that it is a better one, that in general it will have cost more to produce, and certainly that, in the opinion of the viewers of the film, it should earn the exhibitor a larger sum.[19]

How much larger? Rowson suggested that the growth in revenue which accrued correlatively with the fractional increments in film marks up to 7 or 8 would be 'extremely slow', but 'thereafter until a ten mark is reached the resumed progression of values is very rapid.'[20] This, it should be noted, matches closely the pattern of POPSTAT frequency distributions established in Table 4.2.

This scoring system was used by Mr Fennelly to analyse British films divided according to distributor type, to show that those films which were handled by the major domestic distributors achieved on average a higher-quality rating than those handled by American renters.[21] The CEA scores presented to the Moyne Committee are found in column 2 of Table 4.6. Rather disappointingly, his investigation did not include an examination of American films. In order to fill this gap, a 20 per cent sample of all films put out on general release in Britain during 1934 was taken, and a set of marks awarded drawn from the 'review and box-office advice' given to exhibitors in the *Kine Weekly* trade journal, using the scoring system outlined above. Confidence in this methodology is confirmed by comparability of the sampling results for domestic films, given in the first column of Table 4.6, with the CEA markings found in column 2.[22]

It is apparent from Table 4.6, for 1934 at least, that the perceived box-office potential of films produced by the main domestic producers was broadly the same as that of US films produced by the major

Hollywood studios. This is in agreement with the interpretation of the earlier reported mean POPSTAT scores per film discussed above. The lowest scoring category comprised those British films made to enable American renters to fulfil their Quota obligations—the 'Quota Quickies'. However, the mean for these films lies only slightly lower than that of those films produced by secondary American studios, which were for the most part distributed by secondary British renters, such as ABFD and Pathé. As has been observed in the POPSTAT results, secondary British film producers did not have a monopoly of 'poor' film production.

Table 4.6: *A comparison of quality ratings attributed to British and US films put into general release in Britain in 1934*

		Mean 'score' per film[a]	CEA mean 'score' per film[b]
A	British films distributed by an in-house distributor or United Artists[c]	8.68 (18)	8.25 (59)
B	British films distributed by secondary domestic distributors[d]	7.75 (9)	7.59 (22)
C	British films distributed by US distributors[e]	7.35 (32)	7.25 (101)
D	US films distributed by in-house distributors[f]	8.33 (108)	
E	US films distributed by British renters + four films from minor US studios distributed by Universal[g]	7.72 (27)	

Sources: *Minutes of Evidence* (1936); *Kine Weekly* editions for 1934.

Notes:

a. Derived from a sample of 199 films put into general release in Britain in 1934. (The figures in parentheses represent the number of films assessed.)

b. Taken from Mr Fennelly's presentation to the Moyne Committee. (The figures in parentheses represent those films trade shown in 1934.)

c. Includes films made by Gaumont-British/Gainsborough, BIP, British Lion, Twickenham and ATP films distributed by their respective distribution arms and the B&D and London Films distributed by United Artists.

d. Includes films made by Pathé, Butchers, Equity-British, International Productions, Zenifilms, and PDC

e. Includes films distributed by Columbia, Fox, MGM, Paramount, RKO-Radio, Universal, Warners/First National.

f. Includes films made by those major US producers listed in note (e).

g. Includes films distributed by Pathé, Wardour, Gaumont-British, Butchers, Equity-British, PDC, B&N, and Universal.

Conclusion

It will be remembered that Rachael Low's objection to the 1927 Cinematograph Act, set out in Chapter 2, was that the imposition of Quotas encouraged the production of a multitude of domestic films of little intrinsic worth, or popularity, and as a consequence seriously damaged the reputation of British film production as a whole. Her argument stands or falls on the question of the number of 'quality' British films produced. If that number, as perceived by audiences, is significant in relation to the number of films in total, as demonstrated in this chapter, her hypothesis must be rejected or at the very least be heavily qualified. In any form of artistic activity the bad, the mediocre and the good are concomitant. Why should Low have thought film-making would be any different? By not prescribing what should be made, or how—which, of course, is quite different from the activity of prescribing what should not be made, through censorship—the Act in effect gave film-makers their lead. The environment of protection stimulated film-making on an unprecedented scale. This chapter provided two sets of quantitative evidence, the POPSTAT and the CEA scoring systems, to support Simon Rowson's argument that by 1934 significant numbers of British films were being made which were genuinely attractive to domestic audiences. This is not, of course, to deny the hegemony practised by Hollywood—the difference in the volume of output is indicative of that—but it does refute the commonly held belief expressed by writers such as Peter Stead, who asks rhetorically 'for who could doubt that it was the Americans who made the best films'[23] and asserts that 'British films were unpopular (with the notable exceptions of those made by the ex-music hall comedians) because they sounded so awful'.[24] Rather, the statistics presented show that during the period 1932–37, 96 domestic films achieved Top 50 status, with 167 altogether making the Top 100 classification. This constitutes a substantial body of work for an industry that had been regarded as moribund six years earlier. It is these films that should form the basis for a re-evaluation of the strengths and weaknesses of the British film industry and be cited in support of Landy's epigraph to this chapter.

5

Popular Films and their Stars in Bolton (Worktown)

> For a film fanatic, Bolton was almost like Mecca. At one time there lay within my easy reach no fewer than forty-seven cinemas of varying size, quality and character. None was more than five miles from Bolton's town hall and twenty-eight were in the boundaries of the Borough.
>
> Leslie Halliwell, *Seats in All Parts*[1]

Jeffrey Richards has developed the thesis that 'Each individual has a set of multiple identities which operate at different times and under different circumstances'.[2] Consequently, individuals would simultaneously associate with local, regional, national, social class, ethnic, religious and gender identities (amongst others) and yet hold a common British affiliation. Maintaining that cinema, along with television in the latter part of the twentieth century, was an important instrument in the depiction of national identity, Richards argues that nevertheless important differences in tastes manifested themselves according to the make-up of those identities.

> The evidence from Bolton suggests that Lancashire and national taste in the 1930s were in close alignment, that cinema was in fact nationalizing taste and outlook and attitude. It remains true nevertheless that gender and regional identities could be maintained within an overall national identity and the most popular stars achieved their popularity by appealing to all of these multiple identities.[3]

To evaluate Richards' thesis, a comparative analysis was conducted by contrasting the cinema-going preferences of Boltonians, during the middle years of the 1930s, with those of a national sample audience drawn from the cinema programmes of the sample of leading London West End and provincial city cinemas used previously to establish the POPSTAT Index. The assumption implicit in this approach, first set down in the Introduction, is that audiences were for the greater part discriminating and that, given the wide choice of alternative cinema locations in most urban settings, preferences, once revealed, led to differential film box-office performance.[4] Complementary to this is the further assumption that the existence and extent of choice were sufficient to overcome the structural barriers to competition exercised by the principal American producer-distributors and the two vertically integrated British combines, Gaumont-British and ABPC. The argument here, developed in Chapter 3, is that exhibitors preferred their cinemas to be full rather than empty and, in the absence of the blind booking practices which had been outlawed by the 1927 Cinematograph Act, competed for the 'hits' of the season in their locality at a price.[5] As a general rule it was in neither the distributor's, nor the exhibitor's, interest to handle films of an inferior quality, given the existence, at the margin, of discriminating audiences, and the supply of alternative film programmes available in localities at similar prices. Accordingly, I argue that the question as to what films were popular—why they were popular is another matter—is essentially an empirical issue.

Cinemagoing in Bolton

Bolton (Worktown) plays an important part in British cinema historiography. It was the subject of the first Mass-Observation study into audience tastes and preferences in Britain, conducted between 1937 and 1938.[6] With a population of 180,000, Bolton was a large industrial town, built around spinning and hence an integral part of the Lancashire cotton industry and the culture associated with it.[7] In terms of cinemagoing the town was effectively sealed: the supply of alternative programmes during any single week, not to mention the quantity and quality of first-run cinemas, meant that few would seek film entertainment outside the town. As such, it represents a microcosm of cinemagoing in the industrial north, while being large enough to sustain a cascade-like distribution system down to at least fourth-run level.

Table 5.1: *Characteristics of Bolton cinemas, 1934–1935*

Cinema[a]	In operation on 1 Jan. 1934 or date of opening	Order of run status	Seating capacity	Price range[b]	Cinema weight[c]	Owners
Belle[d]	Yes	4th	580	4d to 9d	0.37	Independent
Capitol[e]	Yes	1st	1,642	7d to 1/6	2.04	ABC
Carlton	Yes	3rd	1,000	4d to 1/-	0.79	Bolton Cine
Crompton[f]	6 Dec. 1934	3rd	1,200	3d to 1/3	1.07	A.Hall
Embassy	2 May 1934	3rd	600	6d to 1/-	0.54	Independent
Empire	Yes	5th	472	3d to 6d	0.21	Independent
Gem	Yes	4th	1,050	4d to 1/-	0.83	Independent
Hippodrome	Yes	1st	1,086	6d to 1/4	1.19	Moorhouse
Majestic	Yes	3rd	1,913	4d to 1/-	1.52	Bolton Cine
Palace	Yes	3rd	1,021	4d to 7d	0.56	Independent
Palladium[g]	Yes	2nd	1,238	4d to 1/-	0.98	A.Hall
Plaza[h]	Yes	4th	650	4d to 9d	0.41	Independent
Queens	Yes	1st	1,480	6d to 1/6	1.76	Rialto Bolton
Regal	Yes	2nd	2,380	4d to 9d	1.53	ABC
Regent	Yes	3rd	944	6d to 1/3	0.98	Independent
Rialto	Yes	1st	1,147	6d to 1/-	1.02	Rialto Bolton
Royal	Yes	4th	761	5d to 1/-	0.64	Independent
Theatre Royal[i]	Yes	1st	1,700	6d to 1/6	2.02	Moorhouse

Sources: *Bolton Evening News*; *Kine Year Books* 1933–39; Eyles (1993); Halliwell (1986) and Richards and Sheridan (1987).

Notes:

a.   The Grand functioned as a variety theatre and has not been included in this analysis. George Formby played two single-week engagements in 1934, during w/c 8 Jan. 1934 and w/c 3 Dec. 1934. The Odeon in Bolton was opened on 21 Aug. 1937 becoming Bolton's largest cinema, with a seating capacity of 2,534 and price range of 6d to 1/6. The Imperial closed in May 1934.

b.   These prices do not reflect the cheaper rates available to matinees audiences.

c.   As with the national survey, the weights given to Bolton cinemas are derived by dividing the revenue potential of each cinema (seats multiplied by mid-range price) by the arithmetic mean revenue potential of all of the cinemas included in the sample. Accordingly, the box-office potential of the Theatre Royal was over twice that of the Palladium and approximately four times that of the Royal. Cinemas which opened after the period of investigation (1934–35) have not been included in these calculations.

Table 5.1 continued

d.   Changed owners in 1937 when seating capacity was reduced to 470 seats.

e.   Became an ABC cinema on 26 July 1935. Prior to this it was independently owned.

f.   Halliwell (1986, p.122) asserts that the Crompton opened in 1937. This is repeated twice by Richards in Richards and Sheridan (1987, p.32) and Richards (1994, p.151) but contradicted by him in Richards and Sheridan (1987, p.27). The cinema occasionally had a single weekly programme: *David Copperfield* w/c 25 Nov. 1935, *Modern Times* w/c 9 Nov. 1936 and *Little Lord Fauntleroy* w/c 1 Feb. 1937 are examples.

g.   Opened in 1919 according to Richards in Richards and Sheridan (1987) op cit. Allen Eyles, *ABC: the Name of Entertainment* (London, 1993) has it as 1922—becoming an ABC cinema when taken over in 1930. Subsequently leased to the Regent Circuit 1933–35 and the sold to Mr A. Hall in 1935—the owner of the Crompton in 1935 and later the Tivoli when opened in 1938.

h.   Changed its name to Windsor in 1937.

i.   Taken over by new owners in 1936 and became part of the Moorhouse Circuit.

Halliwell's map of Bolton cinemas of the 1930s locates twenty-two cinemas in the town, almost all of which placed advertisements with the Bolton Evening News.[8] Table 5.1 adds some details to the vivid descriptions of these cinemas found in Halliwell's book. Of interest is the absence of the Gaumont-British organization from the town, whilst the ABC chain boasted two cinemas—the Capitol and the Regal. Most cinema admissions cost less than a shilling. The higher price-range cinemas were those showing a once-weekly change programme and served as Bolton's first-run houses. Cinemas at the bottom end of the price range are suggestive of George Orwell's observation in his 1937 account of working-class life in the industrial north:

> That—keeping warm—is almost the sole preoccupation of a single unemployed man in winter. In Wigan a favourite refuge was the pictures, which are fantastically cheap there. You can always get a seat for fourpence, and at the matinee you can even get a seat for twopence. Even people on the verge of starvation will readily pay twopence to get out of the ghastly cold of a winter afternoon.[9]

The principal first-run cinemas in Bolton during the 1930s were the Capitol, Hippodrome, Queens, Rialto, and Theatre Royal, with the addition of the Lido and Odeon in 1937. In the period 1932–37, all 126 films which received extended London West End runs (listed in Appendix 2) were subsequently exhibited in Bolton, and almost all had their local premiere in these five cinemas.[10] Thirty-four of these films (over a quarter of the selection) opened in two cinemas simultaneously, with *Sanders of the River* (1935) having the distinction of opening in three—Queens, Rialto and Embassy during the week commencing 23 December 1935. Typically these films opened as single-bill entertainments and played for one week.[11] Following their opening, the films from this selection generally returned as the leading film in a double-bill programme to one of the twice weekly change cinemas listed in Table 5.1 for a second-run approximately four weeks later—commonly with a gap of a three to four weeks between any subsequent runs. Twenty-five of these films, however, played on a single-bill weekly programme for their third run in the town, and in the case of *Captains Courageous* (1937), *Lost Horizon* (1937), *Mutiny on the Bounty* (1936), and *One Night of Love* (1934) this continued for their fourth-run exhibitions.

In his recorded interview for Mass-Observation,[12] Mr Hull, the manager of the Embassy cinema, refers to occasions in which exceptional films went on to play again and again in the town. He specifically mentions *Rosalie*—seventh run, and *The Firefly* and *Maytime*—both achieving an eighth run. He also quotes *The Divorce of Lady X* and *Bluebeard's Eighth Wife*[13] as examples of big budget films which did poorly on their second and third runs. Certainly, this investigation confirms his testimony to differences in the popularity of films, as measured by the number of separate performances in Bolton cinemas. Table 5.2 below lists the thirty films from the selection of 126 'hit' films which recorded six or more distinct appearances in Bolton's cinemas: they were amongst the most popular films shown during these years.

An interesting development in filmgoing during the latter part of the period was the emergence of re-released films on cinema programmes. During the early and mid-1930s this had been an occasional event during the summer months when cinema audiences were traditionally at their lowest. There was, however, a dramatic increase during the late spring and summer of 1938. Twenty-seven of the 126 films referred to above were re-released during the period, playing on 43 separate programmes. The extent of the revival in 'old' films can be gauged by the fact that over half of these performances (22) took place in 1938. This may have been a consequence of the domestic crisis in production in 1937, which resulted in a greatly diminished supply of domestic films marketed in 1937 and 1938. Re-released films may well have relieved the supply pressures on renters and distributors alike.

Table 5.2: *London West End 'hit' films which played at six or more Bolton Cinemas, 1932–1937*

Title	Date of Bolton premiere	Number of first release exhibitions	Number of re-release exhibitions
One Night of Love	11 Feb. 35	11	1
Good Companions	23 Oct. 33	9	5
Lives of a Bengal Lancer	5 Aug. 35	9	2
39 Steps	17 Feb. 36	9	0
Captains Courageous	4 Apr. 38	9	0
It Happened One Night	22 Oct. 34	9	0
Roman Scandals	1 Oct. 34	8	1
Libelled Lady	31 May 37	8	0
House of Rothschild	24 Dec. 34	7	1
Scarlet Pimpernel	7 Oct. 35	7	0
Tale of Two Cities	30 Nov. 36	7	0
Plainsman	12 Jul. 37	7	0
Hell Divers	28 Nov. 32	7	0
Charge of the Light Brigade	4 Oct. 37	7	0
Wings of the Morning	13 Sept. 37	7	0
Sanders of the River	23 Dec. 35	7	0
Devil and the Deep	20 Mar. 33	6	3
42nd Street	2 Oct. 33	6	2
Ruggles of Red Gap	12 Aug. 35	6	2
Soldiers of the King	14 Aug. 33	6	1
Jack's the Boy	25 Dec. 32	6	1
Mutiny on the Bounty	5 Oct. 36	6	0
Jack of All Trades	10 Aug. 36	6	0
Bedtime Story	4 Dec. 33	6	0
Dinner at Eight	30 Apr. 34	6	0
Lost Horizon	31 Jan. 38	6	0
General Died at Dawn	29 Mar. 37	6	0
Theodora Goes Wild	28 June 37	6	0
Queen Christina	1 Oct. 34	6	0
Affairs of Voltaire[a]	2 Apr. 34	6	0

Source: *Bolton Evening News*.

Note: a. US title: *Voltaire*.

Measuring film popularity

To test the hypothesis that significant regional variations in star and film preferences existed at this time, it is necessary to enlarge the film field of reference from the preselected sample of 126 London West End 'hits' to the complete range of films available to Bolton audiences and to contrast their popularity in Bolton with that achieved in the national sample of cinemas. In order to establish an index of relative popularity (POPSTAT) of each film seen in at least one of the cinemas of Bolton listed in Table 5.1 during the years 1934 and 1935, details of the box-office potential of each cinema at which it was screened, its billing status—single or double bill—and length of exhibition were collected.[14] The procedure is, hence, precisely the same as that set down in Chapter 3, but applied to the cinemas of Bolton rather than to those which constitute the national sample.

The exhibition records show that 1,304 films received at least one half-week billing in one of the Bolton cinemas listed in Table 5.1 between 1 January 1934 and 31 December 1935. Table 5.3 provides a contrast with the statistics of releases collected at national level. The discrepancy between the numbers of releases derives from the fact that whilst the number of films *released* nationally was taken from the Board of Trade register, the number of films *screened* refers to those films shown in the 90 or so cinemas in the sample cinema set under the national heading, and the Bolton cinemas listed in Table 5.1, respectively. It is apparent that many more films were shown in the 20 or so Bolton cinemas than in the larger national sample. The explanation for this is to be found in the unrepresentative nature of cinemas in the national sample, based upon the most prestigious and expensive London and provincial city cinemas of the time. These cinemas, for the greater part, would expect to attract 'A' films on the grounds that distributors wished to maximize their earnings and therefore needed their products to play in those cinemas with the greatest box-office revenue potential. Although the practice of double-bill programmes increased as the 1930s wore on, with only super 'A' films playing as single features, it is clear that a sizeable proportion of releases (approximately 15 per cent) was not shown at all at these cinemas, entering the cascade-type distribution system at a lower level.

The Bolton study differs from the national study for which POPSTAT was initially conceived in that it follows the population of films through the various cinema levels in a single locality to the point where the local exhibition potential is exhausted. From this it is possible to get a much better picture of the exhibition profile of those films, made primarily by 'poverty row' studios in Hollywood or second-rate Quota Quickie producers in Britain, which failed to register in the national sample but which played at lower-level Bolton cinemas as second features.

The differences in magnitude of the arithmetic mean and standard deviation POPSTAT statistics between the two populations of cinemas, shown in Table 5.3, is not important. The national sample is much larger (90 cinemas to 20); consequently its films, because on average they appear more often, generate larger exhibition scores. Later these populations are commonly indexed for the purpose of comparison. However, the difference between the standard deviation of the two samples, once standardized by the coefficient of variation, is marked with the higher national POPSTAT results reflecting the practice of giving potential 'hit' films the opportunity of extended London West End runs at box-office rich cinemas.[15] Although the most popular films in Bolton were held over for a second or very rarely a third week, this was neither as extensive nor as common as in the West End. As a consequence, the POPSTAT scores generated for Bolton were not as widely dispersed as those derived from the national sample of cinemas.

Whilst Table 5.2 lists those 30 films from the 126 'hits' which between 1932 and the early months of 1938 appeared in Bolton on six

Table 5.3. *Contrast between national and Bolton summary statistics*

	National		Bolton	
	1934	*1935*	*1934*	*1935*
Films registered[a]	664	701		
Films shown	584	601	694[b]	610
Mean POPSTAT	7.06	7.39	1.28	1.37
Standard deviation	7.16	7.99	1.08	1.07
Coefficient of variation variation	1.01	1.08	0.84	0.78

Sources: *Bolton Evening News*; *Kine Year Books*, 1932–37; Eyles (1993, 1996); Eyles and Skone (1991).

Notes:
a. Films registered with the Board of Trade in compliance with the 1927 Cinematograph Act.
b. More films were shown in Bolton in 1934 than actually released nationally. This is explained by the inclusion of a large number of films released in 1933.

or more separate occasions, the frequency distribution in Table 5.4 below makes it clear that it was not just London West End 'hits' which were popular with Bolton audiences. What were these films which appeared so frequently in Bolton cinemas over the two years 1934 and 1935 and to what extent did they differ from those in the list of films derived from the national sample? The list of Top 100 films shown in Bolton for 1934 and 1935 respectively and their comparative national sample performance found in Table 5.7, presented as an appendix to this chapter, provides answers to these questions. The comparison is made possible by standardizing the Bolton and national sample series. This is achieved for each of the years of the investigation by giving the mean POPSTAT score in each of the two sample series the value 100, and indexing the POPSTAT scores of each film exhibited at least once

Table 5.4: *Frequency distribution of exhibition of 1,304 films appearing in Bolton cinemas in 1934 and 1935*

No. of distinct runs/exhibitions	No. of films
1	1,304
2	964
3	684
4	411
5	214
6	107
7	43
8	16
9 and more	3

Source: Bolton Evening News.

Note: The films with the largest number of distinct bookings were: *One Night of Love* (11), *Love, Life and Laughter* (10), *It Happened One Night* (9), *20 Million Sweethearts* (8), *Babes in Toyland* (8), *Dancing Lady* (8), *Footlight Parade* (8), *The Lives of a Bengal Lancer* (8), *The Mighty Barnum* (8), *My Song For You* (8), *Police Car No 17* (8), *Roman Scandals* (8), *Sing as We Go* (8), *The Thin Man* (8), *Things are Looking Up* (8), *Tugboat Annie* (8), *The Bowery* (7), *Brewster's Millions* (7), *Broadway Thro' A Keyhole* (7), *Christopher Bean* (7), *Flirtation Walk* (7), *Fraternally Yours* (7), *Fugitive Lovers* (7), *Here Comes the Navy* (7), *House on 56th Street* (7), *I Cover the Waterfront* (7), *Kid Millions* (7), *Looking for Trouble* (7), *The Merry Widow* (7), *Now and Forever* (7), *Off the Dole* (7), *Only Yesterday* (7), *Peg O' My Heart* (7), *Ring Up the Curtain* (7), *Sanders of the River* (7), *The Scarlet Pimpernel* (7), *Those Were the Days* (7), *Treasure Island* (7), *Trouble* (7), *We're not Dressing* (7), *A Wicked Woman* (7), *The Wrecker (7)*.

in either sample relative to this value. Thus, a film with an index value 200 will be twice as popular in either sample as a film with an index value equal to the mean of that sample. Column 9 of Table 5.7 measures the ratio between the two POPSTAT series where a value of 1.0 indicates an identical performance; a value > 1.0 suggests that the Bolton box-office performance was stronger than that achieved nationally; and a value < 1.0 that the national performance was stronger than the Bolton performance. Another form of comparison can be obtained from the ranked order of POPSTAT scores. In this case, the results in column 8 of Table 5.7 are obtained by deducting the national ranking from the Bolton ranking. Where the result is positive, the film was more popular in the national sample cinemas, while a negative result indicates that the film was more popular in Bolton.

Bolton and national comparisons

The most obvious observation stemming from the data collected in the Bolton Top 100 lists found in Table 5.7 is the high levels of popularity associated with the films starring Gracie Fields. Although the Motion Picture Review Poll listed Fields as the number one British star in the mid-1930s, it can be seen from the performance of her films amongst the national sample set of cinemas that Fields' popularity was not uniform across the country. Undeniably, however, as far as Bolton audiences were concerned, Fields was their favourite. *Sing As We Go* and *Love, Life and Laughter* were the two most popular films shown in Bolton in 1934, and *Look Up and Laugh* achieved a Top 20 position in 1935. In all three cases her poll position—up 36, 63 and 97 places respectively—and the POPSTAT ratio result—2.12, 2.64 and 1.83 times greater than the respective national result—reflect strongly a marked bias in affection for the star. The Lancashire factor was undoubtedly important in this popularity,[16] with Fields displaying a strong regional accent and mannerisms, compounded in *Sing As We Go* as she participates in the traditional 'Wakes' holiday at Blackpool. Indeed, the local factor is even stronger with this film because the mill scenes were filmed on location in Bolton.[17] Gracie Fields' relatively poor performance in the more middle-class cinemas of the national survey suggests strongly the existence of distinctive class and regional preferences amongst audiences.[18]

Table 5.5 lists the comparative winners and losers as selected by Bolton audiences. In recognizing that neither difference in ranking nor ratio of popularity is sufficient by itself to serve as a reliable indicator, a composite measure of popularity has been created by: (1) in cases where values of the POPSTAT ratio are ≥ 1, multiplying the two values for any single film found in columns 8 and 9 of Table 5.7 in the Appendix to this chapter; and (2) where values of the ratio are <1, multiplying the reciprocal of the value of the ratio by the difference in the ranking order.[19] What we are looking for here are extremes of value: that is, either those films in Bolton which were significantly more popular than suggested by the national POPSTAT result or vice versa. The absolute value of the composite statistic, then, is a measure of the degree of difference between national and Bolton survey results, where the lower the negative value the greater the relative popularity of the film in Bolton and the higher the positive value the greater its relative popularity amongst national sample audiences.

As we have seen, Gracie Fields' three films shown in Bolton during the years 1934 and 1935 generate a composite measure of relative popularity which is strongly negative. But other films have even more extreme values. The most extraordinary result is that of George Formby's *Off the Dole*, made by Mancunian Films in a room over a Manchester garage, which received little in the way of national distribution, but was the 27th ranking film in Bolton in 1935, ahead of now famous productions such as *The Thin Man* (33rd) and *The Gay Divorcee* (57th) amongst others.[20] Its Bolton ranking was 539 places higher than that recorded in the national survey, with a POPSTAT statistic some 19 times higher. With seven distinct screenings, the film's success can be attributed to local factors.[21] Although this was only Formby's second sound film he was at the height of his music-hall fame and, indeed, had twice played on the stage of Bolton's regular variety theatre, The Grand, in 1934.[22]

Of the remaining comparative winners, it is apparent that Bolton audiences appreciated fairly earthy domestic comedy, compared with the more sophisticated/southern middle-class type product associated with Jack Hulbert. Stanley Lupino's musical comedy vehicle *Happy*, and *You Made Me Love You*, Sidney Howard's *It's a Cop*, as well as *Night of the Garter* and *Trouble*, Will Hay's *Those Were the Days* and *Dandy Dick*, as well as *Radio Parade of 1935* in which he made a star guest appearance, and Winifred Shotter's *D'Ye Ken John Peel* were all Bolton Top 100 productions. If we add to this list Ralph Lynn's *Summer Lightning* as well as the aforementioned *Off the Dole*, domestic comedy productions dominate the comparative winners' sections: these were films very much more enjoyed by Bolton audiences than by national sample audiences.

Table 5.5: *Comparative film 'winners' and 'losers' amongst Bolton audiences*

Film title	Star 1	Star 2	Bolton: national difference in rank[a]	Bolton: national POPSTAT ratio[b]	Bolton: national relative popularity[c]	Composite measure of
	(2)	*(3)*	*(4)*	*(5)*	*(6)*	
Fifteen Bolton comparative winners 1934						
Happy	Lupino, S.	Cliff, L.	-248	4.00	-992.55	
Lily of Killarney	Garrick, J.	Malo, G.	-263	3.49	-918.35	
Scotland Yard Mystery	Du Maurier, G.	Curzon, G.	-252	3.47	-874.79	
It's a Cop	Howard, S.	Bouchier, D.	-241	3.20	-771.32	
On the Air	Fox, R. + Band		-211	3.30	-695.68	
Stage Mother	Tone, F.	O'Sullivan, M.	-214	2.95	-631.61	
Wild Cargo	(Adventure documentary)		-203	2.70	-547.55	
Those Were the Days	Hay, W.	Hoey, A.	-164	3.21	-526.85	
Return of Bulldog Drummond	Richardson, R.	Todd, A.	-163	2.89	-471.53	
Service[d]	Barrymore, L.	Hume, B.	-172	2.48	-426.83	
You Can't Buy Everything	Robson, M.	Stone, L.	-166	2.46	-408.09	
You Made Me Love You	Lupino, S.	Todd, T.	-153	2.26	-345.46	
Counsellor at Law	Barrymore, J.	Daniels, B.	-141	2.31	-325.54	
Summer Lightning	Lynn, R.	Shotter, W.	-144	2.21	-318.56	
Kennel Murder Case	Powell, W.	Astor, M.	-138	2.19	-301.93	
Ten comparative Bolton losers 1934						
Cleopatra	Colbert, C.	William, W.	79	0.52	153.13	
Little Women	Hepburn, K.	Bennett, J.	57	0.50	113.19	
Invisible Man	Rains, C.	Stuart, G.	62	0.61	101.86	
Song of Songs	Dietrich, M.	Aherne, B.	60	0.62	96.04	
Wandering Jew	Veidt, C.		59	0.63	93.15	
Private Life of Henry VIII	Laughton, C.		28	0.33	84.24	
My Song For You	Kiepura, J.	Hales, S.	49	0.71	68.54	
Evergreen	Matthews, J.	Balfour, B.	41	0.61	67.45	
Bitter Sweet	Neagle, A.	Graavey, F.	43	0.65	65.98	
College Humour	Crosby, B.	Arlen, R.	46	0.89	51.43	
Fifteen comparative Bolton winners 1935						
Off the Dole	Formby, G.	Shooter, C.	-512	19.47	-9969.00	
D'Ye Ken John Peel	Shotter, W.	Holloway, S.	-353	5.07	-1788.84	
Java Head	Wong, A.M.	Allan, E.	-291	4.23	-1230.07	
Dandy Dick	Hay, W.		-260	3.68	-956.22	
Laddie	Beal, J.	Stuart, G.	-236	3.02	-713.23	
Girl in Pawn[e]	Temple, S.	Menjou, A.	-223	2.95	-658.79	
Wicked Woman	Christians, M.	Bickford, C.	-178	2.93	-522.39	
School for Girls	Shirley, A.	Fox, S.	-206	2.52	-519.92	
Great Defender	Lang, M.	Bannerman, M.	-203	2.56	-519.74	
Trunk Mystery[f]	Tone, F.	Merkel, U.	-190	2.62	-498.27	

Table 5.5 continued Film title	Star 1 (2)	Star 2 (3)	(4)	(5)	(6)
Student's Romance	Goodner, C.	Natzler, G.	-191	2.46	-469.89
George White's 1935 Scandals	Faye, A.	Dunn, J.	-194	2.39	-463.48
Sequoia	Parker, J.		-176	2.37	-417.44
Society Doctor	Morris, C.	Bruce, V.	-183	2.27	-414.82
Living on Velvet	Francis, K.	William, W.	-159	2.34	-372.06
Ten comparative Bolton losers 1935					
Iron Duke	Arliss, G.	Cooper, Gladys	86	0.30	288.91
Jew Süss	Veidt, C		84	0.32	264.11
Clive of India	Colman, R.	Young, L.	76	0.35	215.12
Escape Me Never	Bergner, E.	Sinclair, H.	67	0.37	181.53
Painted Veil	Garbo, G.	Marshall, H.	58	0.55	104.68
Gay Divorcee	Astaire, F.	Rogers, G.	38	0.61	61.83
Nell Gwyn	Neagle, A.	Hardwicke, C.	32	0.55	57.77
Unfinished Symphony	Eggerth, M.	Jaray, H.	39	0.73	53.59
Count of Monte Cristo	Donat, R.	Landi, E.	35	0.68	51.29
Transatlantic Merry-Go- Round[g]	Raymond, G.	Carroll, N.	30	0.77	38.87

Source: Derived from Table 5.7 found in the Appendix to this chapter.

Notes:

a. Column 8, Table 5.7. Obtained by subtracting the national rank from the Bolton rank. Accordingly a negative difference indicates that the film is relatively more popular in Bolton and vice versa for a positive difference.

b. Column 9, Table 5.7.Obtained by dividing the Bolton POPSTAT statistic for each film by its national POPSTAT statistic. The two POPSTAT series are standardized by giving the mean POPSTAT value for each series the value of 100 and indexing all other POPSTAT values around this.

c. Obtained by multiplying column 5 by column 4 where the ratio values in column 5 are >1, but where <1 using the reciprocal of column 5 values.

d. US title, *Looking Forward*.

e. US title, *Little Miss Marker*.

f. US title, *One New York Night*

g. The performance of Sidney Howard, fourth billed in this, his only Hollywood film, was evidently not sufficient to recommend the film to Bolton audiences.

Of the domestic dramas, *The Scotland Yard Murder Mystery* (32nd in 1934), *The Return of Bulldog Drummond* (12th in 1934), and *Java Head* (15th in 1935) all performed dramatically better in Bolton than nationally, whilst bigger budget costume productions such as *The Private Life of Henry VIII* (30th in 1934), *Bitter Sweet* (59th in 1934), *Jew Süss* (89th in 1935), *Escape Me Never* (77th in 1935), *The Iron Duke* (90th in 1935), *Nell Gwyn* (42nd in 1935), and *The Unfinished*

Symphony (88th in 1935), all relatively under-performed in Bolton.[23] Elizabeth Bergner's starring vehicle *Catherine the Great* is perhaps the most extreme example of this, placed 4th in the national survey but only 140th in Bolton in 1934. If the analysis is extended to Hollywood films, this pattern continues with Boltonians ranking *Cleopatra* (91st in 1934), *Little Women* (65th in 1934), *Clive of India* (85th in 1935) and *The Count of Monte Cristo* (62nd in 1935), much lower than their national counterparts.[24] However, a note of caution should be sounded, since this apparent dislike of the historical costume genre on the part of Bolton audiences did not prevent *The Lives of a Bengal Lancer* from taking top spot in Bolton in 1935, as it did also in the national sample. This point is taken up and developed in the conclusion to this chapter.

In contrast to the relative under-performance of these high budget Hollywood productions, it is noticeable that many of the most notable comparative winners in Bolton emanating from Hollywood studios were middle-budget 'A' film dramas which appeared in the national sample of cinemas, for the most part, on double-feature programmes. Films such as *Stage Mother, You Can't Buy Everything, Counsellor at Law, The Kennel Murder Case, A Wicked Woman, School for Girls, The Great Defender, The Trunk Mystery, Sequoia, Society Doctor*, and *Living on Velvet* did not receive extended London West End runs and yet seem to have been to the particular liking of Bolton audiences.

Another genre-based observation is the relatively weak showing of a number of musicals. The operettas *Unfinished Symphony, My Song for You*, and *Bitter Sweet,* the ballet drama *Escape Me Never*, together with the musicals *Transatlantic Merry-Go-Round*, Jessie Matthews' star vehicle *Evergreen* and Astaire and Rogers' *The Gay Divorcee* all make the lists as 'relative losers'. As in the case of costume films, however, it is not possible to draw the obvious conclusion from this observation, since evidence is presented in Table 5.7 to show that operettas and musicals were among the most popular films enjoyed in Bolton. Again this is taken up in the conclusion.

Almost half of the thirty 'relative winners' were British films: nine in 1934 (including the top five places) and five in 1935—the top five places! This is almost exactly matched in the 'relative losers' chart where half of the ten of the positions are taken by British productions. In Chapter 4 it was estimated that British producers' share of the domestic market was approximately 25 per cent during the mid-1930s. From this, it might be expected that the number of British films in these comparative 'winners' and 'losers' charts should reflect this share. The fact that in both cases the proportions are twice the level of this expectation, leads to the tentative supposition that, in Bolton at least, there was a strength of feeling towards British films which was greater (both positively and negatively) than that manifest amongst audiences attending the cinemas featured in the national sample.

Finally, Table 5.6 presents an aggregate picture of the differences between those films which made up the Bolton Top 100 (found in Table 5.7) for each of the years 1934 and 1935 and their position in the national survey. Should a film be identically placed in each survey, the sum of the differences would add to zero. What Table 5.6 shows is that, on average, the films which appeared in the Bolton Top 100 were placed approximately 50 places lower in the national cinema sample rankings.

Table 5.6: *Aggregate measures of performance of Bolton's Top 100 films in comparison with their performance nationally*

	Difference in rank	POPSTAT ratios
1934		
Total[a]	-4,811.00	151.26
Average	-48.11	1.52
Standard deviation	79.31	0.78
Coefficient of variation	1.65	0.51
1935		
Total[b]	-5,527.00	158.89
Average[c]	-55.83	1.61
Standard deviation	99.36	2.00
Coefficient of variation	1.78	1.24

Source: Derived from Table 5.7.

Notes: The results for 1934 are slightly different to those found in Table VI of Sedgwick (1998b) where it was reported that *Aunt Sally* was a re-issue. The mistake has been corrected and the national POPSTAT performance of the film included in Table 5.7.

a. Obtained by summing the rank differences (column 8) and POPSTAT ratios (column 9) for Bolton's Top 100 films listed in Table 5.7.

b. As with note a, but excluding the re-released *Jenny Lind* which does not appear in any of the national sample of cinemas. This was the British title of the MGM biopic *A Lady's Morals* (1930) which starred opera singer Grace Moore.

c. Derived from dividing the total by 99, rather than 100 on account of the *Jenny Lind* factor explained in the note above.

These results suggest distinct patterns of popularity amongst audiences of the two sample sets of cinemas. Care should be taken with these statistics, however, since the two populations being compared are not equivalent. A film which appears in the Bolton Top 100 belongs to a truncated population. Its position in the national listings is not confined to a similarly truncated population, but to the whole population of films marketed. Accordingly, a film which is ranked 100th in Bolton might be ranked 500th in the national sample—a difference of 400 places—or 1st—a difference of just 99 places. This clearly will bias differences in rank and POPSTAT scores. Further, the high level of variance reflected in the standard deviation and coefficient of variation statistics indicates, as has been shown, wildly differing levels of popularity of particular films in the two samples; implying that for analytical purposes, as much attention should be given to the performance of individual films and their stars as to these aggregated differences. This conclusion is given weight by an analysis of those 'hit' productions equally popular amongst both sets of audiences. Of the twenty films that make up the Bolton Top 10 for 1934 and 1935 respectively, thirteen are similarly popular with national audiences—they take a Top 20 position in the national sample in either of the two years. These are: *Roman Scandals*, *The House of Rothschild*, *Footlight Parade*, *Blossom Time*, and *It Happened One Night* in 1934; and *The Lives of a Bengal Lancer*, *One Night of Love*, *David Copperfield*, *The Merry Widow*, *Sanders of the River*, *Roberta*, *Brewster's Millions* and *The Scarlet Pimpernel* in 1935. If this analysis is continued, so as to account for Top 20 films, *Wonder Bar*, *The Masquerader*, and *Queen Christina* in 1934; and *Treasure Island*, *Kid Millions*, and *The Barretts of Wimpole Street* in 1935 are also similarly placed.

One immediate observation from this list is the wide variety of genre in evidence: comedy/romantic comedy, drama/melodrama/family saga, adventure, musical, operetta, romantic comedy, and British Empire, all feature. Further, many of these films have a historical (costume) context and are set in Britain. Of these thirteen Top 10 films for 1934 and 1935, four were made in British studios, which fact suggests that major Hollywood productions continued to dominate British screens at the national, regional and local level, but not without a significant indigenous competitive presence.

Conclusion

It is clear from the 'winners' and 'losers' listed in Table 5.5 and the summary statistics found in Table 5.6 that a distinctive cinemagoing culture prevailed in Bolton. This should not be over-emphasized, however. Although wide disparities exist between the composition of the lists of the most popular films seen in the cinemas of Bolton and the national sample, this is much less pronounced at the top end of the 'hit' range. Of the Top 10 films exhibited in Bolton in 1934 and 1935, all but seven were similarly popular with national/middle-class audiences, leaving a set of disparate films in which the comedy element was pronounced, including two Gracie Fields' films, *Sing As We Go*, and *Love, Life and Laughter*, an early Will Hay film, *Those Were The Days*, and Laurel and Hardy's *Babes in Toyland*. (Stanley Lupino's *Happy* was 11th in 1934.)

The Bolton sample differs from its national counterpart in that films are allowed to exhaust their distribution potential, whereas in the national sample films are distributed, cascade-like, down and out of the sample from their initial level of entry. Accordingly, the tastes of audiences attending lower-order (cheaper) cinemas are much better represented in the Bolton survey. In particular the attraction of Bolton audiences to distinctive brands of humour—much of which was indigenous—is noticeable. However, it is clear from the analysis of Top 10 productions for the two years, that the bulk of films which secured extensive West End runs and so headed the national sample list of 'hits' were also 'hits' in Bolton.

Furthermore, these films included those genres which, on the basis of the analysis of Table 5.5, appeared to be unpopular with Bolton audiences. Thus, *The House of Rothschild*, *Queen Christina*, *The Lives of a Bengal Lancer*, *David Copperfield*, *Blossom Time*, *The Merry Widow*, *The Scarlet Pimpernel*, and *The Barretts of Wimpole Street* are films found in the Top 20 of both lists and counter the earlier impression that Bolton audiences did not enjoy period settings. What might be more to the point is that they may have enjoyed these less when produced by British studios, with only *The Scarlet Pimpernel* and *Blossom Time* from this list made in Britain. The same might be also said for musicals. Bolton audiences clearly had their favourites in Gracie Fields and George Formby. Also in this vein it is noticeable that Table 5.5 lists *D'Ye Ken John Peel*, with Winifred Shotter and Stanley Holloway, in the 'winners' section, a film which crept into the Bolton Top 100 for 1935 but was placed 353 places lower in the national sample. However, although Bolton audiences do not seem to have enjoyed greatly other British musicals, of either the revue (*Evergreen*) or operetta (*Bitter Sweet*) type, this was not true of rival Hollywood films in the same genre: *Footlight Parade, Wonder Bar, Gold Diggers of 1933, One Night of Love, The Merry Widow, Roberta, Kid Millions* and *Flirtation Walk* were among their Top 20 favourites.

The purpose of the Bolton investigation was to explore Jeffrey Richards' claim that although a singular cinema culture pervaded Britain, it is possible to detect distinctively regional and local patterns of film consumption which were not universally shared. He explains this within the context of multiple identities, so that it is possible for a specific audience to have particular favourites, while confirming the broader national culture preferences.

The investigation proceeded by contrasting the pattern of cinemagoing, for the years 1934–35 in Bolton, Lancashire with that of a national sample drawn from a set of higher-level cinemas located in the West End of London and the cities of Bristol, Edinburgh, Glasgow, Leeds, Liverpool, Manchester, Newcastle and Sheffield. The Bolton survey reflects a complete and sealed local film distribution network, which captures the performance of each film shown at least once from its point of entry to that of its exit: from the relatively expensive first-run cinemas of the town to the extremely cheap third- and fourth-run cinemas. This contrasts with the national sample where films are monitored as they cascade down through a set of upper-level cinemas, prior to their becoming available to localities such as Bolton. National sample cinemas are more expensive, particularly in the West End where prices were as high as 11/6d and may therefore be more representative of a national middle-class cinema.

The results provide unequivocal support for Richards' thesis. As pointed out, thirteen of Bolton's Top 10 'hits' for the two years were similarly popular with national sample audiences. These 'hits' were spread widely across the genre range and split between Hollywood and British studios in the ratio of 9:4. It is with the set of seven films not common to the top listings of the two sample audiences that the case can be made for regional and local distinctiveness. Further, this distinctiveness becomes more marked in the lower-ranked areas of the charts. From these results it may be judged that Bolton audiences appear to have enjoyed British costume films and musicals much less than the comparable genre product emanating from Hollywood, and much less also than their national sample audience counterparts. In their place, Bolton audiences preferred British films characterized by earthy working-class British humour with obvious music-hall antecedents and fast-moving contemporary dramas from either side of the Atlantic.

119

Appendix to Chapter 5

Table 5.7: *The Annual Top 100 films shown in Bolton for 1934 and 1935, compared with their performance in the national sample survey.*

Top 100 films released in Bolton in **1934**

POP = POPSTAT where 100 = mean POPSTAT	Star 1	Star 2	Bolton rank	Bolton POP index	Nat'l rank	Nat'l POP index	Diff. of rank (col 4 − col 6)	Bolton: nat'l index ratio (col 5/ col 7)
	(2)	(3)	(4)	(5)	(6)	(7)	(8)	(9)
Sing As We Go	G. Fields	J. Loder	1	542.24	37	255.66	-36	2.12
Love, Life and Laughter	G. Fields	–	2	514.82	65	195.29	-63	2.64
Roman Scandals	E. Cantor	–	3	409.80	3	656.42	0	0.62
House of Rothschild	G. Arliss	–	4	409.49	1	900.29	3	0.45
Footlight Parade	J. Cagney	R. Keeler	5	387.32	12	384.17	-7	1.01
Blossom Time	R. Tauber	–	6	362.00	6	523.52	0	0.69
Those Were the Days	W. Hay	A. Hoey	7	360.51	171	112.22	-164	3.21
It Happened One Night	C. Gable	C. Colbert	8	347.59	9	447.32	-1	0.78
Red Wagon	C. Bickford	R. Torres	9	347.00	32	292.88	-23	1.18
Dancing Lady	J. Crawford	C. Gable	10	338.47	31	303.71	-21	1.11
Happy	S. Lupino	L. Cliff	11	336.31	259	84.03	-248	4.00
Return of Bulldog Drummond	R. Richardson	A. Todd	12	321.97	175	111.30	-163	2.89
Wonder Bar	K. Francis	A. Jolson	13	321.50	17	370.27	-4	0.87
I Cover the Waterfront	C. Colbert	B. Lyon	14	319.33	114	149.01	-100	2.14
Masquerader	R. Colman	E. Landi	15	314.94	18	348.29	-3	0.90
Tugboat Annie	M. Dressler	W. Beery	16	312.81	35	267.54	-19	1.17
Gold Diggers of 1933	W. William	R. Keeler	17	312.56	29	321.19	-12	0.97
On the Air	R. Fox + his Band	–	18	304.29	229	92.29	-211	3.30
Fraternally Yours[a]	S. Laurel & O. Hardy	–	19	297.67	126	137.62	-107	2.16
Queen Christina	G. Garbo	–	20	294.10	7	467.75	13	0.63
Bowery	W. Beery	F. Wray	21	293.68	20	347.57	1	0.85
Tarzan and His Mate	J. Weissmuller	M. O'Sullivan	22	287.06	124	138.15	-102	2.08
This Is the Life	G. Harker	B. Hale	23	286.96	61	210.79	-38	1.36
Ring Up the Curtain[b]	A. Brady	F. Morgan	24	286.64	97	160.63	-73	1.78
That's a Good Girl	J. Buchanan	E. Randolph	25	284.85	28	175.20	-3	1.63
I'm No Angel	M. West	–	26	284.75	7	514.51	19	0.55
Riptide	N. Shearer	H. Marshall	27	283.13	18	358.64	9	0.79
Hold Your Man	C. Gable	J. Harlow	28	275.66	100	157.78	-72	1.75
Mystery of Mr X	R. Montgomery	–	29	271.60	125	137.93	-96	1.97
Private Life of Henry VIII	C. Laughton	–	30	271.34	2	816.36	28	0.33
Dinner at Eight	M. Dressler	J. Barrymore	31	270.82	17	353.51	14	0.77
Scotland Yard Mystery	G. Du Maurier	G. Curzon	32	269.14	284	77.53	-252	3.47

120

*Table 5.7 continued: Top 100 films released in Bolton in **1934***

	(2)	(3)	(4)	(5)	(6)	(7)	(8)	(9)
Service[c]	L. Barrymore	B. Hume	33	261.06	205	105.20	-172	2.48
Cat and the Fiddle	J. MacDonald	R. Novarro	34	259.52	40	244.98	-6	1.06
Lily of Killarney	J. Garrick	G. Malo	35	258.39	298	74.00	-263	3.49
Only Yesterday	M. Sullivan	J. Boles	36	254.80	27	324.58	9	0.79
Paddy the Next Best Thing	J. Gaynor	W. Baxter	37	254.55	44	238.19	-7	1.07
Stage Mother	F. Tone	M. O'Sullivan	38	253.77	252	85.98	-214	2.95
Moonlight and Melody[d]	M. Brian	L. Carrillo	39	253.57	158	125.47	-119	2.02
It's a Cop	S. Howard	D. Bouchier	40	253.32	281	79.15	-241	3.20
Manhattan Melodrama	C. Gable	W. Powell	41	252.77	90	167.07	-49	1.51
Southern Maid	H. Welchman	B. Daniels	42	251.51	120	145.46	-78	1.73
Every Woman's Man[e]	M. Baer	M. Loy	43	251.47	53	218.64	-10	1.15
Counsellor at Law	J. Barrymore	B. Daniels	44	250.02	185	108.29	-141	2.31
Going Hollywood	M. Davies	B. Crosby	45	246.44	72	187.32	-27	1.32
Murder at the Vanities	C. Brisson	J. Oakie	46	246.43	44	238.29	2	1.03
Men in White	C. Gable	M. Loy	47	246.01	77	183.49	-30	1.34
Lady of the Boulevards[f]	A. Sten	–	48	244.79	34	269.46	14	0.91
Lady For a Day	M. Robson	W. William	49	243.95	51	220.78	-2	1.10
You Can't Buy Everything	M. Robson	L. Stone	50	238.64	216	97.07	-166	2.46
Another Language	R. Montgomery	H. Hayes	51	238.64	99	159.06	-48	1.50
Sorrell and Son	H.B. Warner	W. Shotter	52	238.51	56	218.05	-4	1.09
Crooks in Clover	Baxter, W	M. Loy	53	237.97	183	112.73	-130	2.11
Viva Villa	W. Beery	L. Carrillo	54	236.34	48	227.86	6	1.04
Evergreen	J. Matthews	B. Balfour	55	235.46	14	387.36	41	0.61
Looking For Trouble	S. Tracy	J. Oakie	56	235.45	111	146.74	-55	1.60
Orders Is Orders	J. Gleason	C. Greenwood	57	234.53	41	248.25	16	0.94
Fashion Follies of 1934[g]	W. Powell	B. Davis	58	233.95	39	245.41	19	0.95
Bitter Sweet	A. Neagle	F. Graavey	59	233.89	16	358.89	43	0.65
Summer Lightning	R. Lynn	W. Shotter	60	233.50	204	105.55	-144	2.21
Night of the Garter	S. Howard	E. Randolph	61	233.50	101	157.46	-40	1.48
George White's Scandals	R. Vallee	J. Durante	62	232.92	69	190.07	-7	1.23
Bottoms Up	J. Boles	S. Tracy	63	232.92	190	106.83	-127	2.18
Kennel Murder Case	W. Powell	M. Astor	64	232.45	202	106.24	-138	2.19
Little Woman	K. Hepburn	J. Bennett	65	232.15	8	461.01	57	0.50
20 Million Sweethearts	D. Powell	G. Rogers	66	230.83	71	188.73	-5	1.22
When Ladies Meet	R. Montgomery	A. Harding	67	230.59	184	112.64	-117	2.05
This Side of Heaven	L. Barrymore	M. Clarke	68	230.59	166	114.07	-98	2.02
Christopher Bean	M. Dressler	L. Barrymore	69	224.13	70	183.23	-1	1.22
You Made Me Love You	S. Lupino	T. Todd	70	224.07	223	99.24	-153	2.26
Broadway Thro' a Keyhole	C. Cummings	–	71	223.14	55	218.34	16	1.02
Trouble	S. Howard	–	72	223.14	121	145.27	-49	1.54
Gambling Lady	B. Stanwyck	J. McCrea	73	222.75	79	180.60	-6	1.23
Aunt Sally	C. Courtneidge	–	74	222.43	37	265.70	37	0.81

121

*Table 5.7 continued: Top 100 films released in Bolton in **1934***

	(2)	(3)	(4)	(5)	(6)	(7)	(8)	(9)
Up To the Neck	R. Lynn	W. Shotter	75	220.89	149	131.63	-74	1.68
Too Much Harmony	B. Crosby	J. Oakie	76	220.26	47	227.83	29	0.97
Invisible Man	C. Rains	G. Stuart	77	219.31	15	360.32	62	0.61
My Song For You	J. Kiepura	S. Hale	78	219.30	29	306.74	49	0.71
When New York Sleeps	S. Tracy	H. Twelvetrees	79	217.16	128	134.34	-49	1.62
House on 56th Street	K. Francis	R. Cortez	80	216.19	206	104.71	-126	2.06
Fugitive Lovers	R. Montgomery	M. Evans	81	213.82	200	103.82	-119	2.06
Song of Songs	M. Dietrich	B. Aherne	82	212.80	22	340.64	60	0.62
Sitting Pretty	J. Oakie	G. Rogers	83	211.37	87	170.99	-4	1.24
Secret of the Blue Room	G. Stuart	P. Lukas	84	210.57	189	109.23	-105	1.93
Wandering Jew	C. Veidt	–	85	206.57	26	326.12	59	0.63
Night Flight	C. Gable	M. Loy	86	205.68	46	231.81	40	0.89
Song You Gave Me	B. Daniels	V. Varconi	87	205.37	140	135.47	-53	1.52
Wrecker	J. Holt	G. Tobin	88	202.90	217	100.43	-129	2.02
Stand Up and Cheer	W. Baxter	S. Temple	89	202.82	64	197.55	25	1.03
Change of Heart	J. Gaynor	C. Farrell	90	202.82	84	176.05	6	1.15
Cleopatra	C. Colbert	W. William	91	201.25	12	390.09	79	0.52
Wild Cargo	(Adventure documentary)		92	201.03	295	74.53	-203	2.70
SOS Iceberg	R. La Rocque	L. Riefenstahl	93	201.03	230	96.69	-137	2.08
Man's Castle	S. Tracy	L. Young	94	199.88	131	132.44	-37	1.51
Hollywood Party	S. Laurel	O. Hardy	95	199.63	148	123.81	-53	1.61
College Humour	B. Crosby	R. Arlen	96	199.11	50	222.60	46	0.89
I am Suzanne	L. Harvey	G. Raymond	97	197.75	146	123.95	-49	1.60
Death Takes a Holiday	F. March	–	98	196.21	86	172.33	12	1.14
Jimmy the Gent	J. Cagney	B. Davis	99	196.09	149	122.89	-50	1.60
Reunion in Vienna	J. Barrymore	D. Wynyard	100	195.36	72	180.60	28	1.08

*Top 100 films released in Bolton in **1935***

POP = POPSTAT where 100 = mean POPSTAT	Star 1	Star 2	Bolton rank	Bolton POP index	Nat'l rank	Nat'l POP index	Diff. of rank (col 4 − col 6)	Bolton: nat'l index ratio (col 5/ col 7)
	(2)	(3)	(4)	(5)	(6)	(7)	(8)	(9)
Lives of a Bengal Lancer	G. Cooper	F. Tone	1	422.32	1	853.90	0	0.49
One Night of Love	G. Moore	T. Carminati	2	405.20	2	692.04	0	0.59
David Copperfield	F. Bartholomew	L. Barrymore	3	376.22	11	692.04	-8	0.54
Merry Widow	J. MacDonald	M. Chevalier	4	365.67	11	422.87	-7	0.86
Babes in Toyland	S. Laurel & O. Hardy	–	5	356.76	115	144.29	-110	2.47
Sanders of the River	P. Robeson	L. Banks	6	338.01	6	592.80	0	0.57

Table 5.7 continued: Top 100 films released in Bolton in **1935**

	(2)	(3)	(4)	(5)	(6)	(7)	(8)	(9)
Now and Forever	S. Temple	G. Cooper	7	336.43	104	151.50	-97	2.22
Roberta	I. Dunne	F. Astaire	8	328.65	12	472.34	-4	0.70
Brewster's Millions	J. Buchanan	L. Damita	9	320.63	17	408.54	-8	0.78
Scarlet Pimpernel	L. Howard	M. Oberon	10	320.63	3	692.44	7	0.46
Wicked Woman	M. Christians	C. Bickford	11	315.79	189	107.60	-178	2.93
Treasure Island	W. Beery	J. Cooper	12	314.42	22	337.31	-10	0.93
Things Are Looking Up	C. Courtneidge	M. Miller	13	306.46	60	207.44	-47	1.48
Look Up and Laugh	G. Fields	D. Wakefield	14	304.06	111	151.26	-97	2.01
Java Head	A.M. Wong	E. Allan	15	301.81	306	71.40	−291	4.23
Kid Millions	E. Cantor	A. Sothern	16	298.27	14	451.87	2	0.66
Flirtation Walk	D. Powell	R. Keeler	17	297.57	142	133.45	-125	2.23
Barretts of Wimpole Street	N. Shearer	C. Laughton	18	296.70	15	382.45	3	0.78
Mighty Barnum	W. Beery	A. Menjou	19	291.01	28	319.64	-9	0.91
Happiness Ahead	D. Powell	J. Hutchinson	20	283.09	96	160.78	-76	1.76
Devil Dogs of the Air	J. Gagney	P. O'Brien	21	277.97	58	219.01	-37	1.27
Shadow of Doubt	R. Cortez	V. Bruce	22	277.89	162	122.63	-140	2.27
Dandy Dick	W. Hay	–	23	277.66	283	75.50	-260	3.68
My Heart Is Calling	J. Kiepura	M. Eggerth	24	276.69	113	150.44	-89	1.84
Chained	J. Crawford	C. Gable	25	275.24	47	229.64	-22	1.20
Ruggles of Red Gap	C. Ruggles	C. Laughton	26	273.65	29	319.01	-3	0.86
Off the Dole	G. Formby	C. Shotter	27	272.20	539	13.98	-512	19.47
After Office Hours	C. Gable	C. Bennett	28	271.70	141	134.80	-113	2.02
Here Comes the Navy	J. Cagney	P. O'Brien	29	269.34	54	216.52	-25	1.24
Abdul the Damned	F. Kortner	N. Asther	30	267.59	40	260.74	-10	1.03
Little Colonel	S. Temple	L. Barrymore	31	266.96	30	317.24	1	0.84
Dirty Work	R. Lynn	G. Harker	32	265.56	56	214.74	-24	1.24
Thin Man	W. Powell	M. Loy	33	264.75	26	315.39	7	0.84
Camels Are Coming	J. Hulbert	A. Lee	34	256.33	20	347.51	14	0.74
Bulldog Drummond Strikes Back	R. Colman	L. Young	35	255.44	23	323.29	12	0.79
Vanessa	R. Montgomery	H. Hayes	36	251.94	95	161.26	-59	1.56
West Point of the Air	W. Beery	M. O'Sullivan	37	251.94	96	160.86	-59	1.57
Evelyn Prentice	W. Powell	M. Loy	38	251.67	46	235.79	-8	1.07
Last Gentlemen	G. Arliss	E.M. Oliver	39	251.45	24	321.69	15	0.78
Hide Out	R. Montgomery	M. O'Sullivan	40	251.27	105	151.44	-65	1.66
Bulldog Jack	J. Hulbert	F. Wray	41	248.54	21	372.70	20	0.67
Nell Gwyn	A. Neagle	C. Hardwicke	42	241.65	10	436.29	32	0.55
Forsaking All Others	J. Crawford	C. Gable	43	241.34	49	231.75	-6	1.04
Man From Folies Bergère[h]	M. Chevalier	M. Oberon	44	241.32	51	229.32	-7	1.05
Mississippi[u]	B. Crosby	W.C. Fields	45	241.22	47	233.99	-2	1.03
Girl In Pawn[i]	S. Temple	A. Menjou	46	241.20	269	81.65	-223	2.95
100% Pure	J. Harlow	F. Tone	47	240.93	127	134.61	-80	1.79

*Table 5.7 continued: Top 100 films released in Bolton in **1935***

	(2)	(3)	(4)	(5)	(6)	(7)	(8)	(9)
Man Who Knew Too Much	L. Banks	E. Best	48	239.12	42	243.33	6	0.98
Trunk Mystery[j]	F. Tone	U. Merkel	49	238.50	239	90.94	-190	2.62
Lady In Danger	T. Walls	Y. Arnaud	50	234.54	82	179.14	-32	1.31
Phantom Light	G. Harker	B. Hale	51	234.54	182	112.04	-131	2.09
Goin' To Town	M. West	–	52	233.91	39	263.69	13	0.89
Night Is Young	R. Novarro	E. Laye	53	230.29	154	126.30	-101	1.82
Living On Velvet	K. Francis	W. William	54	230.21	213	98.38	-159	2.30
Sweet Adeline	I. Dunne	D. Woods	55	228.87	164	122.55	-109	1.87
Jenny Lind (reissue)[k]	G. Moore	–	56	223.98	–		–	
Gay Divorce	F. Astaire	G. Rogers	57	220.15	19	358.17	38	0.61
Affairs of Cellini	F. March	C. Bennett	58	219.97	73	186.57	-15	1.18
Sequoia	J. Parker	–	59	219.41	235	92.51	-176	2.37
Baby Take a Bow	S. Temple	J. Dunn	60	216.58	135	130.70	-75	1.66
Drake of England	M. Lang	J. Baxter	61	216.29	178	114.26	-117	1.89
Count of Monte Cristo	R. Donat	E. Landi	62	214.90	27	314.92	35	0.68
Bright Eyes	S. Temple	–	63	211.92	36	259.54	27	0.82
Great Defender	M. Lang	M. Bannerman	64	209.63	267	81.88	-203	2.56
Transatlantic Merry-Go-Round	G. Raymond	N. Carroll	65	207.64	35	269.05	30	0.77
Dames	R. Keeler	D. Powell	66	205.74	53	216.96	13	0.95
Oh! Daddy	L. Henson	R. Hare	67	205.18	59	212.04	8	0.97
Old Curiosity Shop	E. Benson	B. Webster	68	204.13	230	91.90	-162	2.22
Biography of a Bachelor Girl	A. Harding	R. Montgomery	69	202.32	140	135.29	-71	1.50
Flame Within	A. Harding	H. Marshall	70	202.29	231	93.27	-161	2.17
Vagabond Lady	R. Young	E. Venable	71	202.15	132	137.56	-61	1.47
Wedding Night	G. Cooper	A. Sten	72	201.54	44	237.20	28	0.85
Laddie	J. Beal	G. Stuart	73	201.48	309	66.67	-236	3.02
Passport To Fame[l]	E.G. Robinson	–	74	201.00	121	141.56	-47	1.42
Woman of the World	H. Marshall	C. Bennett	75	200.95	153	121.56	-78	1.65
Cat's Paw	H. Lloyd	U. Merkel	76	197.75	50	221.98	26	0.89
Escape Me Never	E. Bergner	H. Sinclair	77	194.71	10	527.54	67	0.37
Road House	V. Loraine	G. Harker	78	193.89	150	122.87	-72	1.58
Painted Veil	G. Garbo	H. Marshall	79	191.37	21	345.39	58	0.55
Fighting Stock	T. Walls	R. Lynn	80	191.02	55	221.74	25	0.86
Sadie McKee	J. Crawford	F. Tone	81	190.98	52	217.84	29	0.88
White Parade	L. Young	J. Boles	82	189.76	118	143.09	-36	1.33
One More Spring	J. Gaynor	W. Baxter	83	189.76	159	123.66	-76	1.53
Student's Romance	C. Goodner	G. Natzler	84	189.47	275	77.02	-191	2.46
Clive of India	R. Colman	L. Young	85	188.28	9	532.93	76	0.35
Belle of the Nineties	M. West	R. Pryor	86	188.28	59	212.52	27	0.89
World Moves On	M. Carroll	F. Tone	87	188.28	60	211.60	27	0.89

*Table 5.7 continued: Top 100 films released in Bolton in **1935***

	(2)	(3)	(4)	(5)	(6)	(7)	(8)	(9)
Unfinished Symphony	M. Eggerth	H. Jaray	88	186.77	49	256.65	39	0.73
Jew Süss	C. Veidt	–	89	185.40	5	582.91	84	0.32
Iron Duke	G. Arliss	G. Cooper	90	183.87	4	617.70	86	0.30
Radio Parade of 1935	W. Hay	H. Chandler	91	183.57	63	200.24	28	0.92
We Live Again	A. Sten	F. March	92	181.55	94	163.94	-2	1.11
George White's 1935 Scandals	A. Faye	J. Dunn	93	177.35	287	74.23	-194	2.39
Charlie Chan In Paris	W. Oland	–	94	177.29	255	84.08	-161	2.11
My Old Dutch	B. Balfour	B. Harker	95	176.24	78	182.75	17	0.96
British Agent	K. Francis	L. Howard	96	175.06	86	167.70	10	1.04
Morals of Marcus	L. Velez	–	97	173.72	125	139.78	-28	1.24
D'Ye Ken John Peel	W. Shotter	S. Holloway	98	172.93	451	34.13	-353	5.07
Society Doctor	C. Morris	V. Bruce	99	171.96	282	75.86	-183	2.27
School For Girls	A. Shirley	S. Fox	100	171.55	306	67.97	-206	2.52

Sources: *Bolton Evening News*; *Kine Year Books*, 1932–37; Eyles (1993, 1996); Eyles and Skone (1991).

Notes: the National Index of Column 7 uses the mean of those films shown at least once in the national sample of cinemas, so as to make it comparable to the Bolton Index in column 5, the latter being based solely on those films shown in the cinemas of the town.
a. US title, *Sons of the Desert*.
b. US title, *Broadway to Hollywood*.
c. US title, *Looking Forward*.
d. US title, *Moonlight and Pretzels*.
e. US title, *The Prizefighter and the Lady*.
f. US title, *Nana*.
g. US title, *Fashions of 1934*.
h. US title, *Folies Bergère*.
i. US title, *Little Miss Marker*.
j. US title, *One New York Night*.
k. US title, *A Lady's Morals*.
l. US title, *The Whole Town's Talking*.

6

Comparative Cinemagoing Preferences 1934–1935

National, Bolton and Brighton audiences

The study of cinemagoing in Bolton produces a series of interesting differences when compared to that based upon the national sample of cinemas and suggests that a distinctive but not separate culture prevailed. This raises the question of whether the Bolton experience was exceptional. Clearly, to answer this properly would require a full investigation of local cinemagoing patterns around Great Britain, a task which is beyond the scope of the present work. However, in order to provide an indication of the kind of research potential of such an investigation, I have contrasted the patterns established for national and Bolton audiences with those of Brighton and Hove on the South Coast of England. The methodology used here is identical to that developed in the Bolton study found in the previous chapter, drawing upon the *Brighton Evening Argus* for information of cinema programmes. Knowledge of the number of seats, prices and ownership which characterized each of the cinemas included in the investigation are drawn from the *Kine Weekly Yearbook* and D. Robert Elleray's study of Brighton and Hove cinemas. With a 1931 census population count of 202,421, the combined settlement of Brighton and Hove was a little larger than Bolton. For the years 1934 and 1935 the town boasted eighteen cinemas (the same number of cinemas as listed for Bolton in Table 5.1). Information describing these cinemas is found in Table 6.2.

Brighton's Cinemas

Like Bolton, Brighton can be considered to have been a cinema centre in that few of its inhabitants would have considered it necessary to travel outside the town in search of film entertainment. The pattern of exhibition again affirms the cascade system of distribution/ exhibition described in national and local contexts in Chapters 2 and 4 respectively, with the chief film attractions being screened typically in one of the four first-run cinemas—Regent, Savoy, Astoria or Odeon[1]—and then appearing three to six weeks later at one of four second-run cinemas—Academy, Lido, Granada, Grand. From this level in the distribution/exhibition hierarchy, popular films were then distributed out to a series of third-run and fourth-run cinemas, with a four-week clearance gap commonly between exhibitions. This transition also marked a change from play-dates where weekly shared billings were the norm to those where a shared billing was exhibited twice weekly. Again, as with Bolton, lower-status films which initially failed to make the bottom half of a double-bill programme entered the exhibition hierarchy at a lower point. Accordingly, all cinemas in Table 6.2 premiered films, but most of these films would not have been considered as major attractions by the cinemagoing public. The pattern of distribution is given in Table 6.1, which includes all of those films which achieved at least one exhibition in one of the cinemas listed in Table 6.2. In comparing it with the frequency distribution of exhibition in Bolton found in Table 5.4, the reader will note that although 170 more films were shown in Brighton, owing to differences in exhibition practices, the rate of decline in the number of films achieving an additional billing is remarkably similar.

It is apparent from a comparison of Brighton cinemas with their Bolton counterparts listed in Table 5.1 that Brighton audiences could expect to pay twice as much across the range of cinemas. Further, unlike in Bolton, the practice of opening major film attractions on a single-bill programme was comparatively rare in Brighton, the only examples being *Convention City* (Astoria), *The Crusades* (Regent), *David Copperfield* (Savoy), *Dinner at Eight* (Regent), *Little Women* (Regent), *The Lives of a Bengal Lancer,* (Savoy), *Masquerader* (Regent), and *Queen Christina* (Savoy). *Damaged Lives* (Princes) also achieved this distinction, but this semi-documentary 'sexploitation' feature built around the issue of venereal disease was clearly in a class of its own as an attraction. Along with *The Lives of a Bengal Lancer*, it was the only film to open with two-week billing over the course of these two years.

Another difference in the distribution/exhibition practice in Brighton was the absence of joint openings—where a film opens at more than one cinema. As pointed out in Chapter 5, it was common

Table 6.1: *Frequency distribution of the exhibition of 1,474 films appearing in Brighton and Hove cinemas in 1934 and 1935*

Number of distinct runs/exhibitions	Number of films
One	1,474
Two	1,140
Three	860
Four	522
Five	265
Six	96
Seven	41
Eight	14
Nine or more	3

Source: *Brighton Evening Argus.*

Note: Includes the complete exhibition record of all films shown during 1934 and 1935 in those Brighton and Hove cinemas listed in Table 6.2. For those films opened before the end of 1935 their exhibition records have been traced through to 31 May 1936.

in Bolton for major attractions to open simultaneously in two or, more rarely, three cinemas in the town. This did not happen in Brighton, although a number of the films listed above played simultaneously at two of the second-run theatres.

It is interesting to ponder on the reasons for these differences. Although the patterns of the cascade system were largely similar in both towns, there were distinctive aspects to each. One possible explanation for this is that the community of Brighton and Hove was less homogeneous than its northern counterpart, and pursued a wider range of paid-for entertainments. Away from the cinema there certainly were more attractions at the south coast resort. In the Hippodrome and Theatre Royal respectively, Brighton had a variety theatre which regularly attracted West End musical acts and a legitimate theatre which staged West End productions. In addition to these there were the Palace Pier and West Pier theatres, both specializing in variety and light comedy theatre. Of course the demand for such attractions was considerably bolstered by the number of trippers and holiday-makers who frequented the town. Nevertheless, these attractions were part of the choice set available throughout the year to

Table 6.2: *Characteristics of Brighton and Hove cinemas, 1934–1935*

Cinema	In operation on 1 Jan. 1934	Run status	Seating capacity	Price range	Cinema weight[a]	Owners
Academy	Yes	2nd	1,000	1 to 2/-	0.88	Gaumont-British
Astoria	Yes	1st	2,000	1/- to 2/6	2.05	ABC
Cinema de Luxe	Yes	3rd	529	9d. to 2/-	0.43	Independent
Court	Yes	3rd	1,200	6d. to 2/-	0.88	Independent
Duke of York's	Yes	3rd	1,000	7d. to 2/-	0.76	Sussex Picturedrome
Granada	Yes	2nd	1,592	7d. to 2/-	1.2	Mistlin and Lee
Grand	Yes	3rd	1,140	6d. to 1/4	0.61	Universal Entertainments
King's Cliff	Yes	4th	370	4d. to 9d.	0.12	Independent
Lido	Yes	2nd	2,137	7d. to 2/-	1.61	County Cinemas
Odeon*	No	1st	1,200	1/- to 2/4	1.17	Odeon
Odeon, Kemp Town	Yes	3rd	958	6d. to 1/6	0.56	Odeon
Princes	Yes	misc.	550	6d. to 2s.	0.4	Independent
Palladium*	Yes	2nd	1,200	1/- to 2/4	1.17	Blue Halls
Regal[b]	Yes	3rd	656	9d. to 1/10	0.5	Regal Cinemas
Regent	Yes	1st	2,020	1/- to 3/6	2.66	Gaumont-British
Savoy	Yes	1st	2,630	1/- to 2/6	2.69	ABC
Troxy	Yes	4th	390	4d. to 1/6	0.21	Independent
Tivoli	Yes	4th	398	7d. to 1/10	0.28	Independent

Sources: Elleray (1989); Eyles (1993, 1996, and private documents); *Kine Year Books*, 1935, 1936.

Notes:
* The Palladium closed as such in September 1934 and was reopened as the Odeon on 8 June 1935.
a. As with the national and Bolton surveys, the weights given to Brighton cinemas are derived by dividing the revenue potential of each cinema (seats multiplied by mid-range price) by the arithmetic mean revenue potential of all of the cinemas included in the sample.
b. The seating capacity of the Regal is that given for its replacement the Curzon. See Elleray (1989).

residents. If this factor is combined with the much higher admission prices charged by the cinemas, it may well have been the case that even first-run cinema owners felt it necessary to offer double-billed programmes to attract audiences. Even then, the much rarer occurrence of holdovers in Brighton may indicate that attendances at Brighton's premier cinemas were on average lower than those at Bolton's.

A further difference between the two cinemagoing communities was that in the Princes, Brighton had something approaching an art house cinema: an establishment of which Bolton was unable to boast. During these years the cinema screened a number of French and German classics—*A Nous la Liberté, Blue Angel, Ces Messieurs de la Santé, L'Ordonnance, La Maternelle, Le Petit Rio, Liebelei, Maskerade, Morgenrot, Poil de Carotte,* and *Prenez Garde à la Peinture*; a series of early/earlier sound classic Hollywood productions which included *Disraeli, Blonde Venus, The Devil and the Deep, The Jazz Singer* and *Jenny Lind*, as well as classic British films such as *The Good Companions* and *Goodnight Vienna*; and two silent features—*Doctor Jack* and *Peter Pan*.

As in Table 5.1 the cinema weights in Table 6.2 describe the relative importance of the cinemas, measured in terms of box-office potential. Based upon the arithmetic mean box-office potential of the listed cinemas, the weights indicate the commercial importance of screenings in the town's principal cinemas particularly when contrasted with that of its lower-order cinemas. It is for this reason that the number of distinct runs *per se* is less important than the number of higher-order cinemas that any single film is booked into: for instance, the Regent had a box-office revenue potential of over 12 times that of the Troxy. Nevertheless, there is some worth in listing the most commonly exhibited films, if for no other reason than to identify those films popular at either end of the exhibition hierarchy. Table 6.3 does this, listing all 41 films which appeared on seven or more distinct occasions in Brighton during the study period.

The striking fact revealed by the 'Nationality' column in Table 6.3 is that 25 of the 41 films listed are British, including a set of films—*Going Gay, The Green Pack, In Town Tonight, On the Air, The Ten Minute Alibi*—produced by British Lion which feature in neither the national Top 100 nor, with the exception of *On the Air,* in the Bolton Top 100. In terms of genre, musicals of the operetta type, historical and costume dramas/adventures, films depicting 'the Empire', comedies/revues with songs, and family and romantic dramas all

Table 6.3: *Films exhibited in Brighton and Hove in 1935 and 1936 which played on seven or more distinct billings*

Title	Nationality	Genre	Date of Brighton and Hove premiere	Number of distinct billings
39 Steps	Br.	Romantic comedy thriller	18 Nov. 1935	7
Autumn Crocus	Br.	Romantic drama	30 Apr. 1934	7
Boys Will Be Boys	Br.	Comedy	30 Dec. 1935	7
Brewster's Millions	Br.	Comedy with songs	8 Jan. 1935	7
Bright Eyes	USA	Child drama with songs	22 July 1935	7
Catherine the Great	Br.	Historical drama	2 July 1934	7
Chu Chin Chow	Br.	Musical	1 Oct. 1934	7
Clive of India	USA	'Empire' historical drama	15 July 1935	7
Count of Monte Cristo	USA	Romantic costume adventure	11 March 1934	7
Escape Me Never	Br.	Romantic drama	26 Aug. 1935	8
Evensong	Br.	Musical drama	12 Nov. 1934	7
Fighting Stock	Br.	'Aldwych farce' comedy	16 Sept. 1935	8
Going Gay	Br.	Musical comedy	26 Feb. 1934	7
Green Pack	Br.	Thriller	18 Mar. 1935	7
House of Rothschild	USA	Historical drama	20 Aug. 1934	7
I'm No Angel	USA	Dramatic comedy with songs	19 Mar. 1934	7
In Town Tonight	Br.	Revue comedy	3 June 1935	7
Invisible Man	USA	Fantasy drama	23 Apr. 1934	8
It Happened One Night	USA	Romantic comedy	17 Sept. 1934	8
Kid Millions	USA	Musical	12 Aug. 1935	7
Les Miserables	USA	Costume drama	14 Oct. 1935	7
Little Friend	Br.	Child drama	22 Oct. 1934	8
Little Women	USA	Romantic drama	30 Apr. 1934	7
Lives of a Bengal Lancer	USA	'Empire' historical drama	19 Apr. 1934	7
Love, Life and Laughter	Br.	Romantic comedy with songs	23 Apr. 1934	11
Man from the Folies Bergère	USA	Comedy with songs	23 Sept. 1935	7
My Heart is Calling	Br.	Musical	22 Apr. 1935	7
My Old Dutch	Br.	Romantic drama	29 Oct. 1935	7
My Song For You	Br.	Musical	15 Oct. 1935	8
On the Air	Br.	Revue with songs	21 May 1934	7
One Night of Love	USA	Musical	7 Jan. 1935	10
Only Yesterday	USA	Romantic drama	9 Apr. 1934	8

Table 6.3 continued

Title	Nationality	Genre	Date of Brighton and Hove premiere	Number of distinct billings
Private Life of Henry VIII	Br.	Historical drama	5 Mar. 1934	7
Sanders of the River	Br.	'Empire' drama	7 Oct. 1935	8
Scarlet Pimpernel	Br.	Romantic costume adventure	10 June 1935	9
Sing As We Go	Br.	Dramatic comedy with songs	1 Oct. 1934	8
Song of Songs	USA	Romantic drama	8 Jan. 1934	8
Ten Minute Alibi	Br.	Murder mystery	13 May 1935	7
Things Are Looking Up	Br.	Comedy with songs	13 May 1935	7
Those Were the Days	Br.	Comedy	15 Oct. 1934	7
Wedding Night	USA	Romantic drama	16 Nov. 1935	7

Source: *Brighton Evening Argus*.

feature prominently. It is noticeable that two of Gracie Fields' films are among the 41 films, suggesting a confirmation of *Variety*'s assessment of the universal appeal of the star outside the West End (see note 18, Chapter 5). Perhaps as intriguing, however, are the stars not featured in these films, including Astaire/Rogers, Garbo, Powell/Loy, Beery, MacDonald, and from Britain, Matthews or Hulbert. Of the 42 films (listed in the note to Table 5.4) which received seven or more separate runs in Bolton, *One Night of Love*, *Love, Life and Laughter*, *It Happened One Night*, *The Lives of a Bengal Lancer*, *My Song for You*, *Sing As We Go*, *Things are Looking Up*, *Brewster's Millions*, *Kid Millions*, *Only Yesterday*, *Sanders of the River*, *The Scarlet Pimpernel* and *Those Were the Days* are common to Table 6.3. However, for reasons already explained, the simple expedient of counting separate billings is not a sufficient guide to film popularity as a proxy measure of box-office revenue. Again it is necessary to call upon the POPSTAT methodology to do this.

POPSTAT results for Brighton

Using the methodology developed in Chapter 3, and applied in Chapters 4 and 5, a POPSTAT index of film popularity was obtained from the exhibition records of the Brighton cinemas listed in Table 6.2. The supposition that the number of exhibitions that any single film might have had will not be necessarily an accurate method of establishing its relative box-office performance is borne out by the POPSTAT results, obtained separately for 1934 and 1935, the Top 20 of which are listed in Table 6.4—with those British productions found in Brighton's Top 50 listed in a note to the table.

Table 6.4 provides a basis for comparing the three sample audience sets—Brighton, Bolton and national. To begin with, the results support the conclusion arrived at in Chapter 5, with respect to Bolton/national audiences, that the majority of the most popular films—those found in Top 20 places—enjoyed by Brighton audiences

Table 6.4: *The annual Top 20 films shown in Brighton and Hove, 1934 and 1935, compared to national and Bolton surveys*

Rank Title	Brighton POPSTAT index*	Bolton POPSTAT index*	Bolton rank	National rank
*100 = mean POPSTAT				
1934				
1 Lady of the Boulevards	589.00	244.79	48	34
2 Roman Scandals	500.42	409.80	3	3
3 Little Women	437.33	232.15	65	1
4 House of Rothschild	391.17	409.49	4	8
5 Catherine the Great	361.08	164.06	140	4
6 Queen Christina	358.91	294.10	20	7
7 It Happened One Night	353.19	347.59	8	9
8 Masquerader	331.96	314.94	15	18
9 Dinner at Eight	326.78	270.82	31	17
10 My Song for You	301.28	219.30	78	29
11 Wonder Bar	293.54	321.50	13	17
12 That's a Good Girl	293.03	284.85	25	28
13 Jew Süss	290.21	185.40	89	5
14 Love, Life and Laughter	285.85	514.82	2	65
15 Sing As We Go	284.81	542.24	1	37
16 Those Were the Days	280.94	360.51	7	171
17 Blossom Time	278.54	362.00	6	6
18 Treasure Island	277.07	314.42	12	22
19 Only Yesterday	276.21	254.80	36	27
20 Barretts of Wimpole Street	269.26	296.70	18	15

Table 6.4 continued	Brighton	Bolton	Bolton	National
	POPSTAT	POPSTAT	rank	rank
Rank Title	index*	index*		

1935					
1	Lives of a Bengal Lancer	663.59	422.32	1	1
2	David Copperfield	554.63	376.22	3	11
3	Scarlet Pimpernel	404.93	320.63	10	3
4	Brewster's Millions	332.24	320.63	9	17
5	One Night of Love	315.12	405.20	2	2
6	Mighty Barnum	302.35	291.01	19	28
7	Sanders of the River	301.81	338.01	6	6
8	Escape Me Never	290.60	194.71	77	10
9	Top Hat	282.88	n/a		10
10	Man from the Folies Bergère	282.82	241.32	44	51
11	Wedding Night	282.82	201.54	72	44
12	Kid Millions	271.61	298.27	16	14
13	Crusades	265.86	n/a		14
14	Behind the Evidence	255.11	49.61	427	15
15	39 Steps	254.89	n/a		16
16	Les Miserables	252.46	n/a		17
17	False Faces	249.19	n/a		18
18	Clive of India	248.72	188.28	85	9
19	Last Gentleman	239.31	251.45	39	24
20	Bright Eyes	238.75	211.92	63	36

Sources: *Brighton Evening Argus*; *Bolton Evening News*; *Kine Year Books*, 1932–37; Eyles (1993, 1996); Eyles and Skone (1991).

Notes:

1. n/a refers to those films which had not been released in Bolton before 1 January 1936.

2. British films ranked 21–50 in Brighton were for 1934: *Turkey Time* (22nd), *Aunt Sally* (24th), *Unfinished Symphony* (25th), *Evergreen* (26th), *Autumn Crocus* (27th), *Little Friend* (30th), *Chu Chin Chow* (31st), *Red Wagon* (33rd), *My Old Dutch* (37th), *Evensong* (38th); *Forbidden Territory* (39th), *Sorrell and Son* (40th), *Wild Boy* (41st), *The Battle* (42nd), *Princess Charming* (43rd), *On Secret Service* (44th), *Gallant Lady* (45th), *Friday the 13th* (46th), *Cup Of Kindness* (48th), *Below the Sea* (49th), *It's a Cop* (50th); and for 1935: *My Heart is Calling* (24th); *Nell Gwyn* (25th); *10 Minute Alibi* (26th), *Look Up and Laugh* (27th); *Silent Passenger* (28th), *Things are Looking Up* (29th), *Girls Will Be Boys* (30th), *The Green Pack* (32nd), *Boys Will Be Boys* (33rd), *Heat Wave* (34th), *The Man Who Knew Too Much* (35th), *In Town Tonight* (42nd), *Joy Ride* (44th), *Honeymoon for Three* (45th), *Bulldog Jack* (46th); *Oh! Daddy* (47th); *Doctor's Orders* (48th), *Iron Duke* (49th), *Lady in Danger* (50th).

were similarly popular with audiences that attended those cinemas which formed the basis for the national survey investigation. The 24—out of a possible total of 40—films included in this category are: *Roman Scandals, Little Women, The House of Rothschild, Catherine the Great, Queen Christina, It Happened One Night, Masquerader, Dinner at Eight, Wonder Bar, Jew Süss, Blossom Time* and *The Barretts of Wimpole Street* in 1934; and in 1935, *The Lives of a Bengal Lancer, David Copperfield, The Scarlet Pimpernel, Brewster's Millions, One Night of Love, Sanders of the River, Escape Me Never, Top Hat, Kid Millions, The Crusades, Les Miserables*, and *Clive of India*.

Furthermore, most of Brighton's Top 20 films are also present in the comparable lists assembled for Bolton, presented in the appendix to Chapter 5. The exceptions are the two films starring Elisabeth Bergner, *Escape Me Never* and *Catherine the Great*; the historical/costume dramas, *Lady of the Boulevards* (US: *Nana*), *Little Women, Jew Süss* and *The Man From The Folies Bergère*, as well as *Dinner at Eight, My Song for You, Love, Life and Laughter, Only Yesterday, The Wedding Night, The Last Gentleman* and *Bright Eyes*.

It is clear, then, that the films which are common to the Brighton/national and Brighton/Bolton Top 20 lists for these years are not always the same, and that significant differences may constitute evidence of idiosyncratic local/regional preferences and dislikes. For instance, in Chapter 5, attention was drawn to the relative popularity in Bolton of British comedy films and the unpopularity of British costume drama and operettas. Further, the prominence of Gracie Fields in the lists and the phenomenal success of George Formby's *Off the Dole* suggests a strong liking for things 'northern' amongst Boltonians. The Brighton lists show that, along with national audiences, historical/costume dramas and adventures were the most popular genres at the time, taking five of the Top 6 places in 1934 and the Top 3 places in 1935. 'Empire' and 'English' subjects, particularly when portrayed by Hollywood, feature strongly across a variety of genres in both Top 20 lists.

It would appear that domestic comedy productions were marginally less popular in Brighton. Gracie Fields had two Top 20 successes in 1934 with *Love, Life and Laughter* and *Sing As We Go*, although in lower positions than in Bolton, whilst *Look Up and Laugh* was placed in 28th position in 1935. Other Bolton Top 20 British comedies—Will Hay's *Those Were the Days*, Stanley Lupino's *Happy* and Cicely Courtneidge's *Things Are Looking Up*—all fared less well in Brighton taking 16th, 60th and 29th positions respectively. The two Laurel and

Hardy features, so popular in Bolton—*Fraternally Yours* (19th in 1934) and *Babes in Toyland* (5th in 1935)—fail, as in the national survey, to break into the Top 100, being placed 129th and 113th respectively in Brighton and 126th and 105th in the national survey. The three Astaire/Rogers musicals—*The Gay Divorcee*, *Roberta*, and *Top Hat*—also performed less well in Brighton than might have been expected. Released within six months of one another during the last half of 1935, they were ranked 31st, 196th and 9th respectively. The popularity rank of *Roberta* in particular is puzzling given its Top 20 standing in both Bolton and national charts. The same is true of *The Merry Widow*, which again is a Top 20 film in the Bolton and national charts but is placed 39th in Brighton in 1935. On the other hand, Jack Buchanan's musical comedies—*That's a Good Girl* and *Brewster's Millions*—seem to have been even more popular in Brighton than in Bolton or the national surveys, taking 12th and 4th spots respectively in 1934 and 1935, whilst Eddie Cantor's films—*Roman Scandals* and *Kid Millions*—seem to have been equally popular with all three audience sets.

The comparative productivity of *Queen Christina* and *Sing As We Go*

A final comparative investigation examines the respective diffusion paths of two popular films made in 1934, one at the MGM studios in Hollywood and the other by a British studio (Associated Talking Pictures), out from their premieres in the West End to a set of provincial city-centre cinemas, and out again to the cinemas of Bolton and Brighton and Hove. *Queen Christina* was a melodramatic vehicle for Greta Garbo who played the part of an anguished seventeenth-century monarch who abdicated the throne of Sweden for the love of a man, whilst *Sing As We Go* was a musical comedy, set amongst the Lancashire working-class at work and play, starring the enormously popular Gracie Fields.[2] The two films represent two quite different forms of pleasure, the first historical, introspective and tragic, the second contemporary, vivacious and celebratory of things working-class, built around the spinning works and the Blackpool holiday.

Table 6.5 reports the POPSTAT index results for the two films from the three sets of cinemas, whilst Tables 6.6 and 6.7 follow their distribution paths. The most immediate observation which can be made is that of the 664 films released in 1934[3] both proved to be popular with all three audience sets. *Queen Christina* proved to be not so

136

Table 6.5: *POPSTAT index results for* Queen Christina *and* Sing As We Go *from national sample, Brighton and Bolton cinemas*

Film * 100 = mean POPSTAT	National sample rank	National sample POPSTAT*	Brighton rank	Brighton POPSTAT* index	Bolton rank	Bolton POPSTAT* index
Queen Christina	7	467.74	6	358.91	20	294.1
Sing As We Go	37	255.66	15	284.81	1	542.24

Sources: Brighton Evening Argus; Bolton Evening News; Kine Year Books, 1932–37; Eyles (1993, 1996); Eyles and Skone (1991).

Note: The POPSTAT scores are standardized by giving the mean POPSTAT for all films exhibited in each set of cinemas during 1934 the value 100.

popular with Bolton audiences as it had been in those cinemas making up the national sample. This contrasts with *Sing As We Go,* which proved to be the top ranking film in Bolton but achieved a more moderate reception amongst the national cinema audiences.

Opening at one of Britain's largest and most prestigious cinemas, The Empire, Leicester Square (owned by MGM), *Queen Christina* attracted weekly audiences of 77,403, 64,362, 54,560 and 37,363 during its four-week run, making it the most popular film at that cinema during that year, ahead of other MGM attractions such as *Riptide, Treasure Island, The Barretts of Wimple Street, The Merry Widow* and *The Painted Veil*—the last also starring Garbo.[4] In contrast *Sing As We Go* opened at Paramount's second London cinema, the 1,896–seater Plaza with a two-week run. During the course of 1934, seven other films were held over for a second week—*Design for Living* (Paramount), *Four Frightened People* (Paramount), *Good Girl* (Paramount), *Man of Two Worlds* (RKO), *Pursuit of Happiness* (Paramount), *The Queen's Affair* (British and Dominion) and *Spitfire* (RKO)—with the last of these enjoying a three-week run.

In aggregating the screenings of the two films from amongst the national sample of cinemas, it is noticeable that outside of London their respective performances are comparable. Altogether, *Queen Christina* played at 21 national sample cinemas, with only three double billings, for a total of 33 weeks whereas *Sing As We Go* was screened at 19 of these cinemas, including four double bookings, for a total of 24.5 weeks. If their West End experience is subtracted from these

Table 6.6: *The diffusion patterns of* Queen Christina *(Board of Trade Registration 15 February 1934)*

Week commencing	National cinema sample	Brighton cinemas	Bolton cinemas
19 Feb. 1934	Empire Leicester Square, WE, 4 wks, sf		
30 July 1934	Dominion, WE, 1 wk, df Metropole, WE, 1wk, df		
20 Aug. 1934	Gaumont, Birmingham, 1wk, sf		
27 Aug. 1934		Savoy, 1 wk, sf	
10 Sept. 1934	Davis, Croydon, 1 wk, df Embassy, Bristol, 2 wks, sf La Scala, Glasgow, 1wk, sf New Bedford, Glasgow, 1 wk, sf Regent, Glasgow, 1wk, sf Market St., Manchester, 2 wks, sf New Oxford, Manchester, 2wks, sf Cinema House, Sheffield, 4 wks, sf		
17 Sept. 1934	Scala, Birmingham, 1 wk, sf Assembly Rooms, Leeds, 1 wk, sf Majestic, Leeds, 1 wk, sf Trocadeo, Liverpool, 2wks, sf Pavilion, Newcastle, 1 wk, sf Queens, Newcastle, 1 wk, sf	Grand, 1 wk, df Granada, 1 wk, df	
24 Sept. 1934	Palace, Edinburgh, 2 wks, sf Playhouse, Edinburgh, 2 wks, sf		
1 Oct. 1934		Regal, 1 wk, df	Capitol, 1 wk, sf
22 Oct. 1934			Majestic, 0.5 wk, sf
3 Dec. 1934		Tivoli, 0.5 wk, sf	Carlton, 0.5 wk, sf
10 Dec. 1934	Stoll, WE, 1 wk, df		
7 Jan. 1935			Regent, 0.5 wk, sf
28 Jan. 1935			Belle, 0.5 wk, sf

Sources: *Brighton Evening Argus*; *Bolton Evening News*; *Kine Year Books*, 1932–37; Eyles (1993, 1996); Eyles and Skone (1991).

Note: WE = London's West End; wk = week; sf = single feature; df = double feature.

Table 6.7: *The diffusion patterns of* Sing As We Go *(Board of Trade Registration 13 September 1934)*

Week commencing	National cinema sample	Brighton cinemas	Bolton cinemas
17 Sept. 1934	Plaza, WE, 2 wks, sf		
1 Oct. 1934	Hippodrome, Bristol, 2 wks, sf	Savoy, 1 wk, df	
22 Oct. 1934	Metropole, WE, 1 wk, df		
29 Oct. 1934	Forum, Birmingham, 1 wk, df		
12 Nov. 1934	Market St., Manchester, 2 wks, sf New Oxford, Manchester, 2 wks, sf		
19 Nov. 1934	Empire, Bristol, 1 wk, sf Triangle, Bristol, 1 wk, sf Stoll, Newcastle, 2 wks, sf Stoll, Bristol, 1 wk, df		
3 Dec. 1934	Rialto, Leeds, 1 wk, sf Futurist, Liverpool, 1 wk, df		
10 Dec. 1934		Lido, 1 wk, df	
24 Dec. 1934			Queens, 1 wk, sf Rialto, 2 wks, sf
31 Dec. 1934	Central, Sheffield, 1 wk, sf		
7 Jan. 1935	Tower, Leeds, 1 wk, sf		
21 Jan. 1935		Duke of Yorks, 1 wk, df Princes, 1 wk, sf	Regent, 1 wk, sf
28 Jan. 1935		Odeon KT, 1 wk, df	
4 Feb. 1935	Coliseum, Glasgow, 1 wk, sf Regal, Glasgow, 1 wk, sf		Crompton, 1 wk, sf
18 Feb. 1935	Regent, Glasgow, 1 wk, sf		
4 Mar. 1935	Poole's, Edinburgh, 2 wks, sf Grand, Glasgow, 0.5 wk, sf		Gem, 0.5 wk, sf
18 Mar. 1935			Belle, 0.5 wk, sf
22 April 1935		Tivoli, 0.5 wk, df	
27 May 1935		Troxy, 0.5 wk, df	
1 July 1935			Crompton, 0.5wk, sf
5 Aug. 1935		King's Cliff, 0.5 wk, df	
25 Dec. 1935			Theatre Royal, 1 day, sf

Sources: *Brighton Evening Argus*; *Bolton Evening News*; *Kine Year Books*, 1932–37; Eyles (1993, 1996); Eyles and Skone (1991).

Note: WE = London's West End, wk = week, sf = single feature, df= double feature.

figures, both received 17 distinct screenings, with the MGM film edging an advantage on holdovers. It is clear that the national sample results, listed in Table 6.5, are heavily influenced by the difference in the West End exposures of the two films.

Unlike *Queen Christina*, *Sing As We Go* was not a major West End attraction, appearing only once again on the screen of the Metropole as a double feature before its widespread diffusion out to the provinces. Indeed, its second screening took place in Bristol. It is also interesting to note the unusually short time span between its premiere and subsequent screenings. In contrast, *Queen Christina's* four-week run at the Empire was followed by a five-month break before its second screening, when it appeared simultaneously at the Dominion and Metropole cinemas. The film also later played at the Stoll in the run up to Christmas. These were big cinemas which generated a lot of box-office revenue and hence were important to the overall box-office performance of a film.[5] Another difference between the two is in the patterns of diffusion once outside the West End. In the case of *Queen Christina*, this took place in mid-September. During the three weeks commencing 10, 17 and 24 September 1934, the film played at principal cinemas in all of the provincial cities included in the sample. In comparison, *Sing As We Go* trickled out slowly through the provincial city cinemas taking from October 1934 to March 1935 to reach all of the sample cities, with Edinburgh and Glasgow city-centre cinemas screening the film last.

Both films opened at the 2,630 seat Savoy in Brighton at the very beginning of their general release but were not seen in Bolton until some time later. However, whereas *Queen Christina* was screened as the single attraction at the Savoy, *Sing As We Go* appeared as the main attraction on a double-film programme, co-featuring *You're Telling Me* (Paramount), starring W.C. Fields. This is critically important as far as their POPSTAT scores are concerned since the relatively high POPSTAT score generated by playing at Brighton's largest first-run cinema is halved in the case of *Sing As We Go* because of this billing factor. Hence, even though *Sing As We Go* played at eight Brighton cinemas, compared to the five recorded for *Queen Christina*, this was not sufficient to counterbalance its shared billing status at the Savoy. It is fair to say that *Sing As We Go* had a greater presence in the lower-order cinemas of the town.

Sing As We Go also played at eight cinemas in Bolton. In this instance, its popularity in the town was such that it opened at two first-run cinemas, the 1,480 seater Queens and the 1,147 seater Rialto, on single-feature billings, holding over for a second week at the latter cinema. *Queen Christina*, on the other hand, opened for one week at the 1,642 seater Capitol on a single-feature bill. Thereafter it received a fairly low-key distribution, appearing as the only feature on a half-week billing at a series of third- and fourth-run cinemas in the town. *Sing As We Go* had a further two single-week bookings before playing out its distribution on half weekly programmes, appearing as a single-feature attraction at all of the cinemas at which it was screened.

Conclusion

The case study which closes the chapter builds upon the description of the cascade distribution/exhibition system found in Chapter 3. The reader will be by now familiar with the argument developed in this book that film as a 'system of provision' is built around the potential productivity of each individual film commodity, with the distribution function designed to ensure that popular films returned again and again to the screens of a locality, filtering down over time through the various orders of cinema, until their exhibition potential was exhausted. In tracing the exhibition history of *Queen Christina* and *Sing As We Go* through three sample sets of cinemas it is possible to come to a deeper understanding of the reach of their respective audience receptions and, of course, of the success achieved by the distributors of the two films in placing them in revenue-generating cinemas.

It would appear that Brighton audiences were closer, in their filmgoing preferences, to those attending the national sample of cinemas than to Bolton audiences. Table 6.4 shows that 24 of the 40 films constituting annually the Top 20 most popular films in Brighton and Hove cinemas in 1934 and 1935 were similarly popular nationally. An inspection of Table 5.7 shows that only 18 Top 20 films for the two years were common to both the national and Bolton audiences. The number of British films in Top 20 positions in Brighton was eight in 1934 and five in 1935, rising to 29 and 24 respectively from the annual Top 50 films for the same two years, denoting the very strong presence of British films in the filmgoing diets of Brighton and Hove residents.[6]

This survey of exhibition programmes of Brighton and Hove cinemas in 1934 and 1935, then, adds further support to the market share results set down in Chapter 4, and to the analysis of filmgoing preferences of Boltonians found in Chapter 5: namely, that British producers were making a large number of films which British audiences chose to watch but that, taking any one of the investigations as a benchmark in relation to the other two, its most popular films were not uniformly represented in the other two. It may be supposed that, *mutatis mutandis*, this pattern would be replicated across the British market, although, as indicated at the beginning of this chapter, it would require a full investigation of local cinemagoing patterns around Great Britain to test that conclusion rigorously.

The preceding three chapters provide detailed evidence of the vagaries as well as those more consistent elements of film popularity in Britain during the 1930s. The uncertainty experienced by filmgoers in choosing between films is reflected in the risks faced by producers in attempting to meet those needs not yet fully known and articulated. It is this dichotomy which provides the risk context of film production and is the key to explaining those strategies developed by film producers to address the problem that audiences cannot know what it is that they like until they have experienced it. These strategies provide the subject of the next three chapters.

7

Profits, Film Budgets and Popularity

Across ten thousand miles, these two men (two Jews born in Poland but now American citizens) had seen the one and sixpence in Turgis's pocket and, with a swift gesture, resolving itself into steel and concrete and carpets and velvet covered seats and pay-boxes, had set it in motion and diverted it to themselves.

J.B. Priestley, *Angel Pavement*[1]

In Table 4.2 it is apparent that only a small number of films became the 'hits' of their day. From this it follows that film producers were faced *ex ante* with a problem concerning the level of expenditure they should commit to a film project. In the Introduction it was argued that producers form concepts of their properties during the development phase. Once the necessary investment has been made, they will require particular performance levels from them. Greenwald's (1950) amortization schedules for the principal Hollywood studios of the period—discussed in Chapter 3—indicate that during the 1930s films were given a life-cycle of 12 to 15 months in which to pay for themselves. It follows, then, that a big-budget film would need to be very much more popular than a low-budget film in order to generate the same rate of return for its producer. There appears to be confusion amongst film historians about the distinction between popularity and profitability. A film may be popular and yet make a loss for its producer in that while it receives widespread distribution, it nevertheless fails to ignite that level of word-of-mouth enthusiasm amongst audiences sufficient to generate box-office revenues which at least cover its cost of production. Conversely, a film may not be very

143

popular amongst audiences when compared to a major production, but yet yield a much higher rate of return for the producer on the initial, more modest, investment. In allocating budgets across a portfolio of films the film producer will be concerned to balance risks in pursuit of a target global rate of return on these investments. As John Izod argues:

> Profits have always, from the earliest days, been the primary objective of the American film industry. However it may appear from outside, Hollywood has always been first and foremost a business; and although occasional exceptions have been made for movies that were thought likely to enhance a studio's corporate image, few films are released in the certain knowledge that they will lose money. This is not to say that all American features do make profit—but almost all are intended to do so.[2]

Film profits and rates of return

These points can be illustrated by exploring studio records of production costs and box-office returns of those films most popular in the British market. Unfortunately, to date, systematic evidence is in the public domain only for the films made at the Hollywood studios of MGM, Warners and RKO. Mark Glancy has kindly made available to the author the full sets of production costs and box-office returns of the first two of these, previously only partially reported in Glancy.[3] The information is further enhanced by Richard Jewell's report on RKO films.[4] In all three ledgers US domestic box-office revenue is distinguished from overseas returns, although, alas, the particular contribution of the British market is not made explicit. Given the importance of the latter to Hollywood revenues, however, the overseas figures provide some further clues to film popularity in Britain.

In the following analysis the profit (Π_i) earned by the ith film is defined as the difference between total box-office revenue generated (R_i) and the costs of producing (C_{pi}) and distributing (C_{di}) that film.

$$\Pi_i = R_i - (C_{pi} + C_{di}) \qquad \text{(Equation 7.1)}$$

The cost of production represents the studio's investment in the ith film. The rate of return or rate of profitability (r_i) on the ith film is given as:

144

$$r_i = \Pi_i / (C_{pi} + C_{di}) \qquad\qquad \text{(Equation 7.2)}$$

Finally, as the monetary values are recorded in US dollars it is important to clarify the question of the rate of conversion into £ sterling. For reasons explained in note 5 an exchange rate of £1 = \$4.50 has been adopted for the whole period of this investigation.[5]

The financial performance of MGM films

Table 7.1 presents production and distribution cost and box-office revenue for those MGM films included in the POPSTAT annual Top 100 charts for the years 1932–7, listed in Appendix 3. The films are listed in order of total box-office revenue. It will be observed that although there is a tendency for box-office revenue to increase with production cost, there are many exceptions. Films such as *After the Thin Man, Libelled Lady, Grand Hotel, Tugboat Annie, Tarzan the Apeman, Mata Hari, Forsaking All Others, Dinner at Eight, Double Wedding* cost \$700,000 dollars or less to make but generated in excess of two million dollars at the box office, world-wide. Conversely, a number of expensive film projects performed poorly. Examples of such films include, *Broadway To Hollywood*—a film which was ranked only 103rd in Britain in 1933—*Going Hollywood, Cat and the Fiddle, Eskimo, Rasputin and the Empress, Parnell, Romeo and Juliet, Conquest, A Day at the Races, The Merry Widow* and *The Good Earth*, all of which cost upwards of \$900,000 but made losses for the studio. It is important to recognize that these loss-making films made the annual Top 100 lists and should not be considered unpopular. Indeed the last five can be considered to be amongst the 'hits' of the season in Britain: nevertheless, the extent of their success was insufficient to cover the combination of production and distribution costs.

A further category of performance includes those films which must have surprised the studio chiefs, in that they were relatively inexpensive to make but yielded considerable returns. *Men in White, The Thin Man, Personal Property*, and *Forsaking All Others*, all generated box-office revenues amounting to twice their respective combined production and distribution costs.

Column 6 expresses the ratio of US box office to foreign box office. Values less than 1.0 identify those films for which overseas earnings exceeded those generated in the US domestic market, whereas values greater than 1.0 reflect the opposite. It can be seen that, whereas films such as *Saratoga, Born to Dance, A Day at the Races, Gorgeous Hussy,*

Table 7.1: *Cost and revenue data of all MGM films included in the annual POPSTAT 100 lists, 1932–1937*

Film	British Top 100 rank in year of release	Production cost $000s	Distribution cost $000s	US box-office $000s	Foreign box-office $000s	Ratio of US/foreign box-office	Total box-office $000s	Profit $000s (col.7 − (cols.2+3))	Percentage rate of return col.8/((col.2+3))
	(1)	(2)	(3)	(4)	(5)	(6)	(7)	(8)	(9)
San Francisco	13	1,300	1,736	2,868	2,405	1.19	5,273	2,237	73.68
Great Ziegfeld	3	2,183	1,668	3,089	1,584	1.95	4,673	822	21.35
Mutiny on the Bounty	2	1,905	1,646	2,250	2,210	1.02	4,460	909	25.60
Maytime	14	2,126	1,286	2,183	1,823	1.20	4,006	594	17.41
Good Earth	2	2,816	1,237	2,002	1,555	1.29	3,557	-496	-12.24
Rose Marie	28	875	1,152	1,695	1,820	0.93	3,515	1,488	73.41
Saratoga	42	1,144	962	2,432	820	2.97	3,252	1,146	54.42
After the Thin Man	13	673	976	1,992	1,173	1.70	3,165	1,516	91.93
Captains Courageous	12	1,645	1,133	1,688	1,445	1.17	3,133	355	12.78
David Copperfield	11	1,073	1,210	1,621	1,348	1.20	2,969	686	30.05
Broadway Melody of 1936	16	1,062	1,118	1,655	1,216	1.36	2,871	691	31.70
China Seas	31	1,138	1,076	1,710	1,157	1.48	2,867	653	29.49
Broadway Melody of 1938	39	1,588	997	1,889	967	1.95	2,856	271	10.48
Camille	8	1,486	968	1,154	1,688	0.68	2,842	388	15.81
Libelled Lady	20	603	931	1,601	1,122	1.43	2,723	1,189	77.51
Firefly	65	1,495	1,016	1,244	1,430	0.87	2,674	163	6.49
Queen Christina	7	1,144	843	767	1,843	0.42	2,610	623	31.35
Merry Widow	11	1,605	1,116	861	1,747	0.49	2,608	-113	-4.15
Grand Hotel	2	700	947	1,235	1,359	0.91	2,594	947	57.50
Tugboat Annie	36	614	746	1,917	655	2.93	2,572	1,212	89.12
Tarzan the Apeman	19	660	961	1,112	1,428	0.78	2,540	919	56.69
Born to Dance	42	1,422	850	1,632	781	2.09	2,413	141	6.21
Dancing Lady	31	923	739	1,490	916	1.63	2,406	744	44.77
Barretts of Wimpole Street	15	870	805	1,258	1,085	1.16	2,343	668	39.88
Day at the Races	50	2,016	832	1,602	703	2.28	2,305	-543	-19.07
Anna Karenina	24	1,152	832	865	1,439	0.60	2,304	320	16.13
Tale of Two Cities	10	1,232	929	1,111	1,183	0.94	2,294	133	6.15
Treasure Island	21	825	884	1,164	1,110	1.05	2,274	565	33.06
Mata Hari	29	588	760	931	1,296	0.72	2,227	879	65.21
Forsaking All Others	48	392	675	1,399	800	1.75	2,199	1,132	106.09
Hell Divers	8	821	882	1,244	917	1.36	2,161	458	26.89
Dinner at Eight	17	435	723	1,398	758	1.84	2,156	998	86.18
Conquest	30	2,732	806	730	1,411	0.52	2,141	-1,397	-39.49
Romeo and Juliet	14	2,066	1,001	962	1,113	0.86	2,075	-992	-32.34

Table 7.1 continued

Film	(1)	(2)	(3)	(4)	(5)	(6)	(7)	(8)	(9)
Naughty Marietta	74	782	868	1,058	999	1.06	2,057	407	24.67
Double Wedding	73	678	680	1,314	727	1.81	2,041	683	50.29
Smilin' Through	22	851	653	1,004	1,029	0.98	2,033	529	35.17
Gorgeous Hussy	49	1,119	784	1,458	561	2.60	2,019	116	6.10
Chained	47	544	712	1,301	687	1.89	1,988	732	58.28
Emma	17	350	724	1,409	563	2.50	1,972	898	83.61
Viva Villa	48	1,022	766	941	934	1.01	1,875	87	4.87
Love on the Run	47	578	607	1,141	721	1.58	1,862	677	57.13
Night At The Opera	65	1,057	668	1,164	651	1.79	1,815	90	5.22
Suzy	58	614	691	1,223	580	2.11	1,803	498	38.16
Last of Mrs Cheyney	21	741	596	1,107	690	1.60	1,797	460	34.41
Riptide	18	769	639	1,023	718	1.42	1,741	333	23.65
Personal Property	68	299	560	1,086	645	1.68	1,731	872	101.51
White Sister	39	625	591	750	922	0.81	1,672	456	37.50
Painted Veil	20	947	573	538	1,120	0.48	1,658	138	9.08
No More Ladies	41	765	692	1,117	506	2.21	1,623	166	11.39
Big City	72	621	554	906	695	1.30	1,601	426	36.26
Parnell	43	1,547	666	992	584	1.70	1,576	-637	-28.78
Prosperity	34	628	508	1,166	348	3.35	1,514	378	33.27
I Live My Life	56	586	508	921	557	1.65	1,478	384	35.10
Men in White	77	213	458	890	565	1.58	1,455	784	116.84
Thin Man	26	231	463	818	605	1.35	1,423	729	105.04
Hell Below	30	895	546	634	755	0.84	1,389	-52	-3.61
Rasputin and the Empress	61	1,022	542	677	702	0.96	1,379	-185	-11.83
As You Desire Me	35	469	445	705	658	1.07	1,363	449	49.12
Reckless	82	858	606	847	492	1.72	1,339	-125	-8.54
Emperor's Candlesticks	91	620	454	733	600	1.22	1,333	259	24.12
West Point of the Air	96	591	464	677	640	1.06	1,317	262	24.83
Eskimo	67	935	613	636	676	0.94	1,312	-236	-15.25
Fury	82	604	450	685	617	1.11	1,302	248	23.53
Sadie McKee	52	612	464	838	464	1.81	1,302	226	21.00
Piccadilly Jim	87	466	431	769	503	1.53	1,272	375	41.81
Strange Interval	28	654	493	957	280	3.42	1,237	90	7.85
Manhattan Melodrama	90	355	463	735	498	1.48	1,233	415	50.73
Letty Lynton	36	347	435	754	418	1.80	1,172	390	49.87
Evelyn Prentice	46	498	424	700	466	1.50	1,166	244	26.46
Private Lives	24	500	369	814	311	2.62	1,125	256	29.46
Arsene Lupin	58	433	432	595	515	1.16	1,110	245	28.32
Cat and the Fiddle	40	843	398	455	644	0.71	1,099	-142	-11.44
Petticoat Fever	90	247	365	693	387	1.79	1,080	468	76.47
Night Flight	48	499	404	576	503	1.15	1,079	176	19.49

147

Table 7.1 continued

Film	(1)	(2)	(3)	(4)	(5)	(6)	(7)	(8)	(9)
Night Must Fall	83	589	386	550	465	1.18	1,015	40	4.10
Spy 13	95	880	356	619	391	1.58	1,010	-226	-18.28
Escapade	61	467	365	577	398	1.45	975	143	17.19
Going Hollywood	72	914	317	620	342	1.81	962	-269	-21.85
The Prize Fighter and the Lady	53	682	356	432	501	0.86	933	-105	-10.12
Flesh	93	480	308	487	350	1.39	837	49	6.22
Huddle	87	514	323	476	333	1.43	809	-28	-3.35
Blonde Bombshell	84	344	295	531	230	2.31	761	122	19.09
Gabriel Over the White House	56	216	250	468	201	2.33	669	203	43.56
Flying High	90	634	296	476	181	2.63	657	-273	-29.35
Reunion in Vienna	76	478	299	379	264	1.44	643	-134	-17.25
Stranger's Return	99	300	224	439	191	2.30	630	106	20.23
Vanessa	95	594	278	353	266	1.33	619	-253	-29.01
Skyscraper Souls	76	382	227	444	111	4.00	555	-54	-8.87
What Every Woman Knows	93	428	214	340	162	2.10	502	-140	-21.81
Payment Deferred	86	197	139	169	135	1.25	304	-32	-9.52
Men Must Fight	100	240	169	229	205	1.12	434	25	6.11

Sources: Eddie Mannix Ledger, made available to the author by Mark Glancy; Appendix 3.

Notes: Films are listed with their original US titles. Their British release titles can be found in Appendix 3. The films were released in the US earlier than in Britain. Accordingly, the year of release into the two markets does not always coincide. The records of *Christopher Bean* and *Topper* were not included in the original ledger.

Emma, No More Ladies, Prosperity, Strange Interval, Private Lives, Blonde Bombshell, Gabriel Over the White House, Happy Landing, Another Language, Stranger's Return, Skyscraper Souls and *What Every Woman Knows* were heavily dependent for their popularity on American audiences, the films starring Greta Garbo: *Camille, Queen Christina, Grand Hotel, Anna Karenina, Mata Hari, Conquest, Painted Veil*, as well as the Jeanette MacDonald operettas, *Rose Marie, Firefly, The Merry Widow*, and *The Cat and the Fiddle*, all proved significantly more popular with foreign audiences, and this is also true of *Tarzan the Apeman* and *White Sister*. Not surprisingly, given that the British market was the second largest in the world during this period, those MGM films that performed relatively better in foreign markets tended to earn high POPSTAT rankings—generating a correlation coefficient of 0.78 between the two sets—and were amongst the most popular of their day in Britain.

Finally, attention ought to be given to those middle-budget films produced by MGM ($500–700,000) which fall outside of the POPSTAT Top 100. Most notable failures, all of which lost money for the studio, include *Blondie of the Follies*, *Phantom of Paris*, *West Of Broadway*, *Downstairs*, *Flying High* and *The Squaw Man* from the 1931–32 season; *Fast Workers* and *Today We Live* from the 1932–33 season; *Laughing Boy*, *The Chief* and *Hollywood Party* (a big-budget $932,000 production debacle)[6] from the 1933–34 season; *Outcast Lady*, *Riff-Raff*, *Biography of a Bachelor Girl* and *The Night is Young* from the 1934–35 season; and *Robin Hood of Eldorado* and *A Perfect Gentleman* from the 1935–36 season.

A simple linear regression model of film popularity

An examination of RKO's and Warners' outputs over the same time reveals telling similarities: that 'hit' production was an inherently risky business because although big-budget films could be expected to be more popular than smaller-budget films, they might not be sufficiently popular to warrant the extra production costs and consequent promotional expenditures, thus generating a negative rate of return for the studio. In my analysis of the rates of return on RKO films 1930–41, based upon the accounting information presented by Jewell, I found that 29 of the 51 films with production budgets of $600,000 or more made losses, with all 51 taken together generating a mean rate of return of just 1 per cent, compared with the studio's mean rate of return of 7 per cent from all its films during this period.[7] An investigation of accounting information from the Warners studio, in the form of William Schaefer's ledger, yielded similar results. One could continue in this way, analysing batches of films defined by discrete *ad hoc* budgetary cost criteria, but the procedure would only highlight and not answer the question of the extent to which, stochastically, the size of the production budget determined a film's popularity.[8] This is an important query because it requires the analyst to formalize and test a proposed relationship between film budgets, box-office and profits and rates of return. It provides the key to understanding the risk environment in which film producers operated.

To tackle this question, I have specified and tested a simple linear regression model for the period 1932–37 in which the popularity of

Warners' films (the dependent variable)—represented in the US and British markets respectively by their box-office returns and POPSTAT scores—is functionally determined by film production budgets (the independent or explanatory variable), where film budgets act as a proxy for the difficult to isolate and quantify associated characteristics of production and star values, technical sophistication, writing qualities, directorial influence and length, amongst other things. If the reader were to think of a scatter diagram such as depicted in Figures 7.1 and 7.2 in which the dependent variable is measured on the vertical (Y) axis and the independent variable on the horizontal (X) axis, the model in effect allows us to draw a line of best fit through the data: one which minimizes the sum of the squared differences between the actual scatter point observations and the line itself. Such a model is represented by Equation 7.3.

$$POP_i = \beta_0 + \beta_1 BUDGET_i + \mu_i \qquad \text{(Equation 7.3)}$$

Where POP = popularity as measured by either box-office
receipts or the POPSTAT statistic,
i = ith film (i = 1, 2, ... n,)
BUDGET = production budget in $000s,
μ_i = error term
β_0, β_1 = constants

The results of the test are given in Table 7.2. A first observation is that the Film Budget coefficients are positive and have associated standard errors which pass the 95 per cent confidence test: they are statistically significant. The tests suggests that for the release years 1932–7 an additional $1,000 spent at Warners on production budgets yielded on average $1,130 extra box-office revenue in the American market, whilst in Britain the same increase in budget generated on average an increase POPSTAT of 0.016: for every extra $100,000 Warners added to the budget of a film a further yield of 1.6 points on average was added to its POPSTAT score.[9] The ability of production budgets to explain the success or otherwise of Warners' releases is given by the coefficient of determination (R^2) where $1 - R^2$ represents that proportion of any change in the dependent variable (in this case Warners' box-office gross taken in the American market, or POPSTAT score generated by the British market) which is not explained by a change in the independent variable (in this case, cost of production). Clearly, the R^2 statistic is higher for the US market than for Britain. In both markets

Table 7.2: *The relation between Warners' production budgets and (1) their US box-office grosses and (2) their POPSTAT scores, 1932–37, using ordinary least squares regression techniques*

---

(1) Regression of US box-office grosses (Y) on production budgets (X)

	Constant β_0,	103.12
	Film budget β_1	1.13
		(0.055)

R squared   0.557

No. of observations   331

(2) Regression of POPSTAT scores (Y) on production budgets (X).

	Constant β_0	3.55
	Film budget β_1	0.016
		(0.001)

R squared   0.297

No. of observations   331

Source: William Schaefer Ledger.

Note: The numbers in parentheses are the standard errors of the film budget coefficient estimates.

the size of production budgets evidently mattered in box-office performance, but why apparently more so in the United States? Although one should be careful when comparing R^2 from differently specified models, as they are not strictly comparable, one possible answer for the difference in R^2 statistics is that the principal Hollywood studios wielded greater market power in the American market when compared to its British counterpart: in the American market the major Hollywood studios competed for the most part against one another while in Britain they were compelled to compete further with potential British studio 'hits' without the security of their own cinema chains to hand. With more films to choose from, British audiences were able to privilege indigenous production if they so wished. A cultural and institutional discount in favour of British films would manifest itself in a lower R^2 for Warners' films in Britain.

Although the regression results presented in Table 7.2 indicate that the coefficient values for film budgets meet the 95 per cent confidence interval test it would be surprising if these values were a reliable predictive guide to a relation between budgets and popularity, given what has been said about the substantial financial risks, particularly at the higher budgetary levels associated with film production. While it might be suspected that higher budgets tended to induce higher levels of popularity, they are also accompanied by greater variations in popularity: higher budgets implied greater risks. Where the range of box-office or POPSTAT returns increase with the magnitude of production budgets the error term associated with the film budget coefficient may be expected to depart from being homoscedastic, i.e. to be heteroscedastic.[10] If this is the case, the standard error estimate is invalid, which in turn casts doubt upon the significance test associated with the coefficient values.

Figures 7.1 and 7.2 illustrate the point being made. It is clear that irrespective of whether US box-office grosses, or POPSTAT measures of popularity are used, the data points fan out as film budgets are increased. Tests show that heteroscedasticity exists and analysis suggests that it is an important feature. However, experimenting with alternative functional forms by taking the logarithms or square roots of the dependent variables in order stabilize the variance of Y_i (i.e. re-

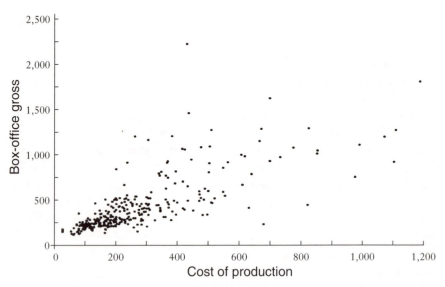

Source: William Schaefer Ledger.

Figure 7.1: *The relation between US box-office grosses ($000s) and film budgets ($000s), for Warners' films 1932–1937*

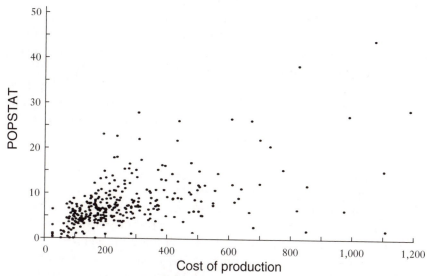

Source: William Schaefer Ledger.

Figure 7.2: *The relation between POPSTAT scores—serving as a proxy for British box-office revenue—and film budgets ($000s), for Warners' Films 1932–1937*

establish homoscedasticity) still produced significant coefficient estimates.

These results confirm a more detailed study into individual film performance based upon the 871 films produced and marketed by Warners (including First National following Warners' acquisition in 1929) between 1921/22 and 1940/41, in which Sedgwick and Pokorny found that although 'higher budget films tended to generate high box-office receipts, they did so with increasing uncertainty'; for 'While box-office revenue might have been a reasonable reflection of film popularity, it was a poor proxy for film profitability.' An important reason for this was that 'The more popular a film was, the higher the distribution costs incurred in exhibiting it'; and from this 'It would appear that the quest for 'hit' production was not only more risky, since the variance of profits increased with production budgets, but also that such productions generated lower average rates of return'.[11]

There is no reason to suppose that the risk characteristics of film production at Warners outlined here did not apply to all the principal studios. The business response of Hollywood to this phenomenon, for the decade dating from the mid-1920s, was to spread risk across a portfolio of products in the expectation that if not all big-budget films were to make positive rates of returns, at least some of them would, and that the more stable returns of lower-budget films could be used, at least partially, to offset the potential losses associated with the former. In the case of the five majors—Paramount, MGM, Warners, Fox/20th Century-Fox and RKO—this strategy complemented the requirement for the film studios to produce product for the distribution and exhibition wings of their organizations.

Conclusion

The use of production budgets as a proxy for production, artistic and star inputs is insensitive to the unique contributions of the contracted workforce to the finished product. It is this intangible element together with the demand of filmgoers for films which are in some way novel which makes film making such a risky activity. Certainly, the R^2 results derived from Warners' accounts confirm the earlier analysis of the MGM ledger concerning the risks involved in 'hit' production, with, overall, 44 per cent (1–0.56) of box-office performance in the US explained by factors other than the film budget. Undoubtedly, the model is simplistically specified. It may well be possible to get closer to the contributions made by particular film inputs through deconstructing the proxy variable—a procedure not attempted in this study—to take into account, for example, genre type and 'star' qualities, the subject of the next two chapters. The use of regression techniques, however, has provided a means of investigating the business environment of film in which only a small number of films in any one season could expect to become 'hits', and in so doing enjoy the disproportionate box-office rewards that this entailed. In particular, the tests showed that although a positive relationship prevailed between the production costs of a film and its box-office performance, this relationship was far from perfect: indeed, the rule appears to have been that the more that was spent on making a film the greater the potential variance of its performance parameters.

8

Genres, Generic Lineages and 'Hits'

...a close study of any long-lasting genre shows either that it changes formally over time, or that the so-called genre had a comparatively short life.

Vincent Porter[1]

In his account of Hollywood's commercial development, John Izod explains that genre classifications perform the essential task of codifying the film product, enabling audiences to easily form expectations, and understand the experience, of cinemagoing. For Izod, genre enables 'the uniqueness of the product to be strikingly de-emphasised.'[2] When it comes to assessing the significance of genre as an element in the financial success or otherwise of films, however, difficulties arise when one attempts to organize a classification schema devoid of imprecision, and to assign films in accordance with it. At an abstract level these difficulties stem from the unique irreducibly artistic form of individual film products which is particularly evident at the 'hit' end of the market. Inevitably, there will always be films which cut across genre classifications, however defined, as well as differences between commentators as to the respective characteristics of particular films: for instance, is Hitchcock's *The 39 Steps* primarily a thriller or a comedy, or should we devise a distinct inclusive classification 'comedy-thriller'?

This chapter addresses these issues, beginning with a simple classification system to measure the frequency of popular genres in Britain during the 1930s. However, the greater part of the chapter is devoted to an analysis of the complex and dynamic nature of genres,

155

concentrating on the popular musical and other genres with prominent musical elements. In proposing a profit-driven model, the work introduces the idea of seminal films, defined as those films which change fundamentally audiences' perceptions, leading to the emergence of stylistic/aesthetic lineages within and across genre.

Popular genres in Britain

A record of the most popular genres in Britain during the 1930s is set down in Table 8.1. It is based on a classification system in which the genre categories of Adventure, Comedy, Drama, Fantasy, Horror, Musical, Romance, Thriller/Crime and Western have been applied to Top 50 films listed in the annual Top 100 films found in Appendix 3 for the period 1932–37. The three main genre categories of the period were drama (inclusive of romantic drama, costume drama, and drama with songs), comedy (inclusive of romantic comedy and comedy with songs), and musicals. It is interesting to note that not a single western made the annual Top 50 category during the period. The only significant shift in the pattern of genre composition occurred in 1934 when the number of musicals making the Top 50 lists doubled, with a compensatory fall in comedies.

The place of music in the affections of domestic audiences is amplified by grouping together musicals with those films which contained singing that was not central to their intent, however entertaining it may have been incidentally.[3] At the margin, however, this line is somewhat arbitrary and different readings will lead to different classifications. For instance, whereas the Eddie Cantor starring vehicles *Kid From Spain* (1933) and *Kid Millions* (1935) are perceived as comedies with songs, his film *Roman Scandals* is classified as a musical. The films starring Shirley Temple, all of which have strong musical elements, are likewise not treated as fully-fledged musicals.

A further point of interest which emerges from Table 8.1 concerns the popularity and regularity of films, made on both sides of the Atlantic, about aspects of the British state—past and present: films which sought to explain, describe and applaud the unique and idiosyncratic nature of British institutions, at peace and at war, and the people who served them.

The extent to which the pattern of genre popularity outlined above is reflected in the 'hit' outputs of British and American studios is set out in Table 8.2. Here it is possible to obtain an idea of relative advantage. For instance, and not surprisingly given the culture-specific nature of much comedy, British studios take a significant, but not a majority, share of Top 50 films in the comedy genre, contributing in total 36 of the 79 films. British comedies were particularly successful during the early part of the period.[4] A feature of many of these British comedies was the inclusion of musical numbers, undoubtedly the consequence of the music-hall roots of many of the comedians.[5] Conversely, domestically-made dramas performed poorly in relation to those of Hollywood origin during the the early years, but became more prominent later, and exceeded the number of domestically made comedies in the Top 50 listings for those films released between 1936 and 1937. It is interesting to note the importance of romance as an integral ingredient in so many American dramas and the contrast with popular British films of this genre.

The contribution of British studios to the 'hit' musical was partial, with the exception of the releases of 1934 when a staggering eight films made the Top 50 category, matching the success of musicals emanating from Hollywood. This had fallen away to zero by 1937, when not even the Jessie Matthews vehicles *Head Over Heels* and *Gangway* made the 'hit' list.[6]

Film lineages: musical 'hits' in Britain, 1932–37

The preceding analysis is based upon the conception of genres as sets of distinct elements (categories) in a film classification system. The designation of these genre categories is a matter of historical convention and judgement but, once abstractly formed, it provides a means of labelling and differentiating films. It may be objected, however, that difficulties of definition and hence classification are made even more problematic because the genre form is itself subject to variation. Set against the backdrop of competitive capitalist production and market relations, those producers in pursuit of 'hit' successes sought either to create new forms within a general genre category— such as the emergence of the 'screw-ball' comedy with Capra's *It Happened One Night* (1934)—to modify existing forms, or to plagiarize the innovatory films, within legal limits. The interplay between all three processes over time meant that the conceptions and standards of intra-genre form were subject to change, as studios sought to establish or narrow competitive advantage. With the possible exception of the western, genre categories at the end of the 1930s had a different style and set of conventions from those at the beginning of the decade. The critical factor in the seemingly organic flux of artistic and technical

Table 8.1: *Genre classification of annual Top 50 POPSTAT films released in Britain, 1932–1937*

Genre	1932	1933	1934	1935	1936	1937	Total
Adventure	4	0	3	1	1	5	14
Comedy	15	15	8	15	14	12	79
Drama	22	22	21	25	24	24	138
Fantasy/science fiction	0	1	0	0	2	1	4
Horror	2	2	0	0	0	0	4
Musicals	4	8	16	7	8	7	50
Thriller/crime	3	2	2	2	1	1	11
Western	0	0	0	0	0	0	0
Total	50	50	50	50	50	50	300
Romantic comedy	1	1	0	2	3	1	8
Romantic drama	13	5	7	8	4	10	47
Romantic interest total	14	6	7	10	7	11	55
Comedy with songs	6	5	3	3	3	6	26
Drama with songs	1	1	2	3	6	0	13
Thriller with songs	0	0	1	0	0	0	1
Adventure with songs	0	0	0	0	0	1	1
Musicals	4	8	16	7	8	7	50
Musical content total	11	14	22	13	17	14	91
British state/Empire	0	2	1	3	1	4	11

Sources: Genre information taken from *The Motion Picture Guide*; Appendix 3.

inputs, which gave rise, in an unpredictable fashion, to new genre conceptions and standards, was the search for profit.

The attempt to uncover the dynamic competitive process in the market for films through an analysis of box-office revenue and production-cost information and genre classification, has produced interestingly indicative, albeit inconclusive, results in this investigation. Whilst positive associations have been uncovered between the scale of film budgets and popularity, the very general specification of the model and its moderate explanatory powers leave much unsaid and may reflect limitations on the extent to which inferential statistical techniques can further elucidate an understanding of relative success,

Table 8.2: *Genre classification of British and US annual Top 50 POPSTAT films released in Britain, 1932–1937*

Genre	1932		1933		1934		1935		1936		1937	
	US	Br	US	Br	US	Br	US	Br	US	Br	US	Br
Adventure	4	0	0	0	3	0	1	0	0	1	2	3
Comedy	6	9	5	10	5	3	8	7	11	3	8	4
Drama	18	3	15	7	15	6	17	8	19	5	16	8
Fantasy/ science fiction	0	0	1	0	0	0	0	0	0	2	1	0
Horror	2	0	2	0	0	0	0	0	0	0	0	0
Musicals	2	1	6	2	8	8	5	2	7	1	7	0
Thriller/crime	2	1	2	0	1	1	1	1	0	1	0	1
Western	0	0	0	0	0	0	0	0	0	0	0	0
Total	34	14	32	19	32	18	32	18	37	13	34	16
Romantic comedy	1	0	1	0	0	0	2	0	3	0	1	0
Romantic drama	11	1	5	0	6	1	5	3	4	0	6	4
Romantic interest total	12	1	6	0	6	1	7	3	7	0	7	4
Comedy with songs	1	5	1	4	1	2	2	1	1	2	5	1
Drama with songs	1	0	0	1	1	1	3	0	4	2	0	0
Thriller with songs	0	0	0	0	1	0	0	0	0	0	0	0
Adventure with songs	0	0	0	0	0	0	0	0	0	0	1	0
Musicals	2	1	6	2	8	8	5	2	7	1	7	0
Musical content total	4	6	7	7	11	11	10	3	12	5	13	1
British state/Empire	0	0	1	1	1	0	2	1	0	1	2	2

Sources: *Motion Picture Guide*; Appendix 3.

Note: The columns for 1932 and 1933 do not add to 50 because three (two in 1932 and one in 1933) German films are included in the annual Top 50 films.

because of the large number of contributory variables and their often unique juxtaposition. The problems associated with assessing the role of genre in the competitive make-up of a film have also been discussed. Whilst in broad terms it is possible to describe what types of film British audiences were attracted to, the more-or-less constant proportions of Top 50 films in the respective genre categories fail to capture dynamic changes within the genre categories and the reasons for them.

A distinctive approach to the evolution of popular films, not necessary bound by 'genre' rigidities, can be formulated from the box-office performances of particularly successful films. It is argued that such films, in revealing consumer taste at a moment in time, act as models for subsequent productions of similar type. Further, this influence is not specific to the originating studio but one which is felt across the production spectrum. These lineages fade as box-office returns decline. An example of this might be the high degree of popularity achieved by the Astaire/Rogers musicals, all made at the same studio (RKO), with common (but not identical) acting, artistic, technical, writing and directorial inputs stretching across a series of films between 1934 and 1939.The films are recognized as classic examples of the Hollywood musical and yet, stylistically and context-ually, they differ appreciably from the backstage musicals produced by Warners in 1933–34 and the successful MGM musicals built around Eleanor Powell from 1936. Jewell's (1994) figures show that after *Top Hat* (1935) the US box-office receipts of *Follow the Fleet* (1936), *Swing Time* (1936), *Shall We Dance* (1937) and *Carefree* (1938) fell whilst production costs rose: their success, defined in either box-office or rate-of-return terms, was in decline and was to end after *The Story of Vernon and Irene Castle* in 1939. Their decline coincided with new and distinctive conceptions of the genre emerging at MGM, just as they themselves had replaced the grittier product produced by Warners at the height of the Depression.

Using the musical as an illustrative field of investigation, the following analysis is based upon those 50 musicals which are ranked in the Top 50 films of the annual POPSTAT Top 100 lists, found in Appendix 3, for the years 1932–37—the most popular musicals of their day.[7] An excellent history of the formation of the musical is found in Barrios who argues that it was not until 1934 with the emergence of the Astaire/Rogers musicals that the genre settled into a narrow set of conventions which remained largely unchanged until the genre's demise in the 1960s.[8] Rather than recount past histories of the genre's development during these years, my investigation identifies a number of distinct lineages which cut across studio boundaries, and the films that were seminal to this development. To be seminal, a film will be innovatory and worthy of imitation. The reasons for this imitation will principally be based upon its box-office performance. Of course, the reasons behind this popularity are to do with its perceived filmic qualities vis à vis the perceived qualities of rival products placed on the market. The seminal film will therefore shape the conceptual, including stylistic, environment in which films are made. The extent of its influence will vary, being subject to both filmic and non-filmic forces. As Vincent Porter has argued,

> genre is little more than a potentially flexible format for the production of films, British or otherwise. What is more difficult to establish are the relationships between this enabling capability and the actual film texts which have been produced. For this, I suggest the critic needs to resist the lures of the synchronic approach adopted by the formalists and structural critics, and pursue a diachronic approach which examines the ebbs and flows within a genre, and the rise and fall of iconography, narrative and ideology over a period of time.[9]

For instance, prior to 1934 the musical had an unsettled history, both artistically and commercially. Following the enormous world-wide success of MGM's *The Broadway Melody* (1929), followed by *Rio Rita* (RKO, 1929) and *The Gold Diggers of Broadway* (Warners, 1929) an explosion of copy-cat production occurred in Hollywood. In the absence of precedent, these films reveal the search for ways in which to integrate narrative with musical expression and dance in a production environment in which the technology was newly conceived and highly restrictive. What followed was a discovery process in which each new musical was simultaneously imitative and innovatory. This process of frantic activity continued apace throughout 1929 and into 1930 when the first severe effects of the Depression were setting in. Suddenly, the demand for musicals dried up. Indeed, such was the scale of rejection of the genre that there are instances of films made as musicals but subsequently issued with the musical element edited out—*50 Million Frenchmen* (1931) and *Reaching for the Moon* (1931) are such examples, illustrating the fact that creative prestige counted for little.[10]

Production of musicals more or less came to a standstill, with the exception of Ernst Lubitsch at Paramount 'whose prestige and clout was such that he could choose his own projects.'[11] Lubitsch filmed *The Smiling Lieutenant* during the early months of 1931, starring Maurice Chevalier, with whom he had worked before on *The Love Parade* (1929), alongside Claudette Colbert and Miriam Hopkins, both still relative newcomers to films at that time. The film was based upon Oscar Straus's operetta *The Waltz Dream* and became Paramount's biggest grossing film of 1931. Barrios maintains that 'there were simply no works of wit or allusion—or musical humour—to compare with it. But the success was seen as a tribute to the strength of the Chevalier–

Lubitsch partnership, not as a bucking of the antipathy toward movie musicals.'[12]

The operetta lineage

This leads to the first musical featured in the POPSTAT Top 50 lists for 1932—the Lubitsch directed *One Hour with You*,[13] again starring Chevalier, but this time partnered by Jeanette MacDonald with whom he had also co-starred in *The Love Parade*. Set in contemporary Paris, it is a film which Barrios describes as the logical successor to Lubitsch's three earlier comedy operettas and one which is 'intended solely as a devastating polished romp and an étude in cinematic fluidity'.[14] Barrios reports that the film cost $1.1 million and was a major box-office success.[15]

The next film in this lineage—*Love Me Tonight*—was directed by Rouben Mamoulian, in the Lubitsch mould. The film was again set in contemporary Paris and starred Chevalier and MacDonald, but this time told the romantic and comic story of a Princess' attachment to a humble tailor. For Barrios, '*Love Me Tonight* was conceived not so much as a film with music, as music itself put onto film, with the textbook elements of melody, harmony, rhythm and texture laid out either in sequence or in conjunction', with 'every scene finding a new way to advance the story, music and image minutely calibrated yet with exuberant lightness... Mamoulian acknowledges his sources, borrows a bit, and then moves beyond them.'[16] However, although the film received a great deal of praise from the critics and did well in the urban centres of the US, it lost money. Clearly, the film was popular but not popular enough.[17]

At this point the lineage, as far as musicals are concerned, moved from Paramount. The studio simply stopped making operettas and opened a new lineage based upon the popular singer, Bing Crosby, who had made an impact in *The Big Broadcast* (1932). The new lineage was overtly more populist, designed to appeal to more general, non-urban, audiences. Crosby's musicals of 1933 *College Humour*, *Too Much Harmony*, and *Going Hollywood* (released in Britain in 1934) all achieved popular success in Britain being ranked 50th, 47th and 72nd respectively. For Barrios, they represented a formulaic approach to the genre: in lamenting the loss of the Lubitsch tradition he comments that 'seldom would the studio regain its spirit and daring'.[18] This apparent discontinuity at Paramount needs to be tempered somewhat through the recognition that whilst Lubitsch was no longer involved in operetta production for the studio, his reversion to non-musical, sophisticated romantic comedies, such as *Trouble in Paradise* (1932) and *Design For Living* (1933), very much continued this style of film-making. We have here, then, an example of a lineage which cuts across genre.[19] Chevalier, in the meantime, had been given films with smaller budgets. His *Bedtime Story* (1933) was immensely popular in Britain taking a POPSTAT Top 10 position. This romantic comedy with songs was his last starring film for Paramount. MGM took up his contract and immediately re-formed the Lubitsch, Chevalier and MacDonald team in *The Merry Widow* (1934).[20]

From this point onwards the operetta lineage was extended in the US principally by MGM and Columbia.[21] The latter bought the contract of Grace Moore—a genuine diva—and made a series of highly successful operettas—*One Night of Love*[22] (1934), *Love Me Forever*[23] (1935), *The King Steps Out* (1935) and *When You're in Love* (1937)[24]— which were placed 2nd, 5th, 35th and 24th respectively in Britain in the annual POPSTAT lists.[25] Of the American box-office performance of the first of these films, Barrios observes, 'True to such prestige events, the grosses were far more impressive in larger cities than elsewhere, yet remained sufficient for rival studios to scramble about for their own photogenic opera stars.'[26]

MGM's contribution to the operetta lineage centres on the films of Jeanette MacDonald. During the period of this study she made seven films, details of which, including box-office performance, are presented in Table 8.3. It is clear that the pairing of Jeanette MacDonald with Nelson Eddy led to a substantial improvement in financial performance for MGM, with domestic box-office increasing to foreign earnings levels. *Rose Marie* yielded the studio a 73 per cent return on production and distribution costs. Although the box-office and POPSTAT indicators suggest that their next production, *Maytime*, proved even more popular, the returns to the studio are much lower owing to the enormous increase in costs over the previous film.[27] MacDonald's next film, this time paired with Allan Jones in *The Firefly*, saw the return of production costs to Rose Marie level. However, both returns and popularity declined, causing MGM to re-form the MacDonald/Eddy partnership. They subsequently made another five films—*The Girl From the Golden West* (1938), *Sweethearts* (1938) (in modern dress), *Bitter Sweet* (1940), *New Moon* (1940) and finally *I Married an Angel* (1942) (in modern dress)—the last of which lost the studio $725,000.

A final strand to the operetta lineage drawn from those POPSTAT

Table 8.3: *MGM operettas 1932–1937, starring Jeanette MacDonald*[a]

Film	US box-office $000s / POPSTAT rank in year of release (1)	US box-office $000s (2)	Foreign box-office $000s (3)	Prod'n + distr'n cost $000s (4)	Profit $000s (5)	Percentage rate of return (6)
The Cat and the Fiddle (1934) Co-star: Ramon Novarro Dir: William K. Howard	40	455	644	1,241	-142	-11.44
The Merry Widow (1934) Co-star: Maurice Chevalier Dir: Ernst Lubitsch	11	861	1,747	2,721	-133	-4.15
Naughty Marietta (1935) Co-star: Nelson Eddy Dir: W.S. Van Dyke II	74	1,058	999	1,650	407	24.67
Rose Marie (1936) Co-star: Nelson Eddy Dir: W.S. Van Dyke II	28	1,695	1,820	2,027	1488	73.41
Maytime (1937) Co-star: Nelson Eddy Dir: Robert Z. Leonard	14	2,183	1,823	3,363	594	17.41
The Firefly (1937) Co-star: Allan Jones Dir: Robert Z. Leonard	65	1,244	1,430	2,511	163	6.49

Source: Table 7.1.

Note: a. The film *San Francisco* (1936), pairing MacDonald with Clark Gable, is classified as a drama with songs. Even though MacDonald sings, the film is only a distant relation to the operetta lineage.

annual Top 50 films, 1932–37, is one which emerged in Britain but was closely associated with German operetta. This association was strengthened by the flight from Germany of whole sections of its intelligentsia following the accession of Hitler in 1933. Seminal to the development of the indigenous strand of not just the operetta lineage, but the British musical as a whole, was *Sunshine Susie* (1931).[28] Made and released in the year before the start of this investigation, the film had been an outstanding success in Britain. Rachael Low comments that 'Cheaply made, the film was one of the most profitable of the period and although not the first British musical it was certainly the best so far'.[29] Shot in Gainsborough's Islington studio, Victor Saville directed this re-make of the German original (*Die Privatesekretärin*), produced by Herman Fellner and re-starring Renate Müller and co-starring Jack Hulbert.

From Appendix 3, the following films can be grouped as the most popular British operettas of the period under investigation: *Tell Me Tonight* (1932)—ranked 18th; *Waltz Time* (1933)—ranked 14th; *Bitter Sweet* (1933)—ranked 16th; *Blossom Time* (1934)—ranked 6th; *Chu Chin Chow* (1934)—ranked 13th; *Evensong* (1934)—ranked 28th; *My Song for You* (1934)—ranked 29th; *Princess Charming* (1934)—ranked 41st; *Unfinished Symphony* (1934)—ranked 49th; *Heart's Desire* (1935)—ranked 26th. Their German connection is evident. The first film in this list, *Tell Me Tonight*, was released as an English-language version of a German production made by Cine Allianz, who were also responsible for *My Song for You* and *Unfinished Symphony* as joint productions with Gaumont-British. *Waltz Time*, taken from the Johann Strauss opera *Die Fledermaus*, was made at the Shepherd's Bush studio of Gaumont-British: the director, William Thiele, producer, Herman Fellner, co-star Fritz Schultz, and art designer, Alfred Junge, were all German. The German connection continues with *Blossom Time* and *Heart's Desire*, both directed by the German director Paul L. Stein and starring the Austrian tenor Richard Tauber. Finally, on this tack, Austrian actor/tenor Fritz Kortner co-starred in *Chu Chin Chow* and *Evensong*.

Unfortunately, no production cost or box-office information concerning these Anglo-German and British operettas has been uncovered. Their POPSTAT ratings suggest that they were as popular with British audiences as their Hollywood counterparts. Clearly, the early demise of British operettas from Top 50 positions after 1935 was not the result of changing British audience taste, as the popularity of the films of Jeanette MacDonald and Grace Moore showed. However, whereas the Hollywood product, although expensive, could depend upon a substantial contribution to its overall box-office receipts from foreign sales, this was not the case for British productions, which were largely dependent upon the much smaller domestic market.[30] Accordingly, budgets were much smaller, although films in this genre continued to be relatively expensive to produce. For instance, the two Tauber films made by British International Pictures were expensive by BIP standards. Rachael Low comments that *Blossom Time* 'was a major event for the company, costing far more than its other films',[31] but even so, she maintains that the studio 'was not prepared to go to the expense of producing a true operetta, of the type for which he was so well known, or of providing him with adequate musical support'.[32]

The studio's other ventures into this form were less successful, with their production of *My Song Goes Round the World* (1934) starring the lesser known Swiss tenor, Joseph Schmidt, flopping in 347th position. *I Give My Heart* and *Invitation to the Waltz* were two further operetta efforts from BIP which failed to make the POPSTAT Top 50 in 1935, being placed 75th and 225th respectively. The lineage could also stretch to include BIP's production of *Abdul The Damned* (1935). The film was again heavily dependent upon German input. Produced by Max Schach, who according to Low part-financed the venture, directed by Karl Grüne and starring Fritz Kortner, the film had a significant music component, composed by Hans Eisler, including a large-scale production number with dancing girls.[33]

Along with the much smaller budgets, the failure to find an indigenous operetta star who could capture the loyalty of domestic audiences worked against the potential of this genre from the middle years of the decade. Of Evelyn Laye, Low writes: 'As for Saville, his *Evensong* in 1934 was Balcon's third and final bid to turn Evelyn Laye, the beautiful English-rose singer into a film star...(after which) this pretty, ladylike singer returned to the stage.'[34] Although all three films were popular, they were not among the most popular of their day and probably did not cover their budgets. Anna Neagle, although undoubtedly a crowd-puller following the success of Nell Gwyn (1933), did not have the quality of voice to carry a lead singing role.[35] Even though considered by many to be the leading female star in British films, her screen presence whether as singer or dancer was not sufficient to make her later musicals, *Limelight* (1936), *The Three Maxims* (1937) and *London Melody* (1937), into major 'hits', these being placed 99th, 93rd and 159th respectively.

The operetta was an obvious model for film-makers to adopt with the coming of sound. Although it re-emerged as a major film form during the 1950s, a break in the lineage can be traced back to the war years, and specifically to the failure of Jeanette MacDonald's and Nelson Eddy's last co-starring film for MGM in 1942. Prior to this, however, operetta had become an expensive and occasional product dominated by the MacDonald/Eddy pairing at MGM and Grace Moore at Columbia. To caricature, films in the lineage were mostly set in Europe, often in Vienna or Paris, and regularly had historical settings. The plots were romances, often built around the principal as a singer, who is discovered, with the romance taking the form of sacrifice, mistaken identity, or amatory misunderstanding. Their singing style was a throwback to a classical tradition, in contrast to the more populist style of the Broadway show and the jazz-inflected music of the dance band. One suspects that these films were more than likely to appeal to the middle aged and middle class, although a classically-tinged singing turn was always an important component in the programmes of the music hall in Britain and vaudeville in the US.

The backstage musical lineage

The collapse in the popularity of the musical genre, which accompanied the onset of the Depression in the US, was ended by a string of films produced by Warners in 1933. In response to corporate losses which peaked at over $14 million during the 1931–32 financial year the studio had dramatically pared down average production budgets from a high of $354,300 during the 1930–31 season to $275,600 during the 1932–33 season.[36] In this context the decision to spend $439,000 on a musical, *42nd Street*, represented a considerable gamble, the more so since the film represented a return to the backstage musical: 'the type of musical most associated with bringing the genre to a premature demise.'[37] However, in the style of its realization, *42nd Street* fitted comfortably into the post-1930 portfolio of films by which Warners came to be recognized:

> films which were topical and hard hitting, with urban subjects and settings such as crime, gangsterism, bootlegging, federal agents, prisons, night clubs, prostitution, newspapers, and backstage intrigues that provide recurring contexts, particularly during the first half of the decade.[38]

As can be seen in Table 8.4 the film was remarkably successful, particularly with US domestic audiences. Released at the height of the Depression, the film was timed to coincide with Roosevelt's inauguration and marketed as 'The Inauguration of a New Deal in Entertainment.'[39] *42nd Street's* mixture of collective exhortation and social realism carried by a flinty, coherent and fast-moving script appeared to strike a nerve with American audiences. The film juxtaposed the awkward but honest and homely qualities of Ruby Keeler to the more 'knowing' behaviour of the other chorus girls, whilst at the same time the hard-headed and often manic reality of putting on a show in Depression-riven America was contrasted with Busby Berkeley's spectacular and escapist song and dance routines.[40]

Barrios argues that *42nd Street* returned the storyline of the musical back to its 1929 origins and 'reestablished formulas that people like

Table 8.4: *Warners' musicals 1932–1937*

Film	POPSTAT rank in year of release (1)	US box-office $000s (2)	Foreign box-office $000s (3)	Ratio US/foreign box-office (4)	Total box-office $000s (5)	Production cost $000s (6)	Distribution cost $000s (7)	Profit $000s (8)	Rate of return (9)
42nd Street (1933)	10	1,438	843	1.71	2,281	439	843.97	998.03	77.79
Gold Diggers of 1933 (1933)	29	2,202	1029	2.14	3,231	433	1,195.47	1602.53	98.41
Footlight Parade (1933)	12	1,601	815	1.96	2,416	703	893.92	819.08	51.29
Dames (1934)	53	1,057	456	2.32	1,513	779	559.81	174.19	13.01
Wonder Bar (1934)	17	1,264	771	1.64	2,035	675	752.95	607.05	42.51
20 Million Sweethearts (1934)	71	821	392	2.09	1,213	202	448.81	562.19	86.38
Flirtation Walk[a] (1934)	142	1,062	471	2.25	1,533	479	567.21	486.79	46.53
Happiness Ahead (1934)	96	485	344	1.41	829	242	306.73	280.27	51.08
Sweet Adeline (1935)	164	396	271	1.46	667	635	246.79	-214.79	-24.36
Broadway Gondolier (1935)	80	795	324	2.45	1,119	397	414.03	307.97	37.97
Sweet Music (1935)	171	684	210	3.26	894	420	330.78	143.22	19.08
Gold Diggers of 1935 (1935)	68	897	468	1.92	1,365	567	505.05	292.95	27.33
Go Into Your Dance[b] (1935)	89	912	489	1.87	1,401	703	518.37	179.63	14.71
In Caliente (1935)	120	529	402	1.32	931	558	344.47	28.53	3.16
Stars Over Broadway (1936)	212	401	181	2.22	582	375	215.34	-8.34	-1.41
I Live For Love[c] (1935)	301	198	116	1.71	314	194	116.18	3.82	1.23
Shipmates Forever (1935)	104	1,070	392	2.73	1,462	508	540.94	413.06	39.38
Colleen (1936)	196	834	255	3.27	1,089	552	402.93	134.07	14.04
Singing Kid (1936)	112	649	238	2.73	887	614	328.19	-55.19	-5.86
Hearts Divided (1936)	256	429	173	2.48	602	826	222.74	-446.74	-42.60
Broadway Hostess (1936)	395	236	97	2.43	333	165	123.21	44.79	15.54
Singing Marine (1936)	233	1,130	270	4.19	1,400	669	518	213	17.94
Cain and Mabel (1936)	78	900	562	1.60	1,462	1,108	540.94	-186.94	-11.34
Ready Willing and Able (1937)	267	451	125	3.61	576	516	213.12	-153.12	-21.00
Gold Diggers of 1937 (1936)	29	954	441	2.16	1,395	736	516.15	142.85	11.41
Stage Struck (1936)	181	607	176	3.45	783	492	289.71	1.29	0.17
Sing Me a Love Song[d] (1937)	274	380	174	2.18	554	426	204.98	-76.98	-12.20
Varsity Show (1937)	439	1,249	216	5.78	1,465	1,114	542.05	-191.05	-11.54
Gold Diggers in Paris (1937)	n/a	541	194	2.79	735	875	271.95	-411.95	-35.92
Hollywood Hotel (1937)	n/a	1,094	255	4.29	1,349	1,141	499.13	-291.13	-17.75
Cowboy From Brooklyn (1938)	n/a	588	179	3.28	767	572	283.79	-88.79	-10.38

Table 8.4 continued

Sources: The Schaefer Ledger; Glancy (1995); Appendix 3.

Notes: The accounting conventions are the same as those followed in Table 8.1. The Schaefer Ledger does not include distribution costs. These have been computed at the rate of 0.37 of Gross Box-Office revenue following Sedgwick's (1994b) analysis of RKO data presented by Jewell (1994). The n/a entry in column 1 for the last three films indicates that their release extended beyond the end point of this study.
a. Released in Britain in 1935.
b. Released in Britain as *Casino de Paree*.
c. Released in Britain as *I Lived for You*.
d. Released in Britain as *Come Up Smiling*.

Lubitsch and Mamoulian had eradicated'. The consequence of its success was that 'a preponderant number of successful musicals for many years afterward would one way or another be direct successors of *42nd Street*'.[41] Certainly, *42nd Street* returned the studio a handsome profit—over three times its production cost—and not surprisingly led Warners to follow this success with two similarly styled musicals—*Gold Diggers of 1933* and *Footlight Parade*, both dealing with the drama of putting on a show in Depression America and featuring Busby Berkeley's song and dance routines.

During the 1930s Warners resembled a theatrical stock company, with contracted personnel appearing time and again in the studio's productions. Ruby Keeler, Dick Powell and Guy Kibbee appear in all three of the above-listed musicals. Lloyd Bacon directed the first and third of the three films, whilst Ginger Rogers appears in the first two and Joan Blondell in the latter two. *Gold Diggers of 1933* proved to be even more financially rewarding for the studio than *42nd Street*, being particularly popular with US audiences: the POPSTAT score suggests that it was a little less popular in Britain. It is noticeable from Table 8.4 that the budget for *Footlight Parade*, starring James Cagney, is 60 per cent greater than those of its two immediate predecessors, a factor which is explained by Berkeley's staging of what Barrios terms 'the most staggering water ballet in the history of liquid. If *Footlight Parade* contained nothing else of merit this number would have been sufficient to make it a hit.'[42] Although its box-office earnings were slightly up on those of *42nd Street*, the additional cost meant that the rate of return to Warners was considerably lower than it had been for the previous two films, although still a very healthy 51 per cent.

The next film in the sequence, *Dames*—another backstage drama, replete with Berkeley staged numbers, again starring Joan Blondell, Ruby Keeler and Dick Powell and featuring Guy Kibbee—was even more expensive to make than *Footlight Parade*, but this time the combination was relatively unsuccessful at the box-office, generating only a modest profit for the studio. Undoubtedly affected by the changing moral climate, brought about by the Catholic Church's Legion of Decency which led to strict enforcement of the 1930 Production Code from July 1934, *Dames* suffered from a downturn in interest in the formula which had made the previous three films so successful. Of the remaining musicals listed in Table 8.4 only *Wonder Bar* and *Gold Diggers of 1937* are placed in the POPSTAT annual Top 50 lists. Both were backstage stories, the first set in Paris and starring Al Jolson, Kay Francis and Dick Powell, and directed by Lloyd Bacon, who was also responsible for the second, again featuring Powell, this time teamed up with Joan Blondell. The post-1933 films move away from the social realism of the Depression and adopt a more escapist and optimistic form, which in the case of Berkeley's various contributions to the genre often crossed into metaphysical paradox.[43] For Barrios Warners' musicals 'increasingly lost their snap'.[44] Although this judgement was reflected in a lower level of box-office performance, the studio itself cut back on production costs, so that apart from the incredibly cheaply made *Flirtation Walk*, designed to exploit the popularity of the Powell/Keeler team, for the most part the films returned modest rates of profit. It is notable, however, that Warner's attempts to stage big-budget musicals in 1936 and 1937 ended when both *Cain and Mabel*, with the unlikely pairing of Marion Davies and Clark Gable, and *Varsity Show* made losses. By this juncture even Dick Powell and Ruby Keeler were unable to guarantee profits for the studio, although Powell proved popular when loaned out to 20th Century-Fox to star in *On the Avenue* in 1937, alongside Madeleine Carroll and Alice Faye—a film placed 31st in Britain according to the annual POPSTAT lists.

The demise of the Warners musical from the high point of 1933 is explained not only in terms of an audience growing tired of a repetitive formula, including waning stars, but also of developments elsewhere in the genre. In particular, the use of the backstage drama, which allowed producers to mount production numbers as if they were actually part of the show, and facilitated the separation between narrative (continuity) and production number (spectacle), was being challenged by the return of a musical form pioneered by Lubitsch and Mamoulian, in which musical numbers/dance were designed to simultaneously carry the narrative and provide spectacle, and revitalized at RKO by the Fred Astaire/Ginger Rogers team.

Rather than absolute decline, the generic lineage was taken up and remodelled by MGM from 1935 with *Broadway Melody of 1936*, followed by *The Great Ziegfeld* and *Born to Dance of 1936* and *Broadway Melody of 1938* in 1937.[45] Unlike MGM's expensive operettas, which were more-or-less equally popular at home and abroad, this second strand of musical was relatively much more popular with US home audiences, with three of the four films mentioned above earning twice as much from this source as from overseas. The first, third and fourth of this quartet were directed by Roy Del Ruth, starred the dancer Eleanor Powell and were built around the tensions of mounting a new Broadway show. *The Great Ziegfeld*, which cost over $2 million to make, took the form of a musical 'biopic' which, according to the credit titles, was 'suggested by romances and incidents in the life of America's greatest showman Florenz Ziegfeld, Jr.' All four films featured extravagantly staged musical numbers, similar in form to Busby Berkeley's contributions to the Warners musical. A number of important differences exist, however. Berkeley's stagings were essentially decadent spatial fantasies dominated by lustful sexual images, whereas the MGM films celebrate the decency of romantic love and the greatness of America, presented in theatrically 'possible' musical numbers.[46] Further, following the relative financial failure of *Dames* in 1934, Warners had cut back on production budgets. If a comparison is made between those budgets listed in Table 8.4 and the MGM budgets found in Table 7.1 it is apparent that Warners was spending less than half that of its rival on musicals. MGM pursued a strategy whereby each of these films was conceived, designed and marketed as an outstanding production: it differentiated its musicals through expense at a time when Warners continued with Powell and Keeler in relatively cheaply made films based upon repetitive romantic situations.

It is interesting to note that in 1933, when the boot was on the other foot, MGM had attempted to position itself as close to the Warners musical as possible by making a hard-hitting, Depression-based musical, *Dancing Lady*, starring Joan Crawford and Clark Gable, with Fred Astaire, in his screen debut, as Crawford's dancing partner. Whilst not as successful as *Gold Diggers of 1933*, the film was comparable, in terms of popularity, with *42nd Street* and *Footlight Parade* and earned the studio a healthy financial return. The fact that MGM then dropped this generic lineage for the next two years in favour of operetta probably relates to the absence of contracted musical stars to carry future productions at the studio: it would appear that Gable was forced to work on the film against his wishes whilst Crawford's performance did not persuade the studio to cast her again as a musical performer until 1937 when she played the less (musically) demanding role of a cabaret singer in *The Bride Wore Red*.

The art deco lineage

Apart from the proletarian *Follow the Fleet*, and the biographical *The Story of Vernon and Irene Castle* with its Edwardian/First World War setting, the films of Astaire and Rogers take place in an environment of wealth, manifest in the sumptuous hotel/ocean liner spaces— decorated in art deco style replete with white telephones—that they occupy during the course of their eventful romances. The characters portrayed by the couple, however, do not represent superior people, but rather ordinary people who happen to operate in these luxurious places. For the most part, Astaire plays the part of a dancer, in various guises, at the height of his profession, and his role (in real life as well as in most of his films) is usually that of a jobbing artist who has access to the upper tiers of society only through performance. It was Astaire's genius that enabled him to define a style which transformed the way in which people thought about the art form. Barrios encapsulates his persona thus:

> His [Astaire's] natural reserve as well as his stage roles opposite his sister had made Astaire uncomfortable with the idea of romantic acting... All his affinities were defined in terms of musicality: dancer, singer, instrumentalist, composer. These, then, were what made sense to him to carry the plots of his films. Romantic pursuit and attainment, elated insouciance, rejection and even loss, were presented in Astaire's films most often as a song followed by a dance.[47]

The seminal film in the series of six made between 1934 and 1939 was the first in which the couple starred—*The Gay Divorcee*.[48] It is seminal because it represented a distinct departure for the musical and created a style, which their later films would follow, at the centre of which was a highly charged romantic intimacy between the two stars expressed in song and through dance.[49] The lineage was made possible, however, because *The Gay Divorcee* represented a good investment for RKO: its popularity with audiences resulted in a substantial profit for the studio, leading the latter to invest more heavily in subsequent productions. Some idea of the couple's popularity had emerged from the public's reaction to their earlier pairing in the conceptually extravagant musical *Flying Down to Rio* (1933), where they were billed as fourth and fifth ranking players. *The Gay Divorcee* represents the first of a series of collaborations between the couple, RKO producer Pandro Berman and studio director Mark Sandrich, who also directed *Top Hat, Follow the Fleet, Shall We Dance* and *Carefree.*[50]

Table 8.5 depicts a remarkable asymmetry of box-office performance around Astaire and Rogers' most successful film, *Top Hat,* the profits from which were more than twice that of the film's production cost. The rise in the films' budgets suggests a studio willing to invest heavily in exploiting the couple's unparalleled popularity. However, the decline in box-office receipts which followed *Top Hat* meant that the studio was increasingly spending more for each dollar earned through the box-office, to the extent that the last two films in the series made losses. Nevertheless, the fact that five of the series grossed over $2 million suggests that the decline in profits should not detract from the recognition that these films were immensely popular, both at home and abroad. In Britain, this popularity is reflected in the fact that four of the films obtained annual Top 10 POPSTAT positions between 1935 and 1937 with *Roberta* narrowly falling outside this band at no.12.

Jessie Matthews occupied a very similar cinematic space to that of Astaire and Rogers. Of her starring films Jeffrey Richards comments:

> It is true that Jessie's six vehicle films from *Evergreen* on were Art Deco fantasies, taking place in a highly stylized, high contrast, hermetically sealed black and white world of ritzy nightclubs, luxury hotels, ocean liners, newspaper offices, radio studios, theatres and mansions, where vast floor spaces were polished to a preternatural brightness, chrome gleamed and angular metallic accoutrements spoke of the influence of modernism. But the films of Fred Astaire and Ginger Rogers took place in exactly the same milieu and they were enormously popular and regarded as quite legitimate escapism.[51]

Like Astaire, Jessie Matthews developed her craft in theatrical musical comedy and revue, which Richards describes as a 'peculiarly middle class form of entertainment'.[52] Indeed, Victor Saville, her director in *Evergreen*, attempted to sign Astaire to play alongside her when he was

Table 8.5: *The Astaire/Rogers musicals*

POPSTAT rank in year of release	Film	Production cost $000s	Distribution cost $000s	US box-office $000s	Foreign box-office $000s	Ratio US/foreign	Total box-office $000s	Profit $000s	Percentage rate of return
43	Flying Down to Rio[a] (1933)	462	603	923	622	1.48	1,545	480	45.07
22	Gay Divorcee[b] (1934)	520	670	1,077	697	1.55	1,774	584	49.08
12	Roberta (1935)	610	955	1,467	868	1.69	2,335	770	49.20
2	Top Hat (1935)	609	1,268	1,782	1,420	1.25	3,202	1,325	70.59
7	Follow the Fleet (1936)	747	1,035	1,532	1,175	1.30	2,707	925	51.91
8	Swing Time (1936)	886	902	1,624	994	1.63	2,618	830	46.42
6	Shall We Dance (1937)	991	764	1,275	893	1.43	2,168	413	23.53
n/a	Carefree (1938)	1,253	546	1,113	618	1.80	1,731	-68	-3.78
n/a	Story of V.&I. Castle (1939)	1,196	546	1,120	705	1.59	1,825	-50	-2.67

Sources: Jewell (1994); Sedgwick (1994b); Appendix 3.

Notes:
Carefree and *The Story of Vernon and Irene Castle* were released outside the POPSTAT period and hence are not ranked.
a. Released in Britain in 1934.
b. Released in Britain as *The Gay Divorce*.

on the London stage in 1933/4 appearing in *The Gay Divorcee*.[53] Nevertheless, she was a genuinely popular star in Britain, although her box-office performance was not in the same league as that of the Astaire/Rogers films—but then very few were. In the period under investigation, the POPSTAT rankings of her films in Britain were: *Evergreen* (1934)[54]—14th; *First A Girl* (1935)[55]—27th; *It's Love Again* (1936)—32nd; *Head Over Heels* (1937)—57th; and *Gangway* (1937)— 70th.[56] Contracted to Gaumont-British, she was directed by Victor Saville in the first three, and in the last two by her husband, Sonnie Hale. Both *Evergreen* and *First A Girl* formed part of a portfolio of films designed to lever the studio into the American market as a major player, the subject of Chapter 10, but Matthews herself was never to appear in a Hollywood musical.[57]

Another highly popular British musical performer sharing a similar style and ethos with Matthews was Jack Buchanan.[58] Comparing the two, Richards observes:

Jessie like Jack, symbolized that carefree Art Deco world, where style was all and where stardom and romance were to be had in return for a tuneful song and a graceful dance.[59]

Of their popularity Rachael Low remarks:

Like Matthews he [Buchanan] became an extremely popular film star and his films, like hers, included many of the song hits which swept the country in the thirties. Records, sheet music and radio performances of these helped publicise the films and like her, again, he was as popular with British audiences as any Hollywood star.[60]

As with Astaire and Matthews, Buchanan had a long theatrical career in musical comedies and revues in London and New York. Prior to his signing with British and Dominions in 1931, beginning a six-year association with the producer/director Herbert Wilcox, Buchanan had completed a successful spell in the US. He appeared in his first talking picture, First National's version of the Broadway musical *Paris* (1929), with co-star Irene Bordoni recreating her stage role; he had also filmed a sequence intended for Warners' all-star *Show of Shows* (1929), which was released separately as the Vitaphone short *Jack Buchanan with the Glee Quartet* (1930). In December 1929 he had starred on Broadway with Jessie Matthews in the Cole Porter musical *Wake Up and Dream* before returning to Hollywood in April 1930 to star for Paramount with Jeanette MacDonald in Lubitsch's *Monte Carlo* (1930).[61] In the genre classification found in Tables 8.1 and 8.2, Buchanan's work has been classified as either 'comedy or drama with songs' on the grounds that the music component, whilst critical to the success of the films, was not essential to their make-up; they could have functioned adequately had the songs not been included, although I accept that this is a fine line to draw between the two types in this case.

Parallelling Matthew's career, Buchanan's earliest films also proved to be his most popular. His first major 'hit' in Britain was *Goodnight Vienna* (1932)—placed 6th in the POPSTAT list for the year—in which he co-starred with Anna Neagle. In the following year Buchanan starred in and directed two films, *Yes, Mr Brown* and *That's A Good Girl*, placed 21st and 28th respectively in the annual charts. Buchanan spent 1934 working on the London stage, but returned to films the following year with the release of *Brewster's Millions* and *Come Out of the Pantry*, co-starring the Hollywood stars Lili Damita and Fay Wray respectively. British and Dominions' large-scale products were now being handled by United Artists, and Low suggests that Wilcox intended that both should make an impact in the American market.[62] In the case of the first, she maintains that the film cost over £100,000 to make. As far as British audiences were concerned the two films confirmed his popularity, securing POPSTAT rankings of 17th and 35th respectively. His last Top 50 production was *When Knights Were Bold* (1936)—placed 41st—which was produced by Max Schach for his new company, Capitol Films, and distributed by J. Arthur Rank's newly formed General Film Distributors, again co-starring Fay Wray. His other musical films in 1936 and 1937 were less successful, with *This'll Make You Whistle* (1936), *Limelight* (1936) and *The Sky's the Limit* (1937) \being placed 64th, 99th, and 86th respectively in the annual POPSTAT lists.[63]

Comedies with songs

From the list of those musicals which were placed in the annual Top 50, but still to be discussed, only two might be considered to be comedies—*Roman Scandals* (1933) starring Eddie Cantor and *Sing As We Go* (1934) starring Gracie Fields. Both stars had built highly successful stage careers from lowly origins and were attracted into films by the salaries that they could command. Further, whilst these two films have been classified as musicals, both stars featured in a string of films in which the song element was a most important feature. In Cantor's case he was the leading musical star at the Goldwyn studio and from *Whoopee!* (1930) onwards was involved in expensive productions which showcased his zany talents. These films appear to have been hugely popular on both sides of the Atlantic. Apart from *Roman Scandals*—placed 3rd in 1934—his other Top 50 'hits' in Britain, during the period of this investigation, were: *The Kid from Spain* (1932)—placed 5th in 1933; *Kid Millions* (1934)—placed 14th in 1935; and *Strike Me Pink* (1936)—placed 16th. His first film for 20th Century-Fox, *Ali Baba Goes to Town* (1937), failed to make the Top 100 films for the year, being ranked 124th.[64]

Gracie Fields' seven films released between 1932 and 1937 were popular but not among the top ranking films of their respective seasons. The films and their POPSTAT rankings were *Looking on the Bright Side* (1932)—placed 63rd; *This Week of Grace* (1933)—placed 48th; *Love, Life and Laughter* (1934)—placed 65th; *Sing As We Go* (1934)— placed 37th; *Look Up and Laugh* (1935)—placed 111th; *The Queen of Hearts* (1936)—placed 44th; and *The Show Goes On* (1937)—placed 88th. Given what is known about Gracie Fields' popularity as a national celebrity, these box-office performances are surprising: this disparity was the subject of a detailed analysis in Chapter 5 and was touched upon again in the following chapter.

Earlier, the musical was defined as a film in which song and dance was integral to its make-up. This can be contrasted with those films in which songs and dance routines featured but were decorative rather than essential to the development of the narrative and the purpose of the film. Of course at the margin the difference between the two will be thin. The films of Eddie Cantor and Gracie Fields, as indeed those of Jack Buchanan, transgress this definition but certainly should be considered as films within the musical lineage. As can be seen from Tables 8.1 and 8.2, the number of films in the annual POPSTAT Top 50 lists rises from 50 to 91 if other generic films with songs are included, with the most important grouping being comedy with songs, many of which might be included as a branch of the musical comedy lineage. Many of these films were British, and between 1932 and 1936 this group was dominated by the vehicles of Jack Hulbert.[65] Again, like Fields, Matthews and Buchanan, Hulbert was a successful stage variety artist before entering films. His buffoonery and comic song and dance acts, coupled with decent production standards, made for films which were very popular amongst British audiences, with *Jack's the Boy* achieving the top spot in the 1932 POPSTAT ranking.

Child musical stars

Finally, mention should be made of the emergence of child stars during this period. The Shirley Temple phenomenon of the little girl who, according to Barrios 'phrased her songs with instinctive charm and danced like a pro'[66] was also experienced by audiences in Britain: between 1934 and 1936, her films were by far the most successful of any emanating from the Fox/20th Century-Fox studio. The spirited teenage star Deanna Durbin performed a similar role for Universal. Her first feature film, the comedy with songs, *Three Smart Girls*, was popular in Britain achieving a 33rd ranking in 1937. She followed this with the very popular backstage musical *100 Men and a Girl*—placed 10th in 1937—a film uniquely involving the activities of a symphony orchestra and featuring the conductor Leopold Stokowski. This teenage vogue peaked with the pairing of Micky Rooney and Judy Garland at MGM outside the period of this investigation.

Conclusion

Going beyond a static view of genre, this chapter has traced the development of the musical during the 1930s and identified three principal lineages: the operetta, the backstage musical and the art deco musical. In delineating the critical paths of each, attention focused on the seminal qualities of their principal films and the financial returns they generated. A life-cycle hypothesis proposed that films become seminal by attracting strongly, and often surprisingly, the attention of audiences, which in turn attracts the attentions of studio heads, and other film-makers, causing films to be made in a similar stylistic/ aesthetic vein. However, given the paramount requirement that audiences demand novelty, film-makers working within a lineage are bound to introduce innovations which move the lineage on from its original conception. This may be for better or worse as far as audiences are concerned. Nevertheless, the characteristics which are common to, and hence define, those films which make up a lineage are likely to decline in attractiveness to audiences over time, particularly in the context of new films emerging from other lineages, some of which will be seminal, which will also be competing for their attention. The selection of musicals discussed in the chapter comprises those that were amongst the 50 most popular films of the year of their release onto the British market, as identified by the POPSTAT index of film popularity.

Films are differentiated according to types as well as by their stars. Sometimes, of course, the two come together in a unique combination, as in the case of the Astaire/Rogers films of the 1930s: films that were differentiated absolutely from other 'dance' musicals through the genius of Fred Astaire and his on-screen relationship with Ginger Rogers. Such distinctiveness was non-imitable. Although Busby Berkeley's contribution to the musical was highly distinctive, he was not without rivals, such as Dave Gould, Bobby Connolly and Sammy Lee. The fantastic spectacles which he brought to the screen were decorative, often surreally so, and juxtaposed to the development of the narrative. In the case of the three 'hit' musicals made by Warners in 1933, Berkeley's numbers were allied to abrasive contemporary narratives of Depression-hit America carried by an ensemble of players. The enforcement of the Production Code during the following year led the studio to tone down its scripts, and in so doing gave greater emphasis to Berkeley's staged extravagances. It would appear from the box-office information presented in Tables 8.4 and 8.5 that in 1934 audiences were moving away from the Warners product in favour of the lighter, more fluid style of musical built around the Astaire/Rogers combination.[67] Arguably, the spectacles associated with the later MGM musicals were even more fantastic, but respectably so, reflecting the more staid outlook of studio head Louis B. Mayer.[68] Eleanor Powell became the focal figure, soloing in three of the four 'hits' made between 1935 and 1937. Jessie Matthews fulfilled a similar role for Gaumont-British in a series of five films made between 1934 and 1937, three of which made the POPSTAT Top 50 lists.

The operettas also required stars—Jeanette MacDonald (first with Chevalier and then Eddy) Grace Moore, and in Britain the Austrian Richard Tauber were particularly popular—but here the premium was on singing. Again MGM attempted to differentiate its product through lavishness but in the case of the operettas the expense was lavished on the general quality of the production values, rather than focused on the construction of elaborate structures for the staged numbers. The style set by Lubitsch at Paramount in the early 1930s was not to continue, at least not within the operetta tradition, but rather was absorbed into the new style of musical being made at RKO from 1934.

The atmosphere associated with the post-1933 'hit' non-operetta musical was generally one of optimism. In the Astaire/Rogers films the players moved in luxurious settings, far removed from the lifestyles of the greater part of the audiences that went to see them. This was less the case with the backstage musical, since the function of putting on a show was akin to 'work'. However, the narratives served the purpose of legitimizing the spectacle of a staged number within the context of a musical production and this allowed the studios to devise fantastic forms of entertainment which at best were imaginative and the antithesis of 'realism'. The operettas, post-Lubitsch, served up a diet of intense romance—sometimes tragic, sometimes fulfilled—often in European settings of the past, mostly involving at least one player who was associated with a career in classical music. In these films the singer and the songs were paramount: dance played a less important role. In contrast to the studio's backstage musicals, the MGM operettas generated as much box-office abroad as in the US home market. The popularity of the operetta form in Britain is measured not just by the success of the Paramount, MGM and Columbia products in Britain over the period but also by the number and success of British films, albeit heavily influenced by German and Austrian personnel, made in this lineage.

9

Stardom and 'Hits'

Her features, I decided, were very much like those of Myrna Loy. Myrna Loy was a Hollywood cinema actress I had seen many times on the silver screen, and up until then she had been my idea of the perfect beauty. But now I took Miss Loy's face and made it even more beautiful and gave it to Mary Welland.

Roald Dahl, *Going Solo*[1]

The economic properties of stars

Stars are human capital. They are the outcome of past investment decisions in the formation of an idiosyncratic persona—a process mediated by audience and publicity preferences—and function as a means of attenuating the financial risk associated with film projects, whilst paradoxically adding to it as a consequence of the high fees they are able to charge for their services. Who they are, what they might contribute to a project in terms of distinction, additional box-office revenue and cost are clearly important questions facing film entrepreneurs. By definition, their qualities are not easily reproduced and hence not readily replaced. This uniqueness makes any investment in them highly asset-specific. For example, the qualities which went together to form precisely Greta Garbo as a star could not be obtained elsewhere: Greta Garbo was, and indeed is, a phenomenon. Given the appreciation of these qualities by film makers and audiences, stars are able to seek rents for their labour in excess of the rewards attainable from their best alternative employment.

Under the classical Hollywood studio system the function of the

180

studio in developing this asset has been well charted.[2] It is easy to comprehend that, in incurring the expenses and risks associated with developing stars, studio executives were concerned with the payback. With the demise of the studio system, the corporate approach to stardom is less obvious. Stars are now much more likely to emerge as a result of a series of one-off bets than from the corporate fostering of a talent such as that of Bette Davis or Elizabeth Taylor. Either way, the explicit purpose served by stars is that of generating box-office returns from the film(s) in which they appear in excess of the extra expense of their employment. For this to happen, the star's screen image will need to be actively sought and consumed by that part of the audience which, at the margin of decision, would otherwise not pay the price of admission. Hence, a star may also be thought of as a commodity: one which is derivative of the set of film commodities in which he or she has appeared.

Sherwin Rosen has set down formally a set of economic properties which define what he terms 'Superstars': 'In certain kinds of economic activity there is a concentration of output among a few individuals, [which leads to] marked skewness in the associated distributions of income and very large rewards at the top.'[3] To apply this idea to the discussion it will be helpful to bear in mind the characteristics of film as a commodity outlined in the Introduction. In this context the term 'film star' refers not to the flesh and blood human being performing in front of the camera, but to the edited sequences of photographic representations of that person. Fundamentally, it is the mode of reception of these sequences by the moviegoers which constitutes, or fails to constitute, or ceases to constitute, that person's stardom. Therefore it follows that the technology which enables film images to be reproduced infinitely—with each print costing only a small fraction of the production costs entailed in making the negative—and consumed jointly without lowering the quality of the experience, applies also to the star-as-sequence-of-images.[4] Askoy and Robins put this well when they write:

> Film production involves producing master copies only once, but producing a different one each time. This means that new rounds of investment have to be dedicated to each new film product. Since there is no guarantee that a film will be a hit, investment can be more or less profitable, or, in the worst case, can be totally lost. [5]

The extent of the market for any particular film is therefore bounded by the existing institutional arrangements which define distribution and exhibition practices, and by its popularity amongst potential audiences. It is clear that the productivity of a film—the ability of a film to meet audience needs—is determined by these two factors. The productivity of a star is similarly determined, leading to the proposition that only a relatively small number of stars is required to meet mass audience needs. To put this differently, to be a film star is to be one of a very small group of actors capable of consistently generating photographic representations of highly idiosyncratic qualities which are extensively known and favoured strongly by audiences more or less everywhere and for which substitution is highly imperfect.

It is clear that the rational producer, in making a film commodity with the purpose of generating a return over costs, will prefer high to low productivity personnel at each salary level.[6] From this it follows that, where producers know about the likely audience appeal of most performers, the market will ensure that high productivity stars earn disproportionate levels of income as producers bid up the prices necessary to acquire their contracts.[7] These features of stardom have been well explained by Baumol and Bowen:

> The stars constitute another special group in short supply. In part, this means only that the very best people in any profession are always eagerly sought after... One of the important factors at work here is the demand of the mass media. A star who captures the affection of the public holds very considerable economic power as a consequence of the extremely large audience to which the mass media cater. If he agrees to appear in a film rather than live play, he may increase the number of viewers (and box-office receipts) by several million, and his earnings may be expected to reflect this fact... Yet, on the whole, the mass media have probably caused a reduction in the demand for (live) performers below the topmost echelon, since a single film or record often replaces thousands of live performances.[8]

At the top end of the market, Rosen argues that the heightened demand for the star, coupled with the reduced numbers of fellows who occupy the same 'talent' neighbourhood, cause 'small differences in talent [to] become magnified in larger earnings differences'.[9] Adler has taken this argument a step further by arguing that there needn't be any difference in talent between stars and non-stars since, once established, stars serve to attenuate audience costs of acquiring information about the variety of talent available. He writes:

> That is, if other artistes are not cheaper by more than the savings in search costs, one is better off patronising the star...Stardom is a market device to economise on learning costs in activities where 'the more you get the more you enjoy'.[10]

Steven Albert makes a similar point, maintaining that stars act as markers for their audiences: 'stars are important because they are the least noisy and most consistent marker for successful film types'.[11] For Albert, stars create particular viewing pleasures for audiences irrespective of genre, director and studio. It is they to whom audiences are attracted. His statistics show that only a very small number of stars can expect to sustain such a profile over time.

Adler's argument (and that of Albert by implication) is based on the principle of increasing returns to consumption, the opposite to the principle of diminishing returns which I maintain is essential to understanding why most consumers prefer not to repeat view a film: audiences get increasing pleasure from seeing the stars that they like in new roles. The volume of fan activity during the classic Hollywood period, including the widespread circulation of film weeklies such as *Picturegoer* in Britain, together with the centrality of stars to the sales pitch of films then and now, suggests there is truth in the Adler/Albert theory. One serious point of criticism of this approach, however, is its failure to deal with the rise and fall of stars and the dynamic nature of stardom.[12] Further, Adler, and for that matter Rosen, is surely wrong to suggest that audiences are not aware of substantial talent differences, and thus filmic contributions, in their appreciation of stars. Indeed, rather than being narrower, it is the case that the difference between top ranking and second ranking stars is greater than that between second and third ranking stars and so on: differences in perceived qualities are increased rather than reduced at the top end. The principal cause of Rosen's and Adler's difficulties lies in the treatment of stars as no more than skilled workers, where incremental differences in talent/skill can be identified and measured. Whilst stars need to be talented, mere talent is not sufficient. Inconveniently for economists, they will also embody some intangible property which can be thought of as charisma and which is the source of their stardom.

My account of the musical in the preceding chapter serves to illustrate the point that stars do have marked idiosyncratic qualities which people enjoy, but only exceptionally over a long period. This contention is further supported by the empirical results presented later in the chapter. For the most part, stars have short life-cycles and those who are able to extend theirs do so by changing the presentation of their peculiar qualities.[13] When they are at the peak of their popularity they represent something that is precious to film audiences in general and it is this famously difficult-to-specify 'something' that enables them to claim such high rewards.

The market value of a star as a commodity is determined predominantly by the relative box-office success of his or her previous films. Therefore, it could be expected that the value of a star who has appeared in a set of films with growing net box-office returns would be rising, whilst that of a star whose films have performed relatively badly at the box-office would be in decline. The ability of a contract to reflect this value is dependent upon its term structure. A seven-year term contract held by a studio during the classical Hollywood period would be re-configured to reflect the rising value of a star.[14] Such a process was cumbersome and favoured the studio, particularly where a significant portion of the term was still to run. A star in decline, on the other hand, was vulnerable to the decision not to continue with the option to retain her or his services.[15] In contrast, the rewards of freelance stars were much more likely to reflect market value, since rival producers would be engaged in a bidding game to secure his or her peculiar qualities.

In the light of the fact that the vertically integrated majors required upwards of 50 films per season during the 1930s and 40 per season during the following decade, it is not surprising that the studios adopted a corporate approach to the resource co-ordination problem: they chose to internalize the process through a set of term contracts, rather than acquire *ad hoc* human resources through the market for the express purpose at hand. This logic is apparent in studios' dealings with stars. The internal authority structure enabled studio executives to systematically plan for and direct the activities of those idiosyncratic assets under contract. (This often led to disagreements between stars and their executives concerning the appropriateness of the film vehicles to which the former were assigned—regularly leading to punishments.)[16] It also reduced the risks associated with not securing the contracts of desired artistes, where substitution was problematic, since it enabled studios to maintain what were in effect stock companies of players. In contrast, even where successful, the competitive market price necessary to secure a bundle of star and player inputs at any one moment, together with the additional transaction costs associated with constantly seeking such idiosyncratic inputs, project after project, through the market mechanism, imposes marked uncertainty upon the film-making process and may significantly and adversely affect the box-office to production-cost ratio. In effect, in the classical period the major studios were able to expropriate a proportion of the economic rents generated by their stars and in so doing attenuate the risks associated with film production. They did this by paying them less through their term contracts than the price which would have been necessary to secure their services on the open market. One measure of this was the fee obtained from 'loaning out' a star to another studio which invariably resulted in a 'wages-plus-payment' to the home studio.[17] As Michael Storper has written:

> Under the 'star system' if an individual achieved star status, the studio reaped the benefits of having him or her under a long term contract whose terms had been established prior to stardom. The studios thus obtained a monopoly over the actor's specific human capital by controlling the access to training at the port of entry to the labour market for stars. Since the maturation of stardom necessitated long-term investments in specific human capital, the star system encouraged vertical integration.[18]

Star identities

Stars not only sell films, they also tell us something important about viewing preferences and thence social attitudes. Such evidence is important to the historian. Jeffrey Richards, writing about British cinema in the 1930s, advances the case that 'the study of stars and their images and their popularity is central to an understanding of how cinema works in the context of society'. He argues that audiences are primarily attracted by stars rather than storylines. He supports this contention by reference to the importance of fan clubs, the plethora of fan magazines and the manner in which 'stars were ...assiduously promoted by the studio publicity machines'. In representing an ideal, stars needed to be 'both ordinary for the purposes of identification and extraordinary for purposes of admiration'. Further, Richards maintains that stars, like films, operate as ideological tools. In promoting a pattern of behaviour concordant with the perceived interests of the establishment, stars 'can be used to gloss over ambiguities and instabilities in society by individualising social and economic problems and resolving them on a personal level by use of their star charisma'.[19]

The first of these attributes seems a little restrictive in that, as a general rule, the storyline of a film was of critical importance in confirming audiences' perceptions of the star. Where a screenplay and accompanying role was at odds with the perceived qualities of a star, such as with Clark Gable's depiction of the Irish nineteenth-century statesman Charles Parnell in *Parnell* (1937), fan loyalty was not sufficient to guarantee box-office success. To put it another way, the 'someone' who was Gable had a certain 'something' which role and script needed to exploit in order that his star quality be re-affirmed. Also, in the case of stars such as Greta Garbo and Marlene Dietrich, the 'ordinary for the purposes of identification' characteristic presumably relates more to their portrayed emotional states and needs *per se* than to their highly unordinary personas. For Richards, Gracie Fields and George Formby personified these star attributes—each idiosyncratically accentuating the quality of 'ordinariness'—in British Cinema during the 1930s and early 1940s, by 'promot(ing) consensus, the values of decency and hard work, and the overcoming of problems by individual effort'.

In identifying stars of the period, Richards makes much use of the *Motion Picture Herald*'s annual chart (starting from the year 1936) of the most popular stars in the US and Britain, and in doing so draws attention to the premier positions taken by Fields and Formby amongst British stars in both the British and International lists. However, in assessing the relative popularity of stars, as was argued in the Introduction, the approach adopted here favours box-office returns in place of sample survey returns. To recast the argument, whereas the former is based on what customers actually paid to watch, the surveys represent more or less accurately the views of a self-selecting sample of customers based upon a selected group of cinemas. For instance, the *Motion Picture Herald* organized surveys of audiences attending programmes in the leading (pre-release and first-release) cinemas in the major US cities. These results were published annually in the yearbook—the *Motion Picture Almanac*. However, the evidence from this source is bounded and complete—it is not possible to further dissect or add to the results. The polls conducted in Britain were not based upon audience surveys but rather selected exhibitor returns on relative box-office success. As it is not known who the exhibitors were, and hence which cinemas were included in the survey, it is not possible to assess the reliability of their collective returns and the subsequent published annual star lists. Accordingly, the scraps of knowledge that have been passed down through social surveys, exit polls and exhibitor returns have been seta aside in favour of a measure based upon the films which audiences actually paid to watch. Put differently, in the absence (in the UK) of detailed box-office breakdowns of film performance, cinema programmes provide a more tractable source of information since they represent the choice available to customers at any one time, within a locality, at similarly priced cinemas.

The POPSTAT methodology provides a means of establishing star popularity. From the POPSTAT score for each of the 4,748 films marketed in Britain between 1932 and 1937, it is a relatively simple step to evaluate the popularity of the stars who appeared in them. A measure of star popularity (STARSTAT) is derived by identifying the leading stars of each of the 600 annual Top 100 films between 1932 and 1937 and attributing to them the POPSTAT scores of the respective films in which they appeared, weighted with the value 1.0 for primary star(s) and 0.5 for co-stars.[20]

The index of star popularity can thus be expressed:

$$STARSTAT_i = \sum_{j=1}^{n} POPSTAT_j * w_{ij}$$

Where STARSTAT = Star popularity statistic,
i = ith star
j = jth film
n = number of annual Top 100 films between 1932 and 1937 in which the ith star appeared
$POPSTAT_j$ = the popularity score of the jth film among the 600 annual Top 100 films, 1932–7
w_{ij} = the billing status of the ith star in the jth film, where the top billing star(s) is given a weight of 1.0 and second billing star(s) a weight of 0.5
* represents 'multiplied by'

The notation should be read as follows: the STARSTAT score of the ith film star—say Clark Gable—is given by multiplying the POPSTAT score of each of the annual Top 100 films (where $j = 1$ to n) in which he appeared by his concomitant billing status as either a first ranking or second ranking star and then summing the n products thus obtained.

The annual frequency distributions of STARSTAT results are set out in Table 9.1, and even though drawn from the annual Top 100 films of the period—rather than from the whole population of films—

Table 9.1: *Annual frequency distribution of STARSTAT scores.*

STARSTAT score intervals	1932	1933	1934	1935	1936	1937
>0–10	60	47	49	62	81	43
>10–20	58	69	63	77	63	67
>20–30	23	30	35	29	21	27
>30–40	20	17	18	20	17	19
>40–50	6	9	11	11	13	14
>50–60	6	10	5	7	9	7
>60–70	6	5	3	5	0	7
>70–80	2	3	2	3	4	2
>80–90	1	0	3	1	6	3
>90–100	0	2	2	3	2	0
>100–110	0	0	0	1	2	0
>110–120	0	0	0	1	0	1
>120–130	0	0	0	0	2	0
Total	182	192	191	220	220	190
Median	14.38	14.93	15.96	14.47	15.20	16.32

Sources: *Motion Picture Guide*; Appendix 3.

they nevertheless resemble the frequency distributions of POPSTAT scores for all films released in Britain, displayed earlier in Table 4.2. From Table 9.1 it is clear that a small number of actors were disproportionately popular with audiences, with the annual Top 10 actors in each year generating STARSTAT scores approximately four or more times that of the median actor.[21] A top star—defined as an actor with particular qualities which are favoured by audiences and difficult to substitute—is somebody who would expect to hold consistently a position in the upper reaches of these distributions.

Table 9.2 presents the truncated distribution of the Top 100 STARSTAT scores from the 568 principal or co-stars who appear in at least one Top 100 film during one of the six years that bound this enquiry. As would be expected, a similar pattern to that established in Table 9.1 emerges, wherein the 28th ranking star, Leslie Banks, generates less than half the STARSTAT score of the top ranking star Clark Gable, while the 77th ranking star, Mae West scores only a

Table 9.2: *The most popular 100 stars in Britain, 1932–1937, by film score*

Rank	Stars	Annual Top 100 films	Primary-billing films	Years in Top 100	STARSTAT score	STARSTAT index (Rank 20=100)
1	C. Gable	20	19	6	411.45	185.27
2	F. March	18	18	6	410.04	184.64
3	G. Cooper	15	15	6	365.54	164.60
4	R. Colman	10	10	6	333.88	150.34
5	W. Powell	15	15	4	318.77	143.54
6	G. Arliss	12	12	6	313.20	141.03
7	G. Rogers	11	11	5	310.15	139.66
8	C. Laughton	11	7	5	281.52	126.76
9	M. Loy	14	12	6	270.93	122.00
10	C. Colbert	14	13	6	267.44	120.42
11	H. Marshall	13	11	6	265.41	119.51
12	R. Young	12	10	5	262.06	118.00
13	R. Montgomery	16	15	6	249.63	112.40
14	M. Carroll	10	9	5	248.05	111.69
15	L. Young	10	9	6	244.79	110.23
16	W. Beery	12	11	5	244.17	109.94
17	T. Walls	13	13	6	240.87	108.46
18	F. Tone	14	5	5	238.91	107.58
19	F. Astaire	6	6	4	234.94	105.79
20	G. Garbo	8	8	4	222.08	100.00
21	J. Hulbert	8	8	6	218.40	98.34
22	M. Dietrich	9	9	6	217.31	97.85
23	J. Crawford	12	9	6	215.65	97.10
24	D. Powell	13	11	5	213.68	96.22
25	J. MacDonald	9	9	5	212.97	95.90
26	R. Lynn	11	11	6	212.30	95.60
27	C. Brook	8	7	5	205.82	92.68
28	L. Banks	9	7	5	204.68	92.16
29	J. Gaynor	10	10	4	203.48	91.62
30	L. Barrymore	16	5	6	203.33	91.55
31	C. Veidt	8	8	6	195.10	87.85
32	M. Hopkins	12	11	6	191.82	86.37
33	J. Matthews	10	9	6	191.58	86.27
34	B. Crosby	13	13	6	190.16	85.63
35	P. Muni	8	8	6	184.03	82.87

Rank	Stars	Annual Top 100 films	Primary-billing films	Years in Top 100	STARSTAT score	STARSTAT index (Rank 20=100)
36	A. Neagle	8	7	6	180.06	81.08
37	S. Temple	9	9	4	179.93	81.02
38	J. Buchanan	8	8	5	176.91	79.66
39	R. Donat	6	5	5	168.08	75.68
40	I. Dunne	6	6	4	166.70	75.06
41	K. Hepburn	10	8	6	166.02	74.76
42	C. Hardwicke	9	4	6	165.44	74.49
43	M. Oberon	8	3	5	165.41	74.48
44	G. Raft	11	9	6	163.52	73.63
45	J. Barrymore	9	7	4	160.92	72.46
46	S. Tracy	8	8	5	160.04	72.07
47	F. Bartholomew	6	5	3	158.33	71.29
48	R. Taylor	8	7	3	156.76	70.59
49	A. Menjou	12	4	5	154.47	69.56
50	J. Cagney	9	9	4	151.19	68.08
51	N. Shearer	6	6	3	147.96	66.62
52	E. Cantor	4	4	4	147.35	66.35
53	L. Rainer	5	4	3	143.52	64.63
54	M. Douglas	10	5	4	142.56	64.19
55	M. Chevalier	6	6	4	138.25	62.25
56	B. Karloff	6	6	5	136.74	61.57
57	G. Moore	4	4	4	136.32	61.38
58	L. Howard	5	5	3	136.27	61.36
59	D. Fairbanks Jnr	6	6	4	134.70	60.65
60	J. Harlow	8	7	4	134.43	60.53
61	J. McCrea	10	7	5	133.40	60.07
62	R. Hare	10	4	5	130.14	58.60
63	C. Grant	9	6	5	128.40	57.82
64	R. Massey	5	4	3	122.30	55.07
65	W. Baxter	7	6	4	120.56	54.28
66	E. Bergner	4	4	4	119.84	53.96
67	J. Bennett	8	6	4	119.57	53.84
68	F. Wray	7	3	4	115.30	51.92
69	K. Francis	7	6	6	112.76	50.77
70	C. Boyer	6	5	4	111.60	50.25
71	J. Arthur	5	5	3	111.56	50.24
72	S. Sidney	8	7	6	110.59	49.80

Table 9.2 continued

Rank	Stars	Annual Top 100 films	Primary-billing films	Years in Top 100	STARSTAT score	STARSTAT index (Rank 20=100)
73	O. de Havilland	4	3	3	108.59	48.89
74	G. Harker	9	4	5	108.40	48.81
75	R. Keeler	5	5	3	104.71	47.15
76	W. Huston	8	5	3	104.54	47.07
77	M. West	6	5	5	103.95	46.81
78	W. Hay	6	6	4	103.50	46.60
79	C. Courtneidge	5	4	4	101.57	45.73
80	F. MacMurray	9	5	3	100.70	45.34
81	D. Wynyard	2	2	1	98.98	44.57
82	H. Hayes	7	6	4	98.85	44.51
83	M. Dressler[a]	5	5	2	96.12	43.28
84	G. Brent	5	5	3	95.42	42.96
85	C. Bennett	7	7	4	93.12	41.93
86	G. Fields	6	6	5	92.48	41.64
87	J. Blondell	8	6	6	92.03	41.44
88	J. Oakie	8	4	5	91.41	41.16
89	E. Landi	6	2	5	91.06	41.00
90	D. Del Rio	5	5	3	84.97	38.26
91	B. Stanwyck	6	6	4	83.41	37.56
92	C. Chaplin	1	1	1	83.26	37.49
93	J. Loder	10	1	5	82.91	37.33
94	E. Flynn	3	3	2	82.88	37.32
95	C. Lombard	5	5	5	80.75	36.36
96	J. Benny	4	4	4	80.67	36.32
97	P. Robeson	3	3	3	79.81	35.94
98	R. Scott	6	1	3	79.73	35.90
99	W.C. Fields	4	4	2	77.82	35.04
100	G. Stuart	5	2	4	77.16	34.74

Sources: *Motion Picture Guide*; Appendix 3.

Note:
a. Marie Dressler died of cancer on 28 July 1934.

quarter of this amount. Another notable feature of the table is that the first eighteen stars listed appear in ten or more annual Top 100 ranking films, with Clark Gable appearing in twice that number. These were all highly productive stars, whose attraction to audiences in the US, Britain and probably the rest of the world was vigorously exploited by the studios which owned their contracts. Of the first twenty, Gable, William Powell, Myrna Loy, Robert Montgomery, and Greta Garbo were all MGM contract stars whilst Gary Cooper and Claudette Colbert were under contract to Paramount, Rogers and Astaire to RKO from 1934, and Ronald Colman to Goldwyn. Men take the first six positions, with women stars taking three of the Top 10, six of the Top 20 and ten of the leading 30 positions. The leading British-born stars either worked full time in Hollywood, such as Ronald Colman, George Arliss before 1935, Herbert Marshall and Clive Brook, or, like Charles Laughton and Madeleine Carroll,[22] commuted between British and Hollywood studios. Leslie Howard, although Hungarian-born, ought to be included in this transatlantic grouping. His five starring performances made him one of the most popular stars of his day, and his relatively lowly status (58th) in Table 9.2 is explained by his rather low output. This factor is dealt with later in the chapter.

The top indigenous stars can be grouped conveniently into three types—comic, dramatic and musical. The most popular over the whole period were the comic actors Tom Walls and Ralph Lynn who were invariably paired with one another in a series of middle-class drawing-room farces which also regularly co-starred Robertson Hare, and Jack Hulbert, the latter a top billing variety artist who was expert at delivering comic song and dance routines, and whose films, although again of the middle-class farce-type, were typically adventures situated in a variety of exotic and urban settings. Will Hay, who became a top ranking star towards the end of this period, and Cicely Courtneidge, who was rather more popular during the earlier years, make up the set of British comic actors in the Top 100 list. Perhaps surprising for many readers is the absence of George Formby from this account.[23] The *Motion Picture Herald* includes Formby in fourth place in its list of those British stars in 1936 (derived from returns collected during the year prior to 1 September 1936) with the greatest box-office appeal. His position is elevated to second in 1937 and thereafter to first place. Yet by the end of 1936, Formby's only film to date to receive universal distribution in the British market was the entertaining spoof about motor-cycle racing in the Isle of Man, *No Limit*, which was released late in 1935 and which is ranked 175th in the POPSTAT listings for that year. It is difficult to see how this performance warranted his high standing in the box-office lists produced by the *Motion Picture Herald*, unless the sample of showmen from which the results were taken represented a quite different grouping of cinemas from that used to generate the POPSTAT Index. His next film, *Keep Your Seats Please*, was released in August 1936 and is placed 122nd in that year's POPSTAT lists, and was followed in 1937 by *Feather Your Nest*, ranked 131st. Of all of the stars appearing in films in Britain during 1936 Formby is placed in 13th position in the *Motion Picture Herald*, higher than Robert Donat, George Arliss, Dick Powell, Bing Crosby, Grace Moore, Jack Buchanan, Gary Cooper, Ronald Colman, Eddie Cantor, Elisabeth Bergner, Claudette Colbert, Leslie Howard, Robert Montgomery, Myrna Loy and Mae West, amongst many other more likely candidates for popularity.

Leslie Banks, Conrad Veidt, Anna Neagle, Robert Donat and Merle Oberon form a raft of Top 50 dramatic actors whose work was either exclusively or for the greater part done in British studios in films which were popular with British audiences. Later in the period this group would be strengthened by Raymond Massey, Laurence Olivier and Vivien Leigh, and immediately outside of the period, Margaret Lockwood. Cecil Hardwicke and Gordon Harker, although not top drawing actors, appeared in large numbers of successful British films, as did John Loder, mostly in support roles. Interestingly, British cinema did not develop a male dramatic star with a screen image to match the more physical presence of top Hollywood stars such as Gable, March and Cooper.[24]

The lineage of the film musical in Britain has been examined in the previous chapter. Table 9.2 lists Jessie Matthews and Jack Buchanan as the leading British musical stars, starring in ten and eight annual Top 100 films respectively, both with rankings in the first 40. Gracie Fields' performance is more problematic. Although she appeared in six Top 100 films during the period, her films invariably secured low Top 100 positions in their respective years suggesting that for those audiences attending cinemas in the national sample set, Gracie Fields was less popular than is commonly thought, especially given her high rating in the *Motion Picture Herald* polls. This issue was the subject of investigation in Chapter 5 where it was shown that Fields was undoubtedly Bolton's favourite actor in 1934 and 1935.

Using the same typology of stars it becomes apparent that a section of very popular Hollywood stars worked within a light romantic comedy/drama milieu: an area which, with perhaps the exception of

Hitchcock's *The 39 Steps* (1935), was curiously under-exploited in British films during the 1932–37 period.[25] In this category it is possible to include William Powell, Ginger Rogers, Myrna Loy, Claudette Colbert, Loretta Young and Fred Astaire from the list of the top twenty performers.[26] The Top 100 list also includes a number of European stars who were known for their exotic/sexual appeal: namely, Greta Garbo, Marlene Dietrich[27] and Maurice Chevalier, all of whom worked from Hollywood, and Elizabeth Bergner and Conrad Veidt, whose careers were based in London.

Among the most popular Hollywood stars was a group of male actors whose names appeared regularly above the titles, but who were not generally the first listed star in their respective films. In this category it is possible to include stars such as Herbert Marshall, Robert Young, Robert Montgomery and Franchot Tone. Apart from Robert Donat there seems to be no equivalent actor amongst British stars. This is also the case with respect to a set of actors specializing in hard-boiled, working-class roles, often entailing criminal or sexually promiscuous activity. In this context, it is possible to think of George Raft, Spencer Tracy, James Cagney, Jean Harlow, Mae West, Joan Blondell and Barbara Stanwyck. It is interesting to note that the highest ranking of these stars—George Raft—occupies the 44th spot in the Top 100 and that therefore most of these stars are placed in the lower half of the ratings. This suggests that while these more 'realist'-type films were integral to Hollywood's output, neither they nor their stars were the most popular of the day. It is also the case that none of the above was contracted to MGM during the period.

Comic actors from Hollywood were much less popular with British audiences than their indigenous counterparts. If Eddie Cantor is counted primarily as a musical artist then only Jack Benny and W.C. Fields coming from this tradition make the Top 100 list and both are ranked in the nineties. Of the Hollywood melodramatic leads, Ronald Colman, Greta Garbo, Marlene Dietrich, Joan Crawford, Janet Gaynor, Irene Dunne, Katherine Hepburn and Norma Shearer feature prominently, whilst in the area of musicals the principal stars were Astaire and Rogers, Jeanette MacDonald, Dick Powell, Bing Crosby and Eddie Cantor.

As argued earlier, the ranking in Table 9.2 is biased in favour of those stars who were not only popular throughout the period but also were heavily engaged in film-making. Clark Gable admirably fulfils such a description. Bette Davis does not. Although she made just under thirty films for Warners during the period, only three were ranked in the Top 100 films of their respective British release year. Of these, she

194

can only be said to have been a primary star in just one—*Fashions of 1934*, alongside William Powell. Consequently, the apparent low productivity of the films in which she appeared, in contrast to the volume of work she performed as a featured contract player for Warners, resulted in her being placed 186th in the stars list and hence outside of the limits covered by Table 9.2.[28]

Table 9.2 is also biased against those stars who consistently appeared in a relatively small number of successful films. Such stars also have a claim to being amongst the most popular, since their successes were of sufficient magnitude to keep their names before the public. Table 9.3 seeks to redress this and, as can be readily seen, by ranking stars according to their mean STARSTAT performance—with the proviso that each appears in at least four Top 100 films during the period—a completely different pecking order emerges.

Apart from Ronald Colman and Ginger Rogers, both of whom retain their previous ranking status, the remaining 12 of the first 14 places in Table 9.3 are taken by stars whose position improves as a result of using a mean STARSTAT rather than an absolute STARSTAT measure. For Eddie Cantor, Grace Moore, Elisabeth Bergner, Luise Rainer and Leslie Howard this improvement is spectacular, and certainly dramatic for Irene Dunne and Robert Donat. Olivia de Havilland's low position in Table 9.2 can be explained by her late emergence as a star during period of this investigation. Each of the top big three in Table 9.2—Gable, Cooper and March—suffers in comparison, illustrating further the distinction between those high volume stars who were typically worked systematically by the studio that owned their contract, and those more occasional stars who tended to be freelance, moving between studios on a film-by-film basis. Table 9.3 shows that those stars who fell back spectacularly in relation to their standing in Table 9.2, such as Robert Montgomery, mostly come under the 'studio workhorse' category.

A note to Table 9.3 lists the most prominent of those stars who appeared in three annual Top 100 productions. The decision to draw the line at four annual Top 100 films over the period is arbitrary and had Table 9.2 been constructed using three rather than four films as criteria Errol Flynn and Paul Robeson, would have made the list with respective aggregate STARSTAT scores of 82.88 and 79.81. Actors who appeared in only three Top 100 films but who were to became major Hollywood stars during the last two years of the 1930s and beyond, were Nelson Eddy, Eleanor Powell, Vivien Leigh, Laurence Olivier, James Stewart, Bette Davis, Tyrone Power and Deanna Durbin.

195

Table 9.3: *The most popular 100 stars in Britain, 1932–1937, by mean film score*

Rank	Stars	Films	STARSTAT score	Mean STARSTAT	Difference in rank
1	F. Astaire	6	234.94	39.16	18
2	E. Cantor	4	147.35	36.84	50
3	G. Moore	4	136.32	34.08	54
4	R. Colman	10	333.88	33.39	0
5	E. Bergner	4	119.84	29.96	61
6	L. Rainer	5	143.52	28.70	47
7	G. Rogers	11	310.15	28.20	0
8	R. Donat	6	168.08	28.01	31
9	I. Dunne	6	166.70	27.78	31
10	G. Garbo	8	222.08	27.76	10
11	J. Hulbert	8	218.40	27.30	10
12	L. Howard	5	136.27	27.25	46
13	O. de Havilland	4	108.59	27.15	60
14	F. Bartholomew	6	158.33	26.39	33
15	G. Arliss	12	313.20	26.10	-9
16	C. Brook	8	205.82	25.73	11
17	C. Laughton	11	281.52	25.59	-9
18	M. Carroll	10	248.05	24.81	-4
19	N. Shearer	6	147.96	24.66	32
20	L. Young	10	244.79	24.48	-5
21	R. Massey	5	122.30	24.46	43
22	C. Veidt	8	195.10	24.39	9
23	G. Cooper	15	365.54	24.37	-20
24	M. Dietrich	9	217.31	24.15	-2
25	J. MacDonald	9	212.97	23.66	0
26	M. Chevalier	6	138.25	23.04	29
27	P. Muni	8	184.03	23.00	8
28	B. Karloff	6	136.74	22.79	27
29	F. March	18	410.04	22.78	-28
30	L. Banks	9	204.68	22.74	-3
31	A. Neagle	8	180.06	22.51	4
32	D. Fairbanks Jnr	6	134.70	22.45	26
33	J. Arthur	5	111.56	22.31	37
34	J. Buchanan	8	176.91	22.11	3
35	R. Young	12	262.06	21.84	-24

Table 9.3 continued	*Films*	*STARSTAT*	*Mean*	*Difference*
Rank *Stars*		*score*	*STARSTAT*	*in rank*
36 W. Powell	15	318.77	21.25	-32
37 R. Keeler	5	104.71	20.94	37
38 M. Oberon	8	165.41	20.68	4
39 C. Gable	20	411.45	20.57	-39
40 H. Marshall	13	265.41	20.42	-30
41 J. Gaynor	10	203.48	20.35	-13
42 W. Beery	12	244.17	20.35	-27
43 C. Courtneidge	5	101.57	20.31	35
44 J. Benny	4	80.67	20.17	48
45 S. Tracy	8	160.04	20.01	0
46 S. Temple	9	179.93	19.99	-10
47 R. Taylor	8	156.76	19.59	0
48 W.C. Fields	4	77.82	19.45	46
49 M. Loy	14	270.93	19.35	-41
50 R. Lynn	11	212.30	19.30	-25
51 M. Dressler	5	96.12	19.22	30
52 J. Matthews	10	191.58	19.16	-20
53 C. Colbert	14	267.44	19.10	-44
54 G. Brent	5	95.42	19.08	28
55 C. Boyer	6	111.60	18.60	14
56 C. Farrell	4	74.38	18.60	41
57 T. Walls	13	240.87	18.53	-41
58 C. Hardwicke	9	165.44	18.38	-17
59 J. Crawford	12	215.65	17.97	-37
60 J. Barrymore	9	160.92	17.88	-16
61 A. Jones	4	70.25	17.56	41
62 M. West	6	103.95	17.33	14
63 W. Hay	6	103.50	17.25	14
64 W. Baxter	7	120.56	17.22	0
65 F. Tone	14	238.91	17.06	-48
66 D. Del Rio	5	84.97	16.99	22
67 J. Harlow	8	134.43	16.80	-8
68 J. Cagney	9	151.19	16.80	-19
69 K. Hepburn	10	166.02	16.60	-29
70 Marx Bros	4	66.34	16.58	37
71 F. Kortner	4	66.06	16.51	37
72 F. Wray	7	115.30	16.47	-5
73 D. Powell	13	213.68	16.44	-50

Table 9.3 continued Rank Stars	Films	*STARSTAT* *score*	*Mean* *STARSTAT*	*Difference* *in rank*
74 B. Barnes	4	65.04	16.26	36
75 C. Lombard	5	80.75	16.15	16
76 K. Francis	7	112.76	16.11	-8
77 M. Hopkins	12	191.82	15.98	-46
78 R. Montgomery	16	249.63	15.60	-66
79 G. Stuart	5	77.16	15.43	16
80 G. Fields	6	92.48	15.41	4
81 M. Sullavan	4	61.50	15.38	31
82 T. Carminati	4	60.78	15.20	31
83 E. Landi	6	91.06	15.18	4
84 J. Bennett	8	119.57	14.95	-18
85 G. Raft	11	163.52	14.87	-42
86 B. Crosby	13	190.16	14.63	-53
87 E.G. Robinson	4	57.57	14.39	32
88 C. Grant	9	128.40	14.27	-26
89 M. Douglas	10	142.56	14.26	-36
90 H. Hayes	7	98.85	14.12	-11
91 A. Harding	4	55.66	13.92	28
92 B. Stanwyck	6	83.41	13.90	-4
93 S. Sidney	8	110.59	13.82	-23
94 J. McCrea	10	133.40	13.34	-35
95 S. Hale	5	66.61	13.32	9
96 H. Fonda	5	66.60	13.32	9
97 C. Bennett	7	93.12	13.30	-15
98 R. Scott	6	79.73	13.29	-6
99 W. Huston	8	104.54	13.07	-23
100 C. Clive	5	65.29	13.06	17

Sources: *Motion Picture Guide*; Appendix 3.

Note: Errol Flynn (with a mean POPSTAT of 27.63), Paul Robeson (26.6), Richard Tauber (24.7), Nelson Eddy (23.15), Eleanor Powell (22.81), Harold Lloyd (22.19), Evelyn Laye (21.2), Vivien Leigh (20.55), Laurence Olivier (19.49) were all prominent stars in three Top 100 films. James Stewart and Bette Davis were less so with 15.55 and 13.83 respectively. Diana Wynyard (49.49), Tyrone Power (30.15), Ralph Richardson (29.44) and Deanna Durbin (26.64) appeared in two. Figures in parenthesis represent their mean STARSTAT score. All would have appeared in the Table 9.3 had the criterion of a minimum of four films been lowered.

A single listing of the stars would require some mechanism of adjustment to integrate the two lists shown in Tables 9.2 and 9.3. It is not clear that the outcome would help clarify the distinct readings obtained from the two tables, and indeed it might blur the differences which emerge. Accordingly, the two listings have been left for the reader to weigh the respective merits of each in making an assessment of the relative popularity of any particular star.

Star profiles

Using the studio financial records from MGM, Warners and RKO, in conjunction with the POPSTAT scores achieved by the films in which they appeared, it is possible to chart the levels of popularity associated with particular stars over time and, in the course of so doing, identify something of their life-cycle as commodities. As argued earlier, the life-cycle of most stars is limited and subject to changes in taste and fashion. The profile of the Astaire/Rogers films for RKO, for instance (set out previously in Table 8.5) shows a concave-downwards pattern of popularity, when measured by box-office receipts. When the rising schedule of production costs of their films is superimposed upon this, the difference between the two schedules (profits) is similarly concave, with their last two films making losses and signalling the end of their filmic relationship. These relations may be stylized as in Figure 9.1.

Figure 9.1 may be conjectured as follows. In placing star A in film S the studio is sufficiently pleased with the profits made on the production to increase the budget of A's next production, film T, including promotion costs. This film proves to be even more success-ful, generating increased box-office revenue and profits.[29] The studio is encouraged to further increase the budgets of A's next film, V, and once again they are rewarded with renewed success, with increased box-office takings and profit. Star A has proven to be a bankable asset for the studio and is now promoted as a top ranking star in the light of the popularity that s/he has generated. However, a further increase in the budgets associated with the making and promotion of film W yields a decline in both box-office receipts and, given the rising cost schedule, profit. This pattern is continued over the next two productions, Y and Z, the last of which makes a loss. An interesting feature of this stylized framework is that the studio bets even more heavily on the star following the reversal of his or her fortune, presumably in an effort to recapture the previous success through

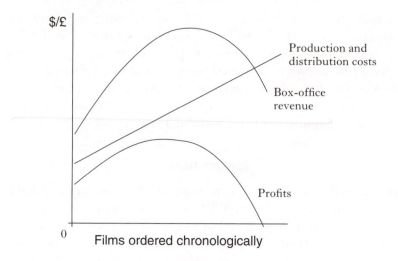

Figure 9.1: *A stylized representation of the life-cycle of a star, based upon the Astaire/Rogers RKO musicals*

enhanced production values. In pursuing such a course the studio is actually increasing its risk stance. Ultimately the evidence of declining popularity generated by the box-office returns convinces the studio that further heavy investment in the star is no longer a sensible bet.

The purpose of this framework is not to offer a template of conformity but rather a standard by which stars can be compared. The choice of stars in this section is unfortunately constrained by the limited availability of financial records, making a detailed assessment of British stars problematic. Clark Gable, Greta Garbo and William Powell were three MGM contract stars. They represent different styles of acting which were exploited through generically distinctive programmes of films: MGM built film vehicles which specifically exploited and propagated their idiosyncratic qualities. Garbo was an established star in 1932. Gable and Powell were both elevated to the status of stardom during the period of this investigation on the back of the box-office performance of their films. Before exploring their profiles it would be instructive to contrast them with that of Bette Davis, who was not a top ranking star during these years but rather a star who appeared in modestly budgeted films, not designed or promoted as top ranking vehicles by her studio, Warners, even though her performance in *Dangerous* (1935) earned her an Academy Award. Tables 9.4, 9.5, 9.6 and 9.7, detailing the financial records of the films featuring these four stars, are located in an Appendix to the chapter.

Bette Davis

The 28 films which Davis appeared in for Warners, released in Britain between 1932 and 1937, are listed in Table 9.4 (found at the end of the chapter), together with box-office and cost information.[30] It is clear that her films were not particularly popular with British audiences with the high US domestic to foreign box-office ratio reinforcing the low POPSTAT rankings of her films in the British market. Indeed, her three Top 100 successes are all in co-staring roles—with George Arliss in *The Man Who Played God* and *Working Man* and William Powell in *Fashions of 1934*. Unlike Gable, Garbo and Powell, Bette Davis appears exclusively in low- to middle-budget films during these years. It was not until 1938 that Warners began to invest heavily in her as a top ranking star, with *Jezebel* and *The Sisters* costing $1,066,000 and $921,000 respectively to make. The mean budget of the 28 films made for Warners was a little over $250,000. A distinct budgetary pattern emerges, showing production costs rising gently over the period interspersed with a small number of more expensive middle-budget films. Warners' failure to develop Davis as a top ranking star, evident in their reluctance to give her special treatment with regard to scripts and budgets, as well as salary, even following her Oscar success with *Dangerous*, led her to walk out of the studio and her contract during the following year.[31] What might have been good for Davis, however, was not necessarily good for Warners. From 1935 onwards, with the exception of *Kid Galahad*, Davis was employed as the leading star in her films, but she continued to be used as a flexible 'enhancement' resource which could be deployed over the range of dramatic properties being developed by the studio. Rather than have product designed for her, Davis was, for the most part, expected to fulfil her contractual obligations by appearing in routine productions of variable quality. It was only following her return to the studio, after the contractual dispute, that the quality of her material became more consistent, with each of the last four listed films in Table 9.4 costing $350,000 or more to make, and *Kid Galahad* (in which she co-starred with Edward G. Robinson) and *Marked Woman* and *That Certain Woman* generating healthy returns for Warners. It was perhaps this profit performance which persuaded the studio to elevate Davis to their slim list of superstars—at that time only Errol Flynn and Olivia de Havilland at Warners could be similarly tagged.

Clark Gable

It is clear from Table 9.5 that Gable was a very successful bankable star for MGM. Apart from the last film in the series, *Parnell*, all of the other 15 films in which he starred for MGM made profits. A distinct profile, which sees him moving gradually from low- and middle-budget films to those with a high budget, can be detected. Of his early high-budget films, his role in *Hell Divers* (1932) was second to that of Wallace Beery, then at the height of his fame—an order that was later reversed in *China Seas* (1935)—whilst *Dancing Lady* (1933) was a musical in which he did not wish to appear and was co-starred with the more established MGM star, Joan Crawford. More typical of these early years were the much lower budget films *Hold Your Man* (1933), *Men In White* (1933), *Manhattan Melodrama* (1934) and *Forsaking All Others* (1935) and a series of middle-budget films—*Strange Interval* (1932), *White Sister* (1933), *Night Flight* (1933) and *Chained* (1934). These films made very healthy returns for the studio, with *Men In White* and *Forsaking All Others* generating over 100 per cent returns. His first million dollar budget film was *China Seas*, which saw him paired with Jean Harlow. Prior to this, Gable had achieved great commercial success and an Academy award when loaned out to low-prestige Columbia where he co-starred with Paramount star Claudette Colbert in *It Happened One Night* (1934), starting the fashion for what became known as 'screwball comedies'. From this point onwards, Gable became one of the studio's top stars, appearing in four million-dollar-plus films during 1936 and 1937, with *Mutiny on the Bounty* and *San Francisco* being extremely popular at the box-office both at home and abroad.

Interestingly, Table 7.1 shows that although *Saratoga* (1937) was enormously popular with American audiences it did very poorly overseas, a phenomenon which is repeated at a lower level of popularity with *Parnell*. Indeed, further investigation shows this to be the general rule, with only *White Sister* proving to be more popular with foreign audiences. Accordingly, while Gable may have been the top ranking star absolutely for British audiences, US domestic box-office data suggests that he was even more popular with North American audiences.[32]

Greta Garbo

Unlike Gable's, Garbo's films, with the exception of *As You Desire Me*, generated greater box-office overseas—primarily in Europe—than in the US domestic market.[33] This popularity is captured strongly in the POPSTAT scores of her films, giving her four annual Top 10 performances in Britain, with her lowest ranking film being only 35th. Unlike Gable, Greta Garbo was in 1932 at the top of her profession,[34] although it is noticeable how much smaller the budgets of her film vehicles were at this time in relation to the end of the period, when perhaps her popularity was in decline relative to a new set of emerging stars. This pattern would seem to accord with the standard model depicted in Figure 9.1 and suggests a studio prepared to bet in order to enhance her standing with US audiences. However, Garbo unquestionably also benefited from the trend increase in the budgets of super 'A' films across Hollywood from the mid 1930s onwards.[35] Table 9.6 shows her 1932 performances to have been particularly strong, earning MGM substantial returns on their investments. Thereafter, her rate of return performance for the studio tails away as production budgets increase, the sequence ending with *Conquest* which proved to be an even bigger disaster than Gable's *Parnell*.

William Powell

A third major MGM star during these years was William Powell. Table 9.7 depicts his successes in the British market from 1934 onwards. Powell signed for MGM during this year after making *Fashions of 1934* for Warners. He was immediately teamed with Myrna Loy in *Manhattan Melodrama*. The film generated a healthy return for the studio and was followed by a second cheaper but even more successful film *The Thin Man*, which settled his star status. Unlike Gable's or Garbo's films, but rather like those of Astaire and Rogers, Powell's films were set in a classless but opulent world in which he 'seemed to alternate only between silk robe and pyjamas and white tie and tails'.[36] His strength as a light comic actor required a female co-star to provide sexual interest and act as a comic foil. For those films listed in Table 9.7 his principal female co-stars during the period were Myrna Loy (7 films), Luise Rainer (3 films), Jean Harlow (2 films) and Bette Davis, Ginger Rogers, Carole Lombard, Jean Arthur and Joan Crawford (one film each).

With the partial exception of *Reckless* and the particular exception of *The Great Ziegfeld*—a film which cost over $2 million to make, owing to the lavish quality of its musical numbers—William Powell's starring vehicles were low to medium budget films. Although there was a tendency for these production budgets to drift upwards during the period, the costs of his four 'hits' in 1937, after a substantial track record of success, fell between $620,000 and $741,000—a figure which was quite modest by MGM standards during the latter part of the 1930s, although high when compared to those films starring Bette Davis made at Warners during the same year. As can be seen from the rate of return figures, Powell was a highly bankable star for MGM with only *Reckless* returning a loss, whilst *The Thin Man* and *After the Thin Man* generated box-office receipts approximately six times, and *Libelled Lady* over four times, their production costs. Although Powell's films were much more popular in the US than Garbo's, the values of the ratio of US to foreign box-office revenue of his 'hit' films listed in Table 7.1 demonstrate that overseas popularity was more important to him than it was to Gable. This success is captured closely by the POPSTAT scores generated by his films which, when aggregated, make him the most popular star in Britain in 1936 and fourth in 1937 behind Ronald Colman, Paul Muni, Robert Taylor.

Conclusion

This chapter set out to explore the economic properties of film stardom before developing a methodology for identifying the most popular film stars in Britain during the 1930s. It has not been concerned with either the meaning of stars to individuals or groups of filmgoers or the reasons behind star preferences. In this I certainly would agree with Richard Dyer's remark that 'the rise and fall of stars indicates that economics alone cannot explain the phenomenon of stardom'. Nevertheless, economic thinking is important to an understanding of stars as a phenomenon-cum-commodity and their essential purpose of selling films.[37]

Tables 9.2 and 9.3 rank stars according to their aggregate and mean STARSTAT scores. Balio suggests that, at the time, Hollywood could muster only some thirty top ranking stars on contract to the major studios, to which may be added a handful or so freelance stars and perhaps a dozen British stars with a strong following amongst domestic audiences.[38] Undoubtedly, the procedure of listing 100 stars exaggerates the supply of star talent, with many of those found in the lower reaches of both tables better thought of as featured players. The evidence presented in these tables supports the findings of Chapter 5 and throws doubt on the claim that Gracie Fields and George Formby were amongst the most popular stars of the 1932–37 period, for national audiences at least.

The Appendix to this chapter makes use of MGM and Warners financial records to examine the life-cycle profiles of three leading top

MGM stars—Greta Garbo, Clark Gable and William Powell—in contrast to that of Warners' Bette Davis, who only became a top ranking star after the period of this book. To do this, the Astaire/Rogers set of musicals for RKO is used to suggest a standard life-cycle profile. The profiles also serve the purpose of relating the British reception of these stars, to the overall box-office performance of the films in which they appeared. Greta Garbo's profile is closest to the standard, whilst Gable and Powell suggest upward profiles where profitability is coupled with expanding budgets. For the most part, all three MGM stars appeared in profitable vehicles, but the losses incurred by Garbo's *Conquest* and Gable's *Parnell* give some indication of the risks entailed in big-budget production: the same star in different films could generate quite different levels of box-office revenue for the studio. Garbo's profile indicates not so much a star in decline as one whose productions became ever more expensive, thus pushing down the rate of return generated by them. The returns on Gable's films were much stronger and explain the studio's decision to assign him to bigger-budget films over the decade. Interestingly, Powell's films generate similarly good returns but he is not given such expensive film properties to appear in. In terms of risk attenuation, Gable appeared able to star in million-dollar-plus films without any diminution of the rate of return performance of his films. The return on Powell's films was from a much lower budgetary base, whereas although Garbo's box-office remained surprisingly constant, over the six years the studio needed to spend an increasingly amount to secure this.

Appendix to Chapter 9

Table 9.4: *Bette Davis' performances, 1932–1937*

Film	POPSTAT rank in year of release	US box-office $000s	Foreign box-office $000s	US/foreign box-office	Total box-office $000s	Production cost $000s	Distribution cost $000s	Total cost $000s	Profit $000s	Rate of return (%)
So Big	212	394	79	4.99	473	228	175.01	403.01	69.99	17.37
Man Who Played God	20	536	299	1.79	835	237	308.95	545.95	289.1	52.94
Dark Horse	220	302	64	4.72	366	185	135.42	320.42	45.58	14.23
Rich Are Always With Us	123	392	94	4.17	486	303	179.82	482.82	3.18	0.66
Ex Lady	249	228	55	4.15	283	93	104.71	197.71	85.29	43.14
Working Man	13	401	421	0.95	822	193	304.14	497.14	324.9	65.35
Parachute Jumper	216	238	156	1.53	394	232	145.78	377.78	16.22	4.29
20,000 Years in Sing Sing	105	504	431	1.17	935	234	345.95	579.95	355.1	61.22
Cabin in the Cotton	354	429	142	3.02	571	341	211.27	552.27	18.73	3.39
Three on a Match	263	338	106	3.19	444	135	164.28	299.28	144.7	48.36
Jimmy the Gent	149	332	135	2.46	467	151	172.79	323.79	143.2	44.23
Housewife	325	254	71	3.58	325	166	120.25	286.25	38.75	13.54
Bureau of Missing Persons	153	338	135	2.50	473	176	175.01	351.01	122	34.75
Fashions of 1934	39	570	395	1.44	965	317	357.05	674.05	291	43.16
Big Shakedown	370	194	65	2.98	259	179	95.83	274.83	-15.8	-5.76
Fog Over Frisco	221	260	129	2.02	389	146	143.93	289.93	99.07	34.17
Of Human Bondage[a]	172	467	125	3.74	592	403	234	637	-45	-7.06
Border Town	176	891	346	2.58	1237	369	457.69	826.69	410.3	49.63
Front Page Girl	247	359	149	2.41	508	198	187.96	385.96	122	31.62
Girl From 10th Avenue	303	322	106	3.04	428	186	158.36	344.36	83.64	24.29
Petrified Forest	116	583	247	2.36	830	503	307.1	810.1	19.9	2.46
Special Agent	179	490	306	1.60	796	168	294.52	462.52	333.5	72.10
Dangerous	186	466	258	1.81	724	190	267.88	457.88	266.1	58.12
Satan Met a Lady	358	266	48	5.54	314	195	116.18	311.18	2.82	0.91
Golden Arrow	197	391	163	2.40	554	291	204.98	495.98	58.02	11.70
Kid Gallahad	112	1037	480	2.16	1517	426	561.29	987.29	529.7	53.65
Marked Woman	218	774	377	2.05	1151	342	425.87	767.87	383.1	49.90
It's Love I'm After	111	578	368	1.57	946	474	350.02	824.02	122	14.80
That Certain Woman	317	749	247	3.03	996	368	368.52	736.52	259.5	35.23

Source: William Schaefer Ledger.

Table 9.4 continued

Notes: The films are listed according to their position in the Schaefer production ledger, reflecting their order of production. A different order will emerge if the films were listed according to release dates. The rate of return is calculated as profit/(production + distribution cost). See Equations 7.1 and 7.2 in Chapter 7 for greater elaboration. POPSTAT measures the popularity of the films in which the star appeared.

a. *Of Human Bondage* (RKO) was Davis's only film made outside Warners' during the 1930s once under contract. The budget data are taken from the Trevlin Ledger, reported in Jewell (1994) and Sedgwick (1994b). Its position in Table 9.4 is derived from its copyright date, given in the Library of Congress Catalog of Copyright Entries, Motion Pictures 1912–1939 (Washington, DC, 1951).

Table 9.5: *Clark Gable's 'hit' performances, 1932–1937*

STARSTAT rank	Top 100 films	First billing	Years in Top 100	STARSTAT score	Mean STARSTAT
1	20	19	6	411.45	20.57

Year	STARSTAT rank	Top 100 films	First billing	STARSTAT
1932	29	2	1	35.19
1933	4	5	5	78.94
1934	6	4	4	72.55
1935	11	3	3	65.63
1936	2	4	4	124.57
1937	43	2	2	34.56

Year	POPSTAT rank	Film	Studio	Production cost $000s	Box-office $000s	Rate of return (%)	POPSTAT
1932	8	Hell Divers	MGM	821	2,161	26.89	31.11
	28	Strange Interval	MGM	654	1,237	7.85	19.63
1933	31	Dancing Lady	MGM	923	2,406	44.77	20.51

207

Table 9.5 continued

Year	POPSTAT rank	Film	Studio	Production cost $000s	Box-office $000s	Rate of return (%)	POPSTAT
	37	White Sister	MGM	625	1,672	37.50	17.60
	46	Night Flight	MGM	499	1,079	19.49	15.66
	57	No Man of Her Own	Paramount	n/a	n/a	n/a	14.52
	100	Hold Your Man	MGM	266	1,073	67.01	10.66
1934	9	It Happened One Night	Columbia	n/a	n/a	n/a	31.58
	47	Chained	MGM	544	1,988	58.28	16.21
	77	Men in White	MGM	213	1,455	116.84	12.96
	90	Manhattan Melodrama	MGM	355	1,233	50.73	11.80
1935	23	Call of the Wild	20th Century	n/a	n/a	n/a	25.56
	31	China Seas	MGM	1,138	2,867	29.49	22.94
	48	Forsaking All Others	MGM	392	2,199	106.09	17.14
1936	2	Mutiny on the Bounty	MGM	1,905	4,460	25.60	59.36
	13	San Francisco	MGM	1,300	5,273	73.68	32.01
	47	Love on the Run	MGM	578	1,862	57.13	18.13
	78	Cain and Mabel	WB	1,108	1,462	-11.34	15.07
1937	42	Saratoga	MGM	1,144	3,252	54.42	17.32
	43	Parnell	MGM	1,547	1,576	-28.78	17.24

Sources: Eddie Mannix Ledger reported in Glancy (1992); for *Cain and Mabel*, William Schaefer Ledger reported in Glancy (1995); Table 8.4.

Note: The films are listed according to their position in the Mannix production ledger, reflecting their order of production. A different order will emerge if the films were listed according to release dates. A more detailed financial profile of these films can be found in Table 7.1. The rate of return is calculated as profit/(production + distribution cost). See Equations 7.1 and 7.2 in Chapter 7 for greater elaboration. STARSTAT measures the relative popularity of the star. POPSTAT measures the popularity of the films in which the star appeared.

Table 9.6: *Greta Garbo's 'hit' performances, 1932–1937*

STARSTAT rank	Top 100 films	First billing	Years in Top 100	STARSTAT score	Mean STARSTAT
20	8	8	4	222.08	27.76

Table 9.6 continued

Year	POPSTAT rank	Film	Studio	Production cost $000s	Box-office $000s	Rate of return (%)	POPSTAT
1932	2	Grand Hotel	MGM	700	2,594	57.50	45.24
	29	Mata Hari	MGM	588	2,227	65.21	19.53
	35	As You Desire Me	MGM	469	1,363	49.12	18.42
1934	7	Queen Christina	MGM	1,144	2,610	31.35	33.03
	20	Painted Veil	MGM	947	1,658	9.08	24.39
1935	24	Anna Karenina	MGM	1,152	2,304	16.13	24.52
1937	8	Camille	MGM	1,486	2,842	15.81	36.64
	30	Conquest	MGM	2,732	2,141	-39.49	20.32

Source: Eddie Mannix Ledger reported in Glancy (1992).

Note: The films are listed according to their position in the Mannix production ledger, reflecting their order of production. A different order will emerge if the films were listed according to release dates. A more detailed financial profile of these films can be found in Table 9.1. The rate of return is calculated as profit/(production + distribution cost). See Equations 7.1 and 7.2 in Chapter 7 for greater elaboration. STARSTAT measures the relative popularity of the star. POPSTAT measures the popularity of the films in which the star appeared.

Table 9.7: *William Powell's 'hit' performances, 1932–1937*

STARSTAT rank	Top 100 films	First billing	Years in Top 100	STARSTAT score	Mean STARSTAT
5	15	15	4	318.77	21.25

Year	STARSTAT rank	Top 100 films	First billing	STARSTAT
1934	8	4	4	68.04
1935	30	3	3	41.10
1936	1	4	4	129.29
1937	4	4	4	80.33

Table 9.7 continued

Year	POPSTAT rank	Film	Studio	Production cost $000s	Box-office $000s	Rate of return (%)	POPSTAT
1934	26	Thin Man	MGM	213	1,423	105.04	22.27
	39	Fashions of 1934	WB	674	965	43.16	17.33
	46	Evelyn Prentice	MGM	498	1,166	26.46	16.65
	90	Manhattan Melodrama	MGM	355	1,233	50.73	11.80
1935	77	Star of Midnight	RKO	280	831	47.00	13.01
	61	Escapade	MGM	467	975	17.19	15.28
	82	Reckless	MGM	858	1,339	-8.54	12.81
1936	3	Great Ziegfeld	MGM	2,183	4,673	21.35	53.29
	21	My Man Godfrey	Universal	n/a	n/a	n/a	27.31
	34	Ex Mrs Bradford	RKO	369	1,084	48.00	21.03
	20	Libelled Lady	MGM	603	2,703	77.51	27.66
1937	13	After the Thin Man	MGM	673	3,165	91.93	31.03
	73	Double Wedding	MGM	678	2,041	50.29	13.62
	91	Emperor's Candlesticks	MGM	620	1,333	24.12	12.15
	21	Last of Mrs Cheyney	MGM	741	1,797	34.41	23.53

Sources: Eddie Mannix Ledger reported in Glancy (1992); for *Star of Midnight* and *The Ex Mrs Bradford*, Trevlin ledger reported in Jewell (1994) and Sedgwick (1994b); for *Fashions of 1934*, William Schaefer ledger reported in Glancy (1995).

Note: The films are listed according to their position in the Mannix production ledger, reflecting their order of production. A different order will emerge if the films were listed according to release dates. A more detailed financial profile of these films can be found in Table 9.1. The rate of return is calculated as profit/(production + distribution cost). See Equations 7.1 and 7.2 in Chapter 7 for greater elaboration. STARSTAT measures the relative popularity of the star. POPSTAT measures the popularity of the films in which the star appeared.

10

Michael Balcon's Close Encounter with the American Market

> The main object of this letter is to let you know that my heart is tied up in America just as much as yours because I know that success for the output stands or falls by its success in that market.
>
> Michael Balcon[1]

The risk environment facing film producers in the 1930s has thus far been portrayed in general terms, wherein the market is depicted as an uncertain environment in which expenditure on production values, genre-type and star inputs can be viewed as mitigating strategies. In contrast, this chapter consists of a study of a particular strategic response by one company to a business problem: namely, the decision of Britain's leading volume producer to tailor films to the perceived tastes of US audiences and to complement this by setting up a distribution wing of the company explicitly to service the American market, in order that it might break free from the constraint of being dependent on the British one.

Michael Balcon was Head of Production at Gaumont-British between 1932 and 1936. During these years Gaumont-British, together with its companion studio Gainsborough, became the leading British studio, increasingly committed to a strategy of quality 'A' film outputs.[2] From its studios at Shepherd's Bush and Islington—marketed respectively under the labels of Gaumont-British and Gainsborough—the company released, as reported in Chapter 4, 125 films during the period 1932–37, achieving 9 nine per cent share of the domestic market in 1934 and 1935, with an average of 7 per cent over the period. Although its output levels were considerably lower than those of the Hollywood majors, its films, on average, were more popular in the British market, with 50 of them obtaining annual Top 50 status and another 29 being placed in the annual Top 100 lists. Its relative performance can be gauged from Table 4.4 (see page 91).

During these years the studio had term contracts with George Arliss, Conrad Veidt, Jessie Matthews, Jack Hulbert, Cicely Courtneidge, Tom Walls, Ralph Lynn, Will Hay, Madeleine Carroll, Gordon Harker, Max Miller, Robertson Hare, Sonnie Hale, Barry Mackay, Frances Day, Anna Lee, Boris Karloff, Constance Cummings and Nova Pilbeam. Other well-known artistes secured by Balcon were Robert Donat, Robert Young, Roland Young, Walter Huston, Paul Robeson, Anna May Wong, Richard Dix, Peter Lorre, Claude Rains, Fay Wray and Edward Everett Horton. The studio's principal contract directors were Walter Forde, Alfred Hitchcock, Milton Rosmer, Victor Saville, Robert Stevenson and Berthold Viertel, all of whom worked either directly for Balcon or for a set of associate producers—Chandos Balcon, Ivor Montagu, Angus Macphail and Edward Black. Maurice Elvey also regularly directed for the studio on a picture-by-picture basis. With outstanding writing, art, camera, music, general and floor management and editing personnel,[3] the production wing of Gaumont-British represented a self confident and ambitious unit.

Balcon's US strategy

Michael Balcon is generally recognized for his stewardship of the Ealing Studios from 1938 and the portfolio of highly esteemed films which emerged until the sale of the premises to the BBC in 1955. Perhaps as a consequence of the critical preoccupation with those films, less attention has been given to his activities as Director of Production at Gaumont-British. Based upon archive material held by the British Film Institute, *The Michael Balcon Special Collection* and the US box-office information contained in *Variety,* this chapter is intended to redress this state of affairs by concentrating on the organization's efforts, during the years 1934–36, to become a major player in the world film industry and therefore to rival in scale and output the principal Hollywood studios. Such a business strategy demanded sustained access to and penetration of the American market.

In order to obtain widespread distribution in the US, the films of Gaumont-British would need to play in those cinemas owned by MGM, Paramount, Warners, Fox or RKO, thus potentially displacing the American studios' own product.[4] To this end, Gaumont-British established a distribution network, headed by Arthur Lee in New York, and set out to sell a set of films specifically addressed to the perceived tastes of American audiences. The strategy failed, and with this the organization went into a decline from which it did not re-emerge.[5] Nevertheless, there is sufficient evidence in the Balcon archive to suggest that the challenge was entirely serious and one to which the whole organization was committed. In the light of Balcon's subsequent championing of a national cinema, the internationalist strategy prosecuted by him in the mid-1930s makes for an intriguing contrast.

Because of the scale and scope of its production plans, the attempt by the corporation to break into the American market was not only brave but also necessary. As a result of the asymmetry of the box-office potentials of the British and American markets, the only strategy available to British producers wishing to make films with high production value inputs, and therefore high unit costs, was to gain access to the American market. The British market was simply not big enough to cover such investments.[6] Even in the depth of the Depression, some 3,640 million Americans paid $518 million to go to the movies in 1934.[7] This contrasts with 903 million admissions in Britain, which generated gross takings of £38.8 million during the same year.[8] Allowing for an exchange rate of £1 to $4.5,[9] American box-office receipts were approximately three times those of the British market at the time. Rachael Low believed this point was fundamental to the prospects of British film producers:

> Even the quality producers had to operate on a scale of production far below that of their competitors in the British market, the Hollywood companies. Only Korda was rash enough to compete on equal terms.[10]

Yet was this true? By 'scale' it is not clear whether Low is referring to qualitative or quantitative differences between Hollywood and British film-makers, although her reference to Korda suggests the former, given the small output of London Films. If so, Warners at this time may be taken as an instructive example for comparison. For each of the 1933/4 and 1934/5 seasons Warners made 54 films at an average cost of $243,900 (£54,222) and $298,700 (£66,444) respectively.[11] During the same two seasons Balcon oversaw the production of 43 films.[12] Unfortunately, systematic budgetary information of the quality found in the Schaefer ledger, from a single source, is not to be found in the Balcon archive, or elsewhere. However, it is possible to piece together a general picture of Gaumont-British budgets from a variety of sources. In an article submitted to the *Film Daily*, Balcon claimed that *Jew Süss* (1933) cost £100,000 to make and, in letters to Mark Ostrer, that *Foreign Affaires* (1935) and *The 39 Steps* (1935) were costed at £47,655 and £58,499 respectively.[13] An internal letter written by Balcon listed the following four cost estimates: *Chu Chin Chow*, £65,000; *Little Friend*, £35,000; *Phantom Light*, £15,000; and *Cup of Kindness*, £47,000.[14] Another internal document costs *The Camels are Coming* at £37,632.[15] A further source of film budget information is found in Balcon's 'Report to the Managing Directors on the 1935 Programme', set out in Table 10.1. An indication of the budgetary tensions pervading the studio may be gained from the correspondence between Balcon and Mark Ostrer concerning the literary property *Tovarich*, later (1937) made into a major feature by Warners starring Charles Boyer and Claudette Colbert. Balcon wanted to make the film, and he sought permission from Ostrer to buy the English-language rights. Ostrer was fearful of the scale of production costs implicit in such a project, calculated by Balcon as in the £100–£120,000 region if Elisabeth Bergner was to be teamed up with Conrad Veidt or, with lower star values, around £60–70,000. Ostrer ruled out the £100,000+ option, especially since 'the foreign rights will already be gone, and that means £20–30,000 must be taken off the gross'.[16]

The evidence suggests that, from what we know of the production values of those projects that came to fruition, standard film budgets at Gaumont-British were approximately a third lower than the average at Warners during the two years in question.[17] Further, we know from Glancy[18] and Jewell [19] that Warners' average film budget exceeded RKO's but was less than MGM's. Accordingly, on a per film basis, it would appear that the film budgets of Gaumont-British were at least comparable to the those of the bulk of films emanating from the major Hollywood studios, although the number of films produced by Gaumont-British was less than half their typical output. In the following chapter, the average box-office return on all films marketed in Britain is calculated as being in the order of £10,000. Although evidence has been presented to show that the studio's films were much more popular to British audiences than the average, it is clear that Gaumont-British required substantial foreign success in order to warrant such film budgets. As the size of the Dominion and Empire markets was relatively small,[20] the Corporation had to succeed in the American market, or else change its production strategy. The clear resolve of Balcon and its implications for the corporation can be found

Table 10.1: *Balcon's production schedule for 1935*

39 Steps	£48,000—thriller.
Redemption	£55,000—drama, Director: Viertel, with Madeleine Carroll and Conrad Veidt—not made.
Youth at the Helm (Jack of All Trades)	£50,000—comedy, bought for Jack Hulbert and Director Walter Forde—made but directed by Hulbert and Robert Stevenson.
Tunnel	£65,000—with Veidt—Veidt's role eventually went to Richard Dix.
Barcarole	£50,000—Director: Victor Saville—not made
Arliss vehicle	£90,000—to be written by J.B. Priestley.
King of the Damned	£65,000—Devil Island Story, Director: Forde, with Veidt.
Pilbeam subject	£40,000.
Passing of the Third Floor Back	£45,000—Director: Viertel, with either John Gielgud or Leslie Howard—made, but starring Veidt.
Untitled	£50,000—Director: Lothar Mendes.
Soldiers Three	£60,000—preliminary location shooting only.
2nd Carroll subject	£55,000—Director: Saville.
2nd Arliss subject	£100,000—possibly Samuel Pepys—not made.
2nd Mendes directed subject	£55,000.
Sam and Sallie	£50,000—Theatrical story, with Jessie Matthews—probably *First a Girl*.
Hitchcock directed subject	£48,000—probably either *Sabotage* or *Secret Agent*.

Source: MBSC/C28/ Report to the Managing Directors on the 1935 Programme, 13 Dec. 1934.

in a report on the 1935 Programme submitted by Balcon to the two joint Managing Directors at the time (Mark Ostrer and C.M.Woolf), in which he argued:

> It is necessary to bear in mind that in order to obtain a firm grip on the American market our pictures must bear comparison, not only with the average Hollywood product, but with the outstanding American films; this is our problem in a nutshell and it cannot be resolved without spending money. Personally, I would prefer not to attempt it under an average of from £55,000 to £60,000 per picture, and even then it would be a contest of David and Goliath.[21]

The point should be made at this juncture that it is possible to make only the most general conjectures from the scanty information available. The need for more reliable data concerning the finances of British film production during these years is paramount for the advancement of knowledge in this area.

International film production

Some idea of the change in Gaumont-British's strategy during 1934 can be found in C.M. Woolf's published address to an AGM of Gainsborough shareholders in December 1934:

> In my speech to you at last year's meeting I spoke of the rise in production costs. This tendency has continued during the year under review, for the very good reason that since our last meeting, America has come across the British film horizon—we are now competing with more expensively made productions on their homeground. We have, therefore, had to increase the scale and the star value of our product, and ...such additional expenditure promises a far more than proportionate return.[22]

To the same audience, Woolf announced the opening of the US distribution wing of Gaumont-British and crowed about the success of *Chu Chin Chow*, which had opened at the 6,200 seater Roxy Theatre, New York, with a two week run.[23] The corporation's films had begun appearing at the independent Roxy regularly from October 1934. The cinema was described by its Managing Director, Howard S. Cullman, in 1936 as having the potential to gross $75,000 per week, comparing it favourably in this respect with all other New York cinemas with the exception of the Radio City Music Hall.[24] Cullman told the Gaumont-British Sales Convention in May of the same year that during the previous two years eighteen films from the company had been shown over 23 weeks and that 'the Roxy Theatre has not had one losing or unprofitable week on Gaumont-British product... You have the pace, stories and certainly production comparable to any American organization.'[25]

Although not too much should be read into these eulogistic remarks, particularly as Cullman had only supply contracts with Universal and Gaumont-British, the promotion and distribution of Gaumont-British's films in the US from late 1934 represents a dramatic change from the earlier situation where Fox had distributed the occasional Gaumont-British film. Indeed, earlier in 1934 Balcon had received a letter from Dixon Boardman in which Sidney Kent (Vice President at Fox) is purported to have commented that *I Was a Spy* was the only Gaumont-British film to date which had the potential for widespread distribution, and was in fact doing well in the American market. Of *Good Companions* Kent is quoted as saying that the film 'was a good English picture but was totally unsuited for distribution in America, due to the fact that nobody in it had ever been heard of over here before and the accent was such that few people could understand it'.[26]

The degree to which the American market influenced Balcon's thinking on both the make-up of his studio's portfolio of films and the means of exploiting them is evident in numerous documents of the period. For instance, in an internal memorandum, Balcon commented on the marketing potential of *The 39 Steps*: 'This is such an obvious international proposition that we must... avoid all phrases which are purely of importance to a British audience.'[27] At the development stage of *Soldiers Three* he instructed: 'This is such a first class property that the very greatest care must be taken not to detract in any way from its international appeal'.[28] In a letter to Harry Lachman, then a director at Fox, Balcon suggests something of the scale of the task before him during 1935, writing, 'next year will tell its own tale. It is quite definite that I have got to make some really big productions if we are going to build up the good will in the States which we are so anxious to acquire.'[29]

In the same vein he wrote to the Joint Managing Directors (Mark Ostrer and C.M.Woolf) when setting out the planned activity for 1935, listed in Table 10.1: 'The attached programme has been framed after a careful consideration of the results of our visit to America. The subjects included are, therefore, those which, besides being of value in the home and dominion market, are also in my opinion, of great international appeal.'[30] The risk of failure was ever present. Writing to Victor Saville in February 1935, Balcon argued that: 'all of us at the Studio are aware the main object of our efforts is to produce the best possible financial results for the Company and to this end we have been trying to get our pictures into the international class. Generally speaking we are not yet certain of success.'[31]

An important feature of the strategy to raise the profile of the studio by making 'international' films was the two-way flow of stars between Gaumont-British and Hollywood. Although Balcon worked hard to implement this he met with only moderate success. Cicely Courtneidge was the only one of his contract stars to make a film in Hollywood, starring with Frank Morgan in *A Perfect Gentleman* (retitled *Imperfect Lady* for its release in Britain), made at MGM in August/September 1935[32]. Writing about Jessie Matthews, Balcon admitted: 'It is obvious to us that *Evergreen*, although a great professional success with fine notices, failed to do the business expected of it owing to the lack of known star value.'[33] Not only was Matthews not known sufficiently widely by American audiences, but also the film did not feature a major Hollywood male lead. This pattern is repeated in her next film, *First a Girl*, which Balcon explained as the consequence of a series of misunderstandings when he was last in the US, although he came to the conclusion that: 'it does seem that it will be helped [i.e. Jessie Matthew's star value], as indeed will also her pictures for us, if she is allowed to make one picture in America'.[34] As is well chronicled, Matthews never got to make a musical film in Hollywood or appear alongside a first-rate American dancing or singing star.[35]

During the spring and summer of 1935, MGM resisted Balcon's efforts to secure Robert Young as a co-star for Matthews in *First a Girl*; similarly, he failed to acquire Spencer Tracy for *Soldiers Three*, James Cagney for *OHMS* and Freddie Bartholomew to star alongside Nova Pilbeam in the project *Lady Jane Grey* (released as *Tudor Rose* (1936)), whilst he turned down the opportunity to take over the property *The Paradine Case* on which MGM had invested in some development work, 'primarily because it calls for a cost which we could not assemble'.[36] Similar failures were recorded with Grace Moore, Leslie Howard [37] and Robert Donat.[38]

The box-office performance of films sent to the US

Gaumont-British decided on a portfolio of sixteen films to be distributed by their American distribution company during the

1934–35 season.[39] From the start it would appear that Balcon was wary of the authority of the US wing and on a number of occasions questioned its sales judgements. In a letter to Mark Ostrer written in November 1934, Balcon expressed his fears of it 'having the right of rejection, particularly in shelving products which will lead to them not being put out at all'. A good example of this sort of debate concerns the distribution of *Bulldog Jack,* released in the US as *Alias Bulldog Drummond.* The archive contains an internal Broadway Office memorandum in which George Weeks argues that:

> With reference to *Bulldog Jack*, I frankly think this is the fastest-moving picture we have received from England and there are many points greatly in its favour. However, as to whether or not we should release the picture in America depends entirely on just how much Hulbert can be eliminated. He definitely is not funny in any of his spots and would not help us in any way with the American public. Unless the picture can be cut in a very satisfactory manner, I would hesitate to release it as I think it would seriously hurt us and doubt if we could gross the cost of the prints…it is evident that Hulbert is never going to be accepted in America in the type of work he is doing on the screen at the present time. They do not like him and do not want him…His comedy is exaggerated to the point where it is pitiful and the marvellous fast action and possibilities of the picture terribly handicapped and hurt by the comedy…I feel that England muffed the chance to give us a very acceptable picture.[40]

In copying this memorandum to Balcon, Arthur Lee informed him that cuts indeed were to be made and reiterated Weekes' sentiment concerning the pace of the film: 'the tempo of this picture is exactly what we want here, so try to keep staff working at that speed.'[41] Balcon responded, in a memorandum to Mark Ostrer, that he thought 'Weekes' criticism 'a little harsh', whilst urging that 'everything possible should be done to put this picture over in America'.[42]

Lee's appraisal of Cicely Courtneidge in *Me and Malborough* echoes Weeks' criticism of *Bulldog Jack.* For him, the film did not have 'one bit of entertainment for the American public and if we were able to offer it to the exhibitors, I am afraid that it would undo the good which we are now doing with pictures like *The Clairvoyant* and *The 39 Steps.*'[43] In this case it would appear that Balcon agreed with the assessment, writing to Courtneidge whilst she was filming *A Perfect*

Gentleman that 'I was terribly disappointed with the picture'.[44]

As has already been indicated, the Balcon archive contains very little in the way of hard business information. It is possible, however, to obtain a measure of the performance of the corporation's films from the records of box-office takings found in *Variety* for the principal cinemas in the major cities of the United States. This information set has not so far been systematically analysed, yet not only does it allow the researcher to assess the relative performance of films showing in the same cinema over time, but also to gauge the strength of the competition between films playing in different cinemas in the same city at the same time.[45]

Beginning with the two week run of *Chu Chin Chow* at the Roxy theatre, from the last week of September 1934, I have traced the diffusion of Gaumont-British films amongst the leading cinemas of New York, Chicago, Los Angeles, San Francisco, Brooklyn, Detroit, Seattle, Philadelphia, Boston, St Louis, Washington DC, Denver, Buffalo, Pittsburgh, New Haven, Portland, Cincinnati, Kansas City, Tacoma, Montreal (Canada), Minneapolis, Indianapolis, Providence (Rhode Island), and Birmingham, through to the end of 1936. Typically, weekly box-office information for approximately 70 cinemas was tabulated for a four-week period. *Variety's* data set is in someway puzzling, since not only are city records occasionally missing but also the cinemas represented in monthly tabular form are not inclusive of each city's major cinemas. For instance, cinemas such as the Lafayette Theatre, Buffalo, with a seating capacity of 3,400, the Indiana, Indianapolis (3,100 seats), the Boyd, Philadelphia (2,400 seats) and the Allen, Cleveland (3,000 seats), were not represented. Accordingly, the data used is neither comprehensive nor consistent. Also, since it consists, in all but a few cases, of first-run cinemas, it is not possible to obtain an idea of how extensively Gaumont-British's films were diffused to second- and subsequent-run cinemas. A further difficulty is that the cinemas of the southern states are poorly represented in the data set.

Despite these deficiencies, it does not appear that the sample of first-run cinemas is particularly biased with regard to ownership or size, and it does provide valid evidence of the relative popularity of Gaumont-British films. Altogether, 80 single-feature billings and 94 double-feature billings containing a Gaumont-British film were counted amongst these cinemas during this period. For analytical purposes what is important is not the absolute box-office takings recorded for each billing but the comparative performance with other

films. To this end, Gaumont-British box-office results have been compared with the average box-office results of films (including the
Gaumont-British film) showing at the same cinema during the four-
week cycle presented in *Variety*, and the average box-office of films
showing simultaneously at rival cinemas in the same city. The
aggregate results are presented in Table 10.2.

Each of the four arithmetic mean results is negative: Gaumont-
British films on average earned less than the average box-office at both
the cinemas and cities in which they appeared. With both single- and
double-feature billings the intra-comparative cinema performance is
much better than that with rival cinemas. This suggests that the
cinemas at which Gaumont-British films appeared generated relatively
lower box-office results. Indeed, the majority of exhibition venues
were cinemas which were independently owned and hence did not have
first call on the major productions emanating from the MGM,
Paramount, Warners, RKO and Fox/20th Century-Fox studios. The
very large standard deviation and hence coefficient of variation
statistics indicate a highly differentiated level of performance of these
films for the owners of the cinemas taking Gaumont-British product.
This is particularly marked when analysing those films showing at the
same cinema. It is noticeable, however, that the variance in the
differential performance of Gaumont-British films is lower in those
programmes in which its films are part of a double-billed programme,
almost always with a film produced in Hollywood. Details of the
comparative performance of individual films are presented in Table
10.3. The number of exhibitions of any of the films in the list is small,
ranging from 14 for *Transatlantic Tunnel* (distributed in Britain as *The
Tunnel*) to one double billing of *My Song for You*. Therefore, it is not
possible to draw reliable film popularity inferences from the table,
except to say that these films were not amongst the most popular of
the two seasons in which Gaumont-British managed a presence in the
American market. Accordingly, the popularity score, given in column
7, which is obtained by adding together the four percentages found in
columns 2, 3, 5 and 6 (after attributing 0.5 weights to the last two in
order to reflect shared-billing status), should be interpreted with
caution. An indication of the partial nature of Gaumont-British's
penetration into the American market can be gained by the fact that
the 'hit' films of the period—for example *The Lives of a Bengal Lancer*
(Paramount), *Roberta* (RKO), and *G Men* (Warners), released during
the first six months of 1935—secured approximately twice the number
of single-feature bookings amongst the *Variety*-listed cinemas as

Table 10.2: *Comparative aggregate box-office performance of Gaumont-British films in major US city first-run cinemas*

	Percentage difference from films shown at the same cinema	Percentage difference from films shown in rival city cinemas
Eighty single-feature billings		
Mean box-office	-3.69	-12.24
Standard deviation	22.21	32.98
Coefficient of variation	-6.01	-2.69
Maximum	45.25	104.98
Minimum	-72.52	-69.87
Ninety-four double-feature billings		
Mean box-office	-5.44	-22.68
Standard deviation	23.39	26.72
Coefficient of variation	-4.30	-1.18
Maximum	78.64	30.77
Minimum	-74.47	-75.51

Source: *Variety*, 1934–36.

Transatlantic Tunnel—the best Gaumont-British performer in this respect. Further, such films were held over for substantially longer runs than their Gaumont-British counterparts. Indeed, whilst *The 39 Steps*, *Chu Chin Chow*, *It's Love Again*, *Secret Agent* and *Transatlantic Tunnel* all secured two-week runs at the Roxy, only *Evergreen* at the Uptown theatre, Kansas City, and *It's Love Again* at the Music Box, Seattle, secured two-week runs elsewhere as single features, and no film was retained for a third week.

Internal problems

The archive makes it very clear that Balcon felt that the film-making side of the business—the central instrument in his organization's strategy for penetrating the American market—was substantially impeded by internal problems. In a letter to Arthur Lee in December 1934, in which Balcon informed him that Maurice Ostrer was taking charge of the administrative work at the studio, allowing him to

Table 10.3: *Sample US box-office performance of Gaumont-British films 1934–1936*

Film	Single-feature billings (1)	Difference from average (%) cinema (2)	Difference from average (%) city (3)	Double feature billings (4)	Difference from average (%) cinema (5)	Difference from average (%) city (6)	Relative popularity score[a] (7)	Total billings (8)
Transatlantic Tunnel	8	2	-15	6	-13	-14	-26	14
39 Steps	6	14	-15	7	-8	-22	-16	13
It's Love Again	7	-12	-4	6	-5	-21	-29	13
Chu Chin Chow	8	-3	-25	4	-5	5	-29	12
Iron Duke	8	-7	18	3	12	9	21	11
Mister Hobo[b]	4	19	-28	7	4	-17	-15	11
Rhodes Of Africa	4	-3	-28	6	-16	-24	-50	10
Secret Agent	4	14	-22	5	-7	-20	-22	9
First a Girl	4	-4	-11	5	-6	-20	-27	9
Evergreen	6	-22	-19	3	-3	-7	-45	9
Evensong	2	-25	2	6	3	-33	-37	8
East Meets West	4	-9	-39	4	-6	-38	-70	8
Clairvoyant	3	6	2	4	-9	-36	-15	7
Man Who Knew Too Much	1	-9	42	4	8	-30	22	5
Little Friend	1	10	23	3	-21	-35	5	4
Nine Days a Queen[c]	3	-31	-30	1	-74	-76	-135	4
Power[d]	2	0	68	1	-5	-52	39	3
Alias Bulldog Drummond[e]	0	0	0	3	5	-4	0	3
Man of Aran	0	0	0	3	-4	-25	-15	3
King of The Damned	1	-15	-33	2	-21	7	-55	3
My Heart Is Calling	1	-31	-48	2	5	-39	-97	3
Unfinished Symphony	1	-24	-31	1	79	-1	-17	2
Seven Sinners	0	0	0	2	-16	-47	-31	2
Passing of the 3rd Floor Back	0	0	0	2	-51	-62	-56	2
Jack Ahoy	1	-12	-39	1	19	-53	-68	2
Pot Luck	0	0	0	1	18	0	9	1
Camels Are Coming	0	0	0	1	-18	-23	-21	1
My Song For You	0	0	0	1	-10	-35	-22	1

Source: Variety 1934–36.

Table 10.3 continued

Notes:
a. Relative popularity score = col 2 + col 3 + 0.5 (col 5 + col 6).
b. Released in Britain as *The Guv'nor*.
c. Released in Britain as *The Tudor Rose*.
d. Released in Britain as *Jew Süss*.
e. Released in Britain as *Bulldog Jack*.

concentrate on 'production only, with of course a concentration on the pictures required for your market', he alluded to the damaging effect of the 'backwash of other financial matters …involving mergers, production curtailment…and all sorts of things of this kind'. Indeed, he complained:

> that to this day I don't know, and will never know, what has happened. In point of fact, I have never tried to find out. I do know that it will take us a long time to make up for the ground we lost.[46]

It is not clear from the letter which particular incident Balcon was referring to, although it was written when Gaumont-British was attempting to acquire the Union circuit of cinemas and the internal dispute with C.M.Woolf was at its height, causing the latter to leave the Corporation in May 1935.[47]

Several internal communications draw attention to tensions associated with poor standards of internal coordination concerning the promotion of the corporation's name, its films and its stars. In January 1934 Balcon was complaining to Mark Ostrer: 'It is quite clear that we cannot do any star-building unless the other branches of the Corporation, for good or evil, follow the line we take at the studios.'[48] He was critical of the uneven promotion of stars amongst the various exhibition companies controlled by Gaumont-British.[49] Eighteen months later the same frustrations abounded:

> We have a Director of Public Relations, a department at Film House, a department at the Studio, a department I believe at New Gallery House and Palmer Newbould and Co.Ltd., yet look at the Press on *39 Steps*. The Press, although brilliant for the picture, is absolutely useless for Gaumont-British as a whole…We have agreed that the general publicity of the Corporation is at its lowest ebb.[50]

Balcon took up the theme a month later, in July 1935, when he complained to Mark Ostrer that the trailer for *The 39 Steps* failed to:

> ...mention the film being a Gaumont-British picture... Unfortunately the public here think there are two classes of films only: quota quickies and good British pictures all of which are made by Korda. You will see in yesterday's [Daily] 'Express' they gave great prominence to the fact that Korda is the only man who put British production on its feet here and abroad.[51]

In another incident, Balcon bemoaned the close proximity of the London pre-release dates of *Jack of All Trades* and *The Guv'nor*—two films with similar themes. In castigating the distribution wing of the corporation, Balcon wrote to Mark Ostrer:

> I must again point out that this lack of appreciation of film production by film distributors must have serious results. If they treat films merely as so much merchandise to fit in with an arbitrary releasing schedule, the business as a whole must suffer.[52]

Perhaps the most immediate source of difficulty for Balcon as Head of Production was the physical constraints posed by the layout of the Shepherd's Bush studio. Gaumont-British had the capacity to make three films simultaneously—two at Shepherd's Bush and the other at Islington. Production was geared to schedules of five weeks for films destined for the US market and four weeks for those intended for domestic and Dominion destinations only.[53] Although refurbished in 1932, the physical features of the Shepherd's Bush studio were a considerable handicap to the production management team, adding, in Arnold Pressburger's opinion, £10,000 to the cost of each film.[54] Balcon's assessment of the studio facilities was vividly captured in a letter written to C.M. Woolf in 1934 in which he argued that Shepherd's Bush was:

> a studio that should never have been built. It is incredible that in these days it should be expected that modern pictures can be made economically in a studio similar to those existing and given up in New York twenty years ago.

Balcon complained that not one of the five stages was to be found on the ground floor, thus entailing lifts to move everything. Further, there

225

was inadequate dressing-room space, no storage space and no lot. The absence of a lot made it impossible to follow the standard Hollywood practice of maintaining durable standing sets which could be 'dressed' for specific production needs from one film to another. The lack of storage space meant that 'one-off' sets had to be built and then destroyed:

> Every single window and door have to be made specifically for each set, and everything has to be broken down when the set is finished.

He claimed that six theatre sets had been built and destroyed over the past 18 months and concluded:

> These studios are not fit under any circumstances to make more than 12 to 14 pictures a year and those at a much higher cost than need be… Indeed this has only been done by everybody here nearly killing themselves.[55]

A vivid illustration of the sort of problems faced by the production management team is that found in Harold Boxall's response to a memorandum from C.M.Woolf, in October 1934, complaining that actual production costs always exceeded estimates. Boxall gave the example of the studio needing recently to employ 'an entire night staff (of carpenters) during the production of *The Iron Duke*, in order to avoid any delay in shooting which would have been extremely serious, owing to the high daily costs of operating with such a star as Mr. Arliss'.[56]

Conclusion

Michael Balcon left Gaumont-British in December 1936 to work as Director of Production for the British wing of MGM, with the remit to produce annually a small number of high-profile, big-budget films using Britain as the subject context and featuring contracted American stars and/or British stars known to American audiences.[57] These films were targeted at both US and British audiences and distributed by the parent company's distribution arm. Balcon's move represented the culmination of a distinct current in British film-making experience during the 1930s. Access to the American market had become a prime objective for the three most ambitious British production directors during this period, Alexander Korda, Herbert Wilcox and Balcon himself. It spawned the concept of the 'International' film in Britain and spurred each to devise distinctive strategies to that end.

In an important contribution to British film history, Andrew Higson has drawn a distinction between the strategies of direct competition— competition with the major Hollywood studios—and product differentiation, adopted by domestic producers in response to the ubiquitous Hollywood product. Product differentiation is defined as:

> producing films with distinctly indigenous attractions and a qualitatively different regime of experiences and pleasures, generally on a budget small enough to make it feasible to generate a profit from the home market alone.[58]

This depiction of the bulk of film-making in Britain should not be allowed to obscure the reality that most British film-makers were attempting to learn from and follow the Hollywood narrative approach, even if Hollywood's Poverty Row studios proved to be a more appropriate standard for many of them. Higson's choice of *Sing As We Go* to illustrate this differentiated tendency, only serves to show how mainstream the aspirations of most British films actually were. For Higson, that film serves as a point of contrast with the film-making activities of Balcon's studio which, during the mid-1930s, took 'the route of direct competition with Hollywood, tackling it on its own terms and its territories'.[59] In his essay on Jessie Matthews' musical vehicle *Evergreen* he writes:

> The result of Gaumont-British's internationalist policy, its push for ever greater profits, its bid to appeal to domestic and foreign audiences attuned to the pleasures and ideologies of America, is to produce a film which works very successfully within the conventions of that cinema.[60]

Indeed, Higson agrees that *ex ante*:

> As a corporate strategy, Gaumont-British's efforts in the mid-1930s seem to have all the hallmarks of a potentially successful, well directed economic attempt to establish a national film industry capable of operating in the international market-place.[61]

Yet, he argues that, ultimately, the failure of Gaumont-British's attempt on the American market rests squarely with the structural impediments to distribution and exhibition. He agrees with, and indeed quotes, Mark Ostrer's *ex-post* assessment of the 'International' strategy, that its failure was:

> not due to any lack of merit, but to the fact that we are not accorded playing time in the most important situations, these being almost exclusively controlled by American producing interests.[62]

The occasional successes of films such as *The Private Life of Henry VIII* and *The Scarlet Pimpernel* are reduced by Higson to 'short term conditions', and he concludes that 'there was no incentive for American majors to make room'.[63]

In an article written by the columnist William Boehnel, in *The New York World Telegram* in November 1935, on the topic of Gaumont-British's threat to Hollywood's supremacy as the film capital of the world, Balcon is quoted as arguing (with pointed reference to Korda):

> Judge no British organization by what you read or hear of its intended activities. Base your judgement on the quality and regularity of its output.[64]

Evidence of the extent of the distribution of Gaumont-British's films in the American market shows that independent cinemas were much more likely to make screen time available than those owned by the vertically integrated 'majors'. Yet the performance of these films in terms of box-office receipts is generally poor when compared with rival films playing simultaneously or films immediately preceding/following. Ultimately, the studio's output was not sufficiently attractive to the audiences of the leading American cities to persuade the 'American majors to make room'. After all, we should not expect indigenous American film organizations not to take advantage of the uneven playing field on which films were competing for box-office receipts.

In assessing Balcon's contribution to Gaumont-British's efforts to establish a foothold in the US it is difficult not to agree with Dom M. Merereau, General Manager of *Film Daily*, writing from New York in October 1934 that:

> your presence, personality and spirit has been a tremendous factor in establishing in the minds of Americans that your organization is one to be looked up to and respected in this country as well as England.[65]

Although the strategy failed, the very idea that a British film company would be able to mount and sustain a campaign in the American market would have been unthinkable five years earlier and is indicative of the strides made by the British industry and in particular Gaumont-British during this period. In the end film-making potential was undermined by the inadequacies of its own organizational and financial structures and led to Balcon's transfer to MGM-British.[66]

Postscript

The problem of access to the American market for non-American producers of mass-media products is a constant and continuing theme. A recent variant comes from Terry Illot in connection with the failure of the British film production company Goldcrest—the latest in a long line of domestic production businesses which failed to sustain a presence in the American market.

> All over the world, it seems, television producers are prey to a perennial pipe-dream: that somehow the very best of their output—prize winning dramatisations of literary classics, ground-breaking documentaries, acclaimed recordings of ballet and opera, folk dance and song—will find an audience in the vast, rich, and fragmented American market. It doesn't happen.[67]

11

Difficulties Facing the Production Sector of the British Film Industry
During the Late 1930s

Even the quality producers had to operate on a scale of production far below that of their competitors in the British market, the Hollywood companies. Only Korda was rash enough to try to compete on equal terms. The size of the market to which the Americans had unquestioned access, not just for the occasional special picture but for all their films, made a very lavish scale of production economically viable…During the decade every British quality producer tried to break into this market, but circuit distribution and the terms upon which films were distributed were in the control of the big producers and they very naturally did not wish to encourage British competition.

Rachael Low[1]

Rachael Low was in no doubt as to the central problem facing British film producers in the 1930s. The concluding two sentences of her *Film-Making in 1930s Britain* read:

It has been argued in this study that although it is sometimes possible, with a lot of talent, to make good films on modest budgets in general a constant level of high quality is expensive and needs to be sure of a big market not just for isolated films but as a matter of course. The Americans had one and the British did not, and underlying the history of the British film industry is its struggle to come to terms with that fact.[2]

This chapter examines these issues. Clearly the corollary of Low's argument is twofold: that big-budget film-making in Britain as a commercial activity was doomed to failure as long as sustained access to the American market was not forthcoming; and that the only chance of obtaining access was for British film-makers to make films of a standard comparable to that of the best of the Hollywood product.

The Gaumont-British legacy

As we have seen in the case of Gaumont-British, the risks associated with this strategy were considerable for indigenous film-makers. The *Kine Weekly* in December 1934 reported a declaration by the Chairman of Gaumont-British, Mark Ostrer, that contractual arrangements had been made with two Broadway (New York) 6,000 seater cinemas—the Roxy and Radio City Music Hall—to show Gaumont-British/Gainsborough films. This followed the success of *Chu Chin Chow* and *Little Friend* at the former and *Jew Süss* at the latter.[3] Ostrer indicated that the international reputation of its films had led the company to adopt an export orientated sales strategy which in turn required it to establish its own sales staff in the United States. This venture failed disastrously. Thirteen months later, Ostrer was reported in the same journal as stating:

> We have attempted to distribute our films in the American market in the hope that we could capture from that most important territory a return on our films to which we think we are justly entitled. Although our films were reviewed most favourably in that country results have not justified our expectations... This is not due to any lack of merit, but to the fact that we are not accorded playing time in the most important situations, these being almost wholly controlled by American producing interests. At the close of our financial year in 1935 we had in stock a number of films which failed to realise their book values, and consequently considerable losses were incurred not only in respect of these particular films, but also in respect of most of the films subsequently released.[4]

The effect on the British film industry was profound. The optimism voiced by Ostrer and Balcon in 1934 turned to caution. George Arliss wrote an article in which he argued that 'America can afford to spend £200,000 on a film and still make a handsome profit. England cannot spend half that sum without courting disaster.' He proposed a strategy, the first premise of which was that film-makers should make:

less pretentious films and make for the English markets... By making British films at modest prices for the English market, films that depend for their success mainly on story and the acting—and, in time, we could excel in such films as Hollywood excels in the spectacular productions—I think the American market would be automatically opened to us. The companies in the United States that control the kinemas are not likely to be slow in making a bid for any British films out of which they can make money.[5]

George Smith, a British film producer with over fifty Quota films to his credit, also thought that much of the production-side of the industry was too ambitious:

> our films have suffered from a little too much genius and not enough commonsense. That is why I plead that it is the bread and butter pictures which should form the solid background for the film Industry in this country. Including the Empire, we have a great home market which is quite enough to make films pay without a thought to foreign markets: why not, then, make reasonable [sic] priced films for this market—and let those which achieve greatness go out as our ambassadors to America and the rest of the world.[6]

Clearly, Smith did not seem to share Arliss' belief that well-made modest-budget films might find a niche in the American market. However, in writing in praise of the British 'B' picture, he argued that 'Modestly priced films have been, and are, the finest training ground for artists, directors and technicians. Here these young people are given real opportunities to emerge from obscurity', and names the directors Brian Desmond Hurst, David MacDonald and Michael Powell as cases in point.

Alexander Korda and strategic adventure

In sad contrast to the archival riches of the American film industry for this period, the poverty of British studio archive materials, including accounting information, is a serious impediment to our understanding of business behaviour. Fortunately, budget and box-office information has been uncovered for a number of films made by Alexander Korda's London Films, sufficient at least to complement the Gaumont-British data introduced in Chapter 10 and highlight Low's claims about the size of the market and some of the commercial problems faced by British film-makers.[7]

London Films has been subjected to more scrutiny than any other British production company during the 1930s. Its founder and prime-mover—Alexander Korda—is the subject of an authoritative biography by Karol Kulik (1975), and Sarah Street (1986) has written a scholarly account of the company's relations with its principal backer, Prudential Assurance.[8] As Rachael Low points out, Korda is generally represented as a pivotal figure in contemporaneous reports of the film industry in Britain during the period: 'More has been written about Korda than about other producers in Britain, and he has been both praised for restoring British film production and blamed for ruining it.'[9] Kulik claims that:

> from the Autumn of 1933 to early 1937, Alexander Korda was the most important single figure in the film industry in Britain, the man whose progress, whose success and failures were the focus of everyone's attention.[10]

From the time of the critical and commercial success of *The Private Life of Henry VIII* (1933) and for the remainder of the 1930s, Korda, in the words of Ian Dalrymple[11] 'made films in England for international exhibition amongst the best American, French and German product'.

Evidence for this may be found in Table 11.1, which lists London Films' releases for the period of the investigation. To begin with, London Films film budgets were substantially higher than those of Gaumont-British films reported in the previous chapter. Furthermore, there is a clear tendency for film budgets to rise over the period, culminating in the release of the equivalent of two 'million dollar' films in *Things To Come* and *Knight Without Armour* in 1936 and 1937 respectively.[12]

In all cases where domestic revenue figures are available, the company was unable to cover its production costs from domestic sales. Revenues from the domestic market account for only 44 per cent of the production costs, ranging from a high of 87 per cent for the *Private Life of Henry VIII* to a low of 16 per cent for *The Private Life of Don Juan*. Being amongst the Top 10 'hits' of the season in the domestic market, when measured by the POPSTAT index of popularity, was not sufficient to cover costs. Penetration into foreign markets, particularly that of the United States, was critical to the success or otherwise of its big-budget productions.

Korda developed a clear three-pronged strategy including the production of international films—films which were rooted in time and

Table 11.1: *London Films' film budgets and domestic gross box-office revenues information[a]*

Film title	Date of Board of Trade registration (1)	Production cost (2) (£)	British box-office receipts (£) (3)	Col. (3)/col. (2) (4)	POPSTAT rank in year of release (5)
Wedding Rehearsal	11 Aug. 1932	42,080			71
Men of Tomorrow	6 Oct. 1932	30,922			519
That Night in London	10 Nov. 1932	33,428			355
Strange Evidence	2 Feb. 1933	28,350			520
Counsel's Opinion	16 Mar. 1933	25,424			104
Private Life of Henry VIII	22 Aug. 1933	93,710	81,825	0.87	2
Girl From Maxims	24 Aug. 1933	62,578			227
Cash	5 Nov. 1933	22,694			369
Catherine the Great	25 Jan. 1934	127,868	58,308	0.46	4
Private Life of Don Juan	6 Sept. 1934	109,987	18,048	0.16	51
Scarlet Pimpernel	3 Jan. 1935	138,392	108,306	0.78	3
Sanders of the River	4 May 1935	144,161	94,360	0.65	6
Moscow Nights	19 Dec. 1935	57,916			72
Ghost Goes West	17 Jan. 1936	161,362	86,894	0.54	6
Things To Come	24 Feb. 1936	256,028	71,757	0.28	9
Forget Me Not	30 Apr. 1936	74,007	15,163	0.21	147
Man Who Could Work Miracles	27 July 1936	136,604	30,976	0.23	46
Rembrandt	20 Nov. 1936	140,236	34,140	0.24	29
Men Are Not Gods	30 Nov. 1936	92,606	22,308	0.24	81
Elephant Boy	11 Feb. 1937	149,882	54,615	0.36	27
Knight Without Armour	10 June 1937	307,201			19
Squeaker	22 Oct. 1937	92,940	42,854	0.46	90
Return of the Scarlet Pimpernel	2 Nov. 1937	94,433	56,569	0.60	165

Source: London Films Special Collection, Box 5, British Film Institute.

Note: Most of the data on budgets and revenues appear in an internal memorandum dated 7 Jan. 1946 addressed to London Films' Production Manager, Sir David Cunynghame, in response to a request for information on the company's 1930s productions. Unfortunately, the domestic revenue earned by *Knight Without Armour* is not listed. Production costs pertaining to seven of the first eight films in the list—the exception being *The Private Life of Henry VIII*—appear on an internal Cost of Production schedule for 'Films Completed and in the Course of Production as at 30 April 1933'.

place but in a style which was international rather than parochial;[13] the ownership and management of first-rate production facilities; and world-wide distribution, including the American market, through United Artists. In many ways the strategy was brilliantly successful. From a base of almost nothing, Korda and his organization were able to produce a string of films which were critically acclaimed and popular on an international scale up to and beyond the outbreak of the Second World War: projects such as *The Thief of Bagdad* and *That Hamilton Woman* were completed in Hollywood. In the case of London Films, as with its fellow United Artists' American counterpart, Goldwyn Studios, individual film popularity was critical. Both were small-output, big-budget 'hit' producers, making it difficult for either to absorb the losses associated with 'flops' within the annual portfolio of films. Clearly, London Films took on the challenge associated with big-budget film-making. To be successful they needed to make significant and sustained penetration into the American market.

Table 11.2[14] shows that although high by British standards, the budgets which Korda dedicated to his principal films were also comparable to the bulk of Hollywood production. For instance, neither Warners nor RKO made a more expensive film than *Knight Without Armour* in 1937. London Films' production budgets were of the order necessary to ensure the highest production values, with the data displayed in the table providing further evidence of the ambitions of the British studio to compete at the highest level.

John Maxwell and strategic conservatism

Having burnt his fingers on a small number of large-budget productions in the late 1920s and unsuccessfully attempted to market British International Production films in the United States, John Maxwell had developed a quite different approach to film budgets. According to Rachael Low:

> He operated a policy of cut-price window dressing, trying to make cheap films which looked like expensive ones. After determined efforts in the early years to get their films into America had largely failed, costs were kept firmly down in order that the films, still ostensibly first features, might make a profit from the home market alone.[15]

Maxwell was clear minded as far as the balance between revenues and

Table 11.2: *The number of films from the Warners, MGM and RKO studios with greater production budgets than those of London Films' principal box-office attractions during the year of release in descending order of production cost*

Film title	British release year	Warners	MGM	RKO
Knight Without Armour	1937	0	9	0
Things to Come	1936	0	4	0
Ghost Goes West	1936	3	11	2
Elephant Boy	1937	3	12	1
Sanders of the River	1935	3	6	3
Rembrandt	1936	4	13	2
Scarlet Pimpernel	1935	5	6	3
Man Who Could Work Miracles	1936	3	11	2
Catherine the Great	1934	3	12	1
Private Life of Don Juan	1934	6	19	2
Private Life of Henry VIII	1933	2	18	1

Sources: Mannix Ledger (MGM); Schaefer Ledger (Warners); the Trevlin Ledger (RKO); and London Films Special Collection, Box 5, British Film Institute Library (London Films). Also see Glancy (1992,1995) for MGM and Warners Ledgers; and Jewell (1994) for RKO.

costs was concerned. His was the only major business in the film industry in Britain to make profits throughout the 1930s. As early as 1935 he predicted the speculative bubble that broke in late 1936 and so badly affected production levels in 1937. In an article in *Kine Weekly* he warned the trade against the growth in speculative ventures, based upon the spectacular success of *The Private Life of Henry VIII*, and set up by

> inexperienced promoters who, with no particular or intimate knowledge of the business, seem to think that by raising £60,000 from confiding City gentlemen, [they can] plunge into picture making and leave a large loss behind them[16]

In the same article, Maxwell proceeded to give a lesson in industry finance. He declared:

> I have made inquiries which satisfy me that not more than ten

pictures a year gross more than £100,000 in this country. Of these prizes six or more are carried off by our American competitors, leaving four, five or six for British companies. Consider the matter in the light of economies. The total amount of film hire available for feature pictures from the kinemas may be placed at £7.5 millions after making allowance for the amount of available film hire in newsreels and shorts etc. From this £7.5 millions must be deducted roughly one-third as the cost of print distribution, publicity, etc., leaving five millions available for division amongst all the feature pictures put out in this country in one year. As the number of feature pictures released in a year is about 500, it is easy to calculate the average gross per picture. Assuming there are only three or four £100,000 grosses—which means £65,000 or so net to the producer—available for British pictures in the year, and that as against this there are at the moment 30 to 40 pictures of which it is claimed to have cost £60,000 to £70,000, and [sic] it will be seen that the danger of heavy losses to which I have drawn attention is in no way exaggerated.

The size of the British market

It is interesting to contrast the figures set down by Maxwell with those presented to the British Association by Simon Rowson a year earlier, in September 1934.[17] Based upon Entertainment Tax returns and a massive sample of ticket sales from 2,000 cinemas for the first six months of 1934, Rowson estimated that the British public paid £40,200,000 in cinema admissions during that year.[18] Net of tax he maintained that total admission revenues were about £35 million including £1.3 million from Irish exhibitor receipts. Of this, Rowson calculated that renters received £11.8 million which after overhead and operating expenses left them with £8.1 million. This is some £3 million more than Maxwell estimated for feature film revenue only. Of this, Rowson estimated that the sum paid by renters to domestic film-makers was of the order of £2.4 million—including shorts and newsreel outputs—with another £0.6 million coming from overseas earnings. Given that the renters generated profits of between £0.4 and £0.5 million, Rowson calculated that the amount being remitted to American film-makers was £5.3 million. These final estimates are presented in Table 11.3.

Comparison of the Maxwell and Rowson calculations is made more complex by Rowson's inclusion of all film output, whilst Maxwell

Table 11.3: *Rowson's estimates of net remittances from the trade in Britain in films during 1934*

	USA (£m)	Other countries (£m)	Total (£m)
Remittances for foreign films	5.3	0	5.3
Receipts from British films shown abroad	0.1	0.5	0.6
Net remittances	5.2	0.5	4.7

Source: Rowson (1934).

attends only to feature films. Intuitively, it is difficult to believe that over a quarter of producers' net revenues—the difference between the two estimations after Rowson's estimate of renters' profits has been deducted—came from non-feature film sources. If we accept Rowson's calculations as being the more scientific in origin and assume that a tenth of film revenues was generated by 'shorts', cartoons, documentaries, newsreels, etc., this leaves a net income of £6,790,000 to be shared amongst the film producers.[19] Altogether, 664 feature films were released in Britain in 1934. Taking the number of these films as a denominator, an arithmetic mean revenue per film of £10,226 is generated, which is of the same order of magnitude as the £10,000 per film inferred by Maxwell.[20]

It is possible to obtain an estimation of how the net box-office revenue calculated by Rowson was distributed across these 664 films by adopting the POPSTAT index of film popularity. Table 4.2 shows the frequency distribution of POPSTAT scores generated by feature films for the period 1932–37. The distribution is characterized by a marked concentration of films around the modal score, which lies well below the value of the arithmetic mean. By transforming the POPSTAT scores generated by 1934 releases, on a *pro rata* basis, into imputed revenue figures based upon the assumed £6,790,000 revenue earned by the producers of feature films, it is possible to obtain an idea of the scale of net box-office takings per film. These are presented in Table 11.4 and would appear to broadly confirm Maxwell's assessment of net box-office returns and risks associated with British big-budget films being largely dependent upon the domestic market.[21] It is evident from Table 11.4 that only 26 films made upwards of £20,000 at the box-office and only 13 films earned £30,000 or more for their makers, with an arithmetic mean box-office for those 161 British films securing a least one booking in the sample cinema set of just over £10,000.

Clearly, the frequency distribution presented in Table 11.4 is crudely arrived at. Maxwell provides no source for his claim concerning box-office performance. Rowson avoids making such estimations. The London Films budgets used earlier in this paper are found in a single archive document and are not supported by details of their composition. In general, evidence is hard to come by and poor in quality. Indeed, these factors provided the principal impetus for formulating the POPSTAT index. The little evidence that is forthcoming supports the validity of the index and Low's claim concerning the commercial reality which confronted film producers dependent upon the British market.

The 1938 Cinematograph Films Act

The 1938 Cinematograph Films Act attempted to address some of these issues. It was based on an exhaustive inquiry into the domestic industry which resulted in the Moyne Committee Report of 1936, leading to the White Paper of 1937.[22] The 1927 Films Act was regarded within the Board of Trade as a success and the Quota was retained to provide a cushion of security for domestic producers.[23] As has been shown, however, it had been difficult for domestic film-makers to cover costs, given the size and slow growth of the domestic market.

An important new element in the 1938 Act was the reciprocity clause by which foreign renters could obtain Quota credits by buying the distribution rights to British films for £20,000 or more. Its inclusion in the Act was the consequence of the obvious structural asymmetry between the British and American market for film producers.[24] The American market, with a population rising from 123 million to 132 million between 1930 and 1940, and with a significantly higher per caput income than Britain, was dominated by the Hollywood product, whereas in Britain, these same American producers were joined by indigenous film-makers in a more competitive scramble for box office.[25]

The structural problem which faced British studios is highlighted by the fact that the Hollywood studios were able nearly to cover the production and domestic distribution costs of their film output from the revenues earned from the American market. Consequently, overseas markets—of which Britain was by far the most important—were perceived as the source of their profits. Evidence for this is shown in Table 11.5, which records the annual total production budget and

Table 11.4: *Frequency distribution of imputed box-office revenues (net of Entertainment Tax) for all feature films released in Britain in 1934*

Class intervals (£s)	Frequency of all films	Frequency of British films
0	81	27
1–9,999	332	107
10,000–19,999	165	28
20,000–29,999	50	13
30,000–39,999	15	5
40,000–49,999	11	4
50,000–59,999	4	1
60,000–69,999	2	2
70,000–79,999	2	1
80,000–89,999	1	0
90,000–99,999	0	0
100,000–109,999	1	0
Total	664	188

Estimated total box-office revenue for all films = £6,790,000
Arithmetic mean box-office revenue for all films = £10,226

Estimated total box-office revenue for British films = £1,667,385
Arithmetic mean box-office revenue for British films = £8,869
Arithmetic mean box-office revenue for British films with a POPSTAT
    score > 0 = £10,356

Sources: POPSTAT distribution; Rowson (1934).

Note: A number of British films made exclusively for Quota purposes only, failed to obtain a single showing in the national sample cinema set. Their presence has the effect of lowering the mean POPSTAT score for domestic production. If they were removed from the denominator the mean POPSTAT result would rise to a level slightly above that for the whole population of films released in 1934.

US box-office performances of Warners films during this period.

Unfortunately the source of information concerning the performance of Warners output—the William Schaefer Ledger—does not record distribution costs. However, if we assume that the distribution costs were approximately one-third of box-office revenue, then combined production and distribution costs of films produced at

Warners from 1932 and 1937 approximately equal US box-office receipts.[26] Film distribution outside of the American market consequently represented, after the deduction of overseas distribution costs, clear profits for the Hollywood majors. Given that Britain was Hollywood's long-standing principal overseas market, it is not surprising that they took the legislative constraints on their ability to dominate the British market so seriously.[27]

For British firms, access to the American market appeared to be the only way of moving beyond the constraints imposed by the size of the domestic and Empire market and the competitiveness of the Hollywood product. For these reasons, John Maxwell became a champion of the reciprocity idea, maintaining in a 1937 *Kine Weekly* article:

> The object in allowing this barter scheme is to provide the British producer with the extra money he must get from overseas markets if he is to escape extinction, and gradually to build up an outlet for British pictures in the American market...The American market, of course, is three times the size of the British market in money yielding capacity, and if the British producer cannot get a reasonable part of his cost from that market he can never hope to establish his business on a footing that will enable him to compete with foreign film producers who have a world market at their disposal.[28]

Maxwell argued that the size and complexity of the US distribution structure, with its thirty-six distribution centres compared to the eight

Table 11.5: *Warners' annual production costs and US gross box-office, 1932–1937*

	US box-office ($000s)	Production costs ($000s)	Costs/box-office
1932	17,891	11,316	0.63
1933	19,769	11,579	0.59
1934	18,603	12,279	0.66
1935	25,670	16,127	0.63
1936	21,632	14,777	0.68
1937	29,642	21,845	0.74

Source: William Schaefer Ledger.

in Britain, militated against British producer-renters organizing their own distribution company. He alluded to the 'The gallant attempt of Gaumont-British to do this' and explained its failure in terms of 'the lack of a large enough quantity of pictures suitable for that market to justify the very heavy costs of distribution there'.[29] Reciprocation, on the other hand:

> will avoid any British company having to undertake the enormous cost of setting up an organization, and get the American producers to use their own existing organizations to distribute British pictures.[30]

Hence, the key element in this agency arrangement was the financial commitment required from the American renter. Maxwell continued:

> The fact that under the reciprocity scheme the American companies would have a substantial financial interest in putting out these pictures in America would, in my view, completely overcome the difficulties that have hitherto existed. American companies, like any individual, once they have their money invested in a proposition, will do their utmost to get back that money, plus a profit.[31]

There is no evidence that the reciprocity option led to a sizeable increase in the numbers of British films distributed in the United States. However, it must be said that our knowledge of those British films which were popular in the American market is lamentably poor. It would appear that rather than adopt greater numbers of British productions for distribution in US markets, the major American companies responded to the double and triple renters' Quota provision of the 1938 Act either by establishing their own production facilities or by investing heavily in a new set of domestic companies set up to produce small numbers of big-budget films at existing production studios.[32] By doing so, they reduced their need for cheap domestic Quota-fillers. In the 1938–9 renters' year, 10 foreign (American) films were registered as triples and 21 as doubles. This in turn lowered domestic film output levels as this new provision reduced the Quota requirement by 41 films, although the decline in actual exhibition was nothing like as dramatic, with well over 20 per cent of cinema screen space occupied by British films.[33] But, in Rachael Low's words, 'the quota quickie was dead.'[34]

Conclusion

The decade of the 1930s was one of remarkable achievement for British film-makers. Not only had their films taken a 25 per cent share of the market between 1932 and 1937, but by the end of the decade an infrastructure was in place which enabled them to meet much of Britain's war-time needs for entertainment. Between 1928 and 1935/6 the area of stage floor space in British studios had increased over sevenfold from 105,211 to 769,557 square feet. Yet, as the New Year issues of the *Kine Weekly* show, even as late as 1934 there was only 301,584 square feet of studio space available to film-makers, with the real explosion occurring between 1935 and 1937 when studio floor space more than doubled.[35]

Commensurate information on the human capital side of the industry is difficult to find. Low maintains that by the end of 1936 the AC-T trade union claimed to represent virtually all studio technicians, with a membership of 1,200.[36] The Board of Trade Census put the number of those working in the production sector of the film industry on 16 October 1937 at 9,529, of whom 4,125 were artistes.

There appears to have been no shortage of capital coming into the industry during this period. The speculative nature of much industry financing has been the subject of investigation.[37] The increased number of firms entering the industry, given the low levels of profits earned by incumbents, suggests that many investors found the allure of potential profitability which accompanied box-office success—*The Private Life of Henry VIII* factor—sufficient to overcome the reality of the risks entailed. It is clear from Table 11.6 that 1936 saw a spectacular increase in film industry investment which tailed away rapidly, so that levels in 1938 were down by a factor of ten. As noted earlier, the expansion of studio floor space, and hence output capacity, peaked precisely at that moment when the speculative bubble of film industry financing burst, leaving established film-makers with plenty of facilities, but lacking operational finance. In the case of Korda's principal backer, Prudential Assurance, its attempt to gain boardroom control of London Films' costs failed, and by 1938 it was looking to loosen its ties.[38] Both major combines sought to cut back on production, which was increasingly viewed as loss-making.

Klingender and Legg in 1937 developed a hypothesis of 'over extension' to highlight operation of the domestic capital market in financing British film companies. The excess to which they refer was the speculative nature of film finance and the opportunistic behaviour of a number of domestic film production companies. The decline in domestic production in 1937 was the consequence of loans being called in and tumbling share values. For perhaps the first time since the 1927 legislation, there was a shortage of funds available for film production. Undoubtedly, many companies in the industry had been poorly managed at both a commercial and financial level, and major changes were required at a corporate level. Unlike its counterpart in the United States during Hollywood's corporate crises of the early 1930s, the British banking/financial sector failed to take the initiative in restructuring the financial and corporate sides of the British film business. It preferred to extend overdrafts and make and re-schedule loans to new and existing producers, including those new firms speculatively set up in 1935 and 1936 through the Aldgate Trust, where the loans advanced were underwritten by Lloyds insurers.

Ultimately, the reason for the commercial and financial difficulties which beset the British film industry during the late 1930s may boil down to the very simple reality voiced by numerous commentators in this chapter, that the domestic market was simply too small to privilege domestic film-makers. As James Foreman-Peck has written:

Table 11.6: *New film industry companies, 1935–1938*

	1935	1936	1937	1938
Production companies	88	94	73	69
Distribution companies	1	0	0	7
Finance companies	0	2	7	0
Studios	4	5	6	1
Laboratories	1	1	0	1
Recording studios	0	0	0	1
Stills studios	0	0	0	1
Colour companies	0	0	3	0
Newsreel companies	0	0	1	0
Total capital value (£) of new companies	1,070,390	2,102,500	769,100	199,760

Sources: Kine Weekly, 6 January 1938 and 12 January 1939; Wood (1986).

The problem Britain faced in the industries of the 'second industrial revolution' was that she generally lacked rapidly growing markets for the products. When the markets were available, as in the urban markets for processed foods such as biscuits, British companies did grow large enough to require professional managers to a much greater extent than elsewhere. Such firms were internationally competitive.[39]

Given the structural weaknesses of the domestic industry and conversely the strength and resilience of the American 'system of provision' at the time of the 1927 legislation, the contribution of British film-makers to the pleasures enjoyed by cinemagoers in Britain during the 1930s was marked. Although we know little of the operational efficiencies of British studios, there is ample evidence in both the scale of the inputs and the quantity and quality of the outputs to suggest that British studios were able to make significant inroads into domestic market shares. Moreover, British International Pictures (ABPC) and Gaumont-British both adopted multi-divisional and vertically integrated-type organizational structures, although in itself this tells us little *per se* about the quality of internal organization.

From our knowledge of the profit and loss ledgers of films from the MGM, RKO and Warners studios, the contribution of non-American box-office receipts was critically important to the profitability of each season's production portfolio. It would appear that the inability of British film producers to sustain extensive penetration into the American market seriously constrained the revenues and profitability for the top domestic producers and led the two most ambitious and successful of them—Gaumont-British and London Films—into financial loss. The collapse of domestic production in 1937 and the triple and double Quota provisions of the 1938 legislation signalled the absence of a 'grand strategy' on the part of British producers, financial institutions and government. It was as if the emergence of a domestic film industry, occasioned but certainly not planned by the authors of the 1927 legislation, was an experience which was not understood by their 1938 counterparts, in that they were unable to resist the sectional interests of American renters. The provisions of the 1938 legislation certainly proved to be a success for American 'grand strategy' and but for the outbreak of war with Germany in 1939 may have led to a weakening of British production to 'B' movie status only.

12

Conclusion

> The firm ... is not simply the passive respondent to the constraints
> imposed on it from the outside. To a greater extent, it creates its
> own environment.
>
> Paul Auerbach[1]

In addressing Hollywood's historical dominance of the international
market for feature films since the 1920s, Ian Jarvie alludes to the
'structural resilience' of what Fine and Leopold have termed a 'system
of provision'. Jarvie starts his examination of the success of the
Hollywood film at the point of consumption and then works back to
explain the structure which delivered and sustained it over a period of
forty years and beyond into the era of television and video. 'Structural
resilience', is his phrase to describe how Hollywood was largely able
to maintain itself, whilst responding and finding solutions to a set of
emerging uncertainties.

For Jarvie, 'Hollywood and its pictures... set the standard for what
was required to make really big money.'[2] However, whilst a necessary
condition, this was not by itself sufficient to ensure global domination.
Jarvie explains the latter as a consequence of a 'grand strategy', based
on relations between the US government and Hollywood over the
period. He writes:

> It transpires that although market dominance was not gained by
> strategy, it was held by strategy, and challenges were beaten off by
> strategy. Some of that strategy was conscious, some was
> not...Nevertheless 'strategy' is the best name for it.[3]

It is within the context of this 'system of provision', established during the 1910s and early 1920s, that Jarvie analyses the emergence of a film industry in Britain during the 1930s. He maintains that, given the strengths of the 'system', the British effort at securing trade success was 'quite futile'. For Jarvie:

> the British... appreciation of their situation was faulty. The fundamental secrets of the success of the Americans were opaque to them. They put it down to chicanery rather than strategy.[4]

The impediments to trade success for British producers lay not just with the quality of the Hollywood product but also with its world-wide system of distribution and the pro-active commercial and trade policy pursued by the US government. The American distributors had by the late 1910s created a world market for their films. In most countries outside of Europe the market and Hollywood were synonymous, and in Europe Hollywood was dominant. As Thomas Saunders argues with respect to European cinemas during the 1930s:

> In the study of European film cultures there is growing recognition that to treat Hollywood as extrinsic to national cinemas is simply inadmissible. Be it French, German, British, Italian or even Soviet, the culture of interwar cinema was first and foremost American.'[5]

For British firms to match the performance of their Hollywood counterparts, access to this system of distribution was indispensable.

Yet even then this may not have been sufficient. Hoskins, McFadyen and Finn have developed the concept of 'cultural discount' to explain how it is that the relatively large size of the US market leads to significant market advantages for US producers of film and television world-wide. Their premise is that indigenous audiences commonly favour home cultural products to those made elsewhere:

> A cultural discount for traded programmes or films arises because viewers in importing markets generally find it difficult to identify with the way of life, values, history, institutions, myths, and physical environment depicted. Language differences are also an important reason for a cultural discount.[6]

In asking the question 'Why does the US dominate trade?', in Chapter 4 of their book, the authors contrast the hypothetical revenue performance of two producers—one based in a large market and the other in a small market. They assume that in the absence of a cultural discount, both would take identical shares of each other's markets. They then drop this assumption and suppose that both markets are characterized by a common level of discount. Under these circumstances the producer from the small market base performs less well than its counterpart since it loses x per cent (the discount) of the large market whilst the firm from the large market loses the same x per cent, but this time only of the small market. Relatively larger revenues earned by the producer based in the larger market allow it to spend more on budgets which, given a positive link between budgets and quality, leads to a competitive advantage: large-budget producers are able to spend more per minute of film running time. Once made, if products from the two markets are allowed to compete equally in both markets, the 'qualities' of the more resource-intensive product from the large market may prove sufficient to overcome the cultural discount it faces outside of its home base.

The structural explanation for Hollywood's dominance, with its emphasis on continuity over the long period, both in terms of industrial structure and aesthetic form, receives further support from a group of historians contributing to an important appraisal of contemporary Hollywood cinema, edited by Neale and Smith.[7] In their introduction to the book, the editors focus on a division which has emerged over the classical/post-classical depiction of Hollywood, defined in Bordwell, Staiger and Thompson's pioneering work on film industry organization and film structure and aesthetics.[8] They argue that whereas Douglas Gomery and Richard Maltby maintain separately that proponents of the discontinuity thesis dismiss too easily the underlying themes which have characterized Hollywood throughout its history, such as its single-minded pursuit of profits and its pragmatic approach to aesthetics, other contributors to the debate such as Thomas Schatz and Justin Wyatt insist on a break in the hegemony of a dominant (classical) style with the demise of cinemagoing as a leisure activity during the 1950–75 period and its impact upon the studio system. For them, Hollywood, in re-discovering a cinema of genres, together with new ways of marketing and packaging the product, was able to arrest the decline and stabilize its institutional framework.

On the question of how aspects of Hollywood's dominance affected British cinema of the 1930s, I would argue that a major difficulty with Jarvie's approach when applied to British production activities is its retrospection: it is not helpful in explaining *ex ante* the process by which British films were 'pushing back' the market share of their American rivals during the middle years of the 1930s.

> In the UK there was a protracted struggle that at one point seemed
> to be pushing back, but over confidence led to over extension.[9]

Furthermore, his statement that: 'British films owed their existence to, indeed were in a certain way parasitic upon, the exhibition industry created around the American product', undervalues the genuine progress made by the domestic industry during the 1930s, including the growth in production studios and new cinema building.[10]

As has been shown in Chapter 4, British films made a major impact on the domestic market in Britain during the period 1932–37. This was particularly pronounced for the three years 1934, 1935 and 1936, the period during which, it will be remembered from Chapter 10, Gaumont-British—led in this enterprise by Michael Balcon—made its determined bid to market its in-house films onto the American market. At the same time, Alexander Korda's London Films was engaged in producing a series of big-budget films—discussed in Chapter 11—also targeted at the American market. Certainly, these films were influenced greatly by the dominant aesthetic conventions of Hollywood as was most commercially serious film-making in Britain. As should be clear from the discussion found towards the end of Chapter 10, on this point I take issue with Andrew Higson's argument that British production can be divided between those films which consciously aped Hollywood's prestige products and those which were deliberately differentiated from them. This does not mean, however, that I am arguing that films from the two British studios were not without their own idiosyncratic house style and not recognized for this by British audiences—see, for instance, Sue Harper's depiction of the different types of costume drama produced by the two studios.[11]

That the cinemas throughout the length and breadth of Britain in which these British films were shown did the bulk of their business screening Hollywood productions gives rise to Jarvie's 'parasite' claim, the corollary being that in the absence of the Hollywood product, the British market would have not been as developed as it in fact was, thereby lessening the commercial opportunity for domestic production. I would maintain, however, that such speculation fails to throw light onto the dynamic circumstances in which British film-makers found themselves in the 1930s, and how they acted upon them. In social life there is always an antecedent, or rather a complex set of antecedents, to all social phenomena, and in this case the Americans were largely responsible for shaping and giving form to the 'system of provision' built around film as a commodity. However, the argument developed throughout this book is that the 'system of provision' in Britain was profoundly affected by the 1927 Cinematograph Films Act to the extent that British producers developed industrial organizations which allowed them to produce, distribute, and in the case of Gaumont-British and ABPC, exhibit, on a significant scale, a series of films which competed equally for audience affections with films emanating from Hollywood. Furthermore, very many of these films are shown—by means of the POPSTAT index of popularity—to have been genuinely popular with indigenous audiences. In the event of a different set of circumstances, the *ex-ante* environment facing film entrepreneurs would have been different and very likely the decisions taken by them would also have been different. With the perfect vision of hindsight, the failure of Gaumont-British and London Films, in particular, to break out of the constraints of the British market can be ascribed to a faulty strategy on their part. However, with the inevitably imperfect vision of foresight, the risk environment can become known more fully only as a result of such commercial experiments. What functions do entrepreneurs serve if they do not challenge constraints and gamble on hunches?

The vertically integrated model of film organization which was championed by the Hollywood 'majors' was not perhaps the ideal form for British film companies, in that big-budget production was rarely profitable when distribution was confined largely to the British market. However, this organizational structure gave both Gaumont-British and ABPC the base to establish large-scale production facilities from which to challenge Hollywood's hegemony in the British market. London Films developed similarly grand production facilities without the in-house distribution and exhibition links, while British and Dominions allowed United Artists to distribute their major productions. Other principal British film producers such as Associated Talking Pictures and Twickenham Films launched their own in-house distribution companies. The decisions taken and the complex configuration which emerged and then changed was the consequence, for the greater part, of optimistic business decision-making in a novel context—novel in contrast with the moribund state of the British industry in the 1920s.

From this emerged a large body of films, some distinctive genres (Chapter 8) and a set of stars (Chapter 9) which form a most important component of British Cinema *in toto* and, as such, British culture. Had those films not been made by that set of producers, working in a variety of contractual arrangements with distributors and exhibitors, British culture would have been something different from what it has become. Of course, this would not have been of the least concern to those agents working in the industry at that time when deciding which resources to deploy, and how, in their search for a profitable aesthetic. Nevertheless, their activities created structures, networks, organizations and institutions within which actors, artists, tradespeople and managers learned how to do things and earned their livelihoods. That the product of their labour reached out to so many people and affected the popular imagination—in the way in which things were perceived—should be of greatest importance to the cultural historian.

The research project which is the subject of this book is predicated upon the idea that it is important to know which films at the time of their release audiences paid to watch, the types of film that attracted particular audiences, which cinemas they watched them at and where these cinemas were located. This knowledge is captured systematically and transformed into a statistically sound body of data (POPSTAT) which is used to measure audience preferences between films. The methodology behind this measure is set out in Chapter 3. My enquiry therefore differs from those of Janet Staiger and Barbara Klinger—studies which seek to show how readings of films are mediated historically by the circumstances of their consumption—in that it focuses exclusively upon the period of initial release.[12] It is argued that film production was not driven by thoughts about its reception by posterity. Rather, film-makers and their production companies, as well as distributors and exhibitors, were preoccupied with the immediate reception of their film commodities, since it was this, manifest in the form of box-office returns, which determined commercial success.

In not knowing fully what they liked, audiences were engaged in a continuous discovery process from which preferences only became known *ex post*. Moreover, they demanded some level of novelty, the form and extent of which was opaque to them *ex ante*. Film-makers, accordingly were engaged in the most risky business of producing new film-types—the general principles of which are set down in Chapters 7 and 8—which had to be in some respect unique.

That British films were of interest to indigenous audiences is apparent in the POPSTAT results published in Chapter 4 in which it

251

is shown that 96 of the 300 annual Top 50 films for the years 1932–37 were made by home-based production companies. Whilst the book gives some clue to the characteristics of these films, they warrant a fuller investigation by film historians. However, this book is not about British films and their performance *per se*, but rather about the British market for films, and not surprisingly it affirms the dominant collective position occupied by the principal Hollywood studios.

Although the work which has been presented in the book is specific to Britain in the 1930s, it need not be. Indeed, a major claim that I would make for the POPSTAT methodology is its transparency and transferability. For example, a researcher interested in investigating the impact of Hollywood on European societies during the inter-war period, including the differential way in which the respective establishments fashioned protection legislation, or not, as the case may be, would be able to use it to obtain a comparative measure of Hollywood's penetration in each of the markets as well as the performance of particular films. Similarly, the impact of British films in the Australian market during the same period is another study which has intriguing cultural aspects. As has been shown in this study—in Chapters 5 and 6—the POPSTAT methodology also allows the researcher to investigate further all kinds of issues specific to a locality/region, such as the way in which the local 'systems of provision' operated and how this affected choice. In this way, patterns of audience preferences across class, gender and within localities can be more firmly based empirically.

This is a book about film which has not used the texts of films or the personas of stars to investigate their meaning(s). It makes the point that there is a great deal that can be and needs to be discovered about the popularity of films and stars prior to and apart from such topics. Until recently the question 'meaning to whom?' has seldom been asked in relation to the millions of people who weekly paid their money at the box office and thus made possible the production of those films for theorists to theorize about. Yet it was those meanings which determined whether film producers succeeded or failed.

For the time period of the book it is too late to conduct a systematic investigation of those meanings. Apart from oral history accounts, which, however fascinating they may be, are by their nature statistically unrepresentative, first-hand meaning reports are not to be had, but this does not mean that the enterprise is a wholly lost cause.[13] The data assembled in this book provide, for the first time, an objective ordering as to what was popular. This raises the possibility of other fields of enquiry. The question as to why a film highly placed in that ordering was so placed, might be the subject of further investigation using wide-ranging fields of historical enquiry, such as social and/or business history. However, one might be equally interested in middle ranking films—films that were widely distributed, but normally as part of double-billing programmes, little known today because they are seldom revived or shown on television. What were they? What was their subject material? Why did studio heads think that they might appeal to audiences? For instance, *Oil for the Lamps of China* (Warners, 1935—POPSTAT rank, 118) is a film about the career of an 'oil man' whose devotion and uncritical loyalty to his company almost wrecks his marriage. Seen today, the film is most striking for its delineation of the relationship between man and wife, which seems to be 50 years ahead of its time. In contrast to *Top Hat* (RKO, 1935—POPSTAT rank, 2)—a very popular film on release which has become part of the received canon of Hollywood cinema, and which currently appears in television listings many times a year and is widely available on video— the meanings of *Oil for the Lamps of China* are time-localized but no less important than those of the films which have generated multiple meanings over a long period.

Because it can be reclassified, it is my hope that the data in this book will serve as a source of reference for those historians of film interested in the knowledge of audience preferences, at either the macro or micro level. The work is decidedly empirical in flavour and requires that its readers are prepared to accept that knowledge can be acquired through systematic observation and that this is a most valuable source of evidence. It is my intention that its methods and reasoning should be clear and open to criticism and refutation. It is my hope that its explanations may open some conceptual doors for its readers.

Appendix 1

The national sample cinema set

Cinema	City	Owner	Seats	Mid-range price (shillings)	Potential revenue (shillings)	POPSTAT weight
1932						
Forum	Birmingham	ABC	1,259	2.0	2,518.0	0.68
Futurist	Birmingham	Independent	1,223	1.8	2,201.4	0.60
Gaumont	Birmingham	GB	2,092	1.8	3,765.6	1.02
Scala	Birmingham	Independent	800	1.7	1,360.0	0.37
West End	Birmingham	GB	1,385	2.1	2,908.5	0.79
Empire	Bristol	ABC	1,437	1.0	1,437.0	0.39
Hippodrome	Bristol	Independent	2,000	1.3	2,600.0	0.71
Kings	Bristol	ABC	1,485	1.3	1,930.5	0.52
New Palace	Bristol	GB	1,574	1.5	2,361.0	0.64
Regent	Bristol	GB/PCT	2,050	1.5	3,075.0	0.83
Stoll	Bristol	Stoll	1,887	0.9	1,698.3	0.46
Triangle	Bristol	ABC	1,400	1.3	1,820.0	0.49
Whiteladies	Bristol	ABC	1,314	1.3	1,708.2	0.46
Davis	Croydon	Independent	3,712	2.0	7,424.0	2.01
Caley	Edinburgh	Independent	1,900	1.1	2,090.0	0.57
New Picture	Edinburgh	GB/PCT	951	1.6	1,521.6	0.41
New Victoria	Edinburgh	GB/PCT	2,006	1.6	3,209.6	0.87
Palace	Edinburgh	Independent	750	1.5	1,125.0	0.31
Playhouse	Edinburgh	Independent	3,000	1.3	3,900.0	1.06
Rutland	Edinburgh	GB/GTC	2,187	1.3	2,843.1	0.77

Cinema	City	Owner	Seats	Mid-range price (shillings)	Potential revenue (shillings)	POPSTAT weight
St Andrews	Edinburgh	GB	1,399	1.0	1,399.0	0.38
Synod	Edinburgh	Independent	1,470	1.0	1,470.0	0.40
Coliseum	Glasgow	ABC	3,094	1.3	4,022.2	1.09
Cranstons	Glasgow	Independent	750	1.5	1,125.0	0.31
Grand	Glasgow	Independent	733	1.4	1,026.2	0.28
Greens Playhouse	Glasgow	Independent	4,200	1.8	7,560.0	2.05
La Scala	Glasgow	Independent	1,191	1.5	1,786.5	0.48
New Savoy	Glasgow	GB	2,000	1.4	2,800.0	0.76
Picture House	Glasgow	GB/PCT	1,572	0.8	1,257.6	0.34
Regal	Glasgow	ABC	2,359	1.3	3,066.7	0.83
Regent	Glasgow	Independent	1,119	1.5	1,678.5	0.46
Assembly	Leeds	GB/PCT	900	1.4	1,260.0	0.34
Coliseum	Leeds	GB	2,000	1.4	2,800.0	0.76
Majestic	Leeds	GB/PCT	2,392	1.3	3,109.6	0.84
Paramount	Leeds	Paramount	2,550	2.4	6,120.0	1.66
Rialto	Leeds	Independent	1,256	1.5	1,884.0	0.51
Scala	Leeds	GB	1,794	1.5	2,691.0	0.73
Tower	Leeds	Independent	1,125	0.9	1,012.5	0.27
Forum	Liverpool	ABC	1,835	2.0	3,670.0	1.00
Futurist	Liverpool	Independent	1,029	1.7	1,749.3	0.47
Palais de Luxe	Liverpool	Independent	1,300	1.8	2,340.0	0.63
Prince of Wales	Liverpool	ABC	700	1.7	1,190.0	0.32
Rialto	Liverpool	GB/PCT	1,274	1.3	1,656.2	0.45
Royal Hippodrome	Liverpool	GB/PCT	3,200	0.8	2,560.0	0.69
Scala	Liverpool	Independent	650	1.9	1,235.0	0.34
Trocadero	Liverpool	GB/PCT	1,362	1.3	1,770.6	0.48
Adelphi*	London	Independent	1,352	4.3	5,813.6	1.58
Alhambra*	London	Independent	1,438	4.3	6,183.4	1.68
Astoria	London	GB/GTC	1,696	2.0	3,392.0	0.92
Capitol	London	GB/GTC	1,560	5.5	8,580.0	2.33
Carlton	London	Paramount	1,159	6.5	7,533.5	2.04
Dominion	London	GB/APPH	2,835	3.8	10,773.0	2.92
Empire	London	MGM	3,226	4.3	13,871.8	3.76
London Coliseum*	London	Independent	2,089	4.3	8,982.7	2.44
Leicester Square	London	RKO	1,771	5.0	8,855.0	2.40
Hippodrome*	London	Independent	1,392	4.3	5,985.6	1.62

Cinema	City	Owner	Seats	Mid-range price (shillings)	Potential revenue (shillings)	POPSTAT weight
Palace*	London	Independent	1,245	4.3	5,353.5	1.45
Marble Arch Pav.*	London	GB	1,189	3.7	4,399.3	1.19
Metropole	London	Independent	2,000	3.3	6,600.0	1.79
New Gallery	London	GB/PCT	1,450	5.0	7,250.0	1.97
New Victoria	London	GB/PCT	2,786	3.8	10,586.8	2.87
Plaza	London	Paramount	1,896	5.0	9,480.0	2.57
Regal	London	ABC	2,400	5.0	12,000.0	3.26
Rialto	London	Independent	684	5.0	3,420.0	0.93
Stoll	London	Stoll	2,425	2.0	4,850.0	1.32
Tivoli	London	GB/PCT	2,097	5.0	10,485.0	2.84
London Pavilion	London	ABC	1,574	1.5	2,361.0	0.64
Deansgate	Manchester	Independent	866	1.3	1,125.8	0.31
Gaiety	Manchester	ABC	1,434	1.4	2,007.6	0.54
Market Street	Manchester	Independent	620	1.5	930.0	0.25
New Oxford	Manchester	Independent	1,150	1.5	1,725.0	0.47
Paramount	Manchester	Paramount	2,914	2.4	6,993.6	1.90
Piccadilly	Manchester	Independent	2,324	1.7	3,950.8	1.07
Regal	Manchester	Independent	1,600	1.6	2,560.0	0.69
Royal	Manchester	Independent	1,943	1.8	3,497.4	0.95
New Westgate	Newcastle	GB/Denman	1,865	1.0	1,865.0	0.51
Paramount	Newcastle	Paramount	2,608	2.4	6,259.2	1.70
Pavilion	Newcastle	GB/Denman	1,525	1.4	2,135.0	0.58
Stoll	Newcastle	Stoll	1,389	1.7	2,361.3	0.64
Queens	Newcastle	GB/PCT	1,400	1.5	2,100.0	0.57
Albert Hall	Sheffield	GB	1,611	1.5	2,416.5	0.66
Central	Sheffield	Independent	1,539	1.3	2,000.7	0.54
Cinema House	Sheffield	Independent	800	1.0	800.0	0.22
Electra	Sheffield	Independent	587	0.8	469.6	0.13
Hippodrome	Sheffield	ABC	2,445	1.2	2,934.0	0.80
Regent	Sheffield	GB/PCT	2,207	1.5	3,310.5	0.90
Union Street	Sheffield	Independent	970	0.8	776.0	0.21

Note: * refers to the legitimate London theatres which occasionally served as cinemas during the period. The average potential revenue of the set of cinemas is 3,686.33 shillings

Additions to/deletions from the sample
1933

Hippodrome	London	No film programme		
London Pavilion	London	Closes		
Leicester Square	London	United Artists becomes the new lessee. Seating capacity falls to 1760		

1934

Embassy	Bristol	Independent	2,021	1.4
New Bedford	Glasgow	Independent	1,800	1.5
Ritz	Leeds	ABC	1,950	1.5
Adelphi	London	No film programme		
Alhambra	London	No film programme		
Coliseum	London	No film programme		
London Pavilion	London	Re-opens under United Artists lease	1,209	5
Palace	London	No film programme		

1935

Paramount	Glasgow	Paramount	2,784	2.5
Prince of Wales	Liverpool	Programme no longer listed in *Kine Weekly* Closes and then re-opens in 1936		
Paramount	Liverpool	Paramount	2,595	2.5
Gaumont	Manchester	Gaumont-British	2,300	2.4

1936

Olympia	Liverpool	ABC	2,900	1.4
Capitol	London	Closes		
Paramount	London	Paramount	2,568	2.5

1937

Paramount	Birmingham	Paramount	2,424	2.5
Curzon	London	Independent	492	5.5
Gaumont	London	Gaumont-British	1,328	5

Source: *Kine Year Books*, 1932–37; Eyles (1993, 1996); Eyles and Skone (1991).

Appendix 2

126 London West End 'hits' screened between 1 January 1932 and 31 March 1938

Film	Studio	Distributor
100 Men and A Girl	Universal	GFD
39 Steps	Gaumont-British	Gaumont-British
42nd Street	WB	WB
Affairs of Voltaire	WB	WB
Anna Karenina	MGM	MGM
Arrowsmith	Goldwyn	UA
Aunt Sally	Gainsborough	Gaumont-British
Barretts of Wimpole Street	MGM	MGM
Bedtime Story	Paramount	Paramount
Bitter Sweet	B&D	UA
Blonde Venus	Paramount	Paramount
Bowery	20th Century	UA
Broadway Melody of 1936	MGM	MGM
Buccaneer*	Paramount	Paramount
Camels are Coming	Gainsborough	Gaumont-British
Camille	MGM	MGM
Captain Blood	WB	FNP
Captains Courageous	MGM	MGM
Cardinal Richelieu	20th Century	UA
Catherine the Great	London Films	UA
Cavalcade	Fox	Fox
Charge of the Light Brigade	WB	FNP
China Seas	MGM	MGM
Clairvoyant	Gainsborough	Gaumont-British

Film	Studio	Distributor
Constant Nymph	Gaumont-British	Gaumont-British
Crusades	Paramount	Paramount
Cuckoo in the Nest	Gaumont-British	W&F
Damaged Lives	Columbia	Columbia
David Copperfield	MGM	MGM
Devil and the Deep	Paramount	Paramount
Dinner at Eight	MGM	MGM
Dreaming Lips	Trafalgar	UA
Escape Me Never	B&D	UA
Evergreen	Gaumont-British	Gaumont-British
Farewell Again	Pendennis	UA
Follow the Fleet	RKO	Radio
Foreign Affaires	Gainsborough	Gaumont-British
FP1	UFA	W&F
G Men	WB	WB
Garden of Allah	Selznick	UA
General Died at Dawn	Paramount	Paramount
Ghost Goes West	London Films	UA
Goldwyn Follies*	Goldwyn	UA
Good Companions	Gaumont-British/ Welsh-Pearson	Ideal
Good Earth	MGM	MGM
Goodnight Vienna	B&D	W&F
Grand Hotel	MGM	MGM
Great Ziegfeld	MGM	MGM
Green Pastures	WB	WB
Guv'nor	Gaumont-British	Gaumont-British
Hell Divers	MGM	MGM
House of Rothschild	20th Century	UA
Hurricane*	Goldwyn	UA
I Met Him in Paris	Paramount	Paramount
I Was A Spy	Gaumont-British	W&F
I'm No Angel	Paramount	Paramount
Iron Duke	Gaumont-British	Gaumont-British
It Happened One Night	Columbia	Columbia
Jack of All Trades	Gainsborough	GB
Jack's the Boy	Gainsborough	W&F
Jew Süss	Gaumont-British	Gaumont-British
Kid from Spain	Goldwyn	UA

Film	Studio	Distributor
Kid Millions	Goldwyn	UA
King Kong	RKO	Radio
Knight Without Armour	London Films	UA
Libelled Lady	MGM	MGM
Life of Emile Zola	WB	FNP
Little Lord Fauntleroy	Selznick	UA
Little Women	RKO	Radio
Lives of a Bengal Lancer	Paramount	Paramount
Lost Horizon	Columbia	Columbia
Love on Wheels	Gainsborough	W&F
Man of Aran	Gainsborough	Gaumont-British
Man Who Knew Too Much	Gaumont-British	Gaumont-British
Marie Walewska* (US: Conquest)	MGM	MGM
Mary of Scotland	RKO	Radio
Merry Widow	MGM	MGM
Milky Way	Paramount	Paramount
Modern Times	Chaplin	UA
Movie Crazy	Lloyd	Paramount
Mr Deeds Goes to Town	Columbia	Columbia
Mutiny on the Bounty	MGM	MGM
Nell Gwyn	B&D	UA
Night Like This	B&D	W&F
Nothing Sacred*	Selznick	UA
On Wings of Song (US: Love Me Forever)	Columbia	Columbia
One Hour With You	Paramount	Paramount
One Night of Love	Columbia	Columbia
Painted Veil	MGM	MGM
Plainsman	Paramount	Paramount
Pot Luck	Gainsborough	Gaumont-British
Prisoner of Zenda	Selznick	UA
Private Life of Henry VIII	London Films	UA
Queen Christina	MGM	MGM
Riptide	MGM	MGM
Road to Glory	20Fox[a]	20Fox
Roberta	RKO	Radio
Roman Scandals	Goldwyn	UA
Rome Express	Gaumont-British	Gaumont-British

Film	Studio	Distributor
Romeo and Juliet	MGM	MGM
Ruggles of Red Gap	Paramount	Paramount
Sanders of the River	London Films	UA
Scarlet Pimpernel	London Films	UA
Shall We Dance	RKO	Radio
Shanghai Express	Paramount	Paramount
She Married Her Boss	Columbia	Columbia
Show Boat	Universal	GFD
Sign of the Cross	Paramount	Paramount
Soldiers of the King	Gainsborough	W&F
Souls at Sea	Paramount	Paramount
Spitfire	RKO	Radio
Stage Door*	RKO	Radio
Star is Born	Selznick	UA
Strike Me Pink	Goldwyn	UA
Swing Time	RKO	Radio
Tale of Two Cities	MGM	MGM
Theodora Goes Wild	Columbia	Columbia
Things To Come	London Films	UA
Top Hat	RKO	Radio
Tovarich*	WB	WB
Trouble in Paradise	Paramount	Paramount
True Confession*	Paramount	Paramount
Tunnel	Gaumont-British	Gaumont-British
Under the Red Robe	New World	20Fox
Victoria the Great	Imperator	Radio
Wings of the Morning	New World	20Fox

Sources: *Kine Weekly*; *London Evening News*

Notes:
* denotes those films which received extended West End runs but were either not shown in Bolton or had not completed their exhibition circuit there before 31 March 1938. See Chapter 3 for premier dates and cinemas.
a. During the 1930s, 20th Century and Fox merged, so in Appendix 2 and Appendix 3 all three studio names appear, with 20th Century-Fox abbreviated to 20Fox.

Appendix 3

POPSTAT Top 100 films in Britain, 1932–1937

Rank	Film	Studio	Distributor	Nation'y	POPSTAT
Films released in 1932					
1	Jack's the Boy	Gainsborough	W&F	Br.	50.12
2	Grand Hotel	MGM	MGM	USA	45.24
3	Shanghai Express	Paramount	Paramount	USA	41.39
4	Rome Express	Gaumont-British	Gaumont-British	Br.	36.33
5	Arrowsmith	Goldwyn	UA	USA	36.11
6	Goodnight Vienna	B&D	W&F	Br.	34.19
7	One Hour With You	Paramount	Paramount	USA	32.02
8	Hell Divers	MGM	MGM	USA	31.11
9	Love On Wheels	Gainsborough	W&F	Br.	29.66
10	Night Like This	B&D	W&F	Br.	27.99
11	Movie Crazy	Lloyd	Paramount	USA	27.37
12	Dr Jekyll and Mr Hyde	Paramount	Paramount	USA	27.37
13	Thark	B&D	W&F	Br.	27.19
14	Delicious	Fox	Fox	USA	24.53
15	Trouble in Paradise	Paramount	Paramount	USA	23.70
16	Frankenstein	Universal	Universal	USA	23.37
17	Emma	MGM	MGM	USA	23.24
18	Tell Me Tonight	Cine Alliance	W&F	Anglo-German	23.20
19	Tarzan the Apeman	MGM	MGM	USA	22.60
20	Silent Voice (US: The Man Who Played God)	WB	WB	USA	22.55
21	Devil and the Deep	Paramount	Paramount	USA	22.53
22	Smilin' Through	MGM	MGM	USA	22.51
23	Melody of Life (US: Symphony of Six Million)	RKO	Radio	USA	22.42
24	Private Lives	MGM	MGM	USA	21.93

Rank	Film	Studio	Distributor	Nation'y	POPSTAT
25	First Year	Fox	Fox	USA	21.50
26	Bring 'em Back Alive	RKO	Radio	USA	21.21
27	Blonde Venus	Paramount	Paramount	USA	20.77
28	Strange Interval (US: Strange Interlude)	MGM	MGM	USA	19.63
29	Mata Hari	MGM	MGM	USA	19.53
30	Lost Squadron	RKO	Radio	USA	18.97
31	Midshipmaid	Gaumont-British	W&F	Br.	18.92
32	It's a King!	B&D	W&F	Br.	18.76
33	Service For Ladies	Paramount British	Paramount	Br.	18.60
34	Prosperity	MGM	MGM	USA	18.56
35	As You Desire Me	MGM	MGM	USA	18.42
36	Letty Lynton	MGM	MGM	USA	17.93
37	What Price Hollywood?	RKO	Radio	USA	17.74
38	Faithful Heart	Gainsborough	Ideal	Br.	17.66
39	Love Me Tonight	Paramount	Paramount	USA	17.49
40	Flag Lieutenant	B&D	W&F	Br.	17.18
41	Say It with Music	B&D	W&F	Br.	16.76
42	Frightened Lady	Gainsborough	Ideal	Br.	16.74
43	Cheat	Paramount	Paramount	USA	16.68
44	Sky Devils	Caddo	UA	USA	16.57
45	Man I Killed	Paramount	Paramount	USA	16.52
46	Blue Light	Sokal	Universal	Germany	16.27
47	Scarface	Caddo	UA	USA	16.08
48	Tess of the Storm Country	Fox	Fox	USA	15.91
49	Forbidden	Columbia	UA	USA	15.70
50	Leap Year	B&D	W&F	Br.	15.41
51	Successful Calamity	WB	WB	USA	15.38
52	There Goes the Bride	Gainsborough	Ideal	Br.	14.99
53	After the Ball	Gaumont-British	Gaumont-British	Br.	14.98
54	Blessed Event	WB	WB	USA	14.80
55	Maid of the Mountains	BIP	Wardour	Br.	14.78
56	Sherlock Holmes	Fox	Fox	USA	14.74
57	Horse Feathers	Paramount	Paramount	USA	14.53
58	Arsene Lupin	MGM	MGM	USA	14.52
59	Night of June 13	Paramount	Paramount	USA	14.51
60	Mr Robinson Crusoe	Elton	UA	USA	14.50
61	Tonight or Never	Goldwyn	UA	USA	14.45
62	Marry Me	Gainsborough	Ideal	Br.	14.38
63	Looking on the Bright Side	ATP	Radio	Br.	13.92
64	Wet Parade	MGM	MGM	USA	13.61
65	Woman from Monte Carlo	WB	WB	USA	13.49
66	Love Contract	B&D	W&F	Br.	13.29
67	Old Dark House	Universal	Universal	USA	12.98

Rank	Film	Studio	Distributor	Nation'y	POPSTAT
68	A Nous La Liberté	Tobis	Universal	France	12.73
69	Honourable Mr. Wong (US: The Hatchet Man)	FNP	FNFD	USA	12.70
70	Bird Of Paradise	RKO	Radio	USA	12.66
71	Wedding Rehearsal	London Films	Ideal	Br.	12.53
72	Strange Case of Clara Deane	Paramount	Paramount	USA	12.07
73	Around the World in 80 Minutes	Columbia	UA	USA	12.04
74	Divine Love	Columbia	UA	USA	11.91
75	This is the Night	Paramount	Paramount	USA	11.90
76	Skyscraper Souls	MGM	MGM	USA	11.87
77	Lodger	Twickenham	W&F	Br.	11.82
78	Lucky Girl	BIP	Wardour	Br.	11.82
79	Thunder Below	Paramount	Paramount	USA	11.60
80	Night After Night	Paramount	Paramount	USA	11.57
81	Lovers Courageous	MGM	MGM	USA	11.49
82	Bitter Tea of General Yen	Columbia	UA	USA	11.40
83	Bill of Divorcement	RKO	Radio	USA	11.36
84	Reputation	RKO	Radio	USA	11.34
85	Congorilla	Johnson	Fox	USA	11.29
86	Payment Deferred	MGM	MGM	USA	11.28
87	Impossible Lover (US: Huddle)	MGM	MGM	USA	11.25
88	His Woman	Paramount	Paramount	USA	11.23
89	Sporting Widow	Paramount	Paramount	USA	11.17
90	Happy Landing (US: Flying High)	MGM	MGM	USA	11.15
91	Sleepless Nights	BIP	Wardour	Br.	11.14
92	Rain	Feature	UA	USA	11.09
93	Crowd Roars	WB	WB	USA	11.05
94	Big Broadcast	Paramount	Paramount	USA	10.86
95	Merrily We Go	Paramount	Paramount	USA	10.83
96	Lady and Gent	Paramount	Paramount	USA	10.79
97	Winner Take All	WB	WB	USA	10.78
98	Corsair	AC	UA	USA	10.78
99	Two Against the World	WB	WB	USA	10.77
100	Baroud	Ingram	Ideal	Br.	10.68

Films released in 1933

1	Cavalcade	Fox	Fox	USA	92.89
2	Private Life of Henry VIII	London Films	UA	Br.	55.13
3	King Kong	RKO	Radio	USA	42.59
4	Sign on the Cross	Paramount	Paramount	USA	41.73
5	Kid from Spain	Goldwyn	UA	USA	36.87
7	I'm No Angel	Paramount	Paramount	USA	34.75
8	Good Companions	Gaumont-British	Ideal	Br.	31.73

Rank	Film	Studio	Distributor	Nation'y	POPSTAT
9	Bedtime Story	Paramount	Paramount	USA	29.88
10	42nd Street	WB	WB	USA	29.51
11	Falling For You	Gainsborough	W&F	Br.	27.85
12	Footlight Parade	WB	WB	USA	25.94
13	Working Man	WB	WB	USA	25.81
14	Waltz Time	Gaumont-British	W&F	Br.	24.44
15	Invisible Man	Universal	Universal	USA	24.33
16	Bitter Sweet	B&D	UA	Br.	24.24
17	Dinner at Eight	MGM	MGM	USA	23.87
18	Damaged Lives	Columbia	Columbia	USA	23.72
19	Masquerader	Goldwyn	UA	USA	23.52
20	Cuckoo in the Nest	Gaumont-British	W&F	Br.	23.49
21	Bowery	20th Century	UA	USA	23.47
22	Yes, Mr Brown	B&D	W&F	Br.	23.18
23	Song of Songs	Paramount	Paramount	USA	23.01
24	FP1	Universum	W&F	Anglo-German	22.52
25	Affairs of Voltaire	WB	WB	USA	22.50
26	Cynara	Goldwyn	UA	USA	22.07
27	Wandering Jew	Twickenham	Gaumont-British	Br.	22.02
28	Only Yesterday	Universal	Universal	USA	21.92
29	That's a Good Girl	B&D	UA	Br.	21.83
30	Gold Diggers of 1933	FNP	FNFD	USA	21.69
31	Hell Below	MGM	MGM	USA	20.69
32	Dancing Lady	MGM	MGM	USA	20.51
33	State Fair	Fox	Fox	USA	20.35
34	Soldiers of the King	Gainsborough	W&F	Br.	19.95
35	I Am a Fugitive from a Chain Gang	WB	WB	USA	19.12
36	Tugboat Annie	MGM	MGM	USA	18.07
37	Aunt Sally	Gainsborough	Gaumont-British	Br.	18.03
38	Blarney Stone	B&D	W&F	Br.	17.65
39	White Sister	MGM	MGM	USA	17.60
40	Friday the 13th	Gainsborough	Gaumont-British	Br.	18.61
41	It's a Boy!	Gainsborough	W&F	Br.	17.06
42	Adorable	Fox	Fox	USA	16.94
43	Orders is Orders	Gaumont-British	Gaumont-British	Br.	16.77
44	Mystery of the Wax Museum	WB	WB	USA	16.44
45	Just My Luck	B&D	W&F	Br.	16.42
46	Constant Nymph	Gaumont-British	Gaumont-British	Br.	16.11
47	Paddy the Next Best Thing	Fox	Fox	USA	16.09
48	Morning Glory	RKO	Radio	USA	15.71
49	Night Flight	MGM	MGM	USA	15.66
50	Too Much Harmony	Paramount	Paramount	USA	15.39
51	This Week of Grace	Real Art	Radio	Br.	15.24

Rank	Film	Studio	Distributor	Nation'y	POPSTAT
52 This Day and Age	Paramount	Paramount	USA	15.19
53 College Humour	Paramount	Paramount	USA	15.03
54 Lady for a Day	Columbia	Columbia	USA	14.91
55 King's Vacation	WB	WB	USA	14.89
56 Every Woman's Man (US: The Prize Fighter and the Lady)	MGM	MGM	USA	14.77
57 Gabriel Over the White House	MGM	MGM	USA	14.76
58 Broadway Thru' a Keyhole	20th Century	UA	USA	14.75
59 Sorrell and Son	B&D	UA	Br.	14.73
60 No Man of Her Own	Paramount	Paramount	USA	14.52
61 Just Smith	Gaumont-British	W&F	Br.	14.44
62 Rasputin the Mad Monk (US: Rasputin and the Empress)	MGM	MGM	USA	14.37
63 My Weakness	Fox	Fox	USA	14.31
64 This is the Life	British Lion	British Lion	Br.	14.24
65 If I Had a Million	Paramount	Paramount	USA	14.17
66 Alice in Wonderland	Paramount	Paramount	USA	13.78
67 White Woman	Paramount	Paramount	USA	13.77
68 My Lips Betray	Fox	Fox	USA	13.74
69 Farewell to Arms	Paramount	Paramount	USA	13.28
70 Midnight Club	Paramount	Paramount	USA	12.97
71 I Lived With You	Twickenham	W&F	Br.	12.75
72 Turkey Time	Gaumont-British	Gaumont-British	Br.	12.63
73 Ghoul	Gaumont-British	W&F	Br.	12.62
74 Jennie Gerhardt	Paramount	Paramount	USA	12.56
75 Christopher Bean	MGM	MGM	USA	12.37
76 Britannia of Billingsgate	Gaumont-British	Gaumont-British	Br.	12.24
77 Reunion in Vienna	MGM	MGM	USA	12.20
78 Son of a Sailor	FNP	FNP	USA	12.19
79 Havana Widows	FNP	FNP	USA	12.10
80 Hot Pepper	Fox	Fox	USA	12.10
81 Way to Love	Paramount	Paramount	USA	12.05
82 Tonight is Ours	Paramount	Paramount	USA	12.05
83 Employees' Entrance	FNP	FNFD	USA	12.05
84 Prince of Arcadia	NFP	W&F	Br.	12.01
85 Blonde Bombshell (US: Bombshell)	MGM	MGM	USA	12.00
86 Up for the Derby	B&D	W&F	Br.	11.98
87 Mayor of Hell	WB	WB	USA	11.95
88 Crime of the Century	Paramount	Paramount	USA	11.82
89 Power and the Glory	Fox	Fox	USA	11.72
90 Call Her Savage	Fox	Fox	USA	11.70
91 Conquerors	RKO	Radio	USA	11.63
92 King of the Jungle	Paramount	Paramount	USA	11.58
93 Flesh	MGM	MGM	USA	11.49

Rank	Film	Studio	Distributor	Nation'y	POPSTAT
94 International House	Paramount	Paramount	USA	11.25
95 Little Damozel	B&D	W&F	Br.	11.14
96 Dick Turpin	JSP	Gaumont-British	Br.	11.13
97 Three Cornered Moon	Paramount	Paramount	USA	11.13
98 Man from Toronto	Gainsborough	Ideal	Br.	11.12
99 Stranger's Return	MGM	MGM	USA	11.00
100 Men Must Fight	MGM	MGM	USA	10.98

Films Released in 1934

1 House of Rothschild	20th Century	UA	USA	63.57
2 One Night of Love	Columbia	Columbia	USA	48.86
3 Roman Scandals	Goldwyn	UA	USA	46.35
4 Catherine the Great	London Films	UA	Br.	43.61
5 Jew Süss	Gaumont-British	Gaumont-British	Br.	41.16
6 Blossom Time	BIP	Wardour	Br.	36.97
7 Queen Christina	MGM	MGM	USA	33.03
8 Little Women	RKO	Radio	USA	32.55
9 It Happened One Night	Columbia	Columbia	USA	31.58
10 Nell Gwyn	B&D	UA	Br.	30.81
11 Merry Widow	MGM	MGM	USA	29.86
12 Cleopatra	Paramount	Paramount	USA	27.54
13 Chu Chin Chow	Gaumont-British	Gaumont-British	Br.	27.45
14 Evergreen	Gaumont-British	Gaumont-British	Br.	27.35
15 Barretts of Wimpole Street	MGM	MGM	USA	27.00
16 Jack Ahoy	Gaumont-British	Gaumont-British	Br.	26.87
17 Wonder Bar	FNP	FNP	USA	26.14
18 Riptide	MGM	MGM	USA	25.32
19 Camels are Coming	Gainsborough	Gaumont-British	Br.	24.54
20 Painted Veil	MGM	MGM	USA	24.39
21 Treasure Island	MGM	MGM	USA	23.82
22 Gay Divorcee	RKO	Radio	USA	23.29
23 Bulldog Drummond	20th Century	UA	USA	22.83
24 Last Gentleman	20th Century	UA	USA	22.71
25 Strictly Confidential (US: Broadway Bill)	Columbia	Columbia	USA	22.34
26 Thin Man	MGM	MGM	USA	22.27
27 Count of Monte Cristo	Reliance	UA	USA	22.24
28 Evensong	Gaumont-British	Gaumont-British	Br.	21.88
29 My Song for You	Gaumont-British /Cine-Allianz	Gaumont-British	Anglo-German	21.66
30 Cup of Kindness	Gaumont-British	Gaumont-British	Br.	21.25
31 Man of Aran	Gainsborough	Gaumont-British	Br.	21.08
32 Red Wagon	BIP	Wardour	Br.	20.68
33 Duck Soup	Paramount	Paramount	USA	19.46

Rank	Film	Studio	Distributor	Nation'y	POPSTAT
34	Lady of the Boulevards (US:Nana)	Goldwyn	UA	USA	19.03
35	Transatlantic Merry-Go-Round	Reliance	UA	USA	19.00
36	Bright Eyes	Fox	Fox	USA	18.33
37	Sing As We Go	ATP	ABFD	Br.	18.05
38	Scarlet Empress	Paramount	Paramount	USA	17.38
39	Fashions of 1934	WB	WB	USA	17.33
40	Cat and the Fiddle	MGM	MGM	USA	17.30
41	Princess Charming	Gainsborough	Gaumont-British	Br.	17.29
42	Man Who Knew Too Much	Gaumont-British	Gaumont-British	Br.	17.18
43	Flying Down to Rio	RKO	Radio	USA	17.05
44	Murder at the Vanities	Paramount	Paramount	USA	16.83
45	Little Friend	Gaumont-British	Gaumont-British	Br.	16.78
46	Evelyn Prentice	MGM	MGM	USA	16.65
47	Chained	MGM	MGM	USA	16.21
48	Viva Villa	MGM	MGM	USA	16.09
49	Unfinished Symphony	Gaumont-British /Cine-Alianz	Gaumont-British	Anglo-German	15.96
50	Cat's Paw	Lloyd	Fox	USA	15.67
51	Private Life of Don Juan	London Films	UA	Br.	15.61
52	Sadie McKee	MGM	MGM	USA	15.38
53	Dames	WB	WB	USA	15.32
54	Here Comes the Navy	WB	WB	USA	15.29
55	Design for Living	Paramount	Paramount	USA	15.19
56	Dirty Work	Gaumont-British	Gaumont-British	Br.	15.16
57	Spitfire	RKO	Radio	USA	15.13
58	Moulin Rouge	20th Century	UA	USA	15.04
59	Belle of the Nineties	Paramount	Paramount	USA	15.01
60	World Moves On	Fox	Fox	USA	14.94
61	Forgotten Men	BIP	Wardour	Br.	14.87
62	House of Connelly (US: Carolina)	Fox	Fox	USA	14.69
63	Radio Parade of 1935	BIP	Wardour	Br.	14.14
64	Stand Up and Cheer	Fox	Fox	USA	13.95
65	Love, Life and Laughter	ATP	ABFD	Br.	13.79
66	Hi! Nellie	WB	WB	USA	13.78
67	Mala the Magnificent (US: Eskimo)	MGM	MGM	USA	13.77
68	Kidnapped (US: Miss Fane's Baby Is Stolen)	Paramount	Paramount	USA	13.58
69	George White's Scandals	Fox	Fox	USA	13.42
70	Good Girl (US: Good Dame)	Paramount	Paramount	USA	13.38
71	Twenty Million Sweethearts	WB	WB	USA	13.33
72	Going Hollywood	MGM	MGM	USA	13.23

Rank	Film	Studio	Distributor	Nation'y	POPSTAT
73	Affairs of Cellini	20th Century	UA	USA	13.17
74	Desirable	WB	WB	USA	13.14
75	Servants' Entrance	Fox	Fox	USA	13.14
76	Madame Dubarry	FNP	FNP	USA	13.07
77	Men in White	MGM	MGM	USA	12.96
78	My Old Dutch	Gainsborough	Gaumont-British	Br.	12.90
79	Gambling Lady	WB	WB	USA	12.75
80	Bolero	Paramount	Paramount	USA	12.75
81	She Loves Me Not	Paramount	Paramount	USA	12.69
82	Lady in Danger	Gaumont-British	Gaumont-British	Br.	12.65
83	Lilies of the Field	B&D	UA	Br.	12.43
84	Change of Heart	Fox	Fox	USA	12.43
85	Pursuit of Happiness	Paramount	Paramount	USA	12.40
86	Death Takes a Holiday	Paramount	Paramount	USA	12.17
87	Sitting Pretty	Paramount	Paramount	USA	12.07
88	Man of Two Worlds	RKO	Radio	USA	11.88
89	Gallant Lady	20th Century	UA	USA	11.81
90	Manhattan Melodrama	MGM	MGM	USA	11.80
91	Battle	Liono	Gaumont-British	French	11.66
92	Four Frightened People	Paramount	Paramount	USA	11.62
93	What Every Woman Knows	MGM	MGM	USA	11.59
94	We Live Again	Goldwyn	UA	USA	11.58
95	Spy 13 (US: Operator 13)	MGM	MGM	USA	11.46
96	Happiness Ahead	FNP	FNP	USA	11.35
97	Marie Galante	Fox	Fox	USA	11.02
98	Advice to Lovelorn	20th Century	UA	USA	10.97
99	Richest Girl in the World	RKO	Radio	USA	10.87
100	Great Schnozzle (US: Palooka)	Reliance	UA	USA	10.82

Films Released in 1935

Rank	Film	Studio	Distributor	Nation'y	POPSTAT
1	Lives of A Bengal Lancer	Paramount	Paramount	USA	63.14
2	Top Hat	RKO	Radio	USA	54.20
3	Scarlet Pimpernel	London Films	UA	Br.	51.20
4	Iron Duke	Gaumont-British	Gaumont-British	Br.	45.68
5	On Wings of Song (US: Love Me Forever)	Columbia	Columbia	USA	44.71
6	Sanders of the River	London Films	UA	Br.	43.83
7	Dark Angel	Goldwyn	UA	USA	42.73
8	39 Steps	Gaumont-British	Gaumont-British	Br.	40.20
9	Clive of India	20th Century	UA	USA	39.41
10	Escape Me Never	B&D	UA	Br.	39.01
11	David Copperfield	MGM	MGM	USA	35.50
12	Roberta	RKO	Radio	USA	34.93

Rank	Film	Studio	Distributor	Nation'y	POPSTAT
13	Cardinal Richelieu	20th Century	UA	USA	34.55
14	Kid Millions	Goldwyn	UA	USA	33.41
15	Tunnel	Gaumont-British	Gaumont-British	Br.	32.63
16	Broadway Melody of 1936	MGM	MGM	USA	31.68
17	Brewster's Millions	B&D	UA	Br.	30.21
18	Crusades	Paramount	Paramount	USA	29.34
19	Les Miserables	20th Century	UA	USA	28.25
20	G Men	WB	WB	USA	27.72
21	Bulldog Jack	Gaumont-British	Gaumont-British	Br.	27.56
22	Little Minister	RKO	Radio	USA	25.90
23	Call of the Wild	20th Century	UA	USA	25.56
24	Anna Karenina	MGM	MGM	USA	24.52
25	Curly Top	Fox	Fox	USA	24.31
26	Heart's Desire	BIP	Wardour	Br.	23.88
27	First a Girl	Gaumont-British	Gaumont-British	Br.	23.80
28	Mighty Barnum	20th Century	UA	USA	23.64
29	Ruggles of Red Gap	Paramount	Paramount	USA	23.59
30	Little Colonel	Fox	Fox	USA	23.46
31	China Seas	MGM	MGM	USA	22.94
32	Love Affair of the Dictator	Toeplitz	Gaumont-British	Br.	22.82
33	Boys Will Be Boys	Gainsborough	Gaumont-British	Br.	20.66
34	Becky Sharp	Pioneer	Radio	USA	20.39
35	Clairvoyant	Gainsborough	Gaumont-British	Br.	19.96
36	She Married Her Boss	Columbia	Columbia	USA	19.88
37	Come Out of the Pantry	B&D	UA	Br.	19.65
38	Goin' to the Town	Paramount	Paramount	USA	19.50
39	Abdul the Damned	BIP	Wardour	Br.	19.28
40	Foreign Affaires	Gainsborough	Gaumont-British	Br.	19.25
41	No More Ladies	MGM	MGM	USA	18.83
42	Irish in Us	WB	WB	USA	17.97
43	Wedding Night	Goldwyn	UA	USA	17.54
44	Shanghai	Paramount	Paramount	USA	17.49
45	Stormy Weather	Gainsborough	Gaumont-British	Br.	17.48
46	Mississippi	Paramount	Paramount	USA	17.30
47	Guv'nor	Gaumont-British	Gaumont-British	Br.	17.18
48	Forsaking All Others	MGM	MGM	USA	17.14
49	If You Could Only Cook	Columbia	Columbia	USA	17.06
50	Man From the Folies Bergère (US: Folies Bergère)	20th Century	UA	USA	16.96
51	Peg of Old Drury	B&D	UA	Br.	20.65
52	Thanks a Million	20Fox	20Fox	USA	16.89
53	Black Fury	WB	WB	USA	16.77
54	Let 'em Have It	Reliance	UA	USA	16.71

Rank	Film	Studio	Distributor	Nation'y	POPSTAT
55	Fighting Stock	Gainsborough	Gaumont-British	Br.	16.40
56	I Live My Life	MGM	MGM	USA	16.39
57	Big Broadcast of 1936	Paramount	Paramount	USA	16.25
58	Devil Dogs of the Air	WB	WB	USA	16.19
59	Oh! Daddy	Gainsborough	Gaumont-British	Br.	15.68
60	Things Are Looking Up	Gaumont-British	Gaumont-British	Br.	15.34
61	Escapade	MGM	MGM	USA	15.28
62	Dr Socrates	WB	WB	USA	15.06
63	Paris Love Song (US: Paris In Spring)	Paramount	Paramount	USA	14.87
64	Passing of the Third Floor Back	Gaumont-British	Gaumont-British	Br.	14.73
65	So Red the Rose	Paramount	Paramount	USA	14.52
66	Forever England	Gaumont-British	Gaumont-British	Br.	14.51
67	Devil is a Woman	Paramount	Paramount	USA	14.50
68	Gold Diggers of 1935	FNP	FNP	USA	14.43
69	Barbary Coast	Goldwyn	UA	USA	14.40
70	Frisco Kid	WB	WB	USA	14.30
71	Two for Tonight	Paramount	Paramount	USA	14.18
72	Moscow Nights	London Films/Capitol	GFD	Br.	14.11
73	Three Musketeers	RKO	Radio	USA	14.11
74	Naughty Marietta	MGM	MGM	USA	14.07
75	I Give My Heart	BIP	Wardour	Br.	13.11
76	Bride of Frankenstein	Universal	Universal	USA	13.08
77	Star of Midnight	RKO	Radio	USA	13.01
78	Informer	RKO	Radio	USA	12.95
79	Hands Across the Table	Paramount	Paramount	USA	12.94
80	Broadway Gondolier	WB	WB	USA	12.91
81	Alice Adams	RKO	Radio	USA	12.83
82	Reckless	MGM	MGM	USA	12.81
83	Mary Burns Fugitive	Paramount	Paramount	USA	12.60
84	18 Minutes	Allied	Pathé	Br.	12.56
85	Scoundrel	Paramount	Paramount	USA	12.51
86	British Agent	WB	WB	USA	12.40
87	Arms and the Girl (US: Red Salute)	Reliance	UA	USA	12.31
88	Wings In The Dark	Paramount	Paramount	USA	12.24
89	Casino de Paree (US: Go Into Your Dance)	FNP	FNP	USA	12.24
90	Every Night at Eight	Paramount	Paramount	USA	12.18
91	Peter Ibbetson	Paramount	Paramount	USA	12.02
92	Melody Lingers On	Reliance	UA	USA	11.96
93	Gilded Lily	Paramount	Paramount	USA	11.95
94	She Couldn't Take It	Columbia	Columbia	USA	11.93
95	Vanessa	MGM	MGM	USA	11.92

271

Rank	Film	Studio	Distributor	Nation'y	POPSTAT
96	West Point of the Air	MGM	MGM	USA	11.89
97	Good Fairy	Universal	Universal	USA	11.88
98	Private Worlds	Paramount	Paramount	USA	11.81
99	Music in the Air	Fox	Fox	USA	11.80
100	Baxter's Millions (US: Three Kids and a Queen)	Universal	Universal	USA	11.74

Films Released in 1936

Rank	Film	Studio	Distributor	Nation'y	POPSTAT
1	Modern Times	Chaplin	UA	USA	83.26
2	Mutiny on the Bounty	MGM	MGM	USA	59.36
3	Great Ziegfeld	MGM	MGM	USA	53.29
4	Mr Deeds Goes to Town	Columbia	Columbia	USA	47.43
5	Show Boat	Universal	GFD	USA	46.66
6	Ghost Goes West	London Films	UA	Br.	41.60
7	Follow the Fleet	RKO	Radio	USA	41.41
8	Swing Time	RKO	Radio	USA	40.95
9	Things to Come	London Films	UA	Br.	40.65
10	Tale of Two Cities	MGM	MGM	USA	34.18
11	Little Lord Fauntleroy	Selznick	UA	USA	33.63
12	Garden of Allah	Selznick	UA	USA	32.71
13	San Francisco	MGM	MGM	USA	32.01
14	Romeo and Juliet	MGM	MGM	USA	31.56
15	Theodora Goes Wild	Columbia	Columbia	USA	31.35
16	Strike Me Pink	Goldwyn	UA	USA	30.71
17	Secret Agent	Gaumont-British	Gaumont-British	Br.	28.53
18	Anthony Adverse	WB	WB	USA	28.51
19	General Dies at Dawn	Paramount	Paramount	USA	28.47
20	Libelled Lady	MGM	MGM	USA	27.66
21	My Man Godfrey	Universal	GFD	USA	27.31
22	Captain Blood	WB	FNP	USA	27.22
23	Dodsworth	Goldwyn	UA	USA	26.93
24	Desire	Paramount	Paramount	USA	26.85
25	Green Pastures	WB	WB	USA	26.51
26	These Three	Goldwyn	UA	USA	25.11
27	Under Two Flags	20Fox	20Fox	USA	24.84
28	Rose Marie	MGM	MGM	USA	24.84
29	Rembrandt	London Films	UA	Br.	24.12
30	Milky Way	Paramount	Paramount	USA	23.52
31	Poor Little Rich Girl	20Fox	20Fox	USA	23.49
32	It's Love Again	Gaumont-British	Gaumont-British	Br.	22.84
33	Captain January	20Fox	20Fox	USA	21.56
34	Ex Mrs Bradford	RKO	Radio	USA	21.03
35	King Steps Out	Columbia	Columbia	USA	20.75

Rank	Film	Studio	Distributor	Nation'y	POPSTAT
36	Littlest Rebel	20Fox	20Fox	USA	20.52
37	Amateur Gentleman	Criterion	UA	Br.	19.93
38	As You Like It	Interallied	20Fox	Br.	19.86
39	Last of the Mohicans	Reliance	UA	USA	19.57
40	Rhodes of Africa	Gaumont-British	Gaumont-British	Br.	19.21
41	When Knights Were Bold	Capitol	GFD	Br.	19.19
42	Born to Dance	MGM	MGM	USA	19.08
43	Song of Freedom	Hammer	BL	Br.	19.03
44	Queen of Hearts	ATP	ABFD	Br.	18.92
45	Jack of All Trades	Gainsborough	Gaumont-British	Br.	18.44
46	Man Who Could Work Miracles	London Films	UA	Br.	18.24
47	Love On The Run	MGM	MGM	USA	18.13
48	Man Who Broke The Bank at Monte Carlo	20Fox	20Fox	USA	18.10
49	Gorgeous Hussy	MGM	MGM	USA	17.89
50	Country Doctor	20Fox	20Fox	USA	17.87
51	I Dream Too Much	RKO	Radio	USA	17.75
52	Where There's a Will	Gainsborough	Gaumont-British	Br.	17.64
53	Sabotage	Gaumont-British	Gaumont-British	Br.	17.58
54	Trail of The Lonesome Pine	Paramount	Paramount	USA	17.51
55	Anything Goes	Paramount	Paramount	USA	17.07
56	Come And Get It	Goldwyn	UA	USA	17.00
57	Big Broadcast of 1937	Paramount	Paramount	USA	16.76
58	Suzy	MGM	MGM	USA	16.70
59	Tudor Rose	Gainsborough	Gaumont-British	Br.	16.53
60	Woman Rebels	RKO	Radio	USA	16.24
61	Texas Rangers	Paramount	Paramount	USA	16.18
62	Story of Louis Pasteur	WB	WB	USA	16.06
63	Accused	Criterion	UA	Br.	16.04
64	This'll Make You Whistle	Wilcox	GFD	Br.	15.96
65	Night At The Opera	MGM	MGM	USA	15.91
66	Mary of Scotland	RKO	Radio	USA	15.84
67	Case Against Mrs Ames	Paramount	Paramount	USA	15.70
68	Magnificent Obsession	Universal	Universal	USA	15.58
69	Dimples	20Fox	20Fox	USA	15.56
70	Pennies From Heaven	Columbia	Columbia	USA	15.44
71	Yours for the Asking	Paramount	Paramount	USA	15.41
72	Girls' Dormitory	20Fox	20Fox	USA	15.39
73	Road to Glory	20Fox	20Fox	USA	15.32
74	Manhattan Madness (US: Adventure In Manhattan)	Columbia	Columbia	USA	15.27
75	Klondike Annie	Paramount	Paramount	USA	15.20
76	Professional Soldier	20Fox	20Fox	USA	15.15

Rank	Film	Studio	Distributor	Nation'y	POPSTAT
77	Bullets or Ballots	WB	FNP	USA	15.13
78	Cain and Mabel	WB	WB	USA	15.07
79	White Angel	WB	WB	USA	14.95
80	Rhythm on the Range	Paramount	Paramount	USA	14.89
81	Men are not Gods	London Films	UA	Br.	14.88
82	Fury	MGM	MGM	USA	14.81
83	Gay Desperado	Pickford	UA	USA	14.77
84	Pot Luck	Gainsborough	Gaumont-British	Br.	14.73
85	Secret Interlude (US: Private Number)	20Fox	20Fox	USA	14.71
86	Bride Comes Home	Paramount	Paramount	USA	14.64
87	Piccadilly Jim	MGM	MGM	USA	14.60
88	Splendour	Goldwyn	UA	USA	14.59
89	East Meets West	Gaumont-British	Gaumont-British	Br.	14.53
90	Petticoat Fever	MGM	MGM	USA	14.17
91	King of the Damned	Gaumont-British	Gaumont-British	Br.	14.09
92	Seven Sinners	Gaumont-British	Gaumont-British	Br.	14.07
93	Three Maxims	Wilcox/CPE	GFD	Br.	13.96
94	Go West Young Man	Paramount	Paramount	USA	13.71
95	Everything is Thunder	Gaumont-British	Gaumont-British	Br.	13.35
96	Windbag the Sailor	Gainsborough	Gaumont-British	Br.	13.25
97	Pagliacci	Trafalgar	UA	Br.	13.25
98	Moon's Our Home	Paramount	Paramount	USA	13.19
99	Limelight	Wilcox	GFD	Br.	13.11
100	Sweet Aloes (US: Give Me Your Heart)	WB	WB	USA	12.67

Films released in 1937

Rank	Film	Studio	Distributor	Nation'y	POPSTAT
1	Lost Horizon	Columbia	Columbia	USA	86.89
2	Good Earth	MGM	MGM	USA	48.95
3	Star is Born	Selznick	UA	USA	47.89
4	Victoria the Great	Imperator	Radio	Br.	45.85
5	Charge of the Light Brigade	WB	FNP	USA	43.88
6	Shall We Dance	RKO	Radio	USA	40.16
7	Life of Emile Zola	WB	FNP	USA	38.20
8	Camille	MGM	MGM	USA	36.64
9	Souls at Sea	Paramount	Paramount	USA	35.46
10	100 Men and a Girl	Universal	GFD	USA	33.07
11	Plainsman	Paramount	Paramount	USA	32.99
12	Captains Courageous	MGM	MGM	USA	32.41
13	After the Thin Man	MGM	MGM	USA	31.03
14	Maytime	MGM	MGM	USA	30.54
15	Lloyds of London	20Fox	20Fox	USA	29.39

APPENDIX 3

Rank	Film	Studio	Distributor	Nation'y	POPSTAT
16 I Met Him in Paris	Paramount	Paramount	USA	28.69
17 Prisoner of Zenda	Selznick	UA	USA	25.93
18 Fire Over England	Pendennis	UA	Br.	25.22
19 Knight Without Armour	London Films	UA	Br.	24.71
20 History is made at Night	Wanger	UA	USA	23.53
21 Last of Mrs Cheyney	MGM	MGM	USA	23.53
22 Easy Living	Paramount	Paramount	USA	22.72
23 Beloved Enemy	Goldwyn	UA	USA	22.29
24 For You Alone	Columbia	Columbia	USA	22.00
25 One in a Million	20Fox	20Fox	USA	21.43
26 Farewell Again	Pendennis	UA	Br.	20.80
27 Elephant Boy	London Films	UA	Br.	20.75
28 Good Morning Boys	Gainsborough	Gaumont-British	Br.	20.63
29 Gold Diggers of 1937	WB	FNP	USA	20.51
30 Marie Walewska (US: Conquest)	MGM	MGM	USA	20.32
31 On the Avenue	20Fox	20Fox	USA	20.30
32 Love From a Stranger	Trafalgar	UA	Br.	20.21
33 Three Smart Girls	Universal	GFD	USA	20.20
34 Great Barrier	Gaumont-British	Gaumont-British	Br.	20.19
35 Storm in a Teacup	Saville	UA	Br.	19.58
36 OHMS	Gaumont-British	Gaumont-British	Br.	19.54
37 Wings of the Morning	New World	20Fox	Br.	19.04
38 Top of the Town	Universal	GFD	USA	17.69
39 Broadway Melody of 1938	MGM	MGM	USA	17.68
40 Lovely to Look At (US: Thin Ice)	20Fox	20Fox	USA	17.41
41 Dreaming Lips	Trafalgar	UA	Br.	17.36
42 Saratoga	MGM	MGM	USA	17.32
43 Parnell	MGM	MGM	USA	17.24
44 Oh! Mr Porter	Gainsborough	GFD	Br.	17.17
45 King Solomon's Mines	Gaumont-British	GFD	Br.	16.95
47 Dark Journey	Saville	UA	Br.	16.84
48 You Only Live Once	Wanger	UA	USA	16.73
49 Wee Willie Winkie	20Fox	20Fox	USA	16.72
50 Day at the Races	MGM	MGM	USA	16.44
51 Champagne Waltz	Paramount	Paramount	USA	16.29
52 Angel	Paramount	Paramount	USA	16.00
53 Stowaway	20Fox	20Fox	USA	15.99
54 His Affair (US: This is my Affair)	20Fox	20Fox	USA	15.96
55 Vogues of 1938	Wanger	UA	USA	15.85
56 High, Wide and Handsome	Paramount	Paramount	USA	15.76
57 Head Over Heels	Gaumont-British	Gaumont-British	Br.	15.46

275

Rank	Film	Studio	Distributor	Nation'y	POPSTAT
58	Action for Slander	Saville	UA	Br.	15.39
59	Thunder in the City	Atlantic	UA	Br.	15.33
60	Woman Chases Man	Goldwyn	UA	USA	15.32
61	Stella Dallas	Goldwyn	UA	USA	15.29
62	Slave Ship	20Fox	20Fox	USA	15.16
63	Stage Door	RKO	Radio	USA	15.10
64	Waikiki Wedding	Paramount	Paramount	USA	15.07
65	Firefly	MGM	MGM	USA	14.85
66	Ebb Tide	Paramount	Paramount	USA	14.48
67	John Meade's Woman	Paramount	Paramount	USA	14.45
68	Man in Possession	MGM	MGM	USA	14.41
69	Maid of Salem	Paramount	Paramount	USA	14.35
70	Gangway	Gaumont-British	GFD	Br.	14.26
71	Dr Syn	Gainsborough	GFD	Br.	13.85
72	Big City	MGM	MGM	USA	13.84
73	Double Wedding	MGM	MGM	USA	13.62
74	Frog	Wilcox	GFD	Br.	13.51
75	Cafe Metropole	20Fox	20Fox	USA	13.49
76	Jump For Glory	Criterion	UA	Br.	13.48
77	Under the Red Robe	New World	20Fox	Br.	13.47
78	That Girl from Paris	RKO	Radio	USA	13.44
79	Take My Tip	Gaumont-British	GFD	Br.	13.37
80	Swing High Swing Low	Paramount	Paramount	USA	13.23
81	Artists and Models	Paramount	Paramount	USA	13.23
82	Turn Off the Moon	Paramount	Paramount	USA	13.21
83	Night Must Fall	MGM	MGM	USA	13.10
84	For Valour	Capitol	GFD	Br.	12.94
85	Double or Nothing	Paramount	Paramount	USA	12.75
86	Sky's the Limit	Buchanan	GFD	Br.	12.70
87	Mind Your Own Business	Paramount	Paramount	USA	12.58
88	Show Goes On	ATP	ABFD	Br.	12.55
89	Over She Goes	ABPC	ABPC	Br.	12.46
90	Squeaker	Denham	UA	Br.	12.42
91	Emperor's Candlesticks	MGM	MGM	USA	12.15
92	Seventh Heaven	20Fox	20Fox	USA	12.07
93	Sensation	BIP	Wardour	Br.	12.06
94	Stolen Holiday	WB	WB	USA	11.86
95	Prince and the Pauper	WB	WB	USA	11.79
96	Crack Up	20Fox	20Fox	USA	11.76
97	Topper	Roach	MGM	USA	11.70
98	Big Business	20Fox	20Fox	USA	11.15
99	Charlie Chan at the Opera	20Fox	20Fox	USA	11.12
100	Quality Street	RKO	Radio	USA	11.03

Notes

Introduction

1. Priestley, J.B., *They Walk in the City* (London, 1936), p. 399.
2. Vasey, R., *The World According to Hollywood, 1918–1939* (Exeter, 1997), pp. 49–62, shows how profoundly questions of what was literally 'political correctness', often at the level of international protests, affected the global marketability of Hollywood films, and led from the 1920s to self-regulatory codes of content and presentation in which 'foreign' film characters with 'bad' attributes came to be identified as people from nations with low revenue potentials.
3. Rowson, S., 'A statistical survey of the cinema industry in Great Britain in 1934', *Journal of the Royal Statistical Society* 99 (1936).
4. Korda, A., 'British films today and tomorrow', in C. Davey (ed.) *Footnotes to the Film* (London, 1937). I am grateful to Sue Harper for this reference in *Picturing the Past: The Rise and Fall of the British Costume Film* (London, 1994), p.21.
5. Harper, S. and Porter, V., 'Cinema audience tastes in 1950s Britain', *Journal of Popular British Cinema* 2 (1999), p. 67 distinguish between indiscriminate, regular and occasional categories of filmgoer. See Chapter 1 for a fuller discussion of these categories. See also the oral evidence produced by Annette Kuhn, (note 6).
6. Kuhn, A., 'Cinema-going in Britain in the 1930s: report of a questionnaire survey', *Historical Journal of Film Radio and Television* 19 (1999), pp.531–43.
7. Landy, M., *British genres: cinema and society 1930–1960* (Princeton, 1991), p. 484. See also the seminal works of Klinger, B., 'Digressions at the cinema: reception and mass culture', *Cinema Journal* 28, 4 (1989) and *Melodrama and Meaning: History, Culture, and the Films of Douglas Sirk* (Bloomington, 1994); and Staiger, J., *Interpreting Films: Studies in the Historical Reception of American Cinema*, (Princeton, 1992). Richard Maltby provides a brief but scholarly account of the reception approach to film theory in *Hollywood Cinema* (Oxford, 1995), pp. 443–47.
8. Thumim, J., 'The 'popular', cash and culture in the postwar British cinema industry', *Screen* 23 (1991), p.246.
9. Richards, J., *The Age of the Dream Palace* (London, 1984), p.323.
10. Richards, J., 'Cinemagoing in Worktown: regional film audiences in 1930s

277

Britain', *Historical Journal of Film, Radio and Television* 14, (1994), p.164.

11. Richards, J., *Films and British National Identity: From Dickens to Dad's Army* (Manchester, 1997), pp.25–6. Jeanne Allen in 'The film viewer as consumer', *Quarterly Review of Film Studies*, 5, (1980), p.487 makes a similar point about film in the US, arguing: 'Utilizing glamour and dramatic appeal, film presented an attractive vehicle for nationalizing public behaviour and for socializing a regionally and ethnically diversified population into a more homogeneous nation of consumers'.

12. A correspondence may be drawn between this notion of conception and that of 'high concept' defined by Justin Wyatt in *High Concept: Movies and Marketing in Hollywood*, (Austin, 1994), p.7 '...as a form of differentiated product within the mainstream film industry. This differentiation occurs in two major ways: through an emphasis on style within films, and through an integration with marketing and merchandising.' For Wyatt, stars help differentiate the product in conjunction with 'a premise, or a subject matter that is fashionable' while providing an obvious means of marketing it. (ibid, pp. 12–13).

13. For a discussion of the term 'popular' see Hollows, J., and Jancovich, M., 'Popular film and cultural distinctions', in J. Hollows and M. Jancovich (eds) *Approaches to Popular Film* (Manchester, 1995).

14. Jarvie, I.C., *Hollywood's Overseas Campaign: The North Atlantic Movie Trade, 1920–1950* (Cambridge, 1992), p. 2.

15. Harper, S., and Porter, V., 'Moved to tears: weeping in the cinema in postwar Britain', *Screen* 37 (1996), p.173.

16. De Vany, A., and Walls, W., 'Bose-Einstein dynamics and adaptive contracting in the motion picture industry', *Economic Journal* 106 (1996), p.1493.

17. See Table 7.1 for the financial performances of these two films.

18. Fowler, D., *The First Teenagers: The Lifestyle of Young Wage-Earners in Interwar Britain* (London, 1995), p.132. Fowler imputes this view to Jeffrey Richards. However, he overstates his case in that although it is certainly true that Richards op. cit. (1984), p.323 argues that British films served an important social control function, it would be wrong to maintain that he perceived working class audiences during the decade as vacuous. Rather, the case he makes is that the films featuring Gracie Fields and George Formby, in particular, dealt with issues of consensus, reconciliation and hope, and were extremely popular with working class audiences. For Richards the evidence presented by the 1931 and 1935 General Elections, and the absence of a strong revolutionary movement—even in the areas where the recession bit deepest, with perhaps the exception of certain districts of Glasgow—suggests that the images and messages contained in such films were those that rested comfortably with audiences in general.

19. Allen, R.C.,'From exhibition to reception: reflections on the audience in film history', *Screen* 34 (1990), pp. 352–53.

20. See Gomery, D., *Shared Pleasures: A History of Movie Presentation in the United States* (London, 1992) on the Balaban and Katz circuit in Chicago from the late 1910s into the mid-1920s.

21. See Sedgwick, J., and Pokorny, M., 'The risk environment of film-making: Warners in the inter-war period', *Explorations in Economic History* 35 (1998), for an account of how Warners organized its portfolio of films during the 1930s in response to this factor.

22. Landy, M., op. cit., p.5

23. Landy, M., op. cit., p.9. Justin Wyatt makes a similar point: 'Historically as the forces forming the mode of production change across time, so does the product of film, privileging a certain "look and sound" within filmmaking' (Wyatt, op. cit., p.15). And again: '...Hollywood will alter the dominant style of production given the potential for additional box-office revenue.', Wyatt, op. cit., p.198.

24. The classical studio system with its seven year option contract on stars was particularly adept at paying the leading stars less than their market value. See the discussion on stardom in Chapter 9.

25. The following discussion on the distinction between things and commodities is influenced by separate discussions with Photis Lysandrou and Bernard Hrusa-Marlow. See Lysandrou, P., 'The market and exploitation in Marx's economic theory: a reinterpretation', *Cambridge Journal of Economics* 24 (2000).

26. Hayek, F., *The Counter Revolution of Science* (London, 1955), p.27. Also see p.209, note 20.

27. See Carroll, N., *A Philosophy of Mass Art* (Oxford, 1998), pp.212–13 for the development of this idea.

28. Some 'avant-garde' films seem to have been made with little intention or hope of being commodities, and some with the positive intention of being anti-commodities!

29. Marx, K., *Capital: Volume 1* (Harmondsworth, 1976), p.125.

30. Carroll, op. cit., p.224.

31. Of course in defining what something is Carroll should be able to distinguish it from things that it isn't. In this case he is particularly concerned with distinguishing mass art from popular or avant-garde art, whatever its form. In a later discussion of the ontology of mass art, Carroll distinguishes between film and theatre as examples of mass art work and non-mass art work. In doing this, however, he makes the mistake of treating movie audiences as inert in the sense that, unlike with a theatrical production in which the text has been the subject of interpretation, the identical nature of each screening *ipso facto* implies that audiences cannot be alive to particular qualities of the production and performance recorded in the film image. But surely the point is that film audiences are just as intent on deriving pleasure from these qualities during the screening of a film as any theatrical audience is from the staging of a play. As argued in the text it is the witting participation of audiences in consumption which affirms the degree of popularity achieved by any particular film commodity.

    With the exception of pay-per-view television, Radio and TV programmes, including films, are more problematic in that whilst they might well be examples of mass art in Carroll's sense, they are not consumed as commodities by audiences even where they have been acquired by the programmers through market based transactions. This is because they cannot be assigned prices for the reason that the technology which carries their transmission cannot or does not exclude viewers. The commodity aspect to radio and television is the air time purchased by advertisers, the price of which is related to the size and type of audience listening to or viewing programmes around and within which adverts are placed. Accordingly, programmes are made to attract audiences so as to sell air time to advertisers.

32. It is this which leads critics of popular culture to castigate cinema as 'ephemeral'.

33. See Chapter 3 for a detailed discussion on the size and numbers of cinemas in Britain during the 1930s.

34. See Rosen, S., 'The economics of superstars', *American Economic Review* 71 (1981) and the discussion set out in Chapter 9.

35. See Chapter 1 for a detailed consideration of the uncertainty faced by filmgoers.

36. Kerr, C., 'Incorporating the star', *Business History Review* 64 (1990), p. 407. The full text of the prospectus, dated 27 May 1927, can be found in T. Balio, (ed.) *The American Film Industry* (Madison, 1985), ch.8.

37. For an excellent discussion of the historical evolution of these practices see Izod, J., *Hollywood and the Box-Office* (London, 1988), ch.6.

38. Greenwald, W, 'The motion picture industry: an economic study of the history and practices of a business' (PhD dissertation, New York University, 1950), Table VI–2; and *Variety*, 2 October 1935, p.7: 'Write off pix in 15 Mos. Cream Income in 39 weeks.'

39. Sedgwick and Pokorny, op. cit., pp. 319–23.

40. See Bowden, S., and Offer, A., 'Household appliances and their use of time', *Economic History Review* 47 (1994), for a discussion of sensual arousal in a similar context. Bowden and Offer describe television viewing as 'the cheapest and least demanding way of averting boredom'. Their argument is that given that the marginal cost of an additional hour of television viewing is close to zero, audiences will tend to continue watching up to the point of saturation. However, Ben Fine has suggested that television audiences are likely to be less focussed on the sound image and its meaning, and use television in a way which is historically specific to their needs. Fine, B.,'Household appliances and their use of time: a comment', *Economic History Review* 52 (1999), for a critique of Bowden and Offer's argument, together with their rejoinder: Bowden, S., and Offer, A., 'Household appliances and 'systems of provision', *Economic History Review* 52 (1999).

   There are of course some films for some people that defy this rule: films which have been watched numerous times since release but which generate high levels of pleasure on each viewing. Annette Kuhn op. cit. in her oral history study of cinema preferences during the 1930s has discovered evidence of this behaviour concerning the Jeanette MacDonald, Nelson Eddy MGM operetta *Maytime* (1937).

41. This is evident from the complete Eddie Mannix ledger for MGM films during the classical period made available to the author by Mark Glancy. See Glancy, H.M., 'MGM film grosses, 1924–1948: the Eddie Mannix ledger', *Historical Journal of Film, Radio and Television* 12 (1992).

42. Many parents will have observed that young children seem to be able to watch the same video 'endlessly' without a diminished sense of pleasure, perhaps because, being young, a child's experience of life and the world is limited, so that the video provides additional discoveries at each viewing.

43. Fine, B. and Leopold E., *The World of Consumption* (London, 1993).

44. ibid., p.4.

45. ibid., p.19.

46. ibid., p.22.

47. Thumim op. cit.

48. Harper, op. cit.

49. ibid., p.56.

50. See Richards (1984) op. cit., ch.1. For the 1936 and 1937 Motion Picture Herald polls see the *1937–38 Motion Picture Almanac*: 1094 (for the 1936 poll) and the *1938–39 Motion Picture Almanac*: 998 (for the 1937 poll).

51. See Jarvie, I.C., 'Sir Karl Popper (1902–94): essentialism and historicism in film methodology', *Historical Journal of Film, Radio and Television* 15 (1995).

52. Stacey, J., 'Textual obsessions: methodology, history and researching female spectatorship', *Screen* 34 (1993), p.263.

53. Chapter 5 is drawn heavily from Sedgwick, J., 'Film "hits" and "misses" in mid-1930s Britain', *Historical Journal of Film, Radio and Television* 18 (1998b).

54. Sedgwick, J., 'Michael Balcon's close encounter with the American market, 1934–36', *Historical Journal of Film, Radio and Television* 16 (1996); Sedgwick, J., 'British film industry's production sector difficulties in the late 1930s', *Historical Journal of Film, Radio and Television* 17 (1997).

Chapter 1

1. I am extremely grateful to Vincent Porter for his detailed and somewhat sceptical comments in a letter to the author on this approach to consumer choice. The purpose of depicting a rational consumer is not, of course, to argue that choices everywhere conformed strictly to the criteria set down in the theory but to suggest that such criteria underpin the cinemagoing decision, and that through the theory it is possible to explain past and future patterns of behaviour. It should also be said that in theorizing about the choice framework, I am not attempting to explain how it was that cinemagoing became normal social behaviour for large sections of the population at the time.

2. Nelson, R., 'Advertising as information', *Journal of Political Economy*, 81 (1974), p.745.

3. Harper and Porter, 'Cinema audiences in 1950s Britain', *Journal of Popular British Cinema* 2 (1999), p.67.

4. Fine, B. and Leopold, E., *The World of Consumption* (London, 1993).

5. Gilad, B., Kaish, S., and Loab, P., 'Cognitive dissonance and utility maximization: a general framework', *Journal of Economic Behaviour and Organization* 8 (1987).

6. ibid., p.67.

7. Indeed, the filmgoer will not experience identical pleasure from repeat viewing the same film, as each subsequent encounter will be experienced in the light of those previous encounters. Normally, consumers experience rapidly diminishing marginal utility on consumption.

8. Stigler, G., and Becker, G., 'De gustibus non est disputandum,' *American Economic Review* 67 (1977), p. 76.

9. See McFadden, D., and Train, K., 'Consumer's evaluation of new products: learning from self and others', *Journal of Political Economy*, 104 (1996), for an account of the dynamics of learning from others.

10. Earl, P., *Microeconomics for Business and Marketing* (Aldershot, 1995), p.68.

11. From his many books, see Shackle, G., *Imagination and the Nature of Choice* (Edinburgh, 1979), for his theory of choice. An excellent account of Shackle's approach to the problem of 'uncertainty' in economics can be found in Earl, P., 'The economics of G.L.S. Shackle in retrospect and prospect', and in Carter, C., 'George Shackle and uncertainty, a revolution still awaited', both in *Review of*

Political Economy 5 (1993).

12. Shackle, G., *Epistemics and Economics* (New Brunswick, 1992), p.366.

13. Hoskins, C., McFadyen, S., and Finn, A., *Global Television and Film* (Oxford, 1997), p.56.

14. Shackle, G., *Expectations in Economics* (Cambridge, 1948), p. 38.

15. It is possible to situate the subsequent analysis within an indifference curve framework where filmgoers form subjective maps of their trade-off preferences between risk (potential surprise) and potential pleasure. On the gain-side the curves would be concave with higher levels of pleasure to be found towards the pleasure axis of Figure 1.4. The analysis, however, becomes complex since a similar procedure needs to be undertaken on the loss side so that the two sets of curves could then be compared. What follows is a more simple approach developed by Peter Earl.

16. A gain-side focus assumes that filmgoers, in general, will accept a fair gamble i.e. one in which the chance of gain is equal to that of loss. This may be contrasted with decision makers who are risk averse, i.e. those who would not accept a fair gamble. This conjecture is based on the assumption that the film choice is based upon positive perceptions of quality rather than the desire to minimise potential disappointment. These speculations, of course, are capable of being tested empirically.

17. De Vany, A., and Walls, W., 'Bose-Einstein dynamics and adaptive contracting in the motion picture industry', *Economic Journal* 106 (1989), p.1494.

18. *Gone with the Wind* (1939), *The Sound of Music* (1965) and *Titanic* (1998) are examples of big budget films which built audiences.

Chapter 2

1. Priestley, J.B., *Angel Pavement* (London, 1930), p. 71.

2. Hall, S., 'Notes on deconstructing "the popular"', in John Storey (ed.) *Cultural Theory and Popular Culture: A Reader* (Brighton, 1994), p. 458.

3. Priestley, J.B., *English Journey* (London, 1933), p. 410.

4. Stevenson, J., and Cook, C., *Britain in the Depression: Society and Politics 1929–39,* 2nd edition (Harlow, 1994), p. 12.

5. Solomou, S., and Weale, M., 'UK national income, 1920–38: the implications of balanced estimates', *Economic History Review* 49 (1996). If Feinstein's estimates of weekly wage rates are taken, the increase in real wages was only 20 per cent, emphasising the difference in employment income between wage and salary earners. See Feinstein, C., *Statistical tables of national income, expenditure and output of the United Kingdom 1855–1965* (Cambridge, 1976, tab. 65).

6. Stevenson and Cook, op. cit., pp. 13 and 39.

7. Greenwood, W., *Love on the Dole* (London, 1993), ch.18.

8. Fowler, D., *The First Teenagers: The Lifestyle of Young Wage-Earners in Interwar Britain* (London, 1995), tab.1.1. The upper bound of the age classification is raised to 20 in the 1931 census.

9. ibid., tab. 3.1

10. ibid., pp. 97–8.

11. ibid., tab. 2.1, based on the census returns of 1931.

12. ibid., tab. 1.1.

13. ibid., p. 110.

14. ibid., p. 99.
15. ibid., p. 100. Schafer S., *British Popular Films, 1929–39: The Cinema of Reassurance* (London, 1997, pp. 17–20), presents similar evidence, from a review of the letters columns of the popular fan magazines, *Picturegoer Weekly, Film Weekly, Film Pictorial* and *Screen Pictorial*.
16. These are discussed in depth in Richards, *The Age of the Dream Palace* (London, 1984), ch.1.
17. McKibbin, R., *Classes and Cultures: England, 1918–1951: A Study of a Democratic Society* (Oxford, 1998), p. 421.
18. Rowson, S., 'A statistical survey of the cinema industry in Great Britain in 1934', *Journal of the Royal Statistical Society* 99 (1936). Subsequent downward revisions to Rowson's estimates of cinema expenditure are presented in row 10 of Table 2.1 of this chapter.
19. ibid., tab.II.
20. ibid., tab.X.
21. ibid., tab.IX
22. ibid., p. 76. This information is derived from the *Film Daily Yearbooks* and *Motion Picture Almanacs* for the period. The same sources counted the number of wired for sound cinemas in Germany, with its much bigger population, as rising from 4,000 to 5,395 between 1934 and 1938, whilst the numbers in the US actually fell from 19,000 to 16,228. However, the size of German cinemas appears to have been much smaller, with another source listing their combined seating capacity as 2,100,000 in 1937, compared with 3,200,000 in Britain. Altogether, this information is usefully collected in Wood, L., (ed.) *British Films 1927–1939* (London, 1986), pp. 128–30.
23. See De Grazia, V., 'Mass culture and sovereignty: the American challenge to European cinemas, 1920–1960', *Journal of Modern History* 61 (1989). Rowson estimated box-office receipts in Britain to be in the order of £40 million in 1934, in Rowson, S., 'The value of remittances abroad for cinematograph films', *Journal of the Royal Statistical Society*, 97 (1934). This compares with *Film Daily Yearbook/Motion Picture Almanac* comparable estimates for the US of $518 million. Using the exchange rate of £1 = $4.5, it is clear that the British market for films was approximately one-third the size of the American market. See note 5, Chapter 7 for an explanation of how this exchange rate was calculated, based on Dimsdale, N., 'British monetary policy and the exchange rate', *Oxford Economic Papers* 33 (1981).
24. McKibbin, op. cit., p. 419.
25. See Street. S., 'The Hays' Office and the defence of the British market in the 1930s', *Historical Journal of Film, Radio and Television* 5 (1985); Jarvie, I., *Hollywood's Overseas Campaign: The North Atlantic Movie Trade, 1920–1950* (Cambridge, 1992), chs. 4–5; and Vasey, R., *The World According to Hollywood, 1928–1939* (Exeter, 1979), ch. 2.
26. Taylor, A.J.P., *English History, 1914–1945* (Oxford, 1965), p. 313.
27. Richards, op. cit. (1984), p. 158.
28. ibid., p. 159.
29. Unfortunately, this work does not measure the success, or otherwise, of these two stars with Edinburgh and Glasgow audiences, although such a study would prove fascinating reading.

283

30. Thompson, K., *Exporting Entertainment: America in the World Film Market 1907–1934* (London, 1985), appendices 1,2,& 3, pp. 194–230.
31. ibid., p. 127.
32. ibid., p. 2.
33. ibid., pp. 29–30.
34. ibid., p. 49.
35. ibid., pp. 71–3.
36. ibid., p. 83.
37. ibid., pp. 15, 83.
38. See also Gabler, N., *An Empire of Their Own: How the Jews Invented Hollywood* (New York, 1988).
39. Nine volumes if the two volumes on non-feature film production in Britain during the 1930s are included.
40. Low, R., *The History of British Film 1918–1927* (London, 1971), p. 302.
41. ibid., p. 302.
42. Low, R., *The History of British Film 1906–1914* (London, 1948b), pp. 137–8.
43. Low, R., *The History of British Film 1914–1918* (London, 1950), p. 49.
44. Low, R., op. cit. (1971), p. 302.
45. ibid., p. 309.
46. Low, R., op. cit. (1950), p. 64.
47. Low, R., op. cit. (1971), p. 302.
48. ibid., p. 302.
49. Coleman, D. and Macleod, C., 'Attitudes to new techniques: British businessmen 1800–1950', *Economic History Review* 39, (1986), p. 598.
50. ibid., p. 600.
51. Low, R., *Film Making in 1930s Britain* (London, 1985), app., tabs.1–6.
52. Dickinson, M. and Street, S., *Cinema and State: The British Film Industry and the British Government 1927–84* (London, 1985), p. 33.
53. Low, op. cit. (1985), app., tab.1.
54. For the density of cinemas and its impact on choice, see Rowson op. cit. (1936), p. 77; and Browning, H. and Sorrell, A., 'Cinema and cinema-going in Great Britain', *Journal of the Royal Statistical Society* 117 (1954), p. 135.
55. Murphy, R., 'British film and the national interest, 1927–39', in R. Murphy (ed.), *The British Cinema Book* (London, 1997), p. 18.
56. See Napper, L., 'A despicable tradition: Quota Quickies, in the 1930s', in R. Murphy (ed.) op. cit., and Wood, L., 'Low budget British films in the 1930s', in R. Murphy, (ed.) op. cit., for appreciations of the 'Quota Quickie' tradition. Also see Brown, G., 'Money for speed: the British films of Bernard Vorhaus', in J. Richards (ed.) *The Unknown 1930s: An Alternative History of the British Cinema, 1929–39* (London, 1998) on the director Bernard Vorhaus.
57. For example, between 1928 and 1935–6 the area of stage floor space in Britain increased by a factor of 7.5, from 105,211 to 769,557 square feet. See Chapter 11.
58. Ryall, T., 'A British studio system: the ABPC and G-B Corporation', in R. Murphy, (ed.) op. cit. (1997), p. 28.
59. Jarvie's sentence reads: 'In the United Kingdom there was a protracted struggle that at one point seemed to be pushing back, but overconfidence led to overextension.', in Jarvie, op. cit. (1992), p. 8.
60. Low, op. cit. (1985), p. xiv.

Chapter 3

1. Priestley, J.B., *Angel Pavement* (London, 1930), p. 170.
2. ibid., p. 306.
3. The seating capacity and price range of the seats in each of the cinemas is taken from the annual *Kine Year Books* for the period. The mid-range price is derived by taking the mid-point of the range. Hence if the range was one shilling to three shillings the mid-range price would be one shilling and sixpence.
4. A new Act of Parliament with an amended regulatory and administrative framework came into force from 1 April 1938.
5. Greenwald, W., 'The motion picture industry: an economic study of the history and practice of a business' (New York University, 1950), p. 107.
6. See also *Variety*, 2 October 1935, p. 7, for a graphic depiction of amortization. The same page carries a feature on the subject entitled 'Cream Income in 39 Weeks'.
7. Good explanations of the US distribution system during the 1930s can be found in Balio, T., *Grand Design* (Berkeley, 1993), ch.4, Izod, J., *Hollywood and the Box-Office* (London, 1988) and Maltby, R., 'The political economy of Hollywood: the studio system', in P. Davies and B. Neve (eds), *Cinema, Politics and Society in America* (Manchester, 1981).
8. See De Vany, A. and Walls, W., 'Bose-Einstein dynamics and adaptive contracting in the motion picture industry', *Economic Journal* 106 (1996) for an explanation of the economics behind current distribution practices.
9. Sedgwick, J., 'Richard B. Jewell's RKO film grosses, 1929–51: the C.J. Trevlin ledger: a comment', *Historical Journal of Film, Radio and Television* 14 (1994b); Sedgwick, J., 'The Warners' Ledger 1921–22 to 1941–42: a comment', *Historical Journal of Film, Radio and Television* 15 (1995); and Sedgwick, J. and Pokorny, M., 'The risk environment of film-making: Warners in the inter-war period', *Explorations in Economic History* 35 (1998).
10. *Minutes of Evidence taken before the Departmental Committee appointed by the Board of Trade to consider the position of British Films* (1936), chairman: Lord Moyne.
11. Low, R., *Film Making in 1930s Britain* (London, 1985), pp. 3–4, maintained that the commercial odds were firmly stacked in favour of the distributor.
12. Rowson (1936), p. 77. Further on this argument, Browning, H. and Sorrell, A., 'Cinema and cinema-going in Great Britain', *Journal of the Royal Statistical Society* 117 (1954), p. 135, explain that the 'extremely high rate (of cinema attendance) for Britain is due to the high concentration of population ... so that a cinema can be provided within comfortable reach of nearly every household.' Leslie Halliwell, *Seats in All Parts*, (London, 1986), in that part of his memoir depicting cinemagoing as a child in Bolton with his mother during the 1930s, describes the number and proximity of cinemas in Bolton and the reasons for preferring one programme to another.
13. Rowson, op. cit., p. 76; Wood (1986), p. 120. Note these figures are exclusive of cinemas in the Irish Free State (now the Republic of Ireland) and Northern Ireland.
14. Rowson, ibid., p. 78; *Kine Year Books* 1934–5.
15. Rowson, ibid., p. 70. Rowson estimated the arithmetic mean admission price as

10.25 (old) pence in 1934. Two shillings was one-tenth of £1 sterling.

16. Indeed, of these six, three had programmes listed for part of the period, meaning that there were only three sets of records not included in the sample set at some stage. The six cinemas were: the Cameo (Independent), Bear Street, London West End, and listed until April 1932, the Century Theatre (Gaumont-British), Liverpool; the Olympia (ABC), Liverpool, listed for 1937–8; the Plaza (Gaumont-British), Liverpool; the Prince of Wales (ABC), Liverpool, listed for 1932–3; and the Haymarket (ABC), Newcastle listed from August 1936. These cinemas have been identified by their having mid-range prices significantly in excess of one shilling for the provincial city cinemas and three shillings for the London West End cinema. The source of this information is the listings of cinemas in England and Scotland in the *Kine Year Books* 1933–9.

17. Gaumont-British ran the GTC, PCT, and Denman chains, as well as the string of Gaumont cinemas. See Eyles, A., *Gaumont British Cinemas* (London, 1996).

18. Rowson, op. cit., p. 83. These figures are greater than those given by Wood, op. cit., p. 119, where the two groups are listed as having 147 and 302 cinemas respectively.

19. Warners-First National flagship cinema, the Warner Leicester Square, opened on 12 October 1938—just beyond the investigation period.

20. Eyles, A. and Skone, K., *London's West End Cinemas* (Sutton, 1991), p. 47.

21. Eyles, A., 'The Empire that was, 1928–61', *Picture House* 13 (1989).

22. The Paramount, Birmingham, opened in September 1937, which accounts for the small number of the 'hit' films screened in relation to the other Paramount cinemas. More surprising is the small number of 'hits' which passed through the Paramount, Tottenham Court Road, which opened on 10 February 1936. It may well be that given the existence of two West End pre-release cinemas already dedicated to screening the films of the parent American company—the Carlton and Plaza—the Paramount, Tottenham Court Road, concentrated more on its less prestigious film releases.

23. The mid-range price has been calculated by taking the mid-point of the price range for each cinema. This information is available for the greater part in the *Kine Year Books* of the period. Allen Eyles was also a valuable alternative source of information.

24. I am grateful to Mike Walsh and Richard Koszarski for raising these points in correspondence with the author.

25. All dates for cinema exhibitions are taken from the Monday of the first week, following the practice established in the *Kine Weekly*.

26. These calculations are based upon the following logic. For a cinema screening one film a week, the total film screen time for the survey period 1 January 1932 to 31 March 1938 is 325 weeks. Hence, cinemas such as the Carlton where film programmes were *typically* single features recorded an aggregate screen time a little above 325 weeks, whereas cinemas in the sample which *typically* ran double feature programmes with a weekly change would record an aggregate twice that.

27. The feature-length films of Laurel and Hardy were premiered at the Empire. Although popular, none of the nine films played for more than a week. The films were produced by Hal Roach and distributed by MGM and as such have not been recorded or counted as MGM films.

28. *A Yank at Oxford*, which opened on the last day of this survey period—31 March

1938—went on to play for six weeks.

29. Eyles and Skone, op. cit., pp. 68–9; Marshall, M., *Top Hat and Tails: The Story of Jack Buchanan* (London, 1978), pp. 5–6.

30. Eyles and Skone, op. cit., p. 40.

31. ibid., p. 47.

32. Powell, M., *A Life in the Movies* (London, 1986), p. 222.

33. For instance, during the exhibition year 1936–7, 50 films were shown at the Plaza, of which 36 were Paramount, and 9 British; probably just sufficient to meet the 20 per cent required screenings quota.

34. Eyles and Skone, op. cit., p. 44, report that after its acquisition of the cinema in November 1928, Provincial Cinematograph Theatres—itself acquired by Gaumont-British in December 1928—replaced the 1,543 existing stalls and circle seats with 1,553 new seats and closed down the balcony. The figure given in the *Kine Year Book* of 2,092 seats clearly includes the balcony listed in Eyles and Skone as holding 572 seats. The *Kine Year Book* figure has been used in the POPSTAT model.

Chapter 4

1. Landy, M., *British Genres: Cinema and Society, 1930–1960* (Princeton, 1991), p.485.

2. The termination of the study at 31 March 1938 marks the substitution of the 1927 Cinematograph Act by a new set of regulations contained in the 1938 Act. The latter came into force on 1 April 1938 and made for a distinctive rental and exhibition environment.

3. This is a conservative estimate since films scoring less than the arithmetic mean POPSTAT were likely to have been rented at a small flat-rate tariff, whilst main features took up to a 60 per cent share of the box-office take. Further, the POPSTAT index treats films sharing a cinema programme as equal, disregarding the fact that most shared programmes contained a main and a support attraction. This methodological decision in the formulation of the POPSTAT index eliminates the need to make judgements concerning the respective status of the films on shared film programmes, but clearly it biases the results in favour of the lower-status films.

4. This is not the same as saying that all of the films of the major studios were conceived as potential 'hits'. It is clear from Glancy, H.M., 'MGM film grosses, 1924–1948: the Eddie Mannix ledger', *Historical Journal of Film, Radio and Television*, 12 (1992); Glancy, H.M., 'Warner Bros film grosses, 1921–1951: the William Schaefer ledger', *Historical Journal of Film, Radio and Television* 15 (1995); Jewell, R.B., 'RKO film grosses, 1929–1951: the C.J. Tevlin ledger', *Historical Journal of Film, Radio and Television* 14 (1994); Sedgwick, J., 'Richard B. Jewell's RKO film grosses, 1929–51: the C.J. Trevlin ledger: a comment', *Historical Journal of Film, Radio and Television* 14, (1994b), and 'The Warners' Ledger 1921–22 to 1941–42: a comment', *Historical Journal of Film, Radio and Television* 15 (1995) and Sedgwick, J. and Pokorny, M., 'The risk environment of film-making: Warners in the inter-war period', *Explorations in Economic History* 35 (1998) that comparatively few of films from the MGM, RKO and Warners portfolios of the period can be classified as super 'A' films—this is

particularly true with respect to the last two studios.

5. King, B., 'Stardom as occupation', in P. Kerr (ed.) *The Hollywood Film Industry*, (London, 1986), p.162.

6. In 1944 Huettig argued that 'interdependence ...seems a unique characteristic of the motion picture business. In other industries, an exceptionally good product is feared and disliked by other producers or sellers of similar goods. But of the small group of dominant movie companies, it is really true that the good of one is the good of all.' Huettig, M. 'Economic control of the motion picture industry', abridged from a publication of the same title published by University of Pennsylvania Press (1944) and found in T. Balio (ed.), *The American Film Industry* (Madison, 1985), p.291. *Variety* (31 July 1935, p.5) has a news piece entitled 'Loew Takes All of Par Pix for N.Y.. Means RKO May Grab WB Program'. The key fact for understanding this form of business behaviour is that the dominant body of assets owned by the vertically integrated companies was not their production studios but the real-estate value of their cinemas which had to derive competitive levels of return to justify their existence. See also Sedgwick and Pokorny, op. cit. (1998), pp.197, 209.

7. King, op. cit., p.162.

8. The number of zero-rated films for 1937 is likely to be exaggerated owing to the probability that some films released towards the end of the year would have obtained a listing in at least one of the national sample cinema set after 31 March 1938.

9. The Mass-Observation Worktown (Bolton) questionnaires of 1938 suggest that the western genre was more popular amongst audiences at the least prestigious of the three surveyed cinemas—the Palladium—which Richards and Sheridan describe as 'frankly a fleapit', and where 'more action' in film programmes was a more frequently stated demand of the audience surveyed, than was the case at the other two surveyed cinemas, the Odeon and Crompton. See Richards, J. and Sheridan, D., (eds) *Mass-Observation at the Movies* (London, 1987), p. 32.

10. Among which may be included *Westfront 1918* (Germany) released in 1932; in 1933, *Emil Und Die Detektive* (Germany); in 1934, *Liebelei* (Germany); in 1935, *Lac Aux Dames* (France), *Merlusse* (France) and *Die Ewige Maske* (Austria); in 1936, *Battleship Potemkin* (USSR) and *October* (USSR); and in 1937, *Zero de Conduite* (France) and *Les Bas-Fonds* (France).

11. A Herfindahl Index is a measure of industrial concentration commonly used by industrial economists which takes the form:

$$H = \sum_{i=1}^{n} s_i^2$$

where H = Herfindahl Index

s_i = market share of the *i*th firm.

n = the number of firms in the industry supplying the market

The squared term in the equation ensures that market shares sum to less than 1.0, unless the supply side of a market comprises one firm in which case it will equal 1.0. At the same time it exaggerates the contribution to industrial concentration of those firms with large shares relative to those with small shares. For any one industry the greater the market share of the leading firms relative to the remainder the greater the Herfindahl Index and the nearer it will be to 1.0.

The Herfindahl Index thus serves as an indicator of market power within an industry and comparator between industries.

12. In the case of London films this did not happen until 1936, when the Denham Studio complex was opened.

13. Bernard Hrusa-Marlow writes in a letter to the author:

> These producers were not independent in the same sense as Chaplin who was financially independent. Typically the 'occasional' producer was regularly employed by a major studio, either under contract with a clause permitting occasional independent production, or on a package basis to produce, say, *n* pictures for the studio after which he (it was always 'he' in those days) would take time off to shepherd his own production(s) to the screen. Selznick eventually set up his own studio, supplementing his own infrequent productions by constantly loaning out his stars—Ingrid Bergman, Joan Fontaine and Joseph Cotten notably and directors Alfred Hitchcock and Robert Stevenson.

14. Rowson, S., 'A statistical survey of the cinema industry in Great Britiain in 1934' *Journal of the Royal Statistical Society* 99 (1936), p.115.

15. United Artists was unlike the other major American operators in the British market in that it had no backward integration linkage to film production. It distributed the films of two of the leading indigenous independent producers—London Film Productions and B & D (British and Dominions).

16. Rachael Low comments, 'Cinemas showed American-owned Quota films because they had to and British quality films because they wanted to.' Low, R., *Film Making in 1930s Britain* (London, 1985), p.35. See also Dickinson, M., and Street, S., *Cinema and State: The British Film Industry and the British Government 1927–84* (London, 1985), pp.67–8.

17. *Minutes of Evidence taken before the Departmental Committee appointed by the Board of Trade to consider the position of British films,* (1936), pp. 8, 11, 26–7.

18. Rowson, op. cit. (1936), p.112, and *Minutes of Evidence,* op. cit., p.27.

19. Rowson, ibid.

20. ibid., p.112.

21. *Minutes of Evidence,* op. cit., (1936), p.11 (Table L), pp.26–7 (Appendix VI).

22. ibid., p.27.

23. Stead, P., 'The people and the pictures. The British working class and film in the 1930s', in N. Pronay, and D. Spring, *Propaganda, Politics and Film* (London, 1982), pp.81–2.

24. ibid., p.90.

Chapter 5

1. Halliwell, L., *Seats in All Parts* (London, 1986), p. 26.

2. Richards, J., *Films and British National Identity: From Dickens to Dad's Army* (Manchester, 1997), p.1.

3. Richards, J, 'Cinemagoing in Worktown: regional film audiences in 1930s Britain', *Historical Journal of Film, Radio and Television* 14 (1994), p.164.

4. Simon Rowson, 'A statistical survey of the cinema industry in Great Britain in 1934', *Journal of the Royal Statistical Society* 99 (1936), p.77 wrote, 'It is probable

indeed that one of the most valuable contributions to the exceptional popularity of the cinema is the existence of a power of selection among alternative programmes in various accessible houses'.

5. The proportion of the gross specified in the contract between distributor and exhibitor, typically ranging from 25–60 per cent, constituted the price of the film: clearly the greater the anticipated box-office, the greater the price set by the distributor. See *Minutes of Evidence taken before the Departmental Committee appointed by the Board of Trade to consider the position of British films*, (1936), para.57, p.9.

6. The study has been reported in Richards op. cit, (1994, 1997) and Richards, J. and Sheridan, D., *Mass-Observation at the Movies* (London, 1987).

7. See Richards, op. cit. (1997) ch.9 for an account of Lancashire and its cinema tradition.

8. The Hippodrome Moses Gate, and Empire Farnsworth have not been included in the sample count as their programmes were not regularly advertised in the *Bolton Evening News*. The latter enjoyed a daily circulation in excess of 50,000.

9. Orwell, G., *The Road to Wigan Pier* (Harmondsworth, 1962), p.72.

10. The exceptions were *42nd Street*—opened at the Regal and Palladium w/c 2 Oct. 1933, *Damaged Lives*—Palladium w/c 11 Dec. 1933, and *Green Pastures*—Embassy w/c 10 May 1937.

11. The exceptions were *Captain Blood* which played for 1.5 weeks at the Theatre Royal, w/c 3 Aug. 1936, *Damaged Lives*—2 weeks at the Palladium w/c 11 Dec. 1933 and *Sign of the Cross*—2 weeks at the Rialto w/c 9 Oct. 1933. A few films opened as the leading part of a double-bill programme. These were *Affairs of Voltaire* with *Smithy*—Hippodrome w/c 2 Apr. 1934, *Dreaming Lips* with *The Gap*—Lido w/c 25 Oct. 1937, *Painted Veil* with *Bon Voyage*—Capitol w/c 15 July 1935, *Road to Glory* with *Grand Jury*—Capitol w/c 26 Apr. 1937 and *Souls at Sea* with *She's No Lady*—Capitol w/c 14 Mar. 1938.

12. Worktown Box 29E, reported in Richards and Sheridan, op. cit., pp.27–30.

13. Unfortunately all these films played in Bolton outside the period of the investigation.

14. To remind the reader, the methodology is based on the fact that the box-office potentials of cinemas differ. Accordingly, it is not sufficient to count merely the number of exhibitions recorded by any particular film. The POPSTAT score for any particular film among a sample population of cinemas is derived by combining three factors: the relative box-office potential of the cinema; the billing status of the film—was it single or double billed; and finally the length of run. By establishing a score for the exhibition of the ith film at the jth cinema, it is then a simple process to aggregate the scores for that film from all of the cinemas included in the sample population. What is important here is not the absolute score, but the score relative to the scores of all other films.

15. Whilst 'hit' films played for extended runs at London West End cinemas, this pattern was not repeated elsewhere. Once outside the West End it was comparatively rare for films to play at the same cinema for more than two consecutive weeks.

16. But certainly not exclusively so. For evidence of Fields' popularity in Brighton and Hove see Chapter 6. Also see Richards, J., *Thorold Dickinson: The Man and His Films* (Beckenham, 1986), p.9, for Thorold Dickinson's description of the

effect that her singing in *Sing As We Go* had upon a Birmingham audience. See Andrew Higson, *Waving the Flag* (London, 1995), ch. 4, for a detailed textural and technical analysis of *Sing As We Go* as well as an account of the circumstances and conditions under which it was made and received.

17. The opening and closing sequences were shot at Denvale Spinning Mill, Union Road, whilst the interiors were shot at Sir George Holden's mill at Astley Bridge. See *Bolton Evening News*, 8 June 1934, p.6, col.6–7. Gracie Fields was prominent in the life of the town during the week of shooting. For details see *Bolton Evening News*, 4, 6, 8, 9, 11 and 21 June 1934, including photographs.

18. *Variety's* London reviewer of *Love, Life and Laughter* commented 'Although of very little value in the West End as a screen attraction, Gracie Fields is one of the biggest film draws in the provinces', *Variety*, 10 July 1935, p.19.

19. The two sample distributions exhibit an important difference. Although similarly skewed with long tails, indicating that the great bulk of films exhibited in either cinema sample set obtained near to average box-office success, whilst a relative small number of films—the 'hits' of the day—earned disproportionate box-office returns, the tail of the national sample distribution extends beyond that of the Bolton sample. Essentially, the longer tail of the nationally derived results is the consequence of extended runs which 'hit' productions generated in box-office rich London West End cinemas.

20. For an account of the circumstances under which *Off the Dole* was made, see Jeffrey Richards, J., *The Age of the Dream Palace* (London, 1984), pp.196–8; Rachael Low, *Film Making in 1930s Britain* (London, 1985), p.162. Some difference of opinion seems to exist as to whether the location was London or Manchester.

21. *Off the Dole* opened as a single billing at the Capitol for a week on 7 October 1935 and played at a further six venues on half weekly programmes, only one of which was shared with another feature film.

22. See note 'a' to Table 5.1.

23. The definition of a costume film is that employed by Sue Harper, *Picturing the Past: The Rise and Fall of the British Costume Film* (London, 1994), p.10, and includes those films which are given settings prior to 1914.

24. Harper's (ibid., p.11) analysis of the scant information concerning film popularity of film in mid-1930s Britain supports the POPSTAT-derived national rankings of these films.

Chapter 6

1. The Palladium was taken over by Oscar Deutch's organization in September 1934, opening as the town's premier Odeon on 8 June 1935, whilst a purpose-built cinema, not opened until 1937, was being built in West Street. The Palladium had served as a second-run cinema until its closure in 1934, and reverted to its original name following the opening of the West Street Odeon.

2. See the previous chapter, including notes 16 and 17, for an account of aspects of the making and reception of *Sing As We Go*.

3. Long films registered with the Board of Trade during that year.

4. Eyles, A., 'The Empire that was, 1928–61', *Picture House* 13 (1989). Eyles, A., and Skone, K., *London's West End Cinemas* (Sutton, 1991) report that the Empire,

Leicester Square, had a seating capacity of 3,226 and a price range from 2s. 6d. to 6s. 0d. or a mid-range price of 4s. 3d.

5.   The capacity and mid-range price for the Dominion were respectively 2,835 and 3.8s; the Metropole, 2,000 and 3.3s; and the Stoll 2,425 and 2s. The Davis cinema in Croydon, at which *Queen Christina* appeared but *Sing As We Go* did not, had 3,712 seats and a mid-range price of 2s. Eyles and Skone, op. cit.; *Kine Year Books*, 1935 and 1936.

6.   The British films outside of the Top 20 which make up these totals are listed in a note to Table 6.4.

Chapter 7

1.   Priestly, J.B., *Angel Pavement* (London, 1930), pp.174–5.

2.   Izod, J., *Hollywood and the Box-Office* (London, 1988), p.ix.

3.   Glancy, H.M., 'MGM film grosses, 1924–1948: the Eddie Mannix ledger', *Historical Journal of Film, Radio and Television* 12 (1992) and 'Warner Bros film grosses, 1921–1951: the William Schaefer ledger', *Historical Journal of Film, Radio and Television* 15 (1995).

4.   Jewell, R., 'RKO film grosses, 1929–1951: the C.J. Trevlin ledger', *Historical Journal of Film, Radio and Television* 14 (1994).

5.   Ostensibly, the exchange rate of £1 = $4.5 would not appear to closely shadow the Dollar-sterling exchange rate of the period which swung dramatically from a low of $3.24 in December 1931 and $3.14 in November 1932 to $5.10 in January 1934. The annual average exchange rate remained above the Gold Standard parity of $4.86 between 1934 and 1938. However, these rates reflect the considerable instability which existed in the international currency market during these years, as countries adopted dramatic internal measures to adjust to recession, balance of payments difficulties, movements of gold and speculation. Such a complexity of determinants means that exchange rates are not reliable as indicators in making comparisons between the major international economies, with the US dollar being relatively undervalued against the pound for much of the period after 1934.

    A better measure of international competitiveness and, therefore, of the respective strengths and weaknesses of internal economies and underlying trend in exchange rates, can be found in comparative unit labour costs, which reflect relative changes in labour productivity and inflation, as well as exchange-rate movements between economies. Using 1929 as a base year, Dimsdale, N., 'British monetary policy and the exchange rate', *Oxford Economic Papers* 33 (1981), has calculated the index for Britain and the US as 89 and 87 respectively for 1931 and 91 for both countries in 1938, with the index sensitive to domestic policy initiatives during the intervening years. Over the period as a whole it would appear that there was very little change in the relative competitiveness of either economy. Accordingly, a single exchange-rate value to gauge UK and film budgets has been adopted for the period. The choice of $4.50 is very close to the 1931 average after Britain had left the Gold Standard and is near to the underlying exchange rate following the US dollar devaluation of 1933, given that the dramatic nature of the latter, led to an undervalued US dollar until at least 1938.

6.   *Hollywood Party* was a musical which started as *The Hollywood Revue of 1933*, in response to Warners' backstage musical 'hits' of the same year. For an account

of the difficulties which plagued the film, the final version of which was abbreviated to a running time of 69 minutes, see Barrios, R., *A Song in the Dark: The Birth of the Musical* (Oxford, 1995), pp. 188, 396, 417–20.

7. Sedgwick, J., 'Richard B. Jewell's RKO film grosses, 1929–51: the C.J. Trevlin ledger: a comment', *Historical Journal of Film, Radio and Television* 14 (1994b).

8. The *New Oxford English Dictionary* (1998) defines 'stochastic' as: 'a random probability or pattern that may be analysed statistically but may not be predicted precisely'.

9. From Rowson, S, 'The value of remittances abroad for cinematograph films', *Journal of the Royal Statistical Society* 97 (1934), I calculate that for that year, net box-office receipts available to film-makers was in the order of £6,790,000. The sum of the POPSTAT scores distributed to the 664 films released during that year was 4,123.56, implying that each POPSTAT unit was worth £1,646. If this value holds for the whole period of the investigation, the regression equation indicates that for each additional $100,000 (£22,222) invested by Warners in a film, they could expect to earn only £2,637 at the British box-office. This converts back to $11,867. However, given the assumptions behind this calculation and the low value of the R2 statistic, it is clear that this result should be treated with a great deal of caution.

10. To be homoscedastic, the data should fall randomly about the regression line but within boundaries two standard errors of the estimate above and below it. Where the data conform to a clear pattern (i.e. are not randomly distributed about the regression line) or fall regularly outside of these boundaries, the regression is likely to be heteroscedastic.

11. Sedgwick, J. and Pokorny, M., 'The risk environment of film-making: Warners in the inter-war period', *Explorations in Economic History* 35 (1998), pp.205–9.

Chapter 8

1. Porter, V., 'Between structure and history: genre in popular British cinema', *Journal of Popular British Cinema* 1 (1998), p.26.

2. Izod, J., *Hollywood and the Box Office* (London, 1988), p.56.

3. 'The musical film, and the musical theatre from which it is largely derived, was also the product of, and testament to, a decade when musical entertainment *per se* was immensely popular.' Guy, S., 'Calling all stars: musical films in a musical decade', in J. Richards, (ed.) *The Unknown 1930s: An Alternative History of the British Cinema, 1929–1939* London, 1998), p.118.

4. For a major new appraisal of British film comedies during the 1930s, see Sutton, D., *A Chorus of Raspberries: British Film Comedy, 1929–1939* (Exeter, 2000).

5. This preference for domestic comedy is shown to be even stronger in the regional studies of Bolton and Brighton described in chapters 5 and 6.

6. *Head Over Heels* and *Gangway* were placed 59th and 72nd respectively in the POPSTAT listings of 1937 releases.

7. A similar exercise could be carried out for the numerous other lineages which can be identified within and across the standard genre classifications. However, as will become clear from the subsequent analysis of lineages related to the musical genre, this becomes a work in itself, space for which cannot be found in this book.

8. Barrios, R., *A Song in the Dark: The Birth of the Musical* (Oxford, 1995).

9. Porter, V., 'Between structure and history: genre in popular British cinema', *Journal of Popular British Cinema* 1 (1998), p.29.
10. The former's Cole Porter songbook was totally excised, notwithstanding the irony that Warners had fully financed the Broadway stage production. The latter's eight Irving Berlin songs were reduced to one despite the presence of major film stars Douglas Fairbanks and Bebe Daniels and the fast rising radio star Bing Crosby.
11. Barrios, op. cit., p.345.
12. ibid., p.346.
13. George Cukor was responsible for the initial direction as Lubitsch was involved in directing another film—*The Man I Killed*. Lubitsch later became involved in the project and took principal directorial credit, which led Cukor into litigation against Paramount.
14. Barrios, op. cit., p.355.
15. ibid., p.467.
16. ibid., pp.359–60.
17. ibid., p.362. No source is given concerning this financial information.
18. ibid., p.399.
19. Bernard Hrusa-Marlow in correspondence with the author makes the argument:

    > In terms of Lubitsch's career, however, those musicals were an interlude or interruption in an already well established 'lineage' going back to the silent era. Many of these films are lost, but the characteristics of Lubitsch's sophisticated, but mostly kindly and gentle, satire are evident in *The Oyster Princess* (1918).

20. Chevalier was loaned out to the 20th Century studio in 1935 to make *Folies Bergère*, released in Britain as *The Man From the Folies Bergère*, but didn't make another film for MGM.
21. Warners made one attempt at producing an operetta—*Sweet Adeline* (1935). The film cost $635,000 to make but lost the studio over $200,000. See Table 8.4.
22. Barrios, op. cit., p.428, describes *One Night of Love* as a 'mix of Cinderella, *Tosca*, and Ruby Keeler.'
23. Released in Britain as *On Wings of Song*.
24. Released in Britain as *For You Alone*.
25. *I'll Take Romance* (1937) was released in Britain in November 1937. Hence, its distribution amongst the sample set of cinemas has not been fully captured as it will not have ended its distribution run before 31 March 1938.
26. Barrios, op. cit., pp. 428–9. He includes in this list Lily Pons, Nino Martini, Jan Kiepura, Gladys Swarthout, James Melton and Marion Talley, ibid., p. 434.
27. These costs included $800,000 spent on part of a Technicolor version which was cancelled after the death of its producer Irving Thalberg. Studio head Louis B. Mayer ordered a complete restart (in black and white) with a new script more in accord with his conservative moral outlook. Excluding the $800,000 would put the cost of the second, released version at approximately $1.3 million, giving a notional return of 100 per cent. Rich, S., *Sweethearts* (New York, 1994), p.165.
28. Although he does not include *Sunshine Susie* in his analysis of the British musical, Stephen Guy (op. cit.) provides a stimulating overview of the British musical during this period.
29. Low, R., *Film Making in 1930s Britain* (London, 1985), p.131.

30. This theme is taken up in ch. 10.

31. Low, op. cit. (1985), p.123.

32. ibid., pp.124–5.

33. ibid., p.124.

34. ibid., p.139. *One Heavenly Night* (Goldwyn, 1931) and *The Night Is Young* (MGM, 1934) had failed to make her a Hollywood star.

35. ibid., p.147.

36. Sedgwick, J. and Pokorny, M., 'The risk environment of film-making: Warners in the inter-war period', *Explorations in Economic History* 35 (1998), tab.2.

37. Barrios, op. cit., p.373.

38. Sedgwick and Pokorny, op. cit. (1998), p.204. See Roddick, N., *A New Deal in entertainment: Warner Brothers in the 1930s* (London, 1983).

39. Barrios, op. cit., p.377. See also Bette Davis's account in her autobiography, Davis, B., *The Lonely Life* (London, 1962), pp.132–4.

40. Barrios, op. cit., p.377, writes: 'By exercising full license to stage numbers not possible in any theatre, Berkeley gave musical film a fresh complexion. Logic— even dance—were less considerations than spectacle and excitement, as propelled by a special energy that made escapism seem urgent and even relevant.'

41. ibid., p.378.

42. ibid., p.391.

43. Some of Berkeley's most fondly remembered sequences take this form. Typically the curtain opened on to a proscenium stage through which the film's spectators were translated by the camera's viewpoint to a theatrically 'impossible' space in which dozens of chorus girls (and sometimes boys) were configured and transformed in ways defying the laws of physics, and were then returned by the camera, as the curtains closed, to a view from the stalls from which, it is assumed, the applauding members of the theatre audience had been watching all this 'impossibility' happen before their very eyes. In the extreme case of the 'Lullaby of Broadway' number in *Gold Diggers of 1935*, the 'impossibility' takes the form of a complete, cinematically articulated, dramatic musical short story.

44. Barrios, op. cit., p.434.

45. The surge of activity at MGM was signalled by reports in *Variety*. See 28 August 1935, p.3; 16 October 1935, p.3; 20 November 1935, p.3.

46. Metaphysical paradox was not MGM's style. Special effects were used more pragmatically than imaginatively, with 'impossible' transitions employed simply as time-saving devices eliminating theatrical real-time 'quick change' diversionary interludes, e.g. in the final production number of *Dancing Lady* an 'instant' change from 'old fashioned' to 'modern' was effected with an archway set end-on, as a split-screen marker, so that Joan Crawford entering in horse-drawn carriage could emerge seated in a luxurious open-top automobile and dressed in the latest fashions of 1933.

47. Barrios, op. cit., p.430.

48. The film was a reworking of Cole Porter's show *The Gay Divorce*. The different title was the consequence of the Hays Office objection to the idea that a divorce could be a gay affair. Astaire had recently played the show on Broadway and in London.

49. Astaire did not obtain executive control over the manner in which his dance routines were filmed until the following film in the series, *Roberta*, from which

time he uses the longest possible takes. This is in contrast to Mark Sandrich's use of short takes in *The Gay Divorcee*. See Barrios, op. cit., p.431, footnote 18. Also see Astaire, F., *Steps in Time* (London, 1959), p.184; Croce, A., *The Fred Astaire and Ginger Rogers Book* (New York, 1972), p.39; Mueller, J., *Astaire Dancing* (London, 1986), p.59.

50. *Roberta* was directed by William A. Seiter and *Swing Time* by George Stevens.

51. Richards, J., *The Age of the Dream Palace* (London, 1984), p. 209.

52. ibid., p.209.

53. ibid., p.217.

54. Higson, A., *Waving the Flag* (London, 1995) pp.131–42.

55. It was in the full-page advertisement for this film in *Variety*, 1 January 1936, p.71, that Matthews was proclaimed 'The Dancing Divinity'. Thornton (London, 1974), p.132, reports that in *Picturegoer*, 15 August 1936, she was named as 'Britain's first world woman star'.

56. For a detailed and stimulating account of Matthews film career during the 1930s, see Richards, op. cit. (1984), ch. 12.

57. The sad story of botched opportunities to dance with Astaire is told by her biographer Michael Thornton (1974) pp. 110–32, 160.

58. Richards, op. cit. (1984), p. 209.

59. ibid., p.223.

60. Low, op. cit. (1985), p.145.

61. These details are taken from Marshall, M., *Top Hat and Tails: The Story of Jack Buchanan*, (London, 1978), who maintains that Buchanan chose not to develop a career in Hollywood because he was confident that he could, independently, take on the challenge of both starring and directing in British films which would compete effectively with the product of the major studios. Barrios, op. cit. (1995), pp.295–6 is quite scathing of Buchanan's performance in *Monte Carlo*.

62. Low, op. cit. (1985), p.148.

63. Buchanan's other 1937 production for his own short-lived company, *Smash and Grab,* was a crime comedy without musical numbers. It doesn't appear to have made much of an impact with British audiences, being placed 313th in the annual POPSTAT list.

64. This result may be artificially low as a consequence of the film's late release date in Britain (November, 1937) with respect to the terminal date of the investigation (31 March 1938), meaning that the film might not have been fully diffused amongst the cinemas of the sample set by this date.

65. George Formby can be seen to be his successor, taking this lineage through to the mid-War years.

66. Barrios, op. cit., p.421.

67. This was duly reflected in *Variety*, 15 May 1935, p.3, under the headline: 'New Film Musical Trend—End of sets filled with hoofers'.

68. This is perhaps best exemplified by the number 'A Pretty Girl is Like a Melody' in *The Great Ziegfeld* for which the world's largest revolving stage assembly was built, on which sat a towering helicoidal fluted wedding cake-like edifice, its spiral stairway lined with a host of singers and dancers.

Chapter 9

1. Dahl, R., *Boy/Going Solo* (Harmondsworth, 1993), p. 295.
2. See Balio, T., *Grand Design: Hollywood as a Modern Business Enterprise* (Berkeley, 1993), ch. 6; Izod, J., *Hollywood and the Box-Office* (London, 1988), chs 8–9; Maltby, R., *Hollywood Cinema* (Oxford, 1995), pp.252–7; Klaprat, C., 'The star as market strategy: Bette Davis in another light', in T. Balio (ed.) *The American Film Industry* (Madison, 1985).
3. Rosen, S., 'The economics of superstars', *American Economic Review* 71 (1981), p.845.
4. This analysis applies also to stars such as Mickey Mouse and Bugs Bunny where there is no direct causal agent in front of the camera.
5. Askoy, A., and Robins, K., 'Hollywood for the 21st century: global competition for critical mass in image markets', *Cambridge Journal of Economics* 16 (1992), p.12.
6. This is not at all the same as saying that film-makers who make films for other objectives are irrational. However, independent producers do need to raise funds from the capital market and hence must assuage their backers in the conventional manner, if they are to continue making films as a long-term project.
7. Rosen (op. cit., p.846) puts this condition more rigorously but less realistically, stating: 'The distribution of talent is assumed to be fixed in the population of potential sellers and costlessly observable to all economic agents'.
8. Baumol, W. and Bowen, W., *Performing Arts: The Economic Dilemma* (Cambridge, Mass., 1968), pp.229–30.
9. Rosen, op. cit., p. 846.
10. Adler, M., 'Stardom and talent', *American Economic Review* 75 (1985), p.209.
11. Albert, S., 'Movie stars and the distribution of financially successful films in the motion picture industry', *Journal of Cultural Economics* 22 (1998), p.251.
12. See Sedgwick, J., and Pokorny, M., '"Movie stars and the distribution of financially successful films in the motion picture industry": a comment', *Journal of Cultural Economics* 22 (1999), for a critique of Albert's argument.
13. See Balio, op. cit., (1993), p.155.
14. ibid., pp.159–61, for an account of this with respect to the disputes which James Cagney and Bette Davis had with their employer, Warners.
15. Where the star was on 'picture-deal' terms the studio could cast the star in low-budget productions to encourage the star's agent to negotiate 'buying out' the contract: Joan Crawford, for example, paid $200,000 in 1952 to be released from her contract with Warners. Where the contract also had clauses giving the star approval of script and/or director and/or co-star and/or cinematographer and/or working conditions, the studio simply kept up a flow of proposals that would be unacceptable to the star in the hope of forcing a departure. Shipman, D., 2nd edition, *The Great Movie Stars: The Golden Years* (London, 1993), p.134.
16. See Balio, op. cit. (1993), p.158.
17. ibid., pp.157–8, for a general discussion of loan outs. The business could become complicated. Although outside our period, Stine, J., *Mother Goddam* (New York, 1974), p.172, reports that Warners wanted Ingrid Bergman for *Saratoga Trunk*—shot in 1943 but not put on general release until 1945—giving Olivia de Havilland in exchange to David O. Selznick. He, however, had no film for de Havilland and sold her on to RKO to appear in the comedy *Government Girl* (1943). Thomas

Schatz, *The Genius of the System* (London, 1998), ch. 17, elaborates on this aspect of Selznick's business behaviour. He argues (p.322) that 'Selznick redefined the role of both agent and producer, creating something of a prototype for the packaging agents who would dominate the New Hollywood decades later.'

18. Storper, M., 'The transition to flexible specialisation in the US film industry: external economies, the division of labour, and the crossing of industrial divides', in A. Amin (ed.), *Post-Fordism: A Reader* (Oxford, 1994), p.207.

19. Richards, J., *The Age of the Dream Palace* (London, 1984), pp.155–9.

20. The weights 1.0 and 0.5 imply that the principal star(s) is rated as twice as important as the next ranking co-star. Different weights could of course be used to further exaggerate, or lessen, the relative value of the dominant star. That there may be one or more dominant or second billing co-stars in any single film, implies that the weights ascribed to each film will differ between films. For instance with *Grand Hotel* (1932) I have given Greta Garbo the weight of 1.0, assessing that she is the dominant star, whilst her co-stars John L. Barrymore, Lionel Barrymore, Joan Crawford, Wallace Beery and Lewis Stone, are each given the weight of 0.5. The weights here sum to 3.5. This contrasts with *Hell Divers* (1932) in which Wallace Beery is identified as the dominant star with Clark Gable as his second billing co-star. Here the weights sum to 1.5. The implication here is that some films are greater star vehicles than others. This convention differs from that previously used in Sedgwick, J., 'Cinema-going preferences in Britain in the 1930s', in J. Richards, ed., *The Unknown 1930s: An Alternative History of the British Cinema, 1929–39* (London, 1998); and Sedgwick, J., 'The comparative popularity of stars in mid-1930s Britain', *Journal of Popular British Cinema 2* (1999) where only the first and second billed stars were identified, carrying the respective weights of 0.67 and 0.33 thus ensuring that the sum of the weights for each film summed to 1.0.

21. The median is found by ranking all of the stars who record a STARSTAT score greater than zero, and taking the score of the actor whose rank falls halfway in the series.

22. Madeleine Carroll's last film in England was Hitchcock's *Secret Agent* (1936), co-starring John Gielgud.

23. For an excellent account of Formby's contribution to British cinema see Richards, op. cit. (1984), ch.11.

24. Richards maintains that Olivier had the potential to rival such Hollywood stars during the 1930s but was poorly served by a domestic film industry which seemed to be too parochial in its approach to stars, ibid., pp. 164–7.

25. Hitchcock's *The Lady Vanishes* (1938) would also fit this description but, unfortunately, it falls outside the period of investigation.

26. Astaire and Rogers are included in this list because the non-musical aspect of their double act was extremely characteristic of their films. Also, Rogers stars in a number of other Top 100 films during the period.

27. Dietrich did make one film in London during this period, appearing in a Korda production for London Films, *Knight Without Armour* (1937), co-starring Robert Donat, which was shot at the Denham studio.

28. This adds fuel to her claims against Warners' poor management of her talent leading her to walk out of her contract in 1935, only to return having lost a lawsuit in London.

298

29. This does not necessarily mean that the rate of return on the investment has increased. (See equations 7.1 and 7.2 in Chapter 7 for definitions of profit and rate of return.) Where costs rise at a faster rate than profits, profits may well still increase, but the rate of return will actually fall. What was probably more important to the studio executive was that net profits were rising subject to an acceptable rate of return. A simple example should suffice. Let costs rise from 100 to 200 from one film project to another. Let the corresponding box-office receipts rise from 200 to 320. Clearly profits have risen from 100 to 120. However, the rate of return on the two projects has fallen from 100 per cent to 60 per cent.

30. Davis was loaned out to RKO in 1934 to make *Of Human Bondage*, in exchange for Irene Dunne. See Stine, op. cit., p. 57.

31. Balio, op. cit. (1993), pp.159–60.

32. A correlation coefficient of 0.81 was measured between the foreign box-office performance of Gable's films and their respective POPSTAT scores.

33. This is apparent from Table 9.1 and brought out in the text pertaining to the table.

34. Shipman, op. cit., p.241.

35. Glancy, H.M., 'MGM film grosses, 1924–1948: the Eddie Mannix Ledger', *Historical Journal of Film, Radio and Television* 12 (1992) and 'Warner Bros. film grosses, 1921–1951: the William Schaefer ledger', *Historical Journal of Film, Radio and Television* 15 (1995), Sedgwick, J. and Pokorny, M., 'The risk environment of film-making: Warners in the inter-war period', *Explorations in Economic History* 35 (1998).

36. Shipman, op. cit., p. 473.

37. Dyer, R., *Stars* (London, 1980), p.12.

38. Balio, op. cit. (1993), p. 155.

Chapter 10

1. (M)ichael (B)alcon (S)pecial (C)ollection, MBSC/File C55/Letter from Michael Balcon to Jeffrey Bernard—Head of Gaumont-British's distribution wing—dated 8 January 1934.

2. MBSC/D25/Letter to Ian Dalrymple, dated 20 March 1936, in which he writes: 'The policy of the Corporation, as you know from your own experience whilst with us, is not to definitely go out to produce second features, whether for Home Market or World Distribution.' For a general account of Balcon's activities first at Gainsborough in Islington and then at Gaumont-British at Shepherd's Bush during the late 1920s and early 1930s see Low, R. *Film Making in 1930s Britain* (London, 1985), pp.126–42.

3. ibid., for a description of this personnel.

4. See Balio, T., *Grand Design: Hollywood as a Modern Business Enterprise* (Berkeley, 1993), p.145, for a description of the relation between the major studios and their in-house exhibition chains. *Variety*, 24 July 1935, p.7, reported that Gaumont-British was the 'First English film company to be admitted to the New York Film Board [meaning that] all G-B contracts with exhibitors will be enforced by the legal department of the board'.

5. Chapter 11 provides an account of this decline.

6. Chapter 11 provides a full discussion of the asymmetry between the two markets

and the implications for film-makers.

7. US Department of Commerce, Bureau of the Census, *Historical Statistics of the US: Colonial Times to 1970*, (Washington DC, 1975), Series H873 & H874.

8. These figures are taken from Browning, H. and Sorrell, A. 'Cinema and cinema-going in Great Britain', *Journal of the Royal Statistical Society* 117 (1954).

9. See note 5 in Chapter 7, based upon Dimsdale, N., 'British monetary policy and the exchange rate', *Oxford Economic Papers* (1981), for an explanation of this exchange rate.

10. Low, op. cit., (1985), p.114.

11. The Warners' financial season ran from September to August. The Schaefer ledger lists films from date of release under these categories. The films of Gaumont-British have been counted using a January to December year.

12. When compared with the output levels of London Films it is not surprising that Balcon was irked by the media attention accorded to Korda as the symbol of British film renaissance during this period. In a letter to Mark Ostrer (Managing Director of Gaumont-British) dated 11 June 1935, Balcon wrote: 'Korda has placed himself in the front rank with three pictures only—*Henry VIII*, *The Scarlet Pimpernel* and perhaps *Sanders of the River*' (MBSC/C63). A month later, Balcon, again writing to Mark Ostrer, commented: 'He [Korda] is looked upon as *the* authority, he is referred to as the uncrowned king of British films, the man who put British films on the map in America...' (MBSC/C64/letter dated 12 July 1935).

13. See MBSC/C39, C50 and C62 respectively. The last file contains a letter from Michael Balcon to Mark Ostrer (Joint-Managing Director), dated 19 January 1935, in which Balcon writes: 'We did not anticipate playing any other star than Robert Donat in this film, but having failed to obtain a satisfactory leading woman player, it has been decided to cast Madeleine Carroll.' With fees set at £5,000 per film for four films, Carroll's engagement raised the budget of *39 Steps* from £53,949 to £58,449, since originally only £500 had been set aside for the lead female part (MBSC/C5). For a discussion of the cost of making *Jew Süss* see Tegal, S., 'The politics of censorship: "Jew Süss" (1934) in London, New York and Vienna', *Historical Journal of Film, Radio and Television* 15 (1995).

14. MBSC/C14/draft letter, dated 12 January 1934. *The Phantom Light* is listed in the text as *The Haunted Light*—the title of the source stage play.

15. MBSC/C7/ dated 18 May 1934.

16. MBSC/C62/Correspondence between Balcon and Mark Ostrer, dated 20 May, 21 May, 24 May 1935.

17. Sedgwick, J. and Pokorny, M., 'The risk environment of film-making: Warners in the inter-war period', *Explorations in Economic History* 35 (1998), tab. 2, calculate the average production budget at Warners in the 1934/5 season as $372,900, falling back to $335,700 during the following season. Given an exchange rate of $4.5 = £1, the sterling equivalent can be obtained by dividing the annual mean budgets by 4.5.

18. Glancy, H.M., 'MGM film grosses, 1924–1948: the Eddie Mannix Ledger', *Historical Journal of Film, Radio and Television* 12 (1992) and 'Warner Bros. film grosses, 1921–1951: the William Schaefer ledger', *Historical Journal of Film, Radio and Television* 15 (1995).

19. Jewell, R., 'RKO film grosses, 1929–1951: the C.J. Trevlin ledger', *Historical*

Journal of Film, Radio and Television 14 (1994).

20. See *Minutes of Evidence* (1936)—evidence given by Mr Simon Rowson, Appendix, Table III, p.126.

21. MBSC/27b/ 'Report to Joint Managing Directors on the 1935 Programme', dated 13 December 1934.

22. MBSC/C50/Copy of C.M.Woolf's address to Gainsborough's AGM, dated 17 December 1934.

23. Balcon received a telegram from newspaper magnate William Randolph Hearst and film star Marion Davies congratulating Gaumont-British on the quality of *Chu Chin Chow*, MBSC/C23/dated 16 December 1934.

24. MBSC/D9/Letter to Balcon from Howard S. Cullman, dated 19 August 1936.

25. MBSC/D9/Address to the Sales Convention found in letter to Balcon from Howard S. Cullman, dated 18 May 1936. Similar sentiments appear in a cutting of a regular column from the *Wall Street Journal* featuring Cullman, dated 27 July 1935 found in the same file.

26. MBSC/C20/Letter from Dixon Boardman, dated 7 February 1934.

27. MBSC/C2/Internal memorandum dated 26 November 1934.

28. MBSC/C2/Internal memorandum dated 17 December 1934. For a history of the making (or not, in the case of Gaumont-British) of this film see Richards, J., "*Soldiers Three*': the 'lost' Gaumont-British imperial epic', *Historical Journal of Film, Radio and Television* 15 (1995).

29. MBSC/C16/ Letter to Harry Lachman dated 23 November 1934.

30. MBSC/C28/Report to the Managing Directors dated 13 December 1934.

31. MBSC/C19/Letter to Victor Saville, dated 2 February 1935. The letter reminds Saville that his contract with Gaumont-British gives him no right of veto over the films he is asked to make, or, indeed, control over their number.

32. MBSC/C58/Correspondence dated August 1935. Balcon made a considerable effort to smooth the path for Courtneidge, writing a string of letters to Louis B. Mayer and the Gaumont-British representative in Hollywood, Larry Darmour. It is evident from the correspondence between them that Courtneidge found the experience troubling. In Balcon she had a sensitive and concerned mentor. Madeleine Carroll, after the apparent transatlantic success of *I Was a Spy*, had travelled to Hollywood to make *The World Moves On* (1934, Fox) when out of contract with Gaumont-British, and prior to the 'international policy'. It is interesting to note that on this occasion Balcon's response was quite the reverse, writing to her husband, Captain Philip Astley, that 'it is a disappointment to me that she has decided that her career calls for her to go to America rather than stay in England', MBSC/C41/Letter dated 29 January 1934.

33. MBSC/C48/Letter to Arthur Lee, dated 28 June 1935.

34. MBSC/C48/Letter to Arthur Lee, dated 26 June 1935. Judging from a telegram communication between Balcon and the MGM studio, Balcon hoped to secure Robert Young to play alongside Matthews in *First a Girl*. The proposal was rejected because of the short notice given. See MBSC/C61/Telegrams dated 29 April 1935 and 30 April 1935. Matthew's husband and fellow Gaumont-British contract star, Sonnie Hale, eventually took the lead. Young subsequently came to Britain to star with Matthews in *It's Love Again* in 1936.

35. Matthews' only Hollywood appearance came in an episode, filmed in September 1941, in *Forever and a Day* (1943)—an all-star tribute to Britain produced by

RKO in aid of charities with contract co-operation from other studios. For a succinct account of Matthews' career during the 1930s, see Richards, J. *The Age of the Dream Palace* (London, 1984), ch.12.

36. MBSC/C61/Letters to and from Sam Marx dated 27 May 1935 and 25 June 1935. Balcon's stated rejection of *The Paradine Case* was perhaps a smokescreen since the file contains an internal review of the literary property which concludes that the subject 'would not make a popular motion picture'. Bernard Hrusa-Marlow adds: 'When the property finally came to the screen in 1947, directed by Alfred Hitchcock for David O. Selznick, it had an unhappy production history and was poorly received at the box-office and by critics.'

37. Balcon pleaded with Jack Warner to release Howard to star in *Secret Agent* but to no avail. Jack Warner's cabled rejection reads: 'Impossible permit Howard do picture London. We have sold Howard pictures for two years and haven't made one', MBSC/C62/Telegram dated 17 August 1935.

38. Balcon appears to have reluctantly given up on ever getting the services of Donat again following the success of *The 39 Steps*. Wanting him to star in *Sabotage*, Balcon expressed his exasperation in a letter to Mark Ostrer writing: 'We are up against a brick wall with Donat. For years I have not known an artist who had so much concentration on him with so little response …like so many of his type, he is anxious to make a big London stage success and it is difficult for him to understand why this is eluding him when he is such a success on the screen', MBSC/C62/Letter dated 16 September 1935.

39. MBSC/C27b/Note dated 8 November 1934.

40. MBSC/C48 Internal Broadway Office memorandum from George Weeks to Arthur Lee, dated 23 April 1935.

41. MBSC/C48/Letter from Arthur Lee, dated 24 April 1935.

42. MBSC/C48/Memorandum to Mark Ostrer, dated 10 May 1935.

43. MBSC/C48/Letter to Mark Ostrer from Arthur Lee, dated 4 July 1935. In the same letter Lee exalted: 'We are pretty well buoyed up by the success of "39 Steps" at the Roxy. I believe it is putting new life into our sales staff and is going to help tremendously. This is the first time we have made any money for the exhibitors.'

44. MBSC/C58/Letter to Cicely Courtneidge, dated 21 September 1935.

45. The fact that different films performed quite differently at the box-office of the same cinema, although obvious, is of great significance in that it implies that, at the margin, audiences in attending a cinema did so out of a preference for its programme relative to alternative programmes, given prices and location.

46. MBSC/C48/Letter to Arthur Lee, dated 6 December 1934. Philip Kemp has commented in a letter to the author that Balcon is here referring to 'Isidore Ostrer's ill-advised attempts to set up as a press tycoon to rival Beaverbrook. Michael Balcon also strongly resented having temperamental artistes like Arliss and Tom Walls imposed on him, especially when they had been granted contracts that allowed them to interfere in production matters.'

47. For two accounts of the complexities associated with the financial affairs of Gaumont-British, see Low, op. cit. (1985), pp. 126–43 and Dickinson, M. and Street, S., *Cinema and State: The British Film Industry and the British Government 1927–84* (London, 1985), pp.34–9.

48. MBSC/C28a/Letter to Mark Ostrer, dated 8 January 1934.

49. Gaumont-British ran four distinct named circuits with separate management and ownership structures before its partial acquisition of Union Cinemas in 1935: these were Denman, Gaumont, General Theatres Corporation, and Provincial Cinematograph Theatres.
50. MBSC/C63/Letter to Mark Ostrer, dated 11 June 1935.
51. MBSC/C64/Letter to Mark Ostrer, dated 5 July 1935.
52. MBSC/C64/Letter to Mark Ostrer, dated 11 July 1935.
53. MBSC/C3/ Recommendations of the Committee on Production Procedures (no.2), dated 17 November 1935.
54. MBSC/C84/Letter from Arnold Pressberger, dated 27 June 1934. This figure is repeated in a letter Balcon wrote to Maurice Ostrer, Head of the Studio Executive, MBSC/C26/dated 12 September 1934.
55. MBSC/C13/Letter to C.M.Woolf, undated but probably written in the period late April to early May 1934, judging from the position of the letter between other correspondence in the file. This output level represented full capacity for the Shepherd's Bush studio, the implication being that any subsequent expansion of output would require additional production facilities.
56. MBSC/C14/Memoranda dated 9 October and 12 October 1934. Consider Balcon's worries in the context of this announcement from Warners in *Variety*, 11 September 1935: 'Warners on studio construction spree, Up Budget $500,000 for Theatre, Stages...previously a $2,000,000 program had been under way...Studio theatre will have proscenium arch 100ft wide and 90 ft high with a 100 ft deep stage and special concealed camera spots every 40 ft of the stage on both sides, plus special arrangements for cameras in the auditorium...Harry M. Warner ...said the company is not waiting for prosperity to round the corner, but is hurrying it along and believes the industry in general should do the same.'
57. Glancy, H.M., 'Hollywood and Britain: MGM and the British 'Quota' legislation', in J. Richards, (ed.) *The Unknown 1930s: An Alternative History of the British Cinema, 1929–39* (London, 1998), pp.67–8.
58. Higson, A., *Waving the Flag* (London, 1995), pp. 10–11.
59. ibid., p.99.
60. ibid., p.142.
61. ibid., p.125.
62. ibid., p.122. Ostrer's explanation for the failure of the US strategy is reported in *Kine Weekly*, 11 April 1937.
63. Higson, op. cit., p.125.
64. MBSC/C70/Cutting from the *New York World Telegram*, dated 20 November 1935.
65. MBSC/C83/Letter dated 18 October 1934.
66. For an account of this transfer and Balcon's short period at MGM British see Glancy, op. cit. (1998), pp.67–71.
67. Eberts, J. and Ilott, T., *My Indecision is Final: The Rise and Fall of Goldcrest Films* (London, 1990), p.2.

Chapter 11

1. Low, R., *Film-Making in 1930s Britain* (London, 1985), pp.115–16.
2. ibid., p.270.

3. *Kine Weekly,* 13 December 1934.
4. *Kine Weekly,* January 1937. Also see Low (1985), pp. 142–3.
5. *Kine Weekly,* 3 June 1937.
6. *Kine Weekly,* 27 October 1938.
7. London Films Special Collection housed at the BFI Library, London.
8. Kulik, K., *Alexander Korda: The Man Who Could Work Miracles* (London, 1975); Street, S., 'Alexander Korda, Prudential Assurance and British film finance in the 1930s,' *Historical Journal of Film, Radio and Television* 6 (1986).
9. Low, op. cit. (1985), p.165. Michael Balcon's irritation with the attention accorded to Korda is documented in Chapter 10.
10. Kulik, op. cit., p.96.
11. Dalrymple, I., 'Alex', *British Film Academic Journal*, Spring (1956), p.7.
12. The exchange rate of $4.5 = £1 has been used here, as throughout the book.
13. See Kulik (op. cit., ch.9) for a full account of the concept of *Internationalism*. Kulik quotes Korda from an interview recorded in 1933, maintaining that to be international, a film had to 'first of all be truly and intensely national. It must be true to the matter of it.' (p.97).
14. Some discrepancies exist between this table and Table 1 of Sedgwick, op. cit., (1997). In the latter I used Glancy (1992, 1995) and Jewell (1994), for the bulk of the observations. The current table uses the primary sources of the Mannix, Schaefer and Trevlin Ledgers directly for information on MGM, Warners and RKO respectively. These were made available to the author by Mark Glancy and Richard Jewell. Mannix has the effect of considerably enlarging the number of MGM films with budgets greater than those listed from London Films. The differences which exist between the two tables with respect to Warners is explained by relating the Board of Trade registration dates of the London Films with the Warners' accounting year which ended on the 26th of August.
15. Low, op. cit. (1985), pp.116–17.
16. *Kine Weekly*, 5 September 1937.
17. Rowson, S., 'The value of remittances abroad for cinematograph films', *Journal of the Royal Statistical Society* 97 (1934). The calculations of remittances are also reported in *Kine Weekly*, 13 September 1934.
18. Browning, H. and Sorrell, A., 'Cinema and cinema-going in Great Britain', *Journal of the Royal Statistical Society* 117 (1954), revise this estimate downwards to £38.8 million.
19. Rowson's calculation of net revenues taken by renters is £8.1 million. From this subtract £810,000 as the revenue earned by non-feature film producers and £500,000 for renters' profits. This leaves an estimate of £6,790,000 going to the makers of feature films.
20. The 664 films released serves as an approximate denominator since 1934 releases would have continued to earn revenues in 1935, and similarly with 1933 releases. For some reason, Maxwell supposed that the number of feature-length films marketed in Britain was in the order of 500. Given the assumption concerning one-tenth of revenues being earned by non-feature films, the difference between the two denominators is sufficient to explain differences between the means of the two sources.
21. In effect, the aggregate POPSTAT score for 1934, generated from the national sample cinema set for that year, is taken to represent the exhibition sector as a

whole. The performance of the season's 'hits' is likely to be underestimated since the respective box-office percentages negotiated by the renters is not measured in the POPSTAT statistic. As explained in Chapter 3, where an exhibitor booked a double-bill programme, which included a major 'A' and a 'B' feature, it is likely that whilst the former commanded a percentage of the gross box-office revenue, the latter would have been booked at a low flat-rate fee. However, the POPSTAT score for both will be identical, thereby underestimating the popularity of the 'A' film as measured by box-office potential revenue and overestimating the popularity of the 'B' film.

At the other end of the scale, the fact that so many films return a zero POPSTAT amongst the sample cinema set, as shown in Chapter 4, suggests an under-estimation of the performance of the cheaper flat-rate bookings. This is not likely to be very important in terms of market share since the size of the cinemas in which such films predominated and their tariff range imply very small box-office returns.

22. *Minutes of Evidence* (1936); *Report of a Committee appointed by the Board of Trade to consider the Position of British Films*, chairman: Lord Moyne (London, HMSO, Cmd 5320), 1936); Board of Trade, *Proposals for Legislation on Cinematograph Films...* (London, HMSO, Cmd 5529, 1937).

23. See Mr Fennelly's evidence to the Moyne Committee in *Minutes of Evidence,* op. cit.

24. For details of the reciprocity provision of the 1938 Act, see Low, op. cit. (1985), p.50, and Dickinson, M. and Street, S., *Cinema and State: The British Film Industry and the British Government 1927–84* (London, 1985), pp.98–9.

25. For a detailed statistical breakdown of the American market for films, see Sedgwick, J. and Pokorny, M., 'The risk environment of film-making: Warners in the inter-war period', *Explorations in Economic History* 35 (1998), tab.1, itself derived from *Historical Statistics of the* US, op. cit.

26. The assumption of a one-third distribution cost to revenue is supported by data from the Mannix and Trevlin ledgers of MGM and RKO respectively. In my comment on Jewell, op. cit., I produce an Appendix in which column 7 presents distribution costs at RKO as a proportion of gross box-office earnings. These averaged 37 per cent. See Sedgwick, J., 'Richard B. Jewell's RKO film grosses, 1929–51: the C.J. Trevlin ledger: a comment', *Historical Journal of Film, Radio and Television* 14 (1994b). Very similar proportions prevailed at MGM as can be gauged from Table 7.1.

27. See Dickinson and Street, op. cit., ch.5; Jarvie, I., *Hollywood's Overseas Campaign: The North Atlantic Movie Trade, 1920–1950* (Cambridge, 1992), ch.5; and Street, S., 'The "Hays" Office and the defence of the British market in the 1930s', *Historical Journal of Film, Radio and Television* 5 (1985); and Glancy, M., *When Hollywood Loved Britain: The Hollywood 'British' Film, 1939–45* (Manchester, 1999).

28. *Kine Weekly,* 4 November 1937.

29. ibid.

30. ibid.

31. ibid.

32. Glancy, H.M., 'Hollywood and Britain: MGM and the British "Quota" legislation', in J. Richards (ed.), *The Unknown 1930s: An Alternative History of*

the British Cinema, 1929–39 (London, 1998), is good on the double and triple Quota and MGM's decision to produce big-budget films in Britain.

33. The Board of Trade registered 228 British 'long' films submitted by renters in the registration year 1937–8. This fell to 103 and 108 respectively for the registration years 1938–9 and 1939–40. On the other hand the proportion of British 'long' films registered by exhibitors fell from 26.4 per cent to 22.8 per cent. See Low, op. cit. (1985), app., tabs 2 & 6.
34. ibid., p.51.
35. See Wood, L., *British Films 1927–1939* (London, 1986), p.120.
36. Low, op. cit. (1985), pp. 29–30.
37. Klingender, F., and Legg, S., *Money Behind the Screen* (London, 1937); Low, op. cit. (1985), pp.199–208.
38. See Street, S., 'Alexander Korda, Prudential Assurance and British film finance in the 1930s', *Historical Journal of Film, Radio and Television* 6 (1986).
39. Foreman-Peck, J. 'Industry and industrial organization in the inter-war years', in R. Floud and D. McCloskey (eds), 2nd edition, *Economic History of Britain Since 1700*, vol. 2 (Cambridge, 1994), pp. 397–8.

Chapter 12

1. Auerbach, P., *Competition: The Economics of Industrial Change*, (Oxford, 1988), pp.57–9.
2. Jarvie, I., *Hollywood's Overseas Campaign: The North Atlantic Movie Trade, 1920–1950* (Cambridge, 1992), p.143.
3. ibid., pp. 9–10. See also Glancy, H.M., *When Hollywood Loved Britain: The Hollywood 'British' Film, 1939–45* (Manchester, 1999).
4. ibid., p.8.
5. Saunders, T., *Hollywood in Berlin: American Cinema and Weimar Germany* (Berkeley, 1994), p.2.
6. Hoskins, C., McFadyen, S. and Finn, A., *Global Television and Film* (Oxford, 1997), p.4.
7. Neale, S., and Smith, M., *Contemporary Hollywood Cinema* (London, 1998).
8. Bordwell, D., Staiger, J. and Thompson, K., *The Classical Hollywood Cinema: Film Style and Mode of Production to 1960* (London, 1985).
9. Jarvie, op. cit. (1992), p.8.
10. ibid., p.172.
11. Harper, S., *Picturing the Past: The Rise and Fall of the British Costume Film* (London, 1994).
12. Klinger, B., *Melodrama and Meaning: History, Culture and the Films of Douglas Sirk* (Bloomington, 1994); Staiger, J., *Interpreting Films: Studies in the Historical Reception of American Cinema* (Princeton, 1992).
13. The oral history project led by Annette Kuhn is an excellent example of this kind of enterprise. See Kuhn, A., 'Cinema-going in Britain in the 1930s: report of a questionnaire survey', *Historical Journal of Film, Radio and Television* 19 (1999).

References

Official publications

Cinematograph Films Act (1927, 17 & 18 Geo.5 c.29).

Minutes of Evidence taken before the Departmental Committee appointed by the Board of Trade to consider the Position of British Films, chairman: Lord Moyne (London, HMSO, 1936).

Report of a Committee appointed by the Board of Trade to Consider the Position of British Films; chairman: Lord Moyne (London, HMSO, cmd.530, 1936).

Cinematograph Films Act (1938), (1 & 2 Geo.6 c.17).

Library of Congress Catalog of Copyright Entries, Motion Pictures 1912–1939.

Primary sources

Kinematograph Year Books, 1927–1939 (cited as *Kine Year Books*).

Kinematograph Weekly, 1927–1938 (cited as *Kine Weekly*).

Michael Balcon Special Collection, British Film Institute Library

Alexander Korda Special Collection, British Film Institute Library.

Motion Picture Guide.

Eddie Mannix Ledger, copied by Mark Glancy. The original ledger is held in the Howard Strickling Collection, The Margaret Herrick Library of the Academy of Motion Picture Arts and Sciences, Beverly Hills, California.

William Schaefer Ledger, copied by Mark Glancy. The original ledger is held as part of the William Schaefer Collection at the University of Southern California Film and Television Archives in Los Angeles.

C.J. Trevlin Ledger, made available by Richard Jewell. The original ledger is held at the University of Southern California Film and Television Archives in Los Angeles.

US Department of Commerce, Bureau of the Census (1975) *Historical Statistics of the US: Colonial Times to 1970*, Washington DC.

Bibliography

Adler, M., 'Stardom and talent', *American Economic Review* 75 (1985) pp.208–12.

Albert, S., 'Movie stars and the distribution of financially successful films in the motion picture industry', *Journal of Cultural Economics* 22 (1998) pp.249–70.

Allen, J., 'The film viewer as consumer', *Quarterly Review of Film Studies* 5 (1980) pp.481–99.

Allen, R.C., ' From exhibition to reception: reflections on the audience in film history', *Screen* 34 (1990) pp.347–56.

Askoy, A. and Robins, K., 'Hollywood for the 21st century: global competition for critical mass in image markets', *Cambridge Journal of Economics* 16 (1992) pp.1–22

Astaire, F., *Steps in Time* (London, 1959).

Auerbach, P., *Competition: The Economics of Industrial Change* (Oxford, 1988).

Balio, T. (ed.), *The American Film Industry* (Madison, 1985).

Balio, T., *Grand design: Hollywood as a Modern Business Enterprise* (Berkeley, 1993).

Barrios, R., *A Song in the Dark: The Birth of the Musical*, (Oxford, 1995).

Baumol, W. and Bowen, W., *Performing Arts: The Economic Dilemma* (Cambridge, Mass., 1968).

Bordwell, D., Staiger, J. and Thompson, K., *The Classical Hollywood Cinema: Film Style and Mode of Production to 1960* (London, 1985).

Bowden, S., and Offer, A., 'Household appliances and their use of time', *Economic History Review* 47 (1994) pp.725–38.

Bowden, S. and Offer, A., 'Household appliances and 'systems of provision', *Economic History Review* 52 (1999), pp. 563–67.

Brown, G., 'Money for speed: the British films of Bernard Vorhaus', in J. Richards (ed.), *The Unknown 1930s: An Alternative History of the British Cinema, 1929–39* (London, 1998).

Browning, H. and Sorrell, A., 'Cinema and cinema-going in Great Britain', *Journal of the Royal Statistical Society* 117 (1954) pp.133–65.

Carroll, N., *A Philosophy of Mass Art* (Oxford, 1998).

Carter, C., 'George Shackle and uncertainty: a revolution still awaited', *Review of Political Economy* 5 (1993).

Coleman, D. and Macleod, C., 'Attitudes to new techniques: British businessmen 1800–1950', *Economic History Review* 39 (1986) pp.588–611.

Croce, A., *The Fred Astaire and Ginger Rogers Book* (New York, 1972).

Dahl, R., *Boy/Going Solo* (Harmondsworth, 1993).

Dalrymple, I., 'Alex', *British Film Academic Journal*, Spring (1956).

Davies, P. and Neve, B., *Cinema, Politics and Society in America* (Manchester, 1981).

Davis, B., *The Lonely Life* (London, 1962).

De Grazia, V., 'Mass culture and sovereignty: the American challenge to European cinemas, 1920–1960', *Journal of Modern History* 61 (1989) pp.53–87.

De Vany, A. and Walls, W., 'Bose-Einstein dynamics and adaptive contracting in the motion picture industry,' *Economic Journal* 106 (1996) pp.1493–1514.

Dickinson, M. and Street, S., *Cinema and State: The British Film Industry and the British Government 1927–84* (London, 1985).

Dimsdale, N., 'British monetary policy and the exchange rate', *Oxford Economic Papers* 33 (1981) pp.306–49.

Dyer, R., *Stars* (London, 1980).

Earl, P., 'The economics of G.L.S. Shackle in retrospect and prospect', *Review of Political Economy* 5 (1993) pp.127–37.

Earl, P., *Microeconomics for Business and Marketing* (Aldershot, 1995).

REFERENCES

Eberts, J. and Ilott, T., *My Indecision is Final: The Rise and Fall of Goldcrest Films* (London, 1990).

Elleray, D. Robert, *A Refuge From Reality* (Hastings, 1989).

Eyles, A., 'The Empire that was, 1928–61', *Picture House* 13 (1989).

Eyles, A., *ABC: The First Name in Entertainment* (London, 1993).

Eyles, A., *Gaumont British Cinemas* (London, 1996).

Eyles, A. and Skone, K., *London's West End Cinemas* (Sutton, 1991).

Feinstein, C., *Statistical Tables of National Income, Expenditure and Output of the United Kingdom 1855–1965* (Cambridge, 1976).

Fine, B.,'Household appliances and their use of time: a comment', *Economic History Review* 52 (1999), pp. 552–62.

Fine, B. and Leopold E., *The World of Consumption* (London, 1993).

Foreman-Peck, J. 'Industry and industrial organisation in the inter-war years', in R. Floud and D. McCloskey (eds), 2nd edition, *Economic History of Britain Since 1700*, vol. 2 (Cambridge, 1994).

Fowler, D., *The First Teenagers: The Lifestyle of Young Wage-Earners in Interwar Britain* (London, 1995).

Gabler, N., *An Empire of Their Own: How the Jews Invented Hollywood* (New York, 1988).

Gilad, B., Kaish, S. and Loab, P., 'Cognitive dissonance and utility maximization: a general framework', *Journal of Economic Behaviour and Organization* 8 (1987) pp.61–73.

Glancy, H.M., 'MGM film grosses, 1924–1948: the Eddie Mannix ledger', *Historical Journal of Film, Radio and Television* 12 (1992) pp.127–44.

Glancy, H.M., 'Warner Bros film grosses, 1921–1951: the William Schaefer ledger', *Historical Journal of Film, Radio and Television* 15 (1995) pp.55–74.

Glancy, H.M., 'Hollywood and Britain: MGM and the British 'Quota' legislation', in J. Richards (ed.), *The Unknown 1930s: An Alternative History of the British Cinema, 1929–39* (London, 1998).

Glancy, H.M., *When Hollywood Loved Britain: The Hollywood 'British' Film, 1939–45* (Manchester, 1999).

Gomery, D., 'US. film exhibition: the formation of a big business', in T. Balio (ed.) *The American Film Industry* (Madison, 1985).

Gomery, D., *Shared Pleasures: A History of Movie Presentation in the United States* (London, 1992).

Greenwald, W., 'The motion picture industry: an economic study of the history and practices of a business', PhD dissertation, New York University (1950).

Greenwood, W., *Love on the Dole* (London, 1993).

Guy, S.,'Calling all stars: musical films in a musical decade,' in J. Richards (ed.), *The Unknown 1930s: An Alternative History of the British cinema, 1929–39* (London, 1998).

Hall, S., 'Notes on deconstructing "the popular"', in John Storey (ed.), *Cultural Theory and Popular Culture: A Reader* (Brighton, 1994).

Halliwell, L., *Seats in All Parts* (London, 1986).

Harper, S., *Picturing the Past: The Rise and Fall of the British Costume Film* (London, 1994).

Harper, S. and Porter, V., 'Moved to tears: weeping in the cinema in postwar Britain', *Screen* 37 (1996) pp.152–73.

Harper, S. and Porter, V., 'Cinema audience tastes in 1950s Britain', *Journal of Popular British Cinema* 2 (1999) pp.66–82.

309

Hayek, F., *The Counter Revolution of Science* (London, 1955).

Higson, A., *Waving the Flag* (London, 1995).

Hollows, J. and Jancovich, M., 'Popular film and cultural distinctions', in J. Hollows and M. Jancovich (eds), *Approaches to Popular Film* (Manchester, 1995).

Hoskins, C., McFadyen, S. and Finn, A., *Global Television and Film* (Oxford, 1997).

Huettig, M., 'Economic control of the motion picture industry', abridged from a publication of the same title published by University of Pennsylvania Press (1944) and found in T. Balio (ed.), *The American Film Industry* (Madison, 1985).

Izod, J., *Hollywood and the Box-Office* (London, 1988).

Jarvie, I., *Hollywood's Overseas Campaign: The North Atlantic Movie Trade, 1920–1950* (Cambridge, 1992).

Jarvie, I., 'Sir Karl Popper (1902–94): essentialism and historicism in film methodology', *Historical Journal of Film, Radio and Television* 15 (1995) pp.301–5.

Jewell, R., 'RKO film grosses, 1929–1951: the C.J. Trevlin ledger', *Historical Journal of Film, Radio and Television* 14 (1994) pp.37–51.

Kerr, C., 'Incorporating the star', *Business History Review* 64 (1990) pp.383–410.

King, B., 'Stardom as occupation,' in P. Kerr (ed.), *The Hollywood Film Industry* (London, 1986).

Klaprat, C., 'The star as market strategy: Bette Davies in another light', in T. Balio (ed.), *The American Film Industry* (Madison, 1985).

Klingender, F. and Legg, S., *Money Behind the Screen* (London, 1937).

Klinger, B., 'Digressions at the cinema: reception and mass culture,' *Cinema Journal* 28 (1989) pp.3–19.

Klinger, B., *Melodrama and Meaning: History, Culture, and the Films of Douglas Sirk* (Bloomington, 1994).

Kuhn, A., 'Cinema-going in Britain in the 1930s: report of a questionnaire survey', *Historical Journal of Film Radio and Television* 19 (1999), pp.531–43.

Kulik, K., *Alexander Korda: The Man Who Could Work Miracles* (London, 1975).

Landy, M., *British Genres: Cinema and Society, 1930–1960* (Princeton, 1991).

Low, R., *The History of British Film, 1896–1906* (London, 1948a).

Low, R., *The History of British Film, 1906–1914* (London, 1948b).

Low, R., *The History of British Film, 1914–1918* (London, 1950).

Low, R., *The History of British Film, 1918–1927* (London, 1971).

Low, R., *Film-Making in 1930s Britain* (London, 1985).

Lysandrou, P., 'The market and exploitation in Marx's economic theory: a reinterpretation', *Cambridge Journal of Economics* 24 (2000).

McFadden, D. and Train, K., 'Consumer's evaluation of new products: learning from self and others', *Journal of Political Economy* 104 (1996) pp.683–703.

McKibbin, R., *Classes and Cultures: England, 1918–1951: A Study of a Democratic Society* (Oxford, 1998).

Maltby, R., 'The political economy of Hollywood: the studio system', in P. Davies and B. Neve (eds), *Cinema, Politics and Society in America* (Manchester, 1981).

Maltby, R., *Hollywood Cinema* (Oxford, 1995).

Marshall, M., *Top Hat and Tails: The Story of Jack Buchanan* (London, 1978).

Marx, K., *Capital: Volume 1* (Harmondsworth, 1976).

Mueller, J., *Astaire Dancing* (London, 1986).

Murphy, R., 'British film and the national interest, 1927–39', in R. Murphy (ed.) *The British Cinema Book* (London, 1997).

Napper, L., 'A despicable tradition: Quota Quickies, in the 1930s', in R. Murphy (ed.), *The British Cinema Book* (London, 1997).

Neale, S. and Smith, M., *Contemporary Hollywood Cinema* (London, 1998).

Nelson, R., 'Advertising as information', *Journal of Political Economy* 81 (1974) pp.729–45

Orwell, G., *The Road to Wigan Pier* (Harmondsworth, 1962).

Porter, V., 'Between structure and history: genre in popular British cinema', *Journal of Popular British Cinema* 1 (1998) pp.25–36.

Powell, M., *A Life in the Movies* (London, 1986).

Priestley, J.B., *Angel Pavement* (London, 1930).

Priestley, J.B., *English Journey* (London, 1933).

Priestley, J.B., *They Walked in the City* (London, 1936).

Rich, S., *Sweethearts* (New York, 1994).

Richards, J., *The Age of the Dream Palace* (London, 1984).

Richards, J., *Thorold Dickinson: The Man and his Films* (Beckenham, 1986).

Richards, J, 'Cinemagoing in Worktown: regional film audiences in 1930s Britain', *Historical Journal of Film, Radio and Television* 14 (1994) pp.147–66.

Richards, J., '"Soldiers Three": the "lost" Gaumont British imperial epic', *Historical Journal of Film, Radio and Television* 15 (1995) pp.137–14.

Richards, J., *Films and British National Identity: From Dickens to Dad's Army* (Manchester, 1997).

Richards, J. and Sheridan, D. (eds), *Mass-Observation at the Movies* (London, 1987).

Roddick, N., *A New Deal in Entertainment: Warner Brothers in the 1930s* (London, 1983).

Rosen, S., 'The economics of superstars', *American Economic Review* 71 (1981) pp.845–58.

Rowson, S., 'The value of remittances abroad for cinematograph films', *Journal of the Royal Statistical Society* 97 (1934) pp.588–611.

Rowson, S., 'A statistical survey of the cinema industry in Great Britain in 1934', *Journal of the Royal Statistical Society* 99 (1936) pp.67–129.

Ryall, T., 'A British studio system: the ABPC and G-B Corporation', in R. Murphy (ed.), *The British Cinema Book* (London, 1997).

Saunders, T., *Hollywood in Berlin: American Cinema and Weimar Germany* (Berkeley, 1994).

Schafer, S., *British Popular Films, 1929–39: The Cinema of Reassurance* (London, 1997).

Schatz, T., *The Genius of the System* (London, 1998).

Sedgwick, J., 'The market for feature films in Britain, 1934: a viable national cinema', *Historical Journal of Film, Radio and Television* 14 (1994a) 15–36.

Sedgwick, J., 'Richard B. Jewell's RKO film grosses, 1929–51: the C.J. Trevlin ledger: a comment', *Historical Journal of Film, Radio and Television* 14 (1994b) pp.51–59.

Sedgwick, J., 'The Warners' Ledger 1921–22 to 1941–42: a comment', *Historical Journal of Film, Radio and Television* 15 (1995) pp.75–82.

Sedgwick, J., 'Michael Balcon's close encounter with the American market, 1934–36', *Historical Journal of Film, Radio and Television* 16 (1996) pp.333–48.

Sedgwick, J., 'British film industry's production sector difficulties in the late 1930s', *Historical Journal of Film, Radio and Television* 17 (1997) pp.49–66.

Sedgwick, J., 'Cinema-going preferences in Britain in the 1930s', in J. Richards (ed.), *The Unknown 1930s: An Alternative History of the British Cinema, 1929–39* (London, 1998a).

Sedgwick, J., 'Film "hits" and "misses" in mid-1930s Britain', *Historical Journal of Film, Radio and Television* 18 (1998b) pp.333–51.

Sedgwick, J., 'The comparative popularity of stars in mid-1930s Britain', *Journal of Popular British Cinema* 2 (1999) pp.121–28.

Sedgwick, J. and Pokorny, M., 'The risk environment of film-making: Warners in the inter-war period', *Explorations in Economic History* 35 (1998) pp.196–220.

Sedgwick, J. and Pokorny, M., '"Movie stars and the distribution of financially successful films in the motion picture industry", a comment', *Journal of Cultural Economics* 22 (1999), pp. 319–23.

Shackle, G., *Expectations in Economics* (Cambridge, 1948).

Shackle, G., *Imagination and the Nature of Choice* (Edinburgh, 1979).

Shackle, G., *Epistemics and Economics* (New Brunswick, 1992).

Shipman, D., 2nd edition, *The Great Movie Stars: The Golden Years* (London, 1993).

Solomou, S. and Weale, M., 'UK national income, 1920–38: the implications of balanced estimates', *Economic History Review* 49 (1996) pp.105–15.

Stacey, J., 'Textual obsessions: methodology, history and researching female spectatorship', *Screen* 34 (1993) pp.260–74.

Staiger, J., *Interpreting Films: Studies in the Historical Reception of American Cinema* (Princeton, 1992).

Stead, P., 'The people and the pictures: the British working class and film in the 1930s', in N. Pronay and D. Spring (eds), *Propaganda, Politics and Film* (London, 1982).

Stevenson, J. and Cook, C., 2nd edition, *Britain in the Depression: Society and Politics, 1929–39* (Harlow, 1994).

Stigler, G. and Becker, G., 'De gustibus non est disputandum', *American Economic Review* 67 (1977) pp.76–90.

Stine, J., *Mother Goddam* (New York, 1974).

Stone, R. and Row, D., *The Measurement of Consumers' Expenditure in the UK 1920–38* (Cambridge, 1966).

Storper, M., 'The transition to flexible specialisation in the US film industry: external economies, the division of labour, and the crossing of industrial divides', in A. Amin (ed.), *Post-Fordism: A Reader* (Oxford, 1994).

Street. S., 'The Hays' Office and the defence of the British market in the 1930s', *Historical Journal of Film, Radio and Television* 5 (1985) pp.37–55.

Street, S., 'Alexander Korda, Prudential Assurance and British film finance in the 1930s', *Historical Journal of Film, Radio and Television* 6 (1986) pp.161–79.

Sutton, D., *A Chorus of Raspberries: British Film Comedy, 1929–1939* (Exeter, 2000).

Taylor, A.J.P., *English History, 1914–1945* (Oxford, 1965).

Tegal, S., 'The politics of censorship: "Jew Süss" (1934) in London, New York and Vienna', *Historical Journal of Film, Radio and Television* 15 (1995) pp.219–44.

Thompson, K., *Exporting Entertainment: America in the World Film Market 1907–1934* (London, 1985).

Thornton, F., *Jessie Matthews* (London, 1974).

Thumim, J., 'The "popular", cash and culture in the postwar British cinema industry', *Screen* 23 (1991) pp.245–71.

Vasey, R., *The World According to Hollywood, 1918–1939* (Exeter, 1997).

Wood, L., *British Films 1927–1939* (London, 1986).

Wood, L., ' Low budget British films in the 1930s', in R. Murphy (ed.), *The British Cinema Book* (London, 1997).

Wyatt, J., *High Concept: Movies and Marketing in Hollywood* (Austin, 1994).

Index